World's Greatest Financial Frauds

World's Greatest Financial Frauds:

Japanese and U.S. War Plunder

Rodney Stich

War Plunder and Atrocities, Secret Gold Retrieval, Subverting Foreign Governments, Classic Culture of Secret U.S. Government

Library of Congress Catalog Card Number: pending
Stich, Rodney—Author

This book: World's Greatest Financial Frauds.

Print ISBN: 978-0-932438-63-8; E-book ISBN 978-0-932438-64-5

Published and distributed in the United States by Silverpeak Enterprises, a Nevada Corporation, PO Box 5, Alamo, CA 94507 and offices in Nevada.

This printing: July 12, 2010.

To The People

Somewhat like Dan Quixote, the author, Rodney Stich, has attempted since 1978 to provide information and evidence to the American people about the arrogance, greed, and corruption in and out of government that to this day continues to inflict great personal and financial harm to countless numbers of people, and has made possible great harm to national security.

He has written numerous books, and appeared as guest and expert on over 3,000 radio and television shows since 1978.

This book is another frightening story of conduct affecting the uninformed public—including those blissfully happy in that state.

Other books by Rodney Stich with Print book ISBN numbers

America's Housing & Financial Frauds	(978-0-932438-54-6)
Blowback, 9/11, and Cover-Ups.	(978-0-932438-15-7)
Congress and Other U.S. Cesspools	(978-0-932438-29-4)
Crimes of the FBI-DOJ, Mafia, and al Qaeda	(978-0-932438-59-1)
David vs. Goliath: 9/11 & Other Tragedies	(978-0-932438-25-6)
Defrauding America, 4th ed. Vol. One	(978-0-932438-18-8)
Defrauding America, 4th ed. Vol. Two	(978-0-932438-19-5)
Disavow: A CIA Saga of Betrayal	(978-0-932438-17-1)
Drugging America, 2nd Ed.	(978-0-932438-11-9)
Explosive Secrets of Covert CIA Companies	(978-0-932438-23-2)
FBI, CIA, the Mob, and Treachery	(978-0-932438-24-9)
History of Aviation Disasters: 1950 to 9/11	(978-0-932438-65-2)
Iraq, Lies, Cover-ups, and Consequences,	(978-0-932438-22-5)
Lawyers and Judge: American Trojan Horses	(978-0-932438-16-4)
Subverting America, Vol. One	(978-0-932438-20-1)
Subverting America, Vol. Two	(978-0-932438-21-8)
Terrorism Against America,	(978-0-932438-14-0)
Those Ugly Americans: 20th & 21st Centuries	(978-0-932438-01-0)
World's Greatest Financial Frauds	(978-0-932438-63-8)

All books are available as Ebooks and on the Kindle.

World's Greatest Financial Frauds

Table of Contents

INTRODUCTION

From 1937 to 1945, the Japanese Army invaded a dozen Southeast Asian countries, and looted them of gold and other valuables. These countries included, for instance, China, Burma, Singapore, Malaysia, Sumatra, Java, Thailand, and parts of India. The plunder came from banks, financial institutions, wealthy individuals, and consisted of tons of gold bullion and other treasures.

Initially, the plunder was shipped to Japan. But once the sinking of Japanese vessels by U.S. submarines made water transport too hazardous, starting in late 1943, the plunder was shipped to the Philippines. As the Japanese realized that they would lose the war, this plunder was then placed in caves and tunnels, and the entrances sealed with explosive charges. Some treasure, such as gold, were hidden in ships that were intentionally sunk in locations where retrieval was possible.

From Japanese maps that had been recovered, there were 138 documented caves and tunnels, plus 13 underwater deliberately-sunk ships containing the plunder from a dozen nations. The amount of gold buried by the Japanese in the Philippines has been estimated at 4,000 to 6,000 tons. That estimate is in addition to the plunder taken to Japan from about 1937 to 1942.

Japanese Entombing American GI's and Other POWs

The Japanese used American GIs and other POWs to dig the tunnels and to move the plunder into these locations. Upon completion, with the prisoners still inside, the entrances were dynamited shut. In that way there were fewer people that could reveal the location of the various caves and tunnels containing the plunder from a dozen nations which the Japanese hoped they could later retrieve.

Variation from Other Books on the Subject

Several books have been written about the whereabouts of the tons of gold plundered by the invading Japanese. An excellent book on the subject is *Gold Warriors* by Sterling and Peggy Seagrave. I decided to write on the subject because a number of key insiders had provided me information and documents that are not found in other books.

What I have to offer is information and documents that I have obtained during my many years of information gathering on other areas of corruption and the many insiders that had learned of my activities and provided me with insider information that they had learned, or were part of, that related to the trillions of dollars of gold that was retrieved from the hidden gold and other valuables.

These people all contributed segments of information that their positions made them privy to. Among these sources were:

- The widow of Santa Romana, the OSS and CIA operative that discovered many of the hidden caves containing the looted gold and who became a major gatekeeper for distributing the assets in banks throughout the world. She and her husband gave me hundreds of pages of documents, letters and explanation concerning the tons of gold plunder retrieved by U.S. personnel and the initial distribution of it.

- Information and documentation provided to me over the years by my sources in the CIA and other government entities.
- Dozens of documents provided to me relating to one of the trusts in which huge amounts of gold were on deposit in banks throughout the world.
- Information obtained through research.
- Reference to other books by investigative reporters and writers.

The myriad sources of information addresse such matters as:

- The seven years of Japanese looting of treasures of a dozen invaded countries immediately before and during World War II, from 1937 to 1945.
- The story behind the Japanese spoils of war that has become today known as the Yamashita Treasure
- The covert disappearance and use of tens of tons of plundered gold and other valuables retrieved by U.S. personnel.
- The story of what happens to people attempting to expose the schemes involved with the retrieved plunder.
- The great number of people complicit, including banks throughout the world.
- The standard cover-up by America's media personnel and media corporations.
- The use of the sequestered plunder by the secret government in the United States to undermine nations throughout the world.

The facts show the existence of one of he greatest financial frauds in history with at the center, personnel of the CIA, U.S. military, and Washington politicians. While the story is high intrigue, it also reflects the corrupt culture of the people that control key segments of the government of the United States.

Where Is This Enormous plunder?

The location of this vast amount of wealth has been kept from the American people, and from the world, by a literal secret army directed initially by people in the Office of Strategic Services/CIA, by people in U.S. military and government financial sectors, and U.S. politicians. And then by a series of countries and tens of dozens of banks where the gold bullion and other valuables were deposited.

World's Greatest Financial Plunder:

Japan, Marcos, and CIA

Rodney Stich

A True Story Revealing Some of The Tentacles of the Secret Government In the United States

CHAPTER ONE

Japanese Version of The Nazi Holocaust: 1937 to 1945

Japan started invading countries in East and Southeast Asia from 1937 to 1945. During this period, the Japanese plundered banks and other sources of valuables in a dozen countries throughout that area. The Japanese compounded their plunder by committing horrible atrocities. During a six-week period after the Japanese Imperial Army captured Nanking in 1937 (the former capital of the Republic of China), they murdered thousands of civilians and brutally raped thousands of women. That period is known as the Nanking Massacre and the subject of the book, *Rape of Nanking.* The Nanking War Crimes Tribunal estimated the Japanese killed 260,000 people in Nanking.

Initial Japanese Brutality Upon Americans

The Japanese brutality upon U.S. personnel started with its simultaneous sneak attacks upon Pearl Harbor on December 7, 1941 and on Wake Island. I was in the Navy at that time and assigned to a Patrol Plane Squadron VP-71. The U.S. military leadership was unprepared despite the fact that it was known in the Navy and Army that war with Japan was imminent. The ships at Pearl Harbor were lined up in a row, making it easy to wipe out a major part of the U.S. Navy in a single blow. So were the planes at Pearl Harbor and at Kaneohe Bay Naval Air Station, with almost every aircraft totally destroyed.

The same culture was shown as a radar operator in Hawaii reported a hoard of fast-moving aircraft headed toward Hawaii and coming from the Northwest. His urgent telephone report was dismissed, claiming they were a few airplanes arriving from California—from the opposite direction! Even the sighting and sinking of small Japanese submarines near the entrance to Pearl Harbor, several hours before the main Japanese attack, did not result in any reaction. This level of intelligence was repeated time and time again since then, the most publicized being the simultaneous hijacking of four U.S. airliners on September 11, 2001, resulting in nearly 3,000 horrible deaths and resulting in the U.S. being involved in two wars with hundreds of thousands of casualties. This American culture that I would repeatedly witness, to this day, is shown by the facts stated in many of my books.

Japanese Brutality on Americans at Wake Island

The Japanese attacked Wake Island the same day they attacked Pearl Harbor (though it is shown as December 8 since Wake Island is on the opposite side of the International Date Line). As in virtually every other military location against the United States—despite the knowledge that war was imminent—aircraft were lined up in a row making it easy for a single Japanese plane to destroy the entire military aircraft at that location. This stupidity resulted in eight of the twelve fighter aircraft belonging to Marine Corps Fighter Squadron VMF-211 being destroyed. Twenty-three of the 55 Marines associated with that unit were killed. Also killed were ten employees of Pan American Airways. The airline had a refueling facility at Wake Island.

Within a few days, Japanese forces attempted to place military personnel on Wake Island, losing two Japanese destroyers in the failed attempt. Soon, assisted by two aircraft carriers, another attempt was made to land troops on Wake Island, and that time, they succeeded. By December 23, 1941, the U.S. defense failed, resulting in the Japanese capturing 1,603 personnel. Among those were 1,150 civilian contractors employed by the Morrison-Knudsen Company, part of a cooperative of eight construction companies called the Contractors Pacific Naval Air Bases. Headquartered in Boise, Idaho, Morrison-Knudsen was contracted to build an airfield, seaplane base, and submarine base and to dredge a channel into the lagoon to allow access for submarines.

As resistance ceased on Wake, the U.S. Marines, sailors, and contractors were marched to the runway and seated in rows facing a line of Japanese machine guns. The men were certain that they were to be murdered. Indeed, this was the plan of the Japanese Special Naval Landing Force troops who held them. Only the intervention of Rear Admiral Sadamichi Kajioka, who commanded the invasion force, prevented the slaughter. After Kajioka arrived, an interpreter read a proclamation to the prisoners that said, in part: "The Emperor has gracefully presented you with your lives." An unknown voice bellowed from the crowd of Americans: "Well, thank the son-of-a-bitch."

Three weeks after the fall of Wake, the POWs awoke to see a large vessel, the *Nita Maru*, standing off the southern shore, to transport some of the POWs to camps in China. Lee Wilcox, a Morrison-Knudsen employee, wrote in his diary on January 12, 1942: "All but 360 of the contractors have been sent to Japan today. [Wilcox assumed the destination was Japan.] Also the military service men, except 21 Marines who are too badly wounded to go." The 360 contractors who remained were chosen because of their skills in operating heavy equipment. They would continue the military build-up of Wake Island with the same supplies and equipment that they had used for the U.S. Navy.

Wilcox's diary was filled with details about the deaths and brutalities. "30 March 1942—Geo. Proteau died at 5 A.M. this date. Four days ago his son died [Laurence Proteau]. The old man was very weak and had a bad heart"; "May 1942, 12:10 P.M.—Geo. Walker died. He leaves a wife and daughter 4 years old"; "16 July 1942—Buried Bill Miles today at the east end of the runway, in Marine casket." Wilcox wrote about donning his VFW emblem based upon his World War I service to perform VFW services for fellow veterans that had died.

In September 1942, 265 of the prisoners of war, including Wilcox, were loaded onto a Japanese freighter and sent to Yokohama. Ninety-seven Americans remained on Wake to continue their work on construction projects.

For the remaining 97, the monotony was interrupted by U.S. bombing. One of those, caught stealing food in July 1943, was beheaded by a Japanese lieutenant under order by Japanese Rear Admiral Shigimatsu Sakaibara. He had flown in from Kwajalein in December 1942 to become island commander.

U.S. Navy submarines harassed shipping coming in and out of Wake, causing food shortages and increasing the risk of an invasion by U.S. forces. In reality, the plan by U.S. forces was to isolate islands that had no strategic use, limiting occasional attacks to destroying the landing areas and port facilities.

On July 8, 1943, U.S. Liberators from Midway Island bombed the island. On October 5, 1943, the USS *Yorktown* (CV-10) and other ships bombarded Wake with 340 tons of explosives, inflicting considerable damage to the infrastructure and on the Japanese aircraft.

Japanese Rear Admiral Sakaibara, thinking an invasion was imminent, decided to murder the remaining Americans. He ordered Lieutenant Commander Tachibana to move the prisoners to an antitank ditch on the northern tip of Wake Island and on October 7, 1943, lined up the remaining Americans and with machine guns, ended their lives. One American escaped, but was captured and beheaded personally by Admiral Sakaibara. That prisoner, during the short period before his recapture, returned to the execution site and carved the message, *98 US PW 5-10-43* on a large coral rock.

After the Japanese surrendered on September 4, 1945, Admiral Sakaibara, Lieutenant-Commander Tachibana, and 15 other officers were sent to Kwajalein where they stood trial by a military commission for war crimes for the murder of the American POWs. Enroute, two of the officers made written statements describing what happened and then committed suicide. Lieutenant Ito, during the trial, signed a statement describing what happened and then committed suicide.

Admiral Sakaibara and Lieutenant Commander Tachibana were sentenced to death. Rear Admiral Sakaibara was taken to Guam and executed on June 19, 1947, along with five other Japanese war criminals.

Close to the Wake Island Atrocities

While the Wake Island brutality was occurring, I was a crewmember on a PBY Catalina patrol plane flying patrol out of Midway Island toward Wake Island. Once, after reaching the outer limits of our patrol and turning back toward Midway, a vastly superior Japanese Betty bomber started shooting at us. He had approached from the rear and was hard to see because of the aircraft's position in line with the sun. Fortunately, we survived, despite the slow speed and poor defensive weaponry on the aircraft that was more suitable for peacetime patrol.

After about a year in that area of the Pacific, the Navy sent me to train to be a Naval Aviator, which culminated in my becoming a Naval Aviator in December 1943. After additional training, became an instructor in PBY Catalina seaplanes at Jacksonville, Florida. That was followed by being sent to the Naval Air Station at Hutchinson, Kansas for further training as a Patrol Plane Commander in their most modern Privateer and Liberator aircraft. All at the age of 20 and 21!

One of VP-71 Pilots Enabled the Initial Defeat of Japan

After I had left the squadron for pilot training, one of the VP-71 patrol planes, on patrol toward Wake Island, decided to extend the designated area of patrol. The additional area covered revealed the approach of a major Japanese fleet. Remaining out of sight, the PBY crew radioed to base the position of the approaching Japanese fleet.

A major U.S. Navy task force was quickly assembled and without Japanese knowledge, initiated an attack on the approaching Japanese fleet that resulted in major ship and aircraft losses. That battle of Midway changed the outcome of the war. In a peculiar twist, within a year of the implementation of the peace treaty between the United States and Japan, I was a captain for Japan Airlines, sharing the cockpit with former Japanese military pilots who were my copilots.

Japanese Brutality Elsewhere

In the nearly 800-page book, *The Last Empress*, by Hannah Pakula, details of Japanese brutality from 1937 to 1945 was described, which was similar to reports from many other sources. I repeat some of the statements in that book:

> **[The Rape of Nanking]**
>
> With all the odds against him, Tang tried to arrange a truce with

the Japanese, but the terms were rejected by the generalissimo, who ordered Tang to go to the dock, where he would be picked up and taken to safety. The only escape route from Nanking was its harbor—a frantic melee of screaming, pushing citizens and soldiers, all attempting to cross the Yangtze River to the place where junks waited to take them away. Once the boats were filled, some tried to escape by clinging to pieces of wood or swimming. Many drowned in the attempt. Those who remained were left to fend for themselves.

When they arrived in Nanking, the Japanese demanded that the city be surrendered intact, dropping leaflets that said that in order to "protect innocent civilians and cultural relics in the city," the Chinese must give up without a fight. In return for compliance, they promised to be "kind and generous to non-combatants and to Chinese troops who entertained no enmity to Japan," but to those who put up a fight, they would be "harsh and relentless." When the Chinese tried to mount a pathetic defense, the Japanese field commander, an uncle of the emperor, gave his soldiers leave to mutilate, rape, and murder anyone they found. Orders were given to take no prisoners, and what came to be known in the history of holocausts as the Rape of Nanking began.

There were only some 50,000 Japanese soldiers to deal with about 500,000 Chinese civilians and 90,000 Chinese soldiers in the capital. This meant that the Japanese had to deceive those they planned to kill into believing that they would be treated according to international rules of warfare. Posters were put up bearing the message "Trust our Japanese army—they will protect and feed you," but Chinese soldiers who gave up their arms were herded into outlying districts, divided into small groups, and beheaded or shot. With so many bodies, there was a problem of disposal. One Japanese general complained how hard it was to find ditches large enough to take 7,000 or 8,000 corpses. It was difficult to get enough fuel to cremate the vast numbers of bodies, and many were simply thrown into the muddy waters of the Yangtze.

Most of the corpses were already bloated and discolored. And there were many dead horses, their legs sticking up stiffly at grotesque and pathetic angles.... Nearly all the shops had been broken open, and showed the disorder left by hasty looters." Abend wandered around the city until after dinner. "At the hotel there was no water, and no light—not even a candle ... so I went to bed, but not to sleep. Never before had I seen death from violence in the mass. As a newspaper reporter ... I had often arrived with the police. . .. Morgues had become commonplace to me. But Tsinan, on that hot

May afternoon, had shown me wholesale massacre in new and shocking forms. . . . I had been surprised at myself, and rather proud, because during the afternoon I had not felt squeamish about the revolting sights I had seen. But lying there ... I suddenly was seized by a violent attack of retching."

Early in May, an obviously concerned May-ling wired Chiang, "I just heard that a Red Cross doctor who practices Western medicine was imprisoned in Hsuchou and thrown into boiling oil. The first thing the Japanese did was to surround the office of the Chinese diplomatic official who represented the Ministry of Foreign Affairs in Nanking; they cut off his nose and his ears, as well as those of the sixteen members of his staff, and then murdered the official, his wife, and all the others.

Japanese soldiers tearing the clothes off young girls, and Japanese soldiers revoltingly examining the bodies of Chinese women. In one picture of a mass beheading, Japanese camera-fiends have climbed a tree to get better pictures."

The worst suffering was endured by the women of Nanking. In the words of one Japanese soldier, "No matter how young or old, they all could not escape the fate of being raped. We sent out coal trucks ... to seize a lot of women. And then each of them was allocated 15 to 20 soldiers for sexual intercourse and abuse." According to another soldier, "It would be all right if we only raped them, I shouldn't say all right. But we always stabbed and killed them. Because dead bodies don't talk. . . . Perhaps when we were raping her, we looked at her as a woman, but when we killed her, we just thought of her as something like a pig." Iris Chang said that many of the Japanese soldiers believed that raping a virgin would make them more powerful on the battlefield, while some were even known to have the pubic hair of the girls they raped made into amulets to guard them against injury. According to a European observer, "There were girls under the age of 8 and women over the age of 70 who were raped and then, in the most brutal way possible, knocked down and beat up. . . . I saw the victims with my own eyes."

As word of the unspeakable treatment of women drifted out of Nanking, there was, according to Iris Chang, a "massive outcry" from the nations of the West. In response—and in one of the strangest quirks of this or any other war—the Japanese established their infamous comfort houses.

One Japanese doctor who took part as a soldier in the Rape of Nanking and who tried to atone for the rest of his life had this to say: "Few know that soldiers impaled babies on bayonets and tossed them still alive into pots of boiling water. They gang-raped women from the ages of twelve to eighty and then killed them when they could no longer satisfy sexual requirements. I beheaded people, starved them to death, burned them, and buried them alive, over two hundred in all. It is terrible that I could turn into an animal and do these things."

It is estimated that somewhere in the range of 200,000 (some say closer to 300,000) Chinese were butchered in the first six weeks of the massacre.

Under the pretext of searching for soldiers, the Japanese soldiers moved from house to house and store to store, demanding that the doors be opened to welcome the victors and then gunning down the residents and shopkeepers. After looting, they often burned the premises. Even Japanese journalists were shocked by the results of these forays: "On Hsiakwan wharves," one wrote, there was the dark silhouette of a mountain made of dead bodies. About fifty to one hundred people were toiling there, dragging bodies from the mountain of corpses and throwing them into the Yangtze River. The bodies dripped blood, some of them still alive and moaning weakly, their limbs twitching.... On the pier was a field of glistening mud under the moon's dim light. Wow! That's all blood! After a while, the coolies had done their job of dragging corpses and the soldiers lined them up along the river. Rat-tat-tat machine-gun fire could be heard. The coolies fell backward into the river and were swallowed by the raging currents.... A Japanese officer at the scene estimated that 20,000 people had been executed.

There was a great deal of sadism as well. Some Chinese citizens were nailed to wooden boards to be run over by tanks, crucified on trees or electrical posts, stripped of long pieces of skin, or had their eyes put out and noses and ears cut off before being killed. Other prisoners were tied together, thrown into pits, doused with gasoline, and set on fire. In one lethal game, the Chinese were driven to the top stories of buildings, the stairs were removed, and the buildings were incinerated. Still others were buried up to their waist and ripped apart by German shepherd dogs. There were medical experiments carried on in a secret location where scientists fed or injected prisoners with germs, poisons, and various lethal gases, killing about ten people a week.

Photographic evidence of the invaders' inhumanity eventually made its way to the West. It came from snapshots taken by the Japanese themselves and given to Japanese photography shops in the International Settlement of Shanghai to develop. Risking their lives, a few Chinese employees made extra prints, which they sent

> to the Chinese Ministry of Information in Hankow, where the government had fled. These prints were given to an Australian journalist, Rhodes Farmer, who had them reproduced and sent, along with a covering story to *Look* magazine. The pictures, declared spurious by the Japanese, were published around the world, while Farmer's name was added to Japan's death list. He wrote that he had other "pictures that the world will never see: Japanese soldiers in the act of raping Chinese women."

I had first seen pictures of these atrocities when, as a young Navy man, arriving in Hawaii within weeks of the Pearl Harbor attack on December 7, 1941, I saw pictures of women that had their breasts cut off being paraded through the streets by the Japanese.

The following is a sampling of data on the Internet's Wikipedia site about the Japanese brutality:

> Although the Nanking Massacre is generally described as having occurred over a six-week period after the fall of Nanking, the crimes committed by the Japanese army were not limited to that period. Many atrocities were reported to have been committed as the Japanese army advanced from Shanghai to Nanking.
>
> According to one Japanese journalist embedded with Imperial forces at the time, "The reason that the [10th Army] is advancing to Nanking quite rapidly is due to the tacit consent among the officers and men that they could loot and rape as they wish."
>
> Perhaps the most notorious atrocity was a killing contest between two Japanese officers as reported in the Tokyo Nichi Nichi Shimbun and the English language Japan Advertiser. The contest was covered much like a sporting event with regular updates on the score over a series of days. In Japan, the veracity of the newspaper article about the contest was the subject of ferocious debate for several decades starting in 1967.
>
> The International Military Tribunal for the Far East estimated that 20,000 women were raped, including infants and the elderly. A large portion of these rapes were systematized in a process where soldiers would search door-to-door for young girls, with many women taken captive and gang raped. The women were often killed immediately after the rape, often through explicit mutilation or by stabbing a bayonet, long stick of bamboo, or other objects into the vagina.

Reverend James M. McCallum wrote in his diary on December 19, 1937, what he saw:

> *I know not where to end. Never I have heard or read such brutality. Rape! Rape! Rape! We estimate at least 1,000 cases a night, and many by day. In case of resistance or anything that seems like disapproval, there is a bayonet stab or a bullet ... People are hysterical ... Women are being carried off every morning, afternoon and evening. The whole Japanese army seems to be free to go and come as it pleases, and to do whatever it pleases.*

On March 7, 1938, Robert O. Wilson, a surgeon at the American-administered University Hospital in the Safety Zone, wrote in a letter to his family, "A conservative estimate of people slaughtered in cold blood is somewhere about 100,000, including of course thousands of soldiers that had thrown down their arms." The following are excerpts from two of his earlier letters, December 15 and 18, 1937, to his family:

> *The slaughter of civilians is appalling. I could go on for pages telling of cases of rape and brutality almost beyond belief. Two bayoneted corpses are the only survivors of seven street cleaners who were sitting in their headquarters when Japanese soldiers came in without warning or reason and killed five of their number and wounded the two that found their way to the hospital.*
>
> *Let me recount some instances occurring in the last two days. Last night the house of one of the Chinese staff members of the university was broken into and two of the women, his relatives, were raped. Two girls, about 16, were raped to death in one of the refugee camps. In the University Middle School where there are 8,000 people the Japs came in ten times last night, over the wall, stole food, clothing, and raped until they were satisfied. They bayoneted one little boy of eight who have five bayonet wounds including one that penetrated his stomach, a portion of omentum was outside the abdomen. I think he will live.*

In his diary kept during the aggression to the city and its occupation by the Imperial Japanese Army, the leader of the Safety Zone [foreigners enclave], John Rabe wrote many comments about Japanese atrocities. For December 17:

> *Two Japanese soldiers have climbed over the garden wall and are about to break into our house. When I appear they give the excuse that they saw two Chinese soldiers climb over the wall. When I show them my party badge, they return the same way. In one of the houses in the narrow street behind my garden wall, a woman*

was raped, and then wounded in the neck with a bayonet. I managed to get an ambulance so we can take her to Kulou Hospital ... Last night up to 1,000 women and girls are said to have been raped, about 100 girls at Ginling College Girls alone. You hear nothing but rape. If husbands or brothers intervene, they're shot. What you hear and see on all sides is the brutality and bestiality of the Japanese soldiers.

There are also accounts of Japanese troops forcing families to commit acts of incest. Sons were forced to rape their mothers, fathers were forced to rape daughters. One pregnant woman who was gang-raped by Japanese soldiers gave birth only a few hours later. (Robert B. Edgerton, Warriors of the Rising Sun). Monks who had declared a life of celibacy were also forced to rape women.

A boy was killed by Japanese with a butt of a rifle, because he did not take off his hat.

On 13 December 1937, John Rabe wrote in his diary about the Japanese destruction that he witnessed:

It is not until we tour the city that we learn the extent of destruction. We come across corpses every 100 to 200 yards. The bodies of civilians that I examined had bullet holes in their backs. These people had presumably been fleeing and were shot from behind. The Japanese march through the city in groups of ten to twenty soldiers and loot the shops. I watched with my own eyes as they looted the café of our German baker Herr Kiessling. Hempel's hotel was broken into as well, as almost every shop on Chung Shang and Taiping Road.

On February 10, Legation Secretary of the German Embassy, Rosen, in a letter to his Foreign Ministry, he wrote about a film made by Reverend John Magee:

During the Japanese reign of terror in Nanking—which, by the way, continues to this day to a considerable degree—the Reverend John Magee, a member of the American Episcopal Church Mission who has been here for almost a quarter of a century, took motion pictures that eloquently bear witness to the atrocities committed by the Japanese. One will have to wait and see whether the highest officers in the Japanese army succeed, as they have indicated, in stopping the activities of their troops, which continue even today.

On December 13, about 30 soldiers came to a Chinese house at #5 Hsing Lu Koo in the southeastern part of Nanking, and demanded entrance. The door was open by the landlord, a Mohammedan named Ha. They killed him immediately with a revolver and also Mrs. Ha, who knelt before them after Ha's death, begging them not to kill anyone else. Mrs. Ha asked them why they killed her husband and they shot her. Mrs. Hsia was dragged out from under a table in the guest hall where she had tried to hide with her 1 year old baby. After being stripped and raped by one or more men, she was bayoneted in the chest, and then had a bottle thrust into her vagina. The baby was killed with a bayonet.

Some soldiers then went to the next room, where Mrs. Hsia's parents, aged 76 and 74, and her two daughters aged 16 and 14. They were about to rape the girls when the grandmother tried to protect them. The soldiers killed her with a revolver. The grandfather grasped the body of his wife and was killed. The two girls were then stripped, the elder being raped by 2–3 men, and the younger by 3. The older girl was stabbed afterwards and a cane was rammed in her vagina. The younger girl was bayoneted also but was spared the horrible treatment that had been meted out to her sister and mother. The soldiers then bayoneted another sister of between 7–8, who was also in the room. The last murders in the house were of Ha's two children, aged 4 and 2 respectively. The older was bayoneted and the younger split down through the head with a sword.

Pregnant women were a target of murder, as they would often be bayoneted in the stomach, sometimes after rape. Tang Junshan, survivor and witness to one of the Japanese army's systematic mass killings, testified:

The seventh and last person in the first row was a pregnant woman. The soldier thought he might as well rape her before killing her, so he pulled her out of the group to a spot about ten meters away. As he was trying to rape her, the woman resisted fiercely. The soldier abruptly stabbed her in the belly with a bayonet. She gave a final scream as her intestines spilled out. Then the soldier stabbed the fetus, with its umbilical cord clearly visible, and tossed it aside.

Thousands were led away and mass-executed in an excavation known as the "Ten-Thousand-Corpse Ditch", a trench measuring about 300m long and 5m wide. Since records were not kept, estimates regarding the number of victims buried in the ditch range from 4,000 to 20,000. However, most scholars and historians consider the number to be more than 12,000 victims.

[Emperor Hirohito Brutality]

On August 6, 1937, Hirohito had personally ratified his army's proposition to remove the constraints of international law on the treatment of Chinese prisoners. This directive also advised staff officers to stop using the term "prisoner of war".

Immediately after the fall of the city, Japanese troops embarked on a determined search for former soldiers, in which thousands of young men were captured. Many were taken to the Yangtze River, where they were machine-gunned. What was probably the single largest massacre of Chinese troops occurred along the banks of the Yangtze River on December 18 in what is called the Straw String Gorge Massacre.

Japanese soldiers took most of the morning tying all of the POWs hands together and in the dusk divided them into 4 columns, and opened fire at them. Unable to escape, the POWs could only scream and thrash in desperation. It took an hour for the sounds of death to stop, and even longer for the Japanese to bayonet each individual. Most were dumped into the Yangtze. It is estimated that at least 57,500 Chinese POWs were killed.

The Japanese troops gathered 1,300 Chinese soldiers and civilians at Taiping Gate and killed them. The victims were blown up with landmines, then doused with petrol before being set on fire. Those that were left alive afterward were killed with bayonets.

F. Tillman Durdin and Archibald Steele, American news correspondents, reported that they had seen bodies of killed Chinese soldiers forming mounds six feet high at the Nanking Yijiang gate in the north. Durdin, who was working for the New York Times, made a tour of Nanking before his departure from the city. He heard waves of machine-gun fire and witnessed the Japanese soldiers gun down some two hundred Chinese within ten minutes.

Two days later, in his report to the New York Times, he stated that the alleys and street were filled with civilian bodies, including women and children. According to a testimony made by missionary Ralph L. Phillips to the U.S. State Assembly Investigating Committee, he was "forced to watch while the Japs disembowled a Chinese soldier" and "roasted his heart and liver and ate them".

Chairman John Rabe wrote a complaint (December 17) to Kiyoshi Fukui, second secretary of the Japanese Embassy, stating:

In other words, on the 13th when your troops entered the city, we had nearly all the civilian population gathered in a Zone in which there had been very little destruction by stray shells and no looting by Chinese soldiers even in full retreat ... All 27 Occidentals in the city at that time and our Chinese population were totally surprised by the reign of robbery, raping and killing initiated by your soldiers on the 14th. All we are asking in our protest is that you restore order among your troops and get the normal life city going as soon as possible. In the latter process we are glad to co-

operate in any way we can.

"Comfort Women" for Japanese Sexual Use

The terms "comfort women" or "military comfort women" are euphemisms for women in Japanese military brothels in occupied countries, many of whom were recruited by force or deception, and regard themselves as having been sexually assaulted or sex slaves. A *New York Times* editorial on (March 6, 2007) stated:

> *These were not commercial brothels. Force, explicit and implicit, was used in recruiting these women. What went on in them was serial rape, not prostitution. The Japanese Army's involvement is documented in the government's own defense files. A senior Tokyo official more or less apologized for this horrific crime in 1993... Yesterday, he grudgingly acknowledged the 1993 quasi apology, but only as part of a pre-emptive declaration that his government would reject the call, now pending in the United States Congress, for an official apology. America isn't the only country interested in seeing Japan belatedly accept full responsibility. Korea, China, and the Philippines are also infuriated by years of Japanese equivocations over the issue.*

A *Washington Post* article (March 6, 2007) described Japanese soldier Yasuji Kaneko admitting that the women "cried out, but it didn't matter to us whether the women lived or died. We were the emperor's soldiers. Whether in military brothels or in the villages, we raped without reluctance."

The U.S. House of representatives Foreign Affairs Committee passed a resolution (June 26, 2007) asking that Japan "acknowledge, apologize and accept historical responsibility in a clear and unequivocal manner for its military's coercion of women into sexual slavery during the war."

Cannibalism

The Australian War Crimes Section of the Tokyo tribunal found that Japanese personnel in the Pacific and in Asia engaged in cannibalism against Allied prisoners. Some cases were motivated by lack of normal supplies, and sometimes, according to historian Yuki Tanaka,"cannibalism was often a systematic activity conducted by whole squads and under the command of officers".

An Indian POW, Havildar Changdi Ram, testified that: "on November 12, 1944, the Kempeitai beheaded an Allied pilot. I saw this from behind a tree and watched some of the Japanese cut flesh from his arms, legs, hips, buttocks and carry it off to their quarters... They cut it small pieces and fried it." Another Indian POW, Lance Naik Hatam, testified that in New Guinea flesh was cut from living people, adding:

The Japanese started selecting prisoners and every day one prisoner was taken out and killed and eaten by the soldiers. I personally saw this happen and about 100 prisoners were eaten at this place by the Japanese. The remainder of us were taken to another spot 50 miles [80 km] away where 10 prisoners died of sickness. At this place, the Japanese again started selecting prisoners to eat. Those selected were taken to a hut where their flesh was cut from their bodies while they were alive and they were thrown into a ditch where they later died.

Reportedly, one of the most senior Japanese officers involved in cannibalism was Lt Gen. Yoshio Tachibana. He and 11 others were tried (August 1946) in relation to the execution of U.S. Navy airmen, and the cannibalism of at least one of them, during August 1944, in the Bonin Islands. Tachibana was sentenced to death, and hanged.

The Infamous Bataan Death March Fatal for Many Americans

An atrocity that killed thousands of U.S. military personnel in the Philippines occurred shortly after the Japanese attack upon Pearl Harbor and became known as the Death March of Bataan. It was a 60-mile forced march of 75,000 American and Filipino prisoners of war from the Bataan peninsula west of Manila to prison camps. Many died during the march as they were beheaded, their throats cut and left to bleed to death, used for bayonet practice, rape, disembowelment, deprivation of food or water. Any prisoner who stumbled was killed. The death toll during the march is estimated at 18,000, with many more who perished in the prison camps.

Extreme Brutality of the Japanese

Over 30 percent of American GIs that were prisoners of war of the Japanese died, while only about two percent of the POWs of the Nazi died. The Japanese killed American POWs that were forced to dig tunnels or in caves to hide the gold plunder. Americans were denied treatment, or deliberately bayoneted or killed, if they were unable to work.

In addition to those that died from neglect were the hundreds that were deliberately killed, who knew of the plunder being buried because they were forced to move the gold or dig the tunnels. They were killed to prevent them from disclosing the information. The Japanese believed that they would return at some later date to retrieve the hidden gold and valuables.

Mass Killing of American GIs

On August 2, 1945, days before Japan ended hostilities, nearly 400 American POWs were buried alive on the Japanese island of Sado, apparently to prevent them from revealing their work at one of the caves containing the plundered gold. Japanese Lieutenant Tsuda Yoshiro later described the event to investigators, describing the mine operated by Mitsubishi using slave labor. In another mine operated by the company on Sado in the Philippines, a reported one-thousand Koreans slave workers were buried alive.

Horrific Experiments on Live POWs by Japanese Unit 731

A Japanese unit known as Unit 731 under the command of Shirō Ishii conducted medical experiments on prisoners of war. Among the tests using prisoners, without anesthesia, were amputations, testing the effects of biological weapons, vivisection (surgery on living people), placing prisoners in freezing weather while parts of their bodies were drenched with water until frozen, followed by amputation. The process would then be followed by similar freezing on other limbs, until only the head and torso remained.

GlobalSecurity.org reported that these medical experiments on living prisoners of war resulted in 3,000 deaths. The *International Symposium on the Crimes of Bacteriological Warfare* stated in 2002 that the total number of people killed by the Japanese Imperial Army germ warfare and human experiments was close to 580,000. The deaths from biological warfare included the bubonic plague, cholera, and anthrax.

A former Japanese IJN medical officer Akira Makino stated in 2006 that he was ordered—as part of his training—to carry out vivisection on about 30 civilian prisoners in the Philippines between December 1944 and February 1945. A former Japanese military doctor in China, Ken Yuasa, also admitted to similar incidents in which he was compelled to participate.

Among the victims of the human experimentation were the 12 crew members that survived the crash of a U.S. Army Air Forces B-29 bomber on Kyūshū, on May 5, 1945, which was piloted by Lt. Marvin Watkins. The vivisection was conducted at the Kyushu University in Fukuoka.

Comparison of Brutality between Nazi and Japanese

Japanese brutality to America POWs was overwhelmingly horrific compared to that of the Nazi. With the exception of the camps holding Jews, the treatment of American POWs was far more humane. The Japanese, on the other hand, seemed to delight in inflicting horrific harm upon prisoners of war and people in the countries that they invaded. The historian, Chalmers Johnson, wrote about the extreme brutality of the Japanese:

The Germans killed six million Jews and 20 million Russians; the Japanese slaughtered as many as 30 million Filipinos, Malays, Vietnamese, Cambodians, Indonesians and Burmese, at least 23 million of them ethnic Chinese. Both conquerors enslaved millions and exploited them as forced labourers—and, in the case of the Japanese, as forced prostitutes for front-line troops.

If you were a Nazi prisoner of war from Britain, America, Australia, New Zealand or Canada you faced a 4% chance of not surviving the war; by comparison, the death rate for Allied POWs held by the Japanese was nearly 30%. Both nations looted the countries they conquered on a monumental scale, though Japan plundered more, over a longer period, than the Nazis

According to the findings of the Tokyo Tribunal, after March 20, 1943, the Japanese Navy was under orders to execute all prisoners taken at sea [which in most cases were Americans]. Political science professor R. J. Rummel at the University of Hawaii wrote that Japanese military murdered, between 1937 and 1945, nearly 3,000,000 to over 10,000,000 people, including Western prisoners of war. "This democide was due to a morally bankrupt political and military strategy, military expediency and custom, and national culture."

According to Rummel, in China alone, during 1937-45, approximately 3.9 million Chinese were killed, mostly civilians, as a direct result of the Japanese operations and 10.2 millions in the course of the war. The most infamous incident during this period was the Nanking Massacre of 1937-38, when, according to the findings of the International Military Tribunal for the Far East, the Japanese Army massacred as many as 300,000 civilians and prisoners of war, although the accepted figure is somewhere in the hundreds of thousands. A similar crime was the Changjiao massacre. In Southeast Asia, the Manila massacre, resulted in the deaths of 100,000 civilians in the Philippines and in the Sook Ching massacre, between 25,000 and 50,000 ethnic Chinese in Singapore were taken to beaches and massacred. There were numerous other massacres of civilians e.g. the Kalagong massacre.

Hirohito's Sanctioned Practice of Killing Everyone

Historian Mitsuyoshi Himeta reported that Emperor Hirohito sanctioned a scorched earth policy that included what he called a "Three Alls Policy" (*Sankō Sakusen*) in China from 1942 to 1945: "Kill All, Burn All, and Loot All." That directive from Hirohito resulted in "more than 2.7 million" deaths of Chinese civilians.

Rampant Cannibalism by Japanese

The Australian War Crimes Section of the Tokyo tribunal collected numerous written reports and testimonies that were investigated by its future Judge-in Chief, William Webb showing that Japanese personnel throughout the Pacific and Asia committed acts of cannibalism against Allied prisoners of war.

Historian Yuki Tanaka wrote: "Cannibalism was often a systematic activity conducted by whole squads and under the command of officers," that frequently involved murder for that purpose.

U.S. War Crime Trials

Following the model used at the Nuremberg Trials in Germany, the Allies established three broad categories. "Class A" charges alleging "crimes against peace" were to be brought against Japan's top leaders who had planned and directed the war. Class B and C charges, which could be leveled at Japanese of any rank, covered "conventional war crimes" and "crimes against humanity," respectively. However, unlike the Nuremberg Trials, the charge of crimes against peace was a prerequisite to prosecution, that is, only those individuals whose crimes included "crimes against peace" could be prosecuted by the Tribunal.

The indictment accused the defendants of promoting a scheme of conquest that "contemplated and carried out ... murdering, maiming and ill-treating prisoners of war (and) civilian internees ... forcing them to labor under inhumane conditions ... plundering public and private property, wantonly destroying cities, towns and villages beyond any justification of military necessity; (perpetrating) mass murder, rape, pillage, brigandage, torture and other barbaric cruelties upon the helpless civilian population of the over-run countries."

General Douglas MacArthur Protecting Top War Criminals

In November 1945, General Douglas MacArthur made known that he intended to protect Japan's Emperor Hirohito, despite the Emperor's role in approving the invasion of a dozen countries, the attacks upon the United States, and the approval of the brutalities against American POWs. The probable reason for that obscene protection of Japanese war criminals is revealed in later pages.

U.S. personnel commenced a disinformation and cover-up campaign to show Emperor Hirohito as innocent, almost a saintly figure, despite the overwhelming evidence contradicting that position. The same protection—and even rewards—were given to many other Japanese responsible for the brutal torture and deaths of huge numbers of Americans.

U.S. Personnel Suborning Perjury in War Crime Trials

This protection of war criminals that resulted in horrendous brutalities and deaths of American military personnel and others required that actions be secretly taken to slant the testimony of the defendants so that they did not implicate Emperor Hirohito. These tactics gave the Japanese people a different perspective upon their guilt.

Among the war criminals protected and even embraced by U.S. leaders were Emperor Hirohito and all members of the imperial family, such as Prince Asaka, his many cousins; Nobusuke Kishi, later prime minister with covert U.S. help; Nobusuke Kishi, also later prime minister; Yoshisuke Aikawa, later the head of zaibatsu Nissan, and future leader of the Chuseiren; Shiro Ishii, who conducted horrible experiments on live prisoners in unit 731, and was granted immunity by U.S. leaders.

Grants of immunity to Major War Criminals

Prince Asaka was the ranking officer in Nanking at the height of the atrocities. In his deposition to the International Prosecution Section of the Tokyo tribunal Asaka denied the existence of any massacre and claimed never to have received complaints about the conduct of his troops, despite the overwhelming evidence. He was not prosecuted by the International Military Tribunal for the Far East because General MacArthur had a pact with Emperor Hirohito, another major war criminal, that all members of the imperial family were granted immunity from prosecution. Many other major war criminals were never prosecuted.

Denial of the Brutal Massacre by the U.S. Supported Liberal Democratic Party (LDP) of Japan

Encouraged by the U.S. cover-ups, in 2007, a group of around 100 Liberal Democratic Party of Japan (LDP) lawmakers again denounced the Nanjing Massacre as a fabrication, arguing that there was no evidence to prove the allegations of mass killings by Japanese soldiers. They accused Beijing of using the alleged incident as a "political advertisement."

Corrupt Protection by key U.S. Personnel of Japanese War Criminals Compounded by Corrupt Reason for Such Conduct

As will be seen in later pages, the reasons for rewarding the perpetrators of great crimes against American military personnel and others was required so as to maintain secret the secret retrieval of tons of gold plundered by the Japanese from 1937 to 1945, and the corrupt use of that retrieved plunder.

The Contempt for U.S. Prisoners of War by U.S. Politicians Manipulation of the 1951 Peace Treaty

U.S. government personnel protected selected Japanese war criminals responsible for horrific brutality upon American POWs and others by their wording of the 1951 peace treaty, the denial of compensation to American prisoners of War, and protection of Japanese war criminals.

Type of Claims against Japan and Its Corporations

International law recognizes several types of claims:

- The right of one nation against another to claim war reparations.
- The right of one nation against another by invoking diplomatic protection of its nationals.

- The right of an individual—separate from the nation—to claim compensation.

U.S. Manipulation of 1951 Japanese Peace Treaty

For various reasons, as will be seen, U.S. personnel manipulated the peace treaty signed with Japan at San Francisco in 1951. The key manipulations in the treaty

- Claimed that Japan had no assets for paying reparations, or to the many horribly affected prisoners of war and other war victims.
- Covered up for the enormous plunder acquired by the Japanese during the plunder of a dozen nations from 1937 to 1945.
- Relieved the Japanese of any liability for the claims by the United States or its many military personnel that were brutally treated by the Japanese.

Major Articles in the 1951 Peace Treaty

The Treaty of Peace with Japan (commonly known as the Treaty of San Francisco or San Francisco Peace Treaty), was officially signed on September 8, 1951, in San Francisco, California and became effective on April 28, 1952. Neither China, who suffered enormously, nor the Soviet Union, was allowed to participate in the preparation of the peace treaty, and neither signed it.

Waiver of *Reparation* Liability under Article 14 (a)

U.S. personnel sought to bar any claims against Japan by the United States or, as it was interpreted, by any of the Americans grossly affected by the Japanese brutality. This was done under Article 14(a), while falsely claiming that Japan had no funds to pay claims—despite the eight years of looting the assets of a dozen nations that were hidden in Japan and also in the Philippines. Article 14 (a) stated, starting with a lie:

> It is recognized that Japan should pay reparations. Nevertheless it is also recognized that the resources of Japan are not presently sufficient, if it is to maintain a viable economy, to make complete reparation for all such damage and suffering and at the present time meet its other obligations.

Article 14 (b) of the peace treaty prepared by U.S. personnel waived *reparation rights* against Japan as it stated:

Except as otherwise provided in the present Treaty, the Allied Powers waive all reparations claims of the Allied Powers, other claims of the Allied Powers and their nationals arising out of any actions taken by Japan and its nationals in the course of the prosecution of the war and claims of the Allied Powers for direct military costs of occupation.

Protecting Japanese War Criminals While Harming American War Victims

U.S. government personnel in the State Department and elsewhere subsequently held that the treaty barred everyone, including the brutally treated American prisoners of war, from filing claims against the Japanese government and even Japanese corporations that forced American prisoners of war to make war materials. These corporations included those that Americans supported by purchasing their cars and other output.

This contempt for their own citizens was subsequently shown in many ways, as I write in my various books. The protection of Israel during the deadly attack by Israel against the U.S. Navy ship, U.S.S. Liberty, was only one of an endless series of such outrages—made possible by the refusal of Americans to read meaningful books or to react when they know of such conduct.

Federal judges in the United States became complicit in this hoax by repeatedly ruling that Article 14 (a) and (b) barred Americans to file lawsuits against Japan or the Japanese industries that misused American POWs during the war.

Subverting Government Rights to Claims Does Not Invalidate Individuals' Rights to File Claims

Prominent attorney Michael Bazyler wrote that Article 14 (b) addressed only waivers of "reparations," which are legally defined as payments made by one nation to another. The legal claims of an American citizen brutalized by Japan could not be extinguished by employees of the United States government. He wrote that in the case of a state foregoing its rights, the individuals' rights are left unprotected unless they can make claims directly for themselves outside of treaty provisions.

Article 14 (b) addressed only waivers of "reparations," which are legally defined as payments made by one state to another. That did not bar *individuals* from pursuing claims for compensation. Further, Japanese corporations that used American prisoners of war were private for-profit corporations. Further, the peace treaty did not address individual rights and claims.

Additional Right of American Victims to File Claims

In any case, Article 26 of the peace treaty with Japan, which superseded the restrictions of Article 14 (b) stated:

> Should Japan make a peace settlement or war claims settlement with any State granting that State greater advantages than those provided by the present Treaty, those same advantages shall be extended to the parties to the present Treaty.

Japan *did* make bilateral peace treaties after the 1951 peace agreement was signed. These were made with such countries as Denmark, Spain, Sweden, and Greece, that paid compensation to the nationals of those countries. The Philippines ratified the San Francisco Treaty on July 16, 1956, after the signing of a reparations agreement between both countries in May of that year.

U.S. Politicians Violated International Law Protecting Individual Rights to Compensation for War Crimes

Article 3 of the Hague Convention of 1907, followed by the Geneva Convention IV, Article 147, protects an individual's rights to compensation when war crimes are involved. The 1949 Geneva Convention further bars any party to allow another to evade liability for major violations of international humanitarian law (See *Geneva Convention IV Art. 148 and Geneva Convention III Art. 131*).

U.S. politicians lacked authority in writing the 1951 peace treaty with Japan to waive these rights and protections. And this surely was known by the U.S. politicians writing the 1951 peace treaty with Japan who violated these important international rights.

Congressional Remedies for War Victims Also Blocked

Congressman Dana Rohrabacher, introduced a bill, HR 1198, called, Justice for US POWs Act of 2001, requiring that the United States interprets Article 14 (b) as not constituting "a waiver by the United States of claims by nationals of the United States." During a congressional hearing in 2000 before Senate Judiciary Committee chaired by Senator Orrin Hatch on the Japanese peace treaty, employees of the U.S. Department of Justice took a position contrary to the position they took with the Nazi Holocaust.

Appearing as an expert witness, Harold G. Maier[1] testified: "It is my opinion that none of the terms of that Treaty (San Francisco Peace Treaty) precludes these legal actions by the American citizens who were former prisoners of war." At the Committee's urging, the State Department representative agreed to re-evaluate the government's position. Yet, the State Department filed two subsequent Statements of Interest which maintain similar positions, presumably after re-evaluation.

If long overdue corrective action had been taken to finally address

---

[1] Harold G. Maier was a noted scholar in the field of international law, international civil litigation, and conflict of laws. He was Professor of Law Emeritus at Vanderbilt University Law School. He had served as Counselor on International Law to the Legal Adviser at the U.S. Department of State; a member of the U.S. Secretary of State Advisory Committee on Private International Law; a consultant to the Office of the Secretary of the Army. He frequently testified before congressional committees on issues involving international law.

the outrages inflicted by U.S. politicians and government bureaucrats in the State Department and Department of Justice, it would have preserved the POWs' right to file the slave labor lawsuits against Japanese corporations in federal courts. And that would have opened a vast can of worms, as will be revealed by the following pages. The legislation and congressional hearings went nowhere.

U.S. District Judge Vaughn Walker's Contempt for Brutalized American War Victims

In a federal lawsuit filed in San Francisco, U.S. District Judge Vaughn Walker, in 2000, dismissed a slave labor lawsuit against Japanese corporations filed by American and Allied POWs and civilian internees. Walker rubber-stamped the amicus curiae friend-of-the-court brief filed by employees of the U.S. State Department—that played such a major role in the initial cover-up of the secret retrieval of gold and the many other corrupt acts yet to be shown in these pages.

The state department supported the Japanese war criminals while undermining the rights of its own military personnel that were victims of horrific Japanese war crimes. State Department lawyers argued that Article 14 (b) barred individual claims of war crime victims against Japan and the corporations that used American prisoners of war.

As described in several of my books, primarily, *History of Aviation* Disasters: 1950 to 9/11, I show how Judge Walker protected corrupt Justice Department personnel in misconduct that had catastrophic consequences for the United States and its citizens. And this is an understatement!

CHAPTER TWO

Japanese Plunder and Secret U.S. Retrieval

In addition to the enormous atrocities perpetrated by the invading Japanese, they also looted gold and other valuables from every available source in the nations they invaded. The name, *kin no yuri*, or Golden Lily, was given to the plan to plunder the nations invaded by Japanese forces, reportedly the name of one of Emperor Hirohito's favorite poems. That primary control of the looting was given to Hirohito's brother, Prince Chichibu, with other princes having a lesser role.

This plunder was originally shipped to Japan until U.S. submarine attacks caused the plunder to be shipped to the Philippines. Starting in 1944, as defeat appeared imminent, Japan's Field Marshall Count Terauchi of the Japanese Imperial Forces, initially in charge of the Southeast Pacific, ordered Admiral Masaharu, the military commander in the Philippines, to transport and hide the plunder located in the Philippines. Masaharu was later replaced by General Tomoyuki Yamashita and it was Yamashita who personally selected the cave and tunnel sites, and the entrances would be blasted shut to obliterate any evidence of the plunder sites. Yamashita was accompanied by his driver, Major Kashii Kojima. In addition to the major sites selected by General Yamashita, lower ranking Japanese military personnel personally hid small quantities of the loot for later retrieval.

Hiding of Plunder Observed by U.S. Intelligence Operatives

Secretly observing some of the Japanese loading operations was a Philippine-American, Santa Romana, a member of the U.S. Office of Strategic Services (OSS), and later was one of the founding members of the Central Intelligence Agency (CIA). Romana passed the information about the hidden plunder to his superiors, including General Douglas MacArthur, and this information was passed on to Washington. Plans, originating in Washington in 1944, were to withhold information about the Japanese plunder and to secretly retrieve as much of it as they could find and use it to fund covert operations after the war ended. That scheme required protecting and even rewarding Japanese guilty of the most horrific crimes against American personnel and others. Minor problem!

What happened to tons of gold and other plunder is described in the following pages. U.S. leaders—and participants in the secret retrieval of Japanese plunder—protected from prosecution or blame members of the imperial family that were involved in war crimes and should have been prosecuted. These included Emperor Hirohito and his brother Prince Chichibu, his cousins Prince Takeda and Prince Fushimi, and his uncles Prince Kan'in, Prince Asaka, and Prince Higashikuni, who should have been tried for war crimes.

General Douglas MacArthur and other U.S. leaders acted to shield from blame or prosecution the very people responsible for many of the atrocities. Emperor Shōwa [Hirohito] was pictured as a powerless figurehead behaving strictly according to protocol, while remaining at a distance from the decision-making processes.

While the emperor of Japan is known as Emperor Hirohito, his personal name, in the West, in Japan he is known as the Shōwa Emperor, reigning from 1901 to 1989, when he died. It was General Douglas MacArthur who insisted that Emperor Shōwa retain the throne. In that way, MacArthur exonerated the emperor from blame that killed hundreds of thousands of Americans and others, and the indescribable torture inflicted on millions of people.

In 1975, President Gerald Ford entertained the war criminal, Emperor Shōwa (Hirohito) at a White House ceremony, ignoring the horror that the Emperor was guilty of orchestrating many years earlier.

More Corrupt Acts Required for U.S. Personnel To Secretly Retrieve and Misuse War Plunder

The scheme to hide the existence of the billions of dollars of secreted gold required that the people in key positions, including the intelligence agencies and the military, and Washington politicians, act in utmost secrecy to insure that the scheme does not become known. These steps included, for instance:

- Protect and reward and use Japanese that had committed or ordered the brutalities from 1937 to 1945.
- Mount a campaign of lies showing the guilty parties to be blameless for the atrocities.
- During the war crime trials, withhold evidence, and even pay witnesses to withhold testimony about the crimes perpetrated by Japanese that U.S. personnel sought to hold blameless.
- Falsify the statements made in the peace treaty between Japan and the United States to omit any reference to the Japanese plunder that was hidden in Japan and the Philippines.
- The peace treaty had to protect Japan against lawsuits arising from the looting of treasures in the invaded countries and from prisoners

of war and other victims of Japanese aggression.

- Some of the Japanese responsible for the invasions and atrocities had to be protected and made a part of the scheme.
- Threaten, or take action, against any witnesses that would expose the U.S. hoax.

Various Names Given to the Scheme To Secretly Retrieve and Use Japanese Plunder

The scheme by key people in the U.S. government to secretly retrieve as much of the Japanese plunder in the Philippines, the placement of the plunder, its use, was given the name, Black Eagle Trust. The people involved in this operation in the Far East included those associated with U.S. intelligence offices, primarily the OSS and the CIA, military personnel, and presidents of the United States. Within the CIA, the primary division involved was the Secret Intelligence (SI) branch. It is believed that the people in Washington that originated the Black Eagle project included U.S. Secretary of War Henry Stimson and CIA deputy director Ray Cline. One document[2] making reference to the Eagle Project stated:

EAGLE PROJECT
13 July 1945

TO: Lt. Col. Paul Helliwell

PROM: Clyde B. Sargent, Captain, AUS
SUBJECT: Executive or Administrative Officer for Eagle.

1. The development of the Eagle Project increases its need for an Executive, or Administrative, Officer, as provided in the Table of Organization of the approved Eagle Project. The Executive Officer will serve as Vice Field Commander, and in the absence of the Field Commander he will serve as Acting Field Commander. At the same time he will serve as Adjutant and head the Administrative Section of the Eagle Project.

2. It is suggested that availability of Lt. Evan Koger, present S&T representative with Eagle, be explored. It is known that Lt. Koger prefers administrative work to instruction, and he seems to be well-qualified in all respects to meet Eagle's need for an Executive Officer. It is believed that S&T is willing to release him, providing it does not

---

[2] Most of the documents in my possession, shown in this book, have been retyped to be more readable.

present an unfillable vacancy in S&T personnel requirements.

3. If the transfer of Lt. Koger from S&T to Eagle as Executive Officer is possible, I should like to see Lt. Koger be promoted, if possible, as an advantage in his position as Executive Officer, and I shall be glad to recommend promotion if such from me is appropriate.

Clyde B. SARGENT
Captain, AUS
FC, Eagle Project

Scheme and Schemers' Need to Eliminate Gen. Yamashita

One of the first steps needed to protect the scheme—and the schemers—was to eliminate Gen. Yamashita before he revealed the existence of the tons of gold plunder that he had placed in tunnels and caves in the Philippines. Instead of providing him the highly visible trial provided to other Japanese war criminals, U.S. personnel subjected Yamashita to a quick military tribunal in Manila that lasted from October 29, 1945 to December 7, 1945—almost as soon as the Japanese surrendered.

U.S. Executed Yamashita for the Manila Massacre While Protecting the Japanese Admiral Most Responsible

The quick execution of General Yamashita by U.S. forces was allegedly based upon the massacre of civilians just prior to the U.S. attack upon the Philippines. But as the Tokyo Tribunal reported, it was not General Yamashita that committed the atrocities. Yamashita had sought to limit the causalities to his men and the population by ordering all Japanese forces under his command to withdraw from Manila.

Those orders were ignored by Japanese Rear-Admiral Iwabuchi. Under Iwabuchi's command, Japanese forces killed over 100,000 Filipino civilians believed to be members or collaborators of guerrilla groups opposing Japan, and did large-scale raping of women.

He was also charged with war crimes arising from the Sook Ching[3] massacre in Singapore. The primary charges were not that he had actually committed the crimes, but that he had failed to prevent them since

---

[3] The Sook Ching massacre occurred as Japanese forces invaded the British colony of Singapore in 1941. It consisted of the systematic murder of Chinese after the British colony surrendered on February 15, 1942 and continued from February 18 to March 4, 1942.

he was in charge of the forces that did the actual atrocities.

The defense team, headed by U.S. army colonel and lawyer, Harry E. Clarke, Sr., argued that atrocities *were* committed, but that there was a breakdown in communications in the Japanese chain of command during the battles and that Yamashita could not control the troops. Clarke argued:

> *Accused is not charged with having done something or having failed to do something, but solely with having been something.... American jurisprudence recognizes no such principle so far as its own military personnel are concerned.... No one would even suggest that the Commanding General of an American occupational force becomes a criminal every time an American soldier violates the law...one man is not held to answer for the crime of another.*

The military tribunal judged Yamashita guilty and sentenced him to death by hanging. Yamashita's defense team headed by Clarke appealed the sentence to General Douglas MacArthur, who upheld the verdict. Clarke then appealed to the Philippines Supreme Court and to the United States Supreme Court, in *In re Yamashita* 327 U.S. 1 (1946). The majority refused to provide any relief. Supreme Court Justice Murphy dissented from the majority, protesting various procedural issues, including the haste of the proceedings, the lack of professional and legal conduct of the military tribunal, the inclusion of hearsay evidence, and stated in his dissenting opinion:

> *More is at stake than General Yamashita's fate. There could be no possible sympathy for him if he is guilty of the atrocities for which his death is sought. But there can be and should be justice administered according to the law... It is not too early, it is never too early, for the nation steadfastly to follow its great constitutional traditions, none older or more universally protective against unbridled power than due process of law in the trial and punishment of men, that is, of all men, whether citizens, aliens, alien enemies or enemy belligerents.*

Following the Supreme Court decision, Clarke filed an appeal for clemency to U.S. President Harry Truman, who denied clemency. General MacArthur then confirmed the military commission's order of death. Yamashita, as he climbed the thirteen steps to the gallows at Los Baños Prison Camp south of Manila, gave a final statement. Yamashita replied through a translator, repeating that he lacked authority over the people that perpetrated the crimes. Yamashita was executed on February 23, 1946 by hanging.

It is interesting that key people involved in Yamashita's sudden military trial were involved in the operation involving the retrieval of the plundered gold that Yamashita had overseen. They included General Douglas MacArthur and President Harry Truman. Many Japanese that were far guiltier of brutal war crimes against American and other prisoners were *not* prosecuted or sentenced. Many were actually rewarded. Some of the most brutal and guilty war criminals were actually protected and made part of the scheme in Japan to carry out some of the covert activities which included altering the Japanese political process.

Another Step to Protect the Scheme and the Schemers

The peace treaty signed with Japan at San Francisco in 1951 had to be worded in such a way that the Japanese plunder located in Japan and in the Philippines not be identified; that Japan be given immunity against lawsuits resulting from their brutality in the invaded countries; and that none of the nations from which the plunder occurred could sue for its return. That was arranged by Article 14 of the peace treaty that stated as follows:

> It is recognized that Japan should pay reparations to the Allied Powers for the damage and suffering caused by it during the war. Nevertheless it is also recognized that the resources of Japan are not presently sufficient... the Allied Powers waive all reparations claims of the Allied Powers and their nationals arising out of any actions taken by Japan. By signing the treaty, Allied countries waived all rights to any claims, including claims by their citizens and service men forced into slave labor by the Japanese warlords.

San Francisco Peace Treaty

It wasn't until 1951 that the United States signed a peace teaty with Japan, officially ending the war. The Treaty of Peace with Japan, also known as the San Francisco Peace Treaty, or the Treaty of San Francisco, was signed at San Francisco by 49 nations on September 8, 1951, in the War Memorial Opera House. It took effect on April 28, 1952.

Japan accepted the jurisdiction of the International Military Tribunal for the Far East. Under Article 11 of the San Francisco Peace Treaty signed on Sept. 8, 1951, Article 11 of the treaty stated:

> Japan accepts the judgments of the International Military Tribunal for the Far East and of other Allied War Crimes Courts both within and outside Japan, and will carry out the sentences imposed thereby upon Japanese nationals imprisoned in Japan.
>
> The power to grant clemency, reduce sentences and parole with respect to such prisoners may not be exercised except on the decision of the government or governments which imposed the sentence in each instance, and on the recommendation of Japan. In the

case of persons sentenced by the International Military Tribunal for the Far East, such power may not be exercised except on the decision of a majority of the governments represented on the Tribunal, and on the recommendation of Japan.

Japanese War Plunder Hidden in Japan

The U.S. personnel writing the peace treaty knew that the plunder by the invading Japanese, from about 1937 to about 1944, had been transported to Japan and hidden. Instead of making this plunder available to the victims of the Japanese military, or return to the countries from which the plunder was taken, the U.S. personnel falsely stated that Japan was without assets, and thereby could not pay any retribution to the brutalized Japanese victims. To protect the Japanese hiding this plunder, and deny the victims of Japanese brutality any financial compensation, the U.S.-written peace treaty had to be worded to legally block any lawsuit against the Japanese.

Compensation to Allied POWs

Clause 16 of the San Francisco Treaty, referring to compensation for allied prisoners of war, stated:

> As an expression of its desire to indemnify those members of the armed forces of the Allied Powers who suffered undue hardships while prisoners of war of Japan, Japan will transfer its assets and those of its nationals in countries which were neutral during the war, or which were at war with any of the Allied Powers, or, at its option, the equivalent of such assets, to the International Committee of the Red Cross which shall liquidate such assets and distribute the resultant fund to appropriate national agencies, for the benefit of former prisoners of war and their families on such basis as it may determine to be equitable.
>
> The categories of assets described in Article 14(a)2(II)(ii) through (v) of the present Treaty shall be excepted from transfer, as well as assets of Japanese natural persons not residents of Japan on the first coming into force of the Treaty. It is equally understood that the transfer provision of this Article has no application to the 19,770 shares in the Bank for International Settlements presently owned by Japanese financial institutions.

That Clause 16 barred subsequent lawsuits filed by former Allied prisoners of war against Japan. Japan paid $6.6 million U.S. dollars to the Red Cross. Some sources claimed that these funds used were not Japanese funds but relief funds contributed by the governments of USA, UK and Netherlands and sequestered in the Yokohama Specie

Bank during the final year of the war. More about this later.

Media's Culture of Cover-Up

As usual, no questions were raised by media people in the United States about the missing Japanese plunder, the immunity against liability by Japan from claims of those brutalized and the countries from where the plunder came; the quick execution of General Yamashita, the peace treaty provisions.

In a document titled, *Reports of General MacArthur: MacArthur in Japan: The Military Phase*, Library of Congress card number 66-60006,

Property that was acquired by Japan under duress, wrongful acts of confiscation, dispossession or spoliation [and] property found in Japan and identified as having been located in an Allied Country [being China] and removed to Japan by fraud or coercion by the Japanese or their agents [consisted of] hoards of gold, silver, precious stones .... Owned or controlled by the Japanese ... One of the spectacular tasks of the Occupation dealt with collecting and putting under guard the great hoards of gold, silver, precious stones ... and all currency ....

Eighth Army was directed to seize and maintain custody of precious metals and diamond stockpiles owned or controlled by the Japanese or Axis governments in Japan during the war. Eight Army agencies were also authorized to confiscate and deposit precious metals and gems in United States vaults in Tokyo or Osaka whenever such items were found. The disposition of that enormous wealth then became secret.

MacArthur Report on Plunder Located in Japan

A report prepared in 1950 by General Douglas MacArthur's headquarters described the wealth acquired through plunder of the Japanese Army. The following is an excerpt from that report:

> Japanese owned gold and silver...property that was acquired by Japan under duress, wrongful acts of confiscation, dispossession or spoliation...property found in Japan and identified as having been located in an Allied country and removed to Japan by fraud or coercion by the Japanese or their agents...great hoards of gold, silver, precious stones, foreign postage stamps, engraving plates...precious metals and diamonds stockpiles owned or controlled by the Japanese...30,000 carats of diamonds in one stash, and a single find of 52.5 pounds of hoarded platinum ...

In their well-researched book, *Gold Warriors*, Arthurs Sterling and Peggy Seagrave wrote about MacArthur's role in hiding the Japanese plunder:

MacArthur's staff was well aware of the Japanese treasures, including the $2 billion of gold lying on the bottom of Tokyo Bay. Another large hoard, discovered in 1946 by U.S. intelligence was the $13 billion cache of underworld godfather Kodama Yoshio. Yoshio was made a rear admiral during the war and placed in charge of looting the Asian underworld. After the war Kodama was arrested for war crimes and imprisoned. To avoid trial and imprisonment, Kodama offered the CIA a $100 million dollar bribe. The money was added to the M-Fund and Kodama was freed. He later financed the creation of two political parties that later merged into the Liberal Party.

A *Fox News* article (February 24, 2007), made reference to an *Associated Press* article, titled, "CIA Recruited Japanese War Criminals," and stated:

TOKYO—Col. Masanobu Tsuji was a fanatical Japanese militarist and brutal warrior, hunted after World War II for massacres of Chinese civilians and complicity in the Bataan Death March. And then he became a U.S. spy. Newly declassified CIA records, released by the U.S. National Archives and examined by *The Associated Press*, document more fully than ever how Tsuji and other suspected Japanese war criminals were recruited by U.S. intelligence in the early days of the Cold War. The documents also show how ineffective the effort was, in the CIA's view.

The records, declassified in 2005 and 2006 under an act of Congress in tandem with Nazi war crime-related files, fill in many of the blanks in the previously spotty documentation of the occupation authority's intelligence arm and its involvement with Japanese ultranationalists and war criminals, historians say.

[U.S. Funded Operations: the M-Fund]

In addition to Tsuji, who escaped Allied prosecution and was elected to parliament in the 1950s, conspicuous figures in U.S.-funded operations included mob boss and war profiteer Yoshio Kodama, and Takushiro Hattori, former private secretary to Hideki Tajo, the wartime prime minister hanged as a war criminal in 1948.

[Japanese Bilking the Gullible Americans]

The CIA also cast a harsh eye on its counterparts—and institutional rivals—at G-2, the occupation's intelligence arm, providing evidence for the first time that the Japanese operatives often bilked gullible American patrons, passing on useless intelligence and using their U.S. ties to boost smuggling operations and further their efforts to resurrect a militarist Japan.

The assessments in the files are far from uniform. They show evidence that other U.S. agencies, such as the Air Force, were also looking into using some of the same people as spies, and that the CIA itself had contacts with former Japanese war criminals. Some CIA reports gave passing grades to the G-2 contacts' intelligence potential.

But on balance, the reports were negative, and historians say there is scant documentary evidence from occupation authorities to contradict the CIA assessment.

The files, hundreds of pages of which were obtained last month by the AP, depict operations that were deeply flawed by agents' lack of expertise, rivalries and shifting alliances between competing groups, and Japanese operatives' overriding interest in right-wing activities and money rather than U.S. security aims.

"Frequently they resorted to padding or outright fabrication of information for the purposes of prestige or profit," a 1951 CIA assessment said of the agents. "The postwar era in Japan ... produced a phenomenal increase in the number of these worthless information brokers, intelligence informants and agents."

The contacts in Japan mirror similar efforts in postwar Germany by the Americans to glean intelligence on the Soviet Union from ex-Nazis. But historians say a major contrast is the ineffectiveness of the Japanese operations.

The main aims were to spy on Communists inside Japan, place agents in Soviet and North Korean territory, and use Japanese mercenaries to bolster Taiwanese defenses against the triumphant Communist forces in mainland China.

[Comical Competence of U.S. Intelligence Personnel]

Some of the missions detailed by the CIA papers, however, bordered on the comical. The Americans, for instance, provided money for a boat to infiltrate Japanese agents into the Soviet island of Sakhalin; but the money, boat and agents apparently disappeared, one report said. In Taiwan, the Japanese traded recruits for shiploads of bananas to sell on the black market back home.

The operatives also were suspected of having murky links with the Communists they were assigned to undermine, the documents say. The CIA also said some agents sold the same information to different U.S. contacts, increasing their earnings, and funneled information on the American military back into the Japanese nationalist underground.

The files and historians strongly suggest that American lack of knowledge about Japan or interest in war crimes committed in Asia, and a reliance on operatives' own assessment of their intelligence skills, made U.S. officials, in the words of one CIA report, "easy to fool for a time."

[Japanese Taking Army Intelligence for a Ride]

"This was a bunch of Japanese nationalists taking the G-2 for a ride," said Carol Gluck, a specialist in Japanese history at Columbia University and adviser to the archives working group administering declassification of the papers. "One thing that was interesting was how absolutely nonsensical it was, of no use to anybody but the people involved. Almost funny in a way."

The informants, many of whom were held as war criminals after Tokyo's surrender and subsequently released, operated under the patronage of Maj. Gen. Charles Willoughby, a German-born, monocle-wearing admirer of Mussolini, a staunch anti-Communist and, as the chief of G-2 in the occupation government, considered second in power only to his boss, Gen. Douglas MacArthur. Some of Willoughby's protégés were seen as prime war trial material by Allied prosecutors.

But even as the occupation authorities were recrafting Japan into a democracy, their focus was shifting to containing the Soviets. Willoughby saw the military men as key to making Japan an anti-Communist bulwark in Asia—and ensuring that Tokyo would rapidly rearm, this time as a U.S. ally.

Historians long ago concluded that the Allies turned a blind eye to many Japanese war crimes, particularly those committed against other Asians, as fighting communism became the West's priority. Chief among the Japanese operatives was Seizo Arisue, Japan's intelligence chief at the end of the war. Arisue had been a key figure in the pro-war camp and in forging Japan's alliance with Nazi Germany and Fascist Italy in the 1930s.

According to the files, Arisue was soon ensconced in G-2, working with former Lt. Gen. Yorashiro Kawabe, who was a military intelligence officer in China in 1938 - to organize groups of veterans and others for underground operations. These groups consisted of former war buddies and often retained the same chains of command and militarist ideology of the war machine that ground much of Asia into submission in the 1930s and '40s.

"It shows how we acquiesced to the Japanese ... in order to continue to build up Japan as our ally," said Linda Goetz Holmes, author of "Unjust Enrichment: How Japan's Companies Built Postwar Fortunes Using American POWs."

"The whole thing was Cold War fear and an awful lot of postwar compensation issues ... all of that was subservient to our total fear of Russia," said Holmes, also a historical adviser for the declassification project.

[U.S. Personnel Sponsoring Notorious Killers]

Indeed, that new focus brought some of Japan's most notorious wartime killers under U.S. sponsorship. Tsuji, for instance, was wanted for involvement in the Bataan Death March of early 1942, in which thousands of Americans and Filipinos perished, and for allegedly co-signing an order to massacre anti-Japanese Chinese merchants in Malaya.

Yet none of that seemed to matter much to American intelligence personnel. The U.S. Air Force attempted unsuccessfully to recruit him after he was taken off the war crimes list in 1949 and came out of hiding, and CIA and U.S. Army files show him working for G-2. In the 1950s he was elected to Japan's parliament. He vanished in Laos in 1961 and was never seen again.

The Army considered him a potentially valuable source, but the CIA was not impressed with Tsuji's skills as an agent. The files show he was far more concerned with furthering various right-wing causes and basking in publicity generated by controversial political statements.

"In either politics or intelligence work, he is hopelessly lost both by reason of personality and lack of experience," said a CIA assessment from 1954. Another 1954 file says: "Tsuji is the type of man who, given the chance, would start World War III without any misgivings."

Kodama was another unsavory player. A virulent anti-communist and superbly connected smuggler and political fixer, Kodama commanded a vast network of black marketeers and former Japanese secret police agents in East Asia. The CIA, however, concluded he was much more concerned about making money than furthering U.S. interests. A gangland boss, he later played a major role in the Lockheed Scandal, one of the country's biggest post-World War II bribery cases. He died in 1984.

"Kodama Yoshio's value as an intelligence operative is virtually nil," says a particularly harsh 1953 CIA report. "He is a professional liar, gangster, charlatan and outright thief... Kodama is completely incapable of intelligence operations, and has no interest in anything but the profits."

Nowadays, the most powerful legacy of the U.S. occupation is the democratic freedoms and pacifism built into Japan's 1947 constitution. But the U.S. association with Japanese war criminals illustrates how Washington embraced nationalist and conservative forces after World War II, helping them reassert their grip on the government once the occupation ended in 1952.

"It's hard to imagine back in those days how intent the U.S. was on rapid remilitarization of Japan," said John Dower, historian and author of *Embracing Defeat: Japan in the Wake of World War II*. When we talk about the emergence of neo-nationalism or a strong right wing in Japan today, this has very deep roots and it involves a very strong element of American support," he said.

Yet the ex-war criminals failed to rebuild a militarist Japan. "Pre-war right-wing activists who escaped war crime charges in fact did not have much influence in the postwar period," said Eiji Takemae, historian and author of *The Allied Occupation of Japan*. To the Americans, he said, "they were in fact not very useful."

Associated Press investigative researcher Randy Herschaft in New York contributed to this report.

On the Net: U.S. National Archives and Records Administration: http://www.archives.ov/iwg/iapanese-war-crimes/introductory-essays .pdf; and http://www.archives.og v/iwg/reports/japanese-interim-report-march-2002-1.htm

A top secret letter from Philippine business man Natividad Fajardo to First Lady Imelda Marcus made reference to money from the Sanwa Bank in Osaka, Japan consisting of interest from money left in trust by General Douglas MacArthur for Japanese Emperor Hirohito. That would support the many reports that U.S. personnel, through General Douglas MacArthur, used funds—probably the secretly retrieved Japanese plunder in the Philippines—to "reward" one of the architects of the seven years of brutality by the Japanese military. Because of poor readability, the contents of the document, minus the Received stamp and initials, follows:

PERSONAL AND VERY CONFIDENTIAL

Malacanang
Office of the Special Secretary

February 21, 1981 RECEIVED
6/24/81

Her Escellency
Madam Imelda Romuldez Marcos
Malacanang Palace
Manila

Dear Madam:

You will remember your letter to Mr. Kazumi Shinzato dated February 4, 1981, copy hereto attached, which I and my group (five members) used as our authority to contact Japanese officials and to ranking businessmen concerned in connection with what we told you as Japanese financial aid to the Philippines. We left for Japan on February 7, stayed there for 13 days and arrived here on February 19.

The mission was made top secret in Japan, so much so that my group was confined in our room at the Miyako Hotel.

The Japanese financial aid consists of accumulated interest income of dollar fund left in trust by General Mac Arthur to the Imperial family. The trustees are two Americans and one Japanese by the name of Mr. Yutaka Acki who discussed the matter with us several times in our hotel.

We are devising a means of how to bring out the money to Hongkong under the authority of the Ministry of Finance of Japan and that our cooperation is needed. It shall be made to appear that the money will be loaned to a Japanese company doing big business in the Philippines and they found that Kawasaki is qualified. The Trust money in the hands of the Imperial family has already been deposited with the Sanwa Bank in Osaka and is ready for transfer to Hongkong. To do this, it shall be made to appear that it is a loan to Kawasaki without any interest for a period of 30 years. It will be Kawasaki that will release the money to finance the massive economic development projects of the Philippines of the First Lady.

Before the Japanese group takes any decisive step, they want to be sure that Mr. Shinzato and the Filipino group have already discussed this matter with you. It is for this reason that when we left Japan, the Japanese group sent Mr. Shinzato to the Philippines to meet you personally and get assurance that you know the transaction and that it was under your authority that we went to Japan.

Ma'am, would you allow me to bring to you the draft of a letter addressed to Mr. Hirro Iwamura, President of Kawasaki in Tokyo, for your signature.

You must have been inconvenienced by the adverse and massive publicity against me during my absence. I wish to assure you that I am innocent.

Very sincerely yours,

NATIVIDAD M. FAJARDO

Notes:

Eduardo G. Fajardo served as chairman of the Natividad Galang-Fajardo Foundation, Inc., in the Philippines.

CHAPTER THREE

Primary U.S. Gatekeepers For Secret Bank Accounts

After the end of hostilities, Santa Romana, who had observed some of the initial shipment of plunder from Manila was joined by U.S. Air Force Captain Edward Lansdale in searching for the plunder. Lansdale was a member of the Office of Strategic Services (OSS), and was sent to the Philippines by General Charles Willoughby after the war ended. He joined an OSS officer named Severino Garcia Diaz Santa Romana (Santy).

With General Yamashita silenced by hanging following the quick and isolated war crime trial, Santa Romana and Lansdale sought to locate Yamashita's driver, Major Kojima Kashii. After he was located, they had to resort to torture before Kashii revealed several of the plunder sites. One of the largest gold caches was in a series of tunnels at Matsushiro near Nagano in the Philippines. The tunnel stretched for five miles.

The task of blasting open the caves and removing the gold and other treasures was given to the U.S. Army Corps of Engineers. Once inside the caves, they found stacks of gold bars. It had been reported and shown by Japanese plunder maps that the Japanese hid the gold and other valuables in 133 caves and tunnels, and 28 in sunken ships in waters that would later be relatively easy to access.

Disposal of Non-Gold Plunder

The secretly retrieved gold and other plunder was then trucked to Manila and sent by ship and aircraft to banks throughout the world. The banks then provided certificates of gold deposits to the people selected to be straw men for later use in covert activities, some of which had serious blowback consequences for the United States.

The scheme to keep the existence of the Japanese plunder and the secret retrieval of it required numerous steps to be taken that required the cooperation of many people at the highest levels of the U.S. government. And also to protect the participants in the corrupt activities.

These steps included, for instance:

- Quick elimination of General Yamashita. This was done by a quick trial by a military tribunal and quickly putting him to death.
- Protecting some of the Japanese complicit in years of horrible brutality and war mongering.
- Denying the existence of any Japanese plunder, thereby protecting the plunder that was hidden in Japan and the plunder being secretly retrieved and hidden by key people in the government of the United States and those intelligence personnel acting outside of their former official intelligence roles.
- Wording the peace agreement between Japan and the United States that was signed at San Francisco in 1951 to give Japan and individual Japanese war criminals immunity from lawsuits by American and other prisoners of war.
- Entering secret agreements with Japanese war criminals and Japanese criminal groups that would be involved in covert manipulation of the Japanese political process.
- Obtain the cooperation of banks throughout the world, including within the United States, and especially Citibank, in keeping secret the tons of gold deposited in their banks.
- Silencing anyone who had the ability to expose these matters.

High-Level U.S. Personnel Involved in Conspiracy That Protected War Criminals and Against War Victims

Among the architects and key people in the scheme that had the label, Black Eagle Trust, were people from the CIA, the military, the White House, and covert operatives acting outside of government, especially who had formerly been in covert activities in the OSS, CIA, and the military.

The people involved included, for instance, General Douglas MacArthur, General Charles Willoughby, Robert Anderson, Paul Helliwell, John J. McCloy, Robert Lovett, Ray Cline, Henry L. Stimson, Colonel Joseph McMicking, and many others. President Harry Truman was also involved, being first briefed on the Black Eagle plan by Secretary of war Henry Stimson and John McCloy. (McCloy later became head of the World Bank.)

Becoming Rich in the Scheme

McMicking was an aide to General MacArthur and remained in the Philippines after the end of World War II. McMicking suddenly became very wealthy—obviously from diverting some of the Japanese plunder to his own use. He married Mercedes Zobel, a sister to a Philippine millionaire, Enrique Zobel, and helped develop the Zobel-Ayala real estate investments.

In one article, the *Philippine Star* stated that McMicking was the primary supplier of funds for the Zobel-Ayala real estate holdings. It doesn't take too much imagination to know where a U.S. Army officer suddenly acquired tens of millions of dollars after learning of the location of some of the Japanese plunder in the Philippines. The group bought the San Francisco Campton Place Hotel in the early 1980s, refurnished it into a lavish hotel and renamed it, Taj Campton Place.

Hands-On Plunder Retrievers

As previously stated, long-time OSS operative Santa Romana, along with Edward Lansdale, discovered some of the caves with the Japanese plunder. Santa Romana operated under several names, including for instance, Severio Garcia Diaz Sanata ("Santy"), Servino Diaz, Pelagia Garcia and others. He was born in Luzon, the Philippines and reportedly received part of his education in California, where he was also married to a wealthy heiress, Evangeline Compton. Her family owned a hotel in San Francisco that was renamed the Drake-Wilshire, and again renamed the Compton Place Hotel. They later moved to Manila in the 1930s, where with the help of his wife's money he developed a huge fortune in real estate as the Zobel-Ayala group.

During their social activities, Romana met General Douglas MacArthur and one of his staff officers responsible for secret agents, Courtney Whitney. These contacts resulted in Romana becoming one of Whitney's agents inside the Philippines. During the Japanese occupation of the Philippines, Romana observed the loading of gold and other plunder onto trucks in the Manila area.

Another person in the group was the law partner of Courtney Whitney, Joseph McKickling. They all became part of the OSS after the Japanese invaded the Philippines. He was Romana's immediate superior. He also became, suddenly, very wealthy after Santa Romana and Lansdale started discovering and removing the Japanese gold bullion from caves.

Life changed for Santa Romana in 1941, as the Japanese invaded the Philippines. A Japanese aircraft strafing run killed his wife. Santa Romana then went underground and periodically sent messages to General Douglas MacArthur's staff on Japanese activities.

Lansdale's Name on Tons of Bank Gold Certificates

Santa Romana and Edward Lansdale had hands-on responsibility for removing and shipping tons of gold bullion to banks throughout the world. Most of the bank certificates of deposit were in the name of Santa Romana or one of his many aliases or company names. Most also used the same password.

Most of the bank certificates of gold deposits available to me were those that named Santa Romana, plus some with Edward Lansdale's name as owner. Both of them were probably straw men for the tons of gold retrieved under guidance by the OSS and CIA.

Army Captain Edward Lansdale

Everyone involved in the scheme profited. Army Captain Edward Lansdale was made Chief of the CIA Intelligence Division in the Philippines, where he remained for several years. Later he was made Assistant Secretary of Defense for Special Operations in the John F. Kennedy administration. Eventually Lansdale's disagreement with policies in Vietnam caused him to be removed from his position.

When Lansdale was removed following his disagreement over Vietnam, he did as many other CIA personnel did; he went undercover with his activities, using his contacts with people acting in covert activities in and out of government. In the well-researched book, *Marcos Dynasty*, the authors, Sterling and Peggy Seagrave, refer to Lansdale's presence at a secret strategy conference held in Washington in October 1985 concerning U.S. military bases in the Philippines, and other matters.

Santa Ramona, described more fully in later pages, was a member of the World War II Office of Strategic Services (OSS) that became the Central Intelligence Agency (CIA) in 1947.

Army and OSS Paul Helliwell

Paul Helliwell, a lawyer, served in the U. S. Army and OSS during World War II, serving under CIA William Donovan. Helliwell was involved in Far East activities, including creating CIA front companies, proprietaries. These included Civil Air Transport (CAT), later renamed Air America, which was based in Taiwan, and the Sea Supply Corporation based in Bangkok. He sought funds for an invasion of Communist China.

Helliwell[4] established an office in Miami for the CIA's Sea Supply Corporation that used Castle Bank and Trust Company, a bank heavily involved in laundering CIA activities and drug money laundering. The IRS started investigating the bank but higher powers in government halted the investigation. Media articles also wrote about the bank, causing CIA personnel to use another bank, this time located in Australia: Nugan Hand Bank. More about that bank in later pages. That bank was staffed with CIA personnel, including Thomas Clines.

CIA Ray Cline

Ray S. Cline[5] was the chief analyst at the CIA during the Cuban missile crisis. His CIA activities included station chief in Taiwan from

---

[4] Paul Helliwell died from emphysema on December 24, 1976.

[5] Ray Cline died from emphysema on March 16, 1996.

1958 to 1962. He once revealed that between 1945 and 1947 OSS and CIA personnel, Santa Romana and Lansdale, had arranged for the shipment by banks of tons of gold retrieved from the Japanese plunder in the Philippines and placed in over 150 bank accounts in over 40 countries. He helped establish such covert CIA proprietaries as Sea Supply Corporation and Castle Bank.

Placement of Tons of Gold in Banks Throughout the World

Considerable information shows that the tons of gold retrieved by U.S. personnel that constituted the Black Eagle Fund were placed in banks throughout the world in accounts using the various names of the original OSS finders: Edward Lansdale and the various names that Santa Roman used. These included Santa Romana; Severino Sta. Romana; Jose Antonio Diaz; various companies; and Edward Lansdale, among others. The names on these accounts were straw men and easily transferred to others when transfer became necessary—with full cooperation of the many banks that became part of the scheme. There were also various names used for funds based upon the retrieved Japanese plunder.

Former CIA Deputy Director Ray Cline would later reveal that between 1945 and 1947 Santa Romana and Edward Lansdale were responsible for moving recovered gold bullion into nearly 200 bank accounts in several dozen countries.

Funding a Revolution in Iran

Funds were used in Iran in 1953 to bring about a revolution that removed the duly elected Mossadegh with the CIA's Shah. I was staying at a hotel in Abadan, Iran, and watched the revolution develop. My stay in Iran was as an airline captain flying Muslim pilgrims from throughout the Middle East to the holy cities of Mecca and Medina.

Tactics Used to Continue the Cover-Up

Many people and groups profited from the scheme concocted at the end of World War II by people in government positions within the United States. These groups included, for instance:

- The many bankers that became part of the scheme by receiving tons of the plundered gold, and whom also profited by denying the validity of the receipts that they had earlier given for the deposits.
- The covert personnel who played a role in the scheme and in whose name or pseudonym was placed millions or billions of dollars worth of gold.
- People in the government of the United States that played a role in the corrupt activities.

Santa Romana and others in whose names the gold and other retrieved valuables were put were probably straw men to hide the secret retrieval of the gold, and who were allowed to access the funds for personal use. According to the Union Banque Suisse documents, Santa Romana's title holder account was changed from Santa Romana's Crown Commodity Holdings to that of Major General Edward G. Lansdale immediately upon Santa Romana's death, which could be further evidence that Santa Romana was acting as a straw man for much of the Japanese plunder that was secretly retrieved by people in or associated with U.S. covert activities.

Among Santa Romana's accounts and enterprises were Crown Commodity Holdings and Diaz & Poirrotte Enterprises. A primary representative for these accounts was Alfredo P. Ramos. The powerful banks controlling the huge amount of money prevented the heirs of the owners with little funds from claiming the money. Further, it is believed that power of people with CIA and other government connections could easily cause the banks holding the billions of funds to simply deny either the validly of the bank documents or the existence of the accounts. With so much money at stake, the scheme of such major ramifications, and if the adverse effects upon the victims of Japanese wartime brutality became known, powerful forces in the U.S. government had to be used in corrupt schemes to prevent the public from realizing what had been done.

Santa Romana's Subsequent Marriage to Luz Rambano

Eventually Santa Romana married again, this time to a petit Philippine woman 30 years younger: Luz Rambano, who he named in his will as owner of some of the many trusts containing the Japanese plunder. The following are the details from the marriage certificate that she provided to me in 1996:

MARRIAGE CONTRACT

	HUSBAND	WIFE
Parties	SEVERINO G. STA. ROMANA	LUZ C. RAMBANO
Age:	66 YEARS, 8 MOS.	36 YRS. 6 MOS.
Nationality	Filipino	Filipino
Status:	Widower	Single

Official: Municipal Mayor
Date of Marriage: February 15, 1974

Solemnized by Hon. Nestor V. Ponce
Mayor of Patoros, Rizal

Certify that I, Severino G. Sta. Romana and Luz C. Rambano on the date and at the place above given, of our own free will and in the presence of the person solemnizing this marriage and of the two witnesses names, both of age, take each other as husband and wife.

Hon. Nestor V. Ponce

The marriage was short-lived; Santa Romana was a heavy drinker, resulting in his death in 1974.

CERTIFICATE OF DEATH

Province Nueva Eoija
City or Municipality Cab. City

Place of Death:
Province Nuova Beije

Name of Deceased: SEVERINO GARCIA STA. ROMANA
Date of Death: 9-30-74

If Married, Name and Address of Surviving Spouse:
Luz R. Sta. Romana
2300 G.M. Reeto Ave., Manila

Widow of Santa Romana Meeting Her Subsequent Husband

After her husband passed away, and while attempting to exercise the legal rights to the dozens of bank accounts throughout the world containing billions of dollars of gold deposits, she met in Hong Kong a business man, Jim Brown, who started helping her as she exercised her legal right as executrix. That turned into an ordeal and intrigue covering many years.

Years later, in 1996, Santa Romana's widow and her next husband provided me with a copy of the holographic that Santa Romana wrote while in the hospital several days before he died. The following is a typed replica of his handwritten will dated September 21, 1974 (excerpts portions with some unintelligible errors):

Page One

Saturday Oct. 21, 1974[6]
San Juan De Dios Hospital Rm. 210

For the first time in my life—67 yrs more or less—I'm at a loss for words to express my desire to defend or even to offer to rationalize or excuse, to offer an alibi for the things I've left undone—the things I've forgotten to do—things I've neglected to do—for all these and more, I make peace and beg forgiveness from all I caused to be unhappy.

From Father—my old man—he often quoted me the following phrases: "When the work has once began, don't leave it till it's done, be the labor great or small, do it well, or not at all. "

"T's very strange for a man to know how much he has to know in order to know how little he knows. "

I've have only 35 minutes left—I'm pressed for time. No matter how incoherent this pease of note may seem please take it in the light it is given.

----To My Immediate Family----

----Flordeliza-"Tam" $50,000,000.00 U.S.D. with her deposition and discretion to use it as she deems fit.

Page Two

----Pedro and Rolando my sons: $5,000,000.00 each for their own—as they seem fit with proper consultation with Leza [sp ?].

----To my brother Mike, $3,000,000.00 U.S. currency and two million more under Flordeliza's supervision, and to be given only if and when Mike's wife signs a receipt whenever she needs money—only Liza can give it to her.

----To Emily Reyes, a lifelong friend and confidant, and as a sister to a daughter--$1,000,000.00 U.S. currency for five years—a reserve of $5,000,000.00 U.S. cur for my brother-in law, Federico Matec [sp. ?]and his children and my sisters Nancy, Baby, Mary, Flor as Flodeliza [sp ?] may deem fit to give.

----All of the above amount of money shall be deducted from my numbered acc. in my bank, FNCB San Juan Luna Office.

----To Luz, $100,000,000.00 as is duly registered in HKG [Hong Kong] Shanghai Bank—HKG Branch. And should be my next in like and $500,000 for each of her children for all my live deposits excluding the amount in my last will and testament—cooperation and understanding from the Executive Committee is hereby solicited and prayed for.

Page Three

----To my friend and beloved trustee—J. Urlasquez SR. [SP ?]

---

[6] Santa Romana died on September 30, 1974, without days of leaving the hospital. It is probable that in his state of mind that he wrote October instead of September.

whose help I've always depended upon--$50,000,000.00. For him and $300,000.00 for member of his family all in U.S. currency also registered in HKG. Shanghai Bank HKG branch.

To my friend and relative of my wife, Miss Tarciana Rodriguez who I promised to help, but instead and in spite of everything stuck to us and helped me--$50,000,000.00 U.S. currency and shall be confidante of my wife—for without her we could have probably not pushed through what we've planned—also deposited in HKG. Shanghai Bank, registered under her own name.

----To Gil Dr. Leon $25,000,000.00 U.S. currency—HKG—for being a good friend and of the family—who also one or the other helped me and my wife.

----To Loy Torres--$25,000,000.00 U.S. currency also HKG Shanghai HKG Branch—He may use as he deem fit. I don't need to enumerate this further—he knows what I mean.

Page IV

To my compaire Ben Caelac [Sp ?] $25,000,000.00 U.S. currency for his family—and own use, 80% of which is to be in my commadre name.—a good man and a friend. He knows what I mean too. From my personal deposit in FNCB San Juan Luna.

----To my beloved daughters Ethel and Menchit--$50,000,000.00 for Ethel and $40,000,000.00 US currency to Menchit with $10,000,000.00 RP currency—for their use in the P.I. and the U.S. currencies in HKG Shanghai Bank HKG Branch. They may use it as they deem fit.

---- To my doctor who saved my life and true friend, $50,000,000.00 U.S. currency. Also in HKG Shanghai Bank, HKG Branch, and $200,000 for his children.

To my compairb and commadre Atty6 & Mr. Luis Cuevas--$252,000,000.00 and $20,000 to each of his children—for his instingting cooperation and selfless dedication for my welfare.

To atty. Dr Guzman $1,500,000.000 one million five hundred thousand dollars—

To Mr. Fernandez $1,,000,000.00 U.S. currency—also in HKG—

----To Billy, Al, Eugenio Agua—Bert--$500,000 -- $500,000 --- $500,000 plus their allowances and residences.

Page V

----Panopio--$500,000 – Katendoy $400,000 -- BAnbteke $400,000. Cruz $400,000. All inm U.S. currency. Areserve of $20,000,000 for Leyte People to dispose of as my wife may deem useful with the advancement of Loy and my father in-law.

Jose Antonio Diaz

Discritionary on the part of the executive committee.

Luz—J. V. Xoy. Ben Carlao Tarciana Rodriguez, Gil de Leon. Dr. Burndia—legal adviser. Att. Luis Cuevas.

$100,000,000.00—US currency-0-for all the people I've forgotten to mention.

IT is understood that all projects are to continue—as planned—the above are purely for their personal use. Just may our dreams come true.

Banks Throughout the World Blocked Retrieval of the Gold Deposits: Assets Conversion

After Santa Romana died, his wife, Luz C. Robano Romana, filed papers showing her as the executor and heir to the many certificates of gold deposits and other CDs at banks throughout the world. With the huge amount of wealth at their disposal, banks put up roadblocks, either demanding other documents, or claiming the certificates of gold deposits were forgeries. Or that no such account existed.

Widow Denied Access to Safe Deposit Boxes by First National City Bank (FNCB) in Manila, (now Citibank and Cititrust)

Upon the death of Santa Romana, his widow, Luz, sought to gain access to multiple safe deposit boxes at First National City Bank[7] in Manila, using the key that she had used many times earlier. FNCB refused to allow her access to the safe deposit boxes that were in her name and that of Santa Romana.

Later, when she returned with a court document showing her as the administratrix of Santa Romana's assets, she was allowed to use the key for the first box, where multiple keys were located for the other boxes, along with numerous bank certificates of gold deposits, many issued by First National City Bank.

Keys and Bank Certificates of Gold Deposits Missing

Upon opening the first safe deposit box, Luz found all the prior contents missing, which consisted of keys to other safety deposit boxes and dozens of bank certificates of gold deposits. The removal of the contents had to be done with the complicity of First National City Bank (Citibank) and with President Ferdinand Marcus. Someone, or many, became fabulously rich by plundering the safe deposit boxes.

Citibank New York City Continued Asset Conversion

When Citibank in New York City also refused to allow Luz access to the dozens of bank certificates of gold deposits for which she had all the required certificate reference numbers, including codes, she hired a

---

[7] First National City Bank (FNCB) later became Citibank.

New York City attorney to file papers showing her as the administratrix of the Santa Romana estate, followed by filing a lawsuit.

The following 1976 document relates to Santa Romana's widow, Luz, filing intestate proceedings in New York to force Citibank to recognize her as the heir to the bullion Santa Romana placed into that bank.

Artemio M. Lobrin
Attorney-at-Law
Tax Consultant

Suites 314-315 Yuchengco Bldg.
484 Rosario, Manila, Philippines Telephone 40-30-08

9 December 1976

The Clerk of Court,
Court of, First Instance, of Manila,
Branch X,
City Hall, Manila

Sir:

For use in the ancillary intestate proceedings in New York City, New York, U.S.A. concerning; the estate of the deceased Severino Sta. Romana also known as J. Antonio Diaz, I have the honor to request for certified copies of the following pleadings and documents filed and/or issued in Special Proceedings No. 96736 of Branch X of said Court, entitled,

"In the matter of the intestate
Estate of the late Severino
Sta. Romana known also as
J. Antonio Diaz, - Petition
for Letters of Administration,

LUZ RAMBANO STA. ROMANA,
Petitioner.

1) Petition dated February 6, 1976 filed by LUZ RAMBANO STA. ROMANA, in Special Proceedings No. 96736, Court of First Instance of Manila, Branch X, entitled,

In the matter of the intestate Estate of the late Severino
Sta. Romana known also as J. Antonio Diaz, --Petition

For Letters of Administration

LUZ RAMBANO STA.ROMANA,
Petitioner;

2) Amended Petition dated May 15, 1975 filed by Petitioner LUZ RAMBANO STA. ROMANA in aforementioned Special Proceedings No. 96736;

3) Order of the Court dated July 3, 1975 issued in the above-mentioned case (Sp. Proc. No. 96736);

4) Ex Parte Motion to correct clerical error, dated July 9, 1975, filed by counsel,

E. J. MANIPULA, in same case;

5) Order of the court dated August 11, 1975, issued in the above-mentioned Special Proceedings No. 96736;

6) Letter of Administration issued by the Court dated August 14, 1975, appointing Petitioner LUZ RAMBANO STA. ROMANA as Administratrix of the Estate of SEVERINO STA. ROMANA, also known as J. ANTONIO DIAZ;

7) Oath of Office of LUZ RAMBANO STA. ROMANA as Administratrix of the Estate of SEVERINO STA. ROMANI A, also known as J. ANTONIO DIAZ.

Please kindly issue one covering certification for the whole bunch of the aforementioned pleadings and documents, so that only one attestation by the offices concerned need be issued.

Thanking you for your kind attention hereon, I am

Very truly yours,

ARTEMIO M LOBRIN

The following document shows Luz Romana as the heir to Santa Romana's estate and the tons of gold in numerous worldwide banks:

C. F. I. Form No. 24
Republic of the Philippines
Court of First Instance of the City of Manila

No. 96736

In the matter of THE INTESTATE ESTATE
OF SEVERINO STA. ROMANA, also know letters of administration
As J. ANTONIO DIAZ,
Deceased

Know All Men by These Presents:

That by order of this Court dated August 11, 1975, issued by Hon. Jose L. Moya, Judge of the Court of First Instance of Manila, Branch X, Mrs. LUZ RAMBANO STA. ROMANA has been appointed Administratrix of the estate of Severino Sta. Romana/also known as J. Antonio Diaz, deceased, with full authority to take possession of all property of said deceased in any province or provinces in which it may be situated and to perform all other acts necessary for the preservation of said property, she having filed a bond satisfactory to the court.

Said Administratrix shall within three months from the date of this appointment return to the Court a true inventory and appraisal of the real and personal estate of the deceased which come into her possession or knowledge, and shall render a true and just account of her administration the Court within one year and at any other time when required by the Court.

IN WITNESS WHEREOF, I sign and seal these presents in Manila, Philippines, this 14th day of August, A.D. 1975.

Leonardo S. Alcid
Clerk of the Court April 11 1995
By Nicanor E. Silvano

Also showing Luz as the administratrix of the estate was a court order in New York City:

THE PEOPLE OF THE State of New York

Know Ye, that we, having inspected the records of our Surrogate' Court in and for the County of New York, do find that on the 31st day of July in the year one thousand nine hundred and 95,

SEVERANO STA ROMANA AKA
J. ANTONIO DIAZ

Philippines, deceased, were granted unto ELEANOR JACKSON PIEL AND LUZ RAMONA, and that it does not appear by said records that said Letters have been revoked.

In Testimony Whereof, we have caused the Seal of the Surrogate's Court of the County of New York to be herein affixed.

Witness, Honorable Eve Preminger, a xxx of our said County, in the City of New York, the 5th day of August 1992.

Powerful Law Firm Entered the Scheme

A big-gun law firm then filed papers to have New York courts refuse to recognize Santa Romana's widow as the administratrix of the estate, despite her having been so designated in the Philippines and earlier in New York. New York has some of the most corrupt judges in the country, possibly more than Chicago. A new court order refused to recognize the widow, depriving her of even the basic funds for survival.

The pattern of corrupt actions by Citibank that helped fuel the financial meltdown that peaked in 2008 was conduct that was compatible with the culture that Santa Romana's widow encountered. It was also compatible with earlier reports that I had received from some of my CIA and other insider contacts involving Citibank with CIA covert and corrupt activities.

Receiving Documents from Santa Romana's Widow

In 1996, Jim Brown and his wife, Luz, were staying at a hotel near my home in Walnut Creek, California. They asked that I meet with them. During this meeting they provided me with hundreds of documents, letters, and other information, and asked me to help them get publicity.

Several dozen records of bank accounts were in the files given to me by Santa Romana's widow. The following are key portions of several of them, sufficient to establish that Santa Romana had bank accounts throughout the world for tons of gold or over a billion dollars. Several things will become apparent:

- Santa Romana had billions in bank deposits and tons of gold, funds that could only have been from the gold plundered by the Japanese and secretly hidden by people of the CIA, the military, and White House politicians.
- Co-ownership of some of these funds between Santa Romana and such CIA and military personnel as Edward G. Lansdale provides more evidence of these covert activities that constitute possibly the world's greatest financial crime.

At that time I was busy exposing areas of corruption that I had discovered, initially as a key federal airline safety inspector-investigator, and then from the many former government agents and other insiders that contacted me. Among the corruption that I discovered and sought to expose and halt was the unpublicized corruption that made possible several years later the hijackings of four airliners on September 11, 2001.

The information they were providing me showed a serious level of corruption in multiple government positions, but not the type that the public would feel sufficient to help what I was focusing on. So I did not make use of the material.

It wasn't until many years later, starting in 2010, that I was prompted to use not only the information that Santa Romana's widow had provided to me but massive evidence from other sources relating to what is probably the greatest financial hoist in the world's history. And even that will probably not result in any meaningful outrage among the American people.

Development Project

Brown described to me why he was in Hong Kong doing business on another matter and how he had learned about the plundered and missing gold. In the mid 1980s, Brown was working on a project to promote a tax-free zone in Belize that would attract business fleeing Hong Kong upon its return to China. He eventually met people seeking to buy several tons of gold from Ferdinand Marcus. This was after the U.S. military had taken him from his palace and flown him to Honolulu.

During these activities Brown met Santa Romana's widow and eventually married her.

Explanation of Events by Husband of Luz Romana Brown

In a 1996 meeting with Santa Romana's widow and her subsequent husband, Clarence "Jim" Brown, near my Walnut Creek, California home, they gave me hundreds of pages of documents and letters that described the relationship of Santa Romana with the retrieval of Japanese plunder and the placement of it in banks throughout the world. One of the papers was an explanation of events in the following paper provided to me, as written by the husband of Santa Romana's widow. That explanation follows:

> I became involved quite by accident in all of this in the late 1980's. I became acquainted with a Shigeo Kokobun, a wealthy Japanese, and for years, Mr. Kokobun paid my expenses after asking me to help the late Sta. Romana's widow in her efforts to try and recover at least a portion of what had been stolen from her late husband's estate. In 1992, after Mr. Kokobun's death, Mrs. Sta. Romana and I were legally married. I only list what I know has happened. (1) After the late Sta. Romana's death, and while my wife was being appointed by a Manila court as the administrator of her late husband's estate, Ferdinand Marcos, in conjunction with

certain bank officials in what was then known as First National City Bank in Manila, (now Citibank and Cititrust) opened and took the contents from eight commercial size safety deposits boxes my wife and her late husband maintained in First National City Bank. [FNCB]

[Stolen CDS for Tons of Gold, with Citibank's Complicity]

These boxes contained dozens of bearer certificates of precious metal and cash, in addition to their real estate titles, personal jewelry and other items. After being appointed the administrator approximately seven months after the late Sta. Romana's death, when my wife, her attorneys, and a member of the court went to First National City Bank in Manila and demanded they now be allowed access to these boxes, (she had tried before this, but was told she would have to wait on the courts) all they found in the first box, which she always had a key to and which also contained the keys to the other boxes, was a current dated newspaper, dated after her husband's death, and during the time she was being appointed by the court.

[FNCB Blocking Access to Tons of Gold CDs]

First National City Bank at the time denied and took her personal deposits in her maiden name of Luz C. Rambano, which amounted to a three-million dollar time deposit, and 180 thousand U.S. dollar savings account. After Marcos was taken to Hawaii [in 1986], he sent her a tape cassette message by a former aid and Manila newscaster by the name of Rita Gody, stating that he then needed her help, and admitting that he was the one who took these items. He also told her on this taped message that he took them for her and the children's protection.

We were also told in 1996, that Marcos' sister, Baby Babba, admitted holding the original copies of my wife's passbook and this certificate of deposit showing the three-million U.S. dollars.

[NY Courts Appointment Over Accounts at Citibank]

After finding these items missing or denied, and knowing full well that it was only Ferdinand Marcos who, other than the court which at the time was in the process of appointing her, that had the authority to order the bank to open these boxes, my wife left the Philippines and went to New York City, where she knew her late husband had huge deposits of precious metal and cash. Once there, she was soon appointed by the New York court as well as the administrator of the estate of Severino Sta. Romana, also known as Jose Antonio Diaz.

[New York Banks, Including Citibank, Stonewalling]

When her attorney wrote the banks in New York, where my

wife knew and had held actual certificates of deposits and bank book, not one of the banks named by my wife bothered to respond to her New York attorney, Eleanor Jackson Piel.

[Japanese Knowledge of Bank Accounts]

When I first met Mr. Kokobun, he told me that he had confirmed what my wife was stating, having learned this from a mentor and old friend, Ryoichi Sasakowa. Sasakowa knew the late Sta. Romana. He was also one of the World War II criminals that General Douglas MacArthur released shortly after World War II to help form the government in Japan.[Marcos' Theft Used by U.S. and Japanese Personnel to Deny Validity of Tons of Bank Certificates of Gold Deposits]

Mr. Kokobun told me that Mr. Sasakowa reported to him that basically everything my wife was saying was true. However, when many of the banks involved and some within the government of the United States learned what Marcos had done, seizing the dozens of bank certificates, it gave the banks and the U.S. government the opportunity to profit by denying the existence of tens of billions of dollars in CDs held by Santa Romana.

[Part of the Golden Lily Plunder Group]

More significant still is the fact that Kodama worked for the Japanese prince who headed the Japanese secret service and who was overlord of the Japanese plunder teams known as "The Golden Lily." The Golden Lily operated in Mukden in Manchuria, but had its headquarters in Manila, the capital of the Philippines. Kodama was tasked with "shepherding masses of war loot in naval vessels ahead of him under the watchful eye of naval officers seconded to him." The loot had been plundered from all over Asia under Kodama's authority and was moved "up the coast of Borneo through Brunei to the Philippines," where it was eventually buried.

[One Account of Nearly a Billion Dollars]

After Luz was appointed trustee of the Santa Romana estate by New York courts, my wife also told her attorney of one transfer she was personally aware of by her late husband that was close to 800 million U.S. dollars, that the late Sta. Romana transferred on one afternoon, just prior to Marcos declaring martial law in the Philippines, to his main account in then First National City Bank, New York.

[Combined Stonewalling by Bank and U.S. Treasury]

However, when Mrs. Piel wrote to the comptroller of currency and other agencies regarding this and other information she sought, she was totally stonewalled. We now hold evidence showing a part of the late Sta. Romana's accounts in Citibank, and hold other information on Chase Manhattan, Bank of America, Wells Fargo, Melon Bank, Manufactures Hanover, and others.

We also hold evidence which Melvin Belli was able to obtain before his death of many of the late Sta. Romana accounts in the Hong Kong Shanghai Bank in Hong Kong. (Computer print-out taken from the Hong Kong authorities after a bank employee was accused and prosecuted for stealing this print-out to sell to some imposters.

[Records of Half Billion Deposit and 1650 Tons of Gold] We hold evidence, including a copy of a U.S. dollar savings passbook, issued to the late Sta. Romana in March of 1973, clearly showing that on March 16 and 18, 1973, he deposited in these two days close to 500 million U.S. dollars into this U.S. dollar savings account. We also hold other documents showing he also had deposited 1640 metric tons of gold in Sanwa Bank Ltd., Hong Kong.

[Swiss USB Bank Admitted the Account]

I could go on and on listing copies of documents we now hold, listing banks and amounts that are almost unbelievable. I even sat in Switzerland in the early 1990's with my wife and another American gentleman, while she gave a vice-president of Union Bank of Switzerland her late husband's master gold account number with them. This banker not only admitted that it was a correct account number, but also said he was familiar with the account. He went on to tell her, that he also wouldn't recommend her trying to claim this account while she was in Switzerland, because before the bank, or even the government of Switzerland would agree to allow her to take what this account represented, that they were not beyond having her killed first.

He also went on to tell her that he wouldn't recommend her hiring any Swiss attorneys because the bank would simply buy them off. (Therefore, when Mike Wallace, on his 60 Minutes T.V. show recently aired his report on the Jewish victims story, what they had to say was sure no surprise to me.)

In 1995, I was furnished a copy of a letter allegedly written by Ferdinand Marcos to one of his trustees, a Mrs. Santiago, in which he was informing her in 1983 that he was selling some gold bullion which he didn't own, nor the government of the Philippines, deposited in the Po Sang Bank Ltd., Hong Kong, and he was depositing this under her name.

The party who supplied this letter, connected with the Bank of China, also informed us that Marcos did sell this gold to the Rothschild Bank in France in 1983 for close to 53 billion U.S. dollars. However, before Marcos could affect the transfer of these funds, he was taken from power and afterwards these funds were moved to the Bank of China. Upon furnishing us these documents, he also furnished a copy of the gold warehouse receipts under which this gold had been deposited. These receipt numbers matched exactly the gold receipt numbers we had manage to get a copy of the original deposit receipt prior to this, clearly showing the depositor to be Sta. Romana.

In the spring of 1996 I was informed that Imelda Marcos, her children, and her attorneys, and this Mrs. Santiago, were making an attempt to claim these funds from the Chinese Government. (Within days after this, I was offered a personal deal, if I wouldn't try and interfere in what they were doing, whereby they agreed they would pay me personally 2% of the total amount, but absolutely nothing to the estate. I even received a written pay order stating this.) However, prior to this, I had sent copies of these documents to high officials in Beijing.

[Marcos' Lawyers Blocking New York Probate Action]

Within weeks, I was informed that Imelda Marcos and her group had been turned down by the Chinese Government and the Bank of China. Shortly after this, an action was started in New York State to dislodge, discredit, and dismiss my wife's authority in New York State, which had been updated in 1992.

We had already been informed that before leaving office, and without making any attempt to notify my wife or her attorney of record, Marcos had ordered the original Philippine court who had issued the original letters of administration to dismiss them.

[People in All Levels of Government Involved in Cover-Up]

That act was totally illegal even under their laws. Attorney Eleanor Jackson Piel, who was also named as the co-administrator because of residency requirements in 1992, objected to the 1996 New York actions. She and her husband were told in a private meeting that the group now in the process of attempting to do this was headed by a former Security and Exchange Commissioner by the name of James Sargent.[8] The representative the Piels met with went on to tell them that they intended to take the remainder of the late Sta. Romana/Diaz assets and use them for good purposes around the world. Even our former President George H.W. Bush was aware of this.

They used as a front person, a Filipino, who claimed to be a

---

[8] James C. Sargent was chairman on the Securities and Exchange Commission from 1956 to 1960 and a lawyer for many years dealing with SEC matters, and with the law firm of Robert S. Newman, Jack I. Samet, Parr, Doherty, Polk & Sargent.

daughter of the late Sta. Romana, who called herself Flordelisa Sta. Romana. Her real name, which I'm told by my wife that they were able to get documents on, is actually Flordelisa Tanceco.

I'm also told they have even located her real father who is still alive and living in the Philippines. The long and the short of this story is, they made a ridiculous offer if Mrs. Piel would stop objecting to what they were trying to do. After we had turned this offer down, they sent a party to the Philippines to find my wife, who was then and still is recuperating from a paralyzing stroke. They told her that they were working with all the banks, and the governments of the United States and Fidel Ramos, and what they were willing to do was to pay my wife 20% of the entire estate in cash, and the balance would go into a non-profitable trust of which she would be chairman of and have total veto powers over any use of the remainder of these funds.

After reading these things to my wife, she agreed. They then told her they needed to run downstairs in their hotel and get copies made. When they returned, they even videotaped her placing her thumb prints these documents. (She no longer could actually sign her name because of her stroke. They also went as far as to hire the head of the Philippine Bar Association, who my wife had never met, and he also furnished them with a letter stating that my wife knew exactly what she was signing.

However, after returning to New York, what they filed with the court were documents only giving my wife 20 million dollars period, and stating that she had never actually been married to the late Sta. Romana. (The offer we had turned down only days before this, and which my wife was aware of, was for a payment of 100 million dollars.) It was obvious what had happened and was going on, especially after I talked with my wife by telephone and asked her why on earth she would sign, say, and agree to what was presented to the New York court.

When I informed her of what was presented, she went ballistic, and said that was not what she agreed to at all. And furthermore she would never sign anything stating that her and the late Sta. Romana were never legally married, or that this Flordelisa's mother that was married to the late Sta. Romana. Once we had her send a statement of fact, we immediately asked the New York court to delay any action on this case until we could produce proof disputing what was submitted by Sargent's group. Shortly after this, Sargent's people got this case transferred to another New York court, who did dismiss any authority in New York State that my wife and Mrs. Piel held there.

In order to demonstrate just how low these people can be, they even went as far as to threaten Mrs. Piel with taking her to the New York Bar Association and charging her with defrauding the court. If there ever was an example of the kettle calling the pot black, this is one. Not one member of the U.S. press picked up on the story!

The saving grace to all of this is, the late Sta. Romana's will has finally been probated and it clearly states that his wife Luz is to be his next in "like," and to receive all his live accounts, excluding what is named to be paid to others in this will. This will supersedes any other court orders, real or fraudulently obtained.

My wife could not probate this will right after her husband died, because of the high court cost involved due to the amounts stated in this will, and the fact that Ferdinand Marcos and First National City Bank officials had taken and denied even her personal accounts.

We absolutely know there is a real cover-up going on regarding all of this. We know that many don't want this story told. We know that the governments of Cory Aquino, and now Fidel Ramos,[9] have taken the ridiculous official position that the late Sta. Romana/Diaz never even existed and these were just shadow names used by the late Ferdinand Marcos to hide his ill-gotten wealth.

[Powerful Figures Complicit in Cover Up]

Despite some of the bearer documents that have been presented clearly showing these deposit dates long before Ferdinand Marcos was anyone of importance. But, how else could they claim any of the late Sta. Romana/Diaz assets otherwise? We had been told in the early 1990's of an agreement signed in the early 1980's between Marcos, President Ronald Reagan, James Baker on behalf of the U.S. Treasury, John Reed of Citibank, and even Margaret Thatcher for Great Britain, whereby they agreed to take and use the late Sta. Romana/ Diaz's assets for their unauthorized clandestine activities around the world.

This was also a much discussed document on Manila television during 1995. We also know that these people use as a justification that the late Sta. Romana/Diaz's wealth came from what is known as the Japanese spoils of war. However, we have evidence which demonstrates that the late Sta. Romana/Diaz was an extremely wealthy man prior to World War II, and had his first gold account when he was only 12 years of age. Besides, even if this claim were true, which it's not, at least not entirely, what spoils of war did the United States of America lose, or the subsequent governments of

---

[9] President of the Philippines from 1992 to 1998.

Ferdinand Marcos, Cory Aquino, Fidel Ramos, or the government of Japan?

Also, if this justification is true, why didn't anyone having a just claim wait for almost 40 years after the war was over and until after Mr. Sta. Romana's died to make this claim? Why after this, did they wait another few years after the late Sta. Romana died and until the spoils of war act had totally expired to allege his fortune came from this? A cover-up plain and simple, what else?

This is a very hard story to tell in this short form because there is much, much more to tell. My final questions are, "Is freedom of the press dead in America? Is our press so manipulated that the truth can no longer be told and investigated? Is our press so busy chasing 7-11 bandits that they have no time for the biggest on-going theft story in the history of mankind?"

Respectfully C.E. "Jim" Brown 10855 Canby Ave. Northridge, Ca. 91326.

Decades of Cover-Ups by U.S. Media

Jim Brown was wondering why the media was not addressing this matter that revealed a literal secret group, both inside and outside of government, engaging in corruption that has international implications and revealed the culture that openly and unrecognized exists in the United States. Almost every one of my dozen-plus books that I have written since 1978 have detailed the role of U.S. media personnel and media corporations in covering up corruption of key people in government when the gravity of the corruption passes a certain mild state.

This media culture is of far more than academic interest. Several of my books go heavily into how individual Americans have been gravely harmed financially and personally, even death, and how almost every major problem now facing the people and the nation has been caused, or allowed to occur, by documented hardcore corruption that was made known to media people and corporations, which they then "deep-sixth."

If you would like to know the people and groups whose misconduct made the 9/11 hijackings possible, read *Unfriendly Skies: 20th & 21st Centuries*, and also *Crimes of the FBI-DO, Mafia, and Al Qaeda*. The *Unfriendly Skies* book, which is in the fourth edition with the first publication in 1978, shows the behind the scene misconduct that enabled to occur the continuing series of preventable airline disasters—and hundreds of deaths—in the period from 1960 to about 1985. Since I was the FAA airline safety inspector given the assignment to correct the problems resulting in many of those preventable disasters, and documented what I found acting similar to an independent prosecutor, possibly I know what I am talking about! The public isn't totally blameless in these tragedies; many millions of Americans heard the charges during my over 3,000 radio and TV appearances since 1978 and in the thousands of books that were printed.

America's Housing and Financial Frauds is another book I wrote that shows the corrupt culture in the financial field and with such banks as Citibank. UBS or Suisse Bank has also been identified by me in *Defrauding America* and *Drugging America* for their facilitating of drug money laundering. So, the blatant complicity—or outright theft—by Citibank, UBS, Suisse Bank, and others, is right along the type of conduct shown in the past.

Lawyer Betraying a Trust: What Else is New!

After Santa Romana became a gate keeper for some of the recovered gold, he had a young lawyer by the name of Ferdinand Marcos that he also named as trustee for some of the sequestered gold deposits. Marcos was also a young politician at the time, seeking higher political office. When Santa Romana died, his lawyer, Marcos converted many of the certificates of gold deposits into his own name.

The wealth from seizing some of Romana's certificates of gold deposits helped bribe himself to being elected president of the Philippines. And once he became President, Marcos used government personnel in a search for other locations where the Japanese hid the plunder, and covered his tracks by declaring martial law and engaging in brutalities, including eliminating anyone that could be adverse to his actions. Some of the searches discovered huge caches of gold.

During this time, President Ronald Reagan and many members of Congress praised Marcos. (More information on Reagan's "uncomplimentary" covert actions can be seen in my books, *Defrauding America* and *Drugging America.*

Unable to Sell the Plundered Gold

Because gold has certain characteristics, the looted gold that Marcos physically acquired could not easily be sold on the world market. The gold had to be sold at huge discounts. To get around this obstacle, Marcos hired a mining and metallurgic engineer from Nevada to help remelt the gold and change its characteristics and markings.

Philippine Locksmith and Treasure Hunter

Information of the hidden Japanese plunder caused other people and groups to search. A locksmith and treasure hunter, Rogelio Roxas, discovered one of the many sites and inside found a one-ton golden Buddha and numerous gold bars. Word-of-mouth publicity reached President Ferdinand Marcus, resulting in President Marcos using government forces to seize the Roxas' treasure find and to torture Roxas into remaining silent.

Roxas Obtained Federal Judgment for Theft by Marcos

In 1968, a U.S. federal court issued a judgment of $22 billion to the heirs of Rogelio Roxas against the estate of Ferdinand and Imelda Marcus relating to the theft and the torture.

Banks Profited by Denying Claims of Heirs

Banks in which enormous wealth was deposited profited by falsely declaring the certificates of gold deposits as forgeries, or that no such accounts existed. Some of these banks, such as UBS and Citibank, transferred the gold to offshore nations that were beyond the legal reach of the heirs, such as those of Santa Romana.

Many of the largest and most important banks were repositories of Santa Romana gold accounts and these banks *all* rebuffed Santa Romana's heirs. And in the process, enriched themselves by millions or billions of dollars. Since powerful people associated with the U.S. government, and the "secret government " wanted all information on the recovered plunder kept secret, the culture of denying the validity of hundreds of bank accounts was done with support and protection of people in control of key government entities.

Denying Validity of Valid Claims a Part of Banks' Culture

The history of banks worldwide denying the validity of huge bank deposits was in line with the long history of banks engaging in drug money laundering and other criminal activities made the false declaration of forgeries and moving deposits to unreachable offshore locations synonymous cultures. Banks holding billions in gold certificates, especially those that powerful people never wanted exposed, these funds use various devices to never release the wealth. These include labeling bank certificates as forgeries. The massive bank frauds that resulted in the financial scandals that peaked in 2009 are simply an extension of the culture.

Santa Romana's Widow Suffering a Stroke

In November 1995, Luz suffered a stroke and was hospitalized at the San Juan De Dios Educational Foundation hospital in Pasay City, Metro Manila, Philippines. A November 27, 1995, statement written by the facility stated:

Re: Mrs. Luz Brown

To whom it may concern:

This is to certify that Mrs. Luz Brown is presently confined at the San Juan de Dios Hospital under my care because of weakness of the right half of the body and slurred speech.

Diagnosis: Brainstem Infarction
Diabetes Mellitus.
Hypertension

Presently she is incapacitated and unable to write and sign documents.

Philip A. Ramiro, M.D. FPNA
Attending Neurologist

The following are excerpts from the power of attorney that Luz Romana Brown signed to her husband, Clarence Elbert ("Jim") Brown, giving him control over the assets she inherited from Santa Romana's billions of deposits in worldwide banks.

Absolute Power of Attorney

I, the undersigned, LUZ RAMBANO STA. ROMANA-BROWN. Philippine passport number E 262972, being of legal age and of sound mind, individually and as the widow, principal heir, and the legal administrator of my late husband's estate, that of my late husband, SEVERINO GARCIA STA. ROMANA—a/k/a/ JOSE ANTONIOL DIAZ, do hereby appoint and give absolute power of-attorney to my present husband, Clarence ELBERT BROWN, United States Passport Number 034175412, issued in los Angeles, California, on the 13th day of January, 1992, (attested authenticated signature below) to act on my behalf, due to my physical condition, individually, or as the administrator of my late husband's estate under the legal power and authority granted me by the courts, to negotiate, enter into binding agreements and settlements, to establish corporations, open bank accounts and authorize the transfer any funds as he deems proper and see's fit on behalf of me personally and/or for the benefit and on behalf of the estate.

He is further empowered to conduct and make irrevocable decisions regarding the above and any other estate business, such as issuing limited powers of attorneys to those he feels are required to conduct preliminary investigations and negotiations in attempting to uncover accounts and assets. Such powers of attorneys will be limited in scope strictly to discovery and preliminary investigations and negotiations and any and all final agreement/agreements of any actual settlements must be approved by Mr. Brown only.

He is fully empowered to cancel any outstanding power of attorney without recourse.

I hereby confine the above and set my hand of this approval this 22 day of November, 1995, in the City of Manila, Philippines.

/s/________________________
Luz Rambano Sta Romana-Brown

____
Witness
104 Nasrnana—Taclo Baed City

____
Witness 1830 H.
Dommiga St. Pasey City
/s/________________________
Clarence Elbert Brown
Specimen Authenticated Signature

SUBSCRIBED AND SWORN TO before me this 22nd day of November, 1995 at the City of Manila, Philippines.

Jose M Cruz
Doc. No. 735
Page No. 47
Book No. II
Series of 1995

Note: The grantor, Mrs. Luz Rambano Sta. Romana-Brown, cannot write her usual signature because her right hand was severely effected and paralyzed by a stroke that has affected her.

Manila, Philippines
October 17, 1995

To Whom it may concern:

I the undersigned Mrs. LUZ RAMBANO STA. ROMANA - BROWN (Philippine Passport No. E 26297 issued by the Philippine Consulate in Los Angeles California, as the widow administrator and principal heir of the estate of my late husband, SEVERINO GARCIA STA. ROMANA- a/k/a JOSE ANTONIO DIAZ, do hereby appoint and give absolute authority on my behalf to my present husband, MR.

CLARENCE E. BROWN (U.S. Passport # 034175412, issued in Los Angeles California on the 13th day of January 1992.) to conduct preliminary negotiations for me and the estate, with any bank/banks, governments, or any other properly authorized person responsible, for the settlement /settlements of any cash accounts or gold bullion deposits belonging to my late husband. Final approval to any agreements are subject to my final approval in writing confirming any of the preliminary terms required for a peaceful settlement of such accounts and/or precious metal deposits.

Signed and duly notarized this 17, October, 1995 in the
City of Manila, Philippines.

/s/ LUZ RAMBANO STA. ROMANA

SUBSCRIBED AND SWORN to before me this 18th day of Oct. 1995 in Pasay City Metre Manila.

/s/ LUZ RAMBANO STA. ROMANA

Doc. No. 438
/s/ ATTY ARTHIO RATACUTAND (sp ?)
Page No. 88 Notary Public
Book No. 57
Series of 1995

High Price Attorneys Working Without Retainer Indicated Their Confidence in the Validity of the Claims

Working for Santa Romana's widow and new husband were two powerful and expensive law firms, on a contingency basis, without any upfront fees. Such an arrangement only occurs when the attorneys are confident about the validity of the documents. In this case, the documents are the numerous bank account certificates. Among the attorneys seeking to force the banks to recognize Luz Romana Brown as the legal heir and entitled to gain access to the tons of gold shown by the certificates were John Hill of the famous San Francisco law office of Melvin Belli and Jackson Piel[10] of New York City. These attorneys were so convinced of the truthfulness of the claims that they worked without

---

[10] Eleanor Jackson Piel, 36 West 46th Street, New York, New York 10006

up-front payments.

One of the people in Hong Kong helping Santa Romana's widow was Ernie A. Tavaco in Hong Kong. A fax sent by Ernie A. Tavaco in Hong Kong to Clarence "Jim" Brown (May 3 1996), referred to a record of deposit in Citibank New York. (For clarity, excerpts are taken from the actual copies in my possession, and copies of a few are at the end of the book. Also, occasional names or information may be put in bold to focus on especially important information.) That fax identified two of the names used by Santa Romana, and also identified Philippine Gen. Fabian Ver, President Ferdinand Marcos' head of security. Ver's reference is important as it will be seen that upon the death of Santa Romana, Ferdinand Marcos was the attorney used by Romana, and also named as trustee. Marcos converted the certificates of gold deposit from Santa Romana's name to himself. More about this in later pages:

Name of Bank: CITIBANK, 399 Park Ave, New York, NY 100-43 U.S.A.
Bank Officer: Attorney John Emmett or Mr. Hukam Gupsta
Citibank clearing No.:261-88
Principal account No. 787632
Principal account holder: **Diaz and Poirotte Enterprises**
Account name: **Jose Antonio Diaz dela Paz**
Reference code name: Berget Harbour King/Fabeut King Fisher
Full account number: 432-20-11
Tax account number: 4293284-5
Metal control number:UBS number C-2311
Metal account number: (46813525) 430-20-2911-797637
Identity code: 2-28-1908
Safety Deposit Box No.: 77236 Code 28
Code number: YAB No. 42-83-84

In the communication, Ernie Tavaco gave details of the gold that was claimed by Marcos' heirs:

Jim, the volume is 63.766 metric tons in this certificate alone; there are 42 certificates all originals with this group. I believe this is a part and parcel of the Purple Ink Conspiracy. As explained to me, the Coded Number YAB 42-83-84 is YAB is Dr. Olive Bay, her name spelled backward; 42 is the number of certificates 1, 2, 3, to 42 (this is the 42nd certificate); 83-84 is the year it was transacted and or transferred from Central Bank to the CITIBANK in New York. I can get photo copies of these certificates but I need to pay and reward these people. I remember this was the very stock being offered in Hongkong by Major Juancho Perez, Col. Bulos and Romy Guiab. (The Brother in law of Gen Fabian

Ver.) They were able to con some people in Hongkong, including a good friend of mine, Mr. Roy Pate.

This guy I believe will testify against this group if necessary.

Here also is the cash deposit of the old man at National City Bank at Chase Manila. I obtained this from Mrs. Brinas, a wife of the former Central Bank Deputy Governor during Marcos time. I was shown lots of documents. They are willing to cooperate with us but not Luz.

I am arranging the possibility of a conference with General Ver late this month in Amsterdam, Dr. AB Reyes and myself will see him, regarding some metals left and entrusted to him by FM [Ferdinand Marcus]. The General is dying and his group wants an immediate disposal of all these stocks before his demise.

[Keeping Low Profile]

I already bought tickets for Cely and me to Hongkong. We are set to go to Hongkong, Monday. The Chinese Group is not available in Hongkong till Tuesday May 7. With my group will be Attorney Vic Millera (representing Imelda Marcos) Bro. Ben Astillere, (Bishops Conf. of the Phil.), Fr. Rogelio Cortes (representing the interest of the Vatican); Dominador Ortiz representing Candelaria Santiago as signatory and Trustee. Another group will follow after a week: Miss Santiago, Ira AB Rayes, Te Water, Imee Marcos, Irene Marcos and their husbands. We will be staying in different places to conserve the discreetness of the deal and spending on our own.

My warmest personal regards to you and Atty. John Hill [San Francisco law firm of Melvin Belli]. Hope to see you both very soon in Hongkong.

Sincerely yours,

Ernie Tavaco

Portions of a Letter (April 28, 1996) from the group to Ernie concerning the Bank of China funds.

TERMS & CONDITIONS 4/28/1996

Mr. Ian Hendy
International Buying Services
Harbour Crystal Centre
100 Granville Road
Kowloon, Hong Kong

Dear Mr. Hendy, **<u>EXTREMELY SECRET</u>, <u>PRIVATE & CONFIDENTIAL</u>**

Subject: retrieval of cash deposits and/or negotiable bank promissory notes covering interest and capital from the bank of china, Beijing, in the name of Candelaria v Santiago, resultant from the sale of AU, formerly held on deposit by Posan Bank, Hong Kong.

GREETINGS:

Our principals are ready to agree to the following terms and conditions, subject to contract:

- The new deposit account should be domiciled in the Bank or China, London, United Kingdom, offshore account, and evidenced by a basket of hard currency, promissory notes covering capital, payable upon each maturity date and a basket of hard currency promissory notes, covering the interest payable quarterly in arrears, during the period of deposit.
- Due to the age, health and physical condition of Candelaria v. Santiago, we respectfully request that all final negotiations and the table top closing are to be held in Hong Kong, and not Beijing.

Candelaria v. Santiago is ready, willing and able to appear in person, and provide her credentials, passport and personal documentation, which proves her identity and authority.

____

DOMINADOR J. MORTIZ
Trustee Of
CADELARIA V. SANTIAGO

With Passport no. I-840080 issued on March 30 at Manila

____

VICENTE D. MILLORA,
Authorized Mandate of Mrs. IMELDA R. MARCOS.
With Passport no AA-4290954 issued on September 15, 1995 at Manila

WITNESSES:

____

NORMAN K. TEWATER ERNESTO A. TAVACO

Indication of the Scheme Concocted by People in The CIA, U.S. Military, and White House Politicians

One of the copies of certificates of gold deposits given to me by Santa Romana's widow provided proof of the diversion of the Japanese plunder. The certificate was issued by First National Bank, New York, that became Citibank, and names as account holder Maj. Gen. Eduard Lansdale It was Lansdale, with Santa Romana, that first discovered several of the caves containing tons of gold bars and other valuables. Both were members of the OSS, CIA, and in Lansdale case, the U.S. Army. This one document, the contents of which could be confirmed by the U.S. Department of Justice—but never will—shows nearly one trillion dollars in a secret bank account shared by OSS-CIA Santa Romana and U.S. General and CIA Lansdale. The following is the data on the certificate of gold deposit given to me by Santa Romana's widow:

First National City Bank
932 Park Ave., New York
New York, 11143, U.S.A.

Serverino Garcia Sta. Romana **Jose Antonio Diaz de la Paz**
FNCB acct. No. 430037 FNCB Acct. No. 768423
Ref. Code name: Fanerst King Ref. Code name: burgst harbour fischer king

Account: Original gold deposit convertible to cash plus earnings in U.B.S. Bahnhof Strasse 45 Zurich

(1) Account No. 01-402-244
Ref. Code RC Delikon, Schaffhaustenstrasse
AMOUNT - $339M [MILLION]
(2) Account No. 01-621-020
Ref. Code Albisrieden, Alisreidplatz
Amount- $8M
(3) Account No. 01-271-331
Ref. Code Altstten, Badsenarstrasse
Amount - $682M

ASSIGNED SIGNATORY:

-JOSE DIAZ/SEVERINO GARCIA STA. ROMANA

-JOSE ANTONIO de LA PAZ
-MAJ. GEN. **EDUARD LANSDALE**

Another account for Santa Romana with the Wespac Bank in Australia:

Name of Bank: WESPAC BANK --AUSTRALIA

Account No.: 13801 FLAT 11460-555 CASH ACCOUNT.
13801 FLAT 11460-999 CORPORATE ACCOUNT
13801 FLAT 11460-333 ESTATE ACCOUNT

<u>CITIBANK/CITICORP, FORMERLY NATIONAL CITY BANK</u>

Master Account Number: 787632
Principal Account Holder: **Diaz and Poerrote Enterprises**
Account Name: **JOSE ANTONIO DIAZ DE LA PAZ**
Reference: **BERGOT HARBOUR KING**
Full Account Number: 432-20-011
Seller's Metal Account No.: C-2311 (UBS)
Bank Officer: Frank Paul Collins
IDENTITY CODE: 2291908
Tax Account Number: 429-3284-5
Clearing Number: 26188

SEVERINO GARCIA STA. ROMANA
F.N.C.B. Account No. 430037
Reference Code Name: Fanerst King Fischer

JOSE ANTONIO N DIAZ de LA PAZ
FNCB Account No. 768423
Reference Code Name: BURGST HARBOUR KING

SEVERINO GARCIA STA. ROMANA
FNCB Account Name: 654-342

JUAN MARIANITO T. STA. ROMANA
No. 1012301918

RENATO TORRES STA. ROMANA
No. 18201918

WITNESSSES

____________________ ____________________

____

The significance of the following document is that it addresses the tons of gold and the involvement of the Catholic Church and the Vatican. Other reference in the book shows the involvement of the Vatican:

CERTIFICATE OF EXCLUSIVE MANDATE

TO WHOM IT MAY CONCERN:
Be it known that:

Mr. Mabini C. Astillero
Director-Consultant
Office of Bishop Nicolas M. Mondejar, D.D.
Catholic Bishop's Conference of the Philippines
Intramuros, Manila, Philippines.

Is exclusively mandated as my personal Representative-Attorney-in-Fact to negotiate and arrange with any interested party—for the recovery, claim and sale of confidential bullion accounts under my name and trusteeship as heir-beneficiary—deposited at several world prime/bullion banks in Asia, Europe and America.

As such, Mr. Astillero is authorized to enter into agreement and sign his contract with any interested party/foreign institution or any corporation which enjoys the trust and confidence of Mr. Astillero.

Further, Mr. Astillero is also authorized to arrange and negotiate for the required "goodwill funds" from any interested party-buyer/joint venture partner.

The undersigned shall be the final signatory at the bank's...

Any cooperation extended to Mr. Astillero shall be greatly appreciated.

Cordially,

MDE. **CANDELARIA V. SANTIAGO**
HEIR-BENEFICIARY/ACCOUNT HOLDER CON-
FORME

MABINT C. ASTILLERO July 10, 1994
Exclusive Representative Bulacan, Philippines

Subscribed and sworn to before me this 11th day of

CONFIDENTIAL APPOINTMENT

The following is a record of funds in the Dresdner Bank for Santa Roman under the names of Diaz and Poerrote Enterprises and Nannette Cooly Enterprises.

Dresdner Bank, Franfurt, Germany
B.C. 050-005
Dated: 06-141981
Acct: A.I.U. 8256
Book: 140-04715

CODE NAME:	"DERYKON"
Bank Officer:	Chairman of the Board
Acct. No. :	01-484-321
Reference Code Name:	"SCHEFAAUSERTRASSES"
COMPANY:	DIAZ AND POERROTTE ENTERPRISES
OR	
	NANNETTE COOLY ENTERPRISES
OWNER:	DON JOSE ANTONIO DIAZ
BANK ADDRESS:	BAHNHOFSTRASSE
	45, 8001 Zurich, Switzerland

CODE NAME:	"SQUUVANEDIENEN"
Reference Code Name:	"WINTERTHORNESTRASSE"
Bank Officer:	Chairman of the Board
Account No. :	01-402-244
OWNER:	DON ANTONIO DIAZ
COMPANY:	DIAZ AND POERROTTE ENTERPRISES

In Santa Romana' ledger records were the following record:

Or NANNETTE COOLY ENTERPRISES BAHNHOFSSTRASSE
45, 8001 Zurich, Switzerland

BANK ADDRESS:	BAHNHOFSSTSRASSE
	45, 8001 Zurich, Switzerland

UBS ACCOUNT	AMOUNT	CODE NOS.
1. H O I D	$ 1M	AMMARTPLATZ
5. B E L L E V U E	$ 155M	01-737-0131

[In 11 accounts there was shown a total of $416 million.]

UBS	SANWA BANK CENTRAL DISTRICT
Bank Account No.	15-2504011-- Hongkong 75267-C10
Account No.	916-002358-4
Reference Code:	SEEFELDS/SEEFELDS/FRASSE

DEPOSITORY NO. A-112834562-A-7
POSANS BANK, CENTRAL DISTRICT
Hongkong
Account No. 681-112785

Santa Romana's records for the following accounts at First National City Bank in New York City showed a total of $1 billion and $29 million in deposits.

FIRST NATIONAL CITY BANK
932 Park Avenue, New York
New York 11143, U.S.A.

Severino Garcia Sta. Romana	**Jose Antonio Diaz De La Paz**
FNCB Acct. No. 430037	FNCB Acct. No. 768423
Ref. Code Name:	FANERST KING

REF. CODE NAME: BURGST HARBOUR FISCHER KING

Account: Original gold deposit convertible to cash plus earnings in U.B.S. Bahnhofstrasse 45 Zurich.

Account No. 01-402-244
Ref. Code RC DELIKON, Schaffhaustenstrasse
Amount: $339M
(2) Account No. 01-621-020
Ref. Code ALBISRIEDEN, ALBISSREIDENPLATZ
Amount: $8M
(3) Account No. 01-271-331
Ref. Code: ALTSTETTEN, BADEENARSTSRASSE

Amount: $682M

ASSIGNED SIGNATORY:
--JOSE ANTONIO DIAZ/SEVERINO GARCIA STA. ROMANA
--JOSE ANTONIO DE LA PAZ
--MAJ. GEN. EDUARD LANSDALE

Name of Bank: WESPAC Australia
Account Number: 13801 FLAT 11460-555
Cash account.
13801 FLAT 11460-999 Corporate Account.
13801 FLAT 11460-333 Estate Account

CITIBANK/CITICORP, FORMERLY NATIONAL CITY BANK

Master Account Number: 787632
Principal Account Holder: Diaz and Poerrote Enterprises
Account Name: JOSE ANTONIO DIAZ DE LA PAZ
Reference: BERGOT HARBOUR KING
Full Account Number: 432-20-011
Seller's Metal Account Number: C-2311 (UBS)
Bank Officer: Frank Paul Collins
IDENTITY CODE: 2291908
Tax Account Number: 429-3284-5
Clearing Number: 26188

SEVERINO GARCIA STA. ROMANA
F.N.C.B. Account No. 430037
Reference Code Name: Fanerst King Fischer

JOSE ANTONIO N DIAZ de LA PAZ
FNCB Account No. 768423
Reference Code Name: BURGST HARBOUR KING

SEVERINO GARCIA STA. ROMANA
FNCB Account Name: 654-342

JUAN MARIANITO T. STA. ROMANA
No. 1012301918

RENATO TORRES STA. ROMANA
No. 18201918

WITNESSSES

________________________ _________________________

____

In a May 16, 1996, letter to Hong Kong trader Ernesto Tavaco, Santa Romana's widow husband wrote, as it related to Ferdinand and Imelda Marcos:

What we are dealing with here are lies, greed and cover-ups that have gone on for almost twenty years. I personally believe that even Ferdinand Marcos, although not void of personal power and greed, was forced to do many things by powers he even feared. Even when asked, after he was forcefully took to Hawaii did he leave of his own accord, he simply smiled and waved his hand sideways and replied, "I don't want to rock any boats right now."

As far as Imelda Marcos is concerned, I don't believe she knew all that was going on. There is even evidence of this in the letter Marcos wrote to Santiago. This brings us to Sta. Romana. There were simply too many detailed stories indicating that relationship between Imelda and Mr. Sta. Romana. Luz's father told me before he died, that Santy admitted to him that Imelda was his daughter. If you ever saw a picture of the late Sta. Romana, you would have to admit that they did indeed favor. However, Luz claims that Santy always told her that she was only his Goddaughter, although Luz also questions this because of an incident at Nelson Rockefeller house in New York.

Luz also tells of how Imelda didn't want Santy to be with her or marry her. This I believe is not only also true, but understandable.

What Imelda never understood was, Luz loved Santy and he obviously loved her. Because of this, Luz refused to take up arms in the courts against Imelda even after Cory Aquino advised her to do so after Cory was thrust into power.

I believe this was her reason for not doing so. In fact, when Imelda was in danger and put on trial in New York City, I personally flew to New York with Luz, because some bankers came and asked Luz to please try and help Imelda by telling the truth as to where most of the money came from that Ferdinand and Imelda were alleged to have taken.

Santy did place her name on most of his major bank accounts, but Marcos had the darn documents. I also believe, if Luz had not been so stubborn and would have gone to Hawaii when Marcos asked her to, neither Luz or Imelda would still be in the mess they are today.

John Hill, who is head of the Belli Foundation and I hope to be in the Far East by the weekend after next. Let's hope we can work together to solve this mess and put this ridiculous situation back on the tract of reality where it belongs.

Regards,

Jim

cc: Attorney Jackson Piel, New York
Attorney John Hill San Francisco

The following agreement between Luz Romana Brown and Carlos Gonzales, Jr., referred to the contract of sale relating to 40 to 80 metric tons of gold from Santa Romana's estate:

AGREEMENT

This agreement made and entered into by and between Carlos F. Gonzales, Jr., Filipino, of legal age, with residence and postal address at 2463 Aurora St., Pasay city, Metro Manila, Philippines, herein represented by himself and hereinafter called seller/signatory,

AND

Luz Sta. Romana-Brown, likewise of legal age, and with postal address at P.O. Box 2202 Rancho Santa Fe, California 92067 United States of America, herein represented by herself and herein after called buyer/signatory;

WITNESSETH

Whereas, parties have signed this agreement which refers to a contract of sale of 40 thousand – 80 thousand metric tons, more or less depending upon the documents released by the courier of au subject to the stipulations, terms and conditions hereunder enumerated and which are self-explanatory;

Whereas, parties hereto hereby warrant under penalty of existing laws both in the republic of the Philippines and the State of California, USA, that they have full power to enter into this agreement which will be binding between themselves and against third parties;

Whereas, seller/signatory is the duly authorized and legally constituted attorney-in-fact for the actual shippers/holders of precious metal commodities in the form of refined gold and silver' bars, coins, and precious metal concentrates delivered by depositories in the United States of America and elsewhere overseas, through the instance of brinks which holds the documents thereto;

Whereas, seller/signatory has in his sole possession the only sourcing and files in the form of certified facsimiles of the original documents having been deliberately destroyed to preserve the commodities due to "force majuere" political upheavals that took place in the Philippines that has placed the security of the commodities and documents in great danger;

Whereas buyer on its own behalf agrees to buy the commodities on as is, where is basis, or their present state, conditions, depositories and will do its utmost to transact with courier and other necessary parties to consummate this transaction;

ACKNOWLEDGMENT

BEFORE ME, a Notary Public for and in the City of Pasay on this 14th day of February 1992 at Pasay City, Metro Manila, personally appeared Tomas Rodriguez with Residence Certificate

No. 1923936 issued at Pasay on 1-3-92 known to me to be the same person who executed the foregoing General Power of Attorney, who acknowledged to me that the same is his true and voluntary act and deed.

WITNESS MY HAND AND SEAL on the date and at the place first above written.

Doc. No. 211 Page No. Book No. xxx, Series of 1992.

Jesus B. Bongon
Notary Public
Until Dec 1993
Tan No 832xxxxxx
PTR No. xxxxxxxxxx1-6-92

The following letter to Jim Brown from Ernie Tavaco in Manila concerning funds in the Bank of China:

To: Mr. Jim Brown
Fax No. 1 818 3638336

From: Ernie Tavaco
Fax No. 852 25768673
Tel No. 852 28909527

31st March 1996

Dear Jim,

In compliance with the request of Mr. Handy to have a copy of Marcos' letter to Ms. Santiago and a basic requirement of the Bank, I translated the tagalog letter in English, this will be brought to Bank of China-Beijing prior to actual presentation of Ms. Candelaria V. Santiago personally to the bank with all relevant documents relative to this account. I wanted so much to join Mr. Hendy to Beijing not only to protect our commission but to get acquainted with some people in the bank which we can use to help us in our quest with the Sta Romana account. The account in Ms. Santiago's name we were told by a top tank Officer is existing (though it was transferred from Posan Bank to Bank of China in Beijing) all we need is to produce the signatory after proper representation negotiation with the Bank.

Ms. Santiago has received the final instruction from Imelda Marcos last night as to where their money be transferred and banks to be used, the party in due to arrive Hongkong this week, wait for the instruction from the Beijing Bank to proceed.

With these foregoings I am required to stay in Hongkong, proceed to China twice, once with Bendy, then to join Ms. Santiago to protect our commissions. Jim, I am practically dried up; the long wait for Raymund has exhausted all my resources in Hongkong, I am still to settle few days arrears in this Guest House we are staying (Cely, my wife is with me because of my hypertension and erratic blood sugar.) Anyway, I believe this is much quicker than the account of the "old man," also our chance to have plenty of funds to be used in our quest with the Sta Romana Estate. We are looking to at least 3% commission out of 53 billion US Dollars. Please try your very best to help, I need to know the result soonest because time is of the essence.

My warmest regards to you all,

Sincerely years,

Ernie A. Tavaco

This letter comes with other 4 pages.

The following letter (April 11, 1996) from Jim Brown, husband of Santa Romana's widow, to Ernesto Tavaco in Manila, referred to the dual claims by Santa Romana's widow and Imelda Marcus to certificates of gold deposits in the Bank of China.

To Ernesto Tavaco (Manila phone number 826 5159) from: C.E. Brown

Ernie:

Sorry for the forty-eight hour delay in answering your last fax. However, I wanted to really give it a lot of thought. Of course, you are absolutely right regarding Luz screwing up most anything she touches. Although, I don't believe that is her intention necessarily, that's just Luz for you. As you are well aware, that was the opinion expressed even by Ben Alonte last fall and his delighted comments over the fact that she had finally given me the full authority to act legally on her behalf.

This brings me to what you said was being offered. Needless to say, four percent for you and me, especially in view of the amount involved would be excellent. The only problem is, it's simply not fair to Luz and the other heirs.

What always seems to have been the problem with all the people involved is pure and simple greed. Whether it be Luz, Mrs. Marcos, the brokers, lawyers, or whoever. I have proclaimed all along that Mrs. Marcos and Luz should make peace and not only respect one another, but work together. This was why I insisted and went with Luz to New York City when Mrs. Marcos was put on trial and Luz offered to help her through her attorney, Mrs. Piel, in an offer submitted to Jerry Spence.

Regarding this Poson deposit. Here again, it seems to be greed calling the shots instead of common sense. I don't care what the advisors and brokers think regarding the fact that President Marcos was able to take and sell product that we now can prove belonged to Mr. Sta. Romana, then put the proceeds into Mrs. Santiago's name at that time, as being a situation beyond correction. Because, one does not have to be an attorney, but simply use plain old common horse sense to realize that this doesn't give Mrs. Santiago, or Mrs. Marcos the right to claim the proceeds of something which we now can prove was clearly stolen from Mr. Sta. Romana. Simple logic should tell anyone that.

Therefore, they have a right to be concerned. Because, there is no doubt, that we could make a legal claim of the proceeds from such a sale as a just demand for the recovery of assets. But, this would mean that, most likely, it would drag out for who knows how long and every claimant, whether justified or not, who's trying to hog in on Imelda Marcos or Luz would put their two cents in as well. So, the end results would most likely be that neither of them might not live long enough to see anything from this, which in my viewpoint is absolutely stupid. (To heck with pride on either part)

I don't know if the people whom you are talking with actually represent Mrs. Marcos or Mrs. Santiago's interest, or if like so many other in Manila, only hope to.

If they do represent Mrs. Marcos and/or in this case, Mrs. Santiago, I would suggest that we quit fighting one another and make peace.

Therefore, what I intend to propose, you most likely could never get Luz to agree to. However, since I have the power and authority to make a final and binding decision on Luz's behalf, and the estate, ... what I'm suggesting is, that we join forces, stop trying to destroy one another and work together. Not only for the Bank of China funds, but other problems as well.

Regarding the Bank of China, apply together, with their side and ours signing for the release of these funds on whatever time schedule is agreeable by the Bank of China, and payments of the withdrawal in accordance with percentage interest held by all parties, with you and I still getting the 4% as suggested of the gross amount, and 21% to be paid to Luz, as the widow of the late Sta. Romana, the original and true legal administrator of estate. And also in accordance with the terms stated in Mr. Sta. Romana's holographic will. If this is agreeable, I'm willing to sign on behalf of Luz and the estate, a binding agreement with the legal representatives of Mrs. Marcos and/or Mrs. Santiago.

At this percentage, Mrs. Marcos and Mrs. Santiago, would be required to pay from the balance of the 75% any and all other cost, commission and expenses involved, including mine and yours to finalize this arrangement.

This should put an end to any outside interest interference, along with any reservations by China, especially if this can be negotiated and done secretly and quickly, which I have full confidence it can from the Chinese end from what I have been told.

I also believe, it may also open the door to further cooperation between Mrs. Marcos and the estate regarding other questioned accounts which we are all familiar with.

Ernie, I must caution you, to make sure we are dealing with the real authorized people on this. If the people you are dealing fits this necessity in order to truly accomplish anything with them, and not coffee shop hustlers, they are welcome to read this fax. But, under no circumstances are you to leave a copy of this fax with anyone. If the people are genuine and will agree, then I would suggest they come here, or we meet in Hong Kong, and sign a formal agreement to what I believe is more than a fair proposal on our part.

Please advise me A.S.A.P, because you know full well, what I have working here and with who. So, I must slam on the breaks or go full steam ahead. Again I caution, if this proposal is accepted, we must carry through on this in the strictest of confidence and the fewer to know, the better, until everything is done and finished totally at least.

I can't make a better offer in view of other things. Let's hope these people can see the fairness and wisdom in this proposal and what I have written. Let's also see now how real and sincere these people are that you are dealing with.

Regards,

Your pal.

Jim Brown

The following fax from Jim Brown to Ernie Tavaco relates to funds at the Dank Bank of China in Beijing.

1 818 3638336

To : Jim Brown
From : Ernie Tavaco
Date : 10 April 1996

Dear Jim,

I cannot fully get the consensus of Candelaria V. Santiago's Group relative to your suggestions as to the sharing in the 53 USD deposit at the Bank of China in Beijing, I found it hard also with Hanley changing his decision, now be agrees later he won't. The problem lies in the belief of these people that true to the fact the money came from the proceeds of stolen gold but it is now impossible to prove this belongs to the Sta. Romana Estate due to the manipulation of Marcos selling the gold and depositing the proceeds instead.

Anyway, I still would strongly suggest we go on with the on-going negotiation with the daughter of Dong Xiao Ping and top Chinese government officials regarding this claim. They are also trying to ask the assistance of the son of Dong which Te Water said they will top in case Hanley will not cooperate, (which I know he won't). They offered 4% for us as a share if we will not oppose this on-going negotiation. I told them I will consult you on this: 4% is 2.12 billion USD, but again, I said I am leaving the matter to you.

I am still here, I could not reroute our tickets because GG is not here. They wanted me to join them to Hongkong to convince Handy to join us to Beijing. But again I said I am still waiting for your call on this.

Have not seen Tita Luz since I came, I hate giving her any info's anymore. The information I gave her re: .... here (sp.?) deposit under the name of LUZ C. RAMABANO in the computer in Hong Kong Bank is now been circulated in Hongkong; also, with the proposed money from Raymund, Dr. Stanley Ho, I heard went to Manila xxx Clemente Santiago and made queries in this, Tita Luz also is telling me she is going to Hongkong and will make withdrawals in her accounts at Hongkong Bank. I do not know how she can do this, but one thing is sure; she will again madden the bank, thereby making our contacts to shy away from us or even endangering me for that matter.

So much for now, I am awaiting your instruction, please keep me posted.

Regards and thanks,

Ernie Tavaco

Try this number for your fax communications to me:
63 2 521 7225 tel adv. pls. 826 5159. (This is a Globe Telecom number, they will call me.)

The following message from Tavaco to Jim Brown referred to documents showing gold to be that which Ferdinand Marcos discovered:

GLOBE TELECOM TEL NO: 632 521 7225
1 816 3630336 (Northridge. Calif., USA)

To: Mr. Jim Brown
From: Mr. Ernie Tavaco
Date: April 16. 1996

Dear Jim,

I had a long talk with some people involve with CANTELARIA V. SANTIAGO. Luckily, one of the lady funding her is Dr. Amelu Bemitez Reyes, the President and Ex-of Philippine Women Universality, sister of former Ministry Jelly Benitez during Marcos time and my associate in the APA stock of supposed gold left behind by Marcos where I was deeply involved (I showed you letter and pictures regarding this) through her.

I was shown some documents which really confused me as to the veracity of the real guy behind this money at Po Sang Bank (now at Bank of China in Beijing). I was shown pictures of trucks, helicopters hauling gold bars inside a tunnel supposedly in Davao, custodial receipts from Central Bank of the Philippines, bill of ladings from Tamaraw Security, a subsidiary of Brinks Int'l loading gold bars consigned to Drexel Burnham bearing the hallmarks CB RP Metal) proceeds of which was deposited by Marcos with PO Sang Bank Hongkong.

With these forgivings, I cannot insist your idea of giving Luz a share; it is very clearly explained to me that this commodity is part of Yamashita Treasure found in Davao during Marcos time under his absolute control. Worst, I was told the people who actually found this were not given their share but were also massacred by the Special Forces during Martial Law days. The Po Sang Bank Warehouse receipt you gave me had nothing to do with this account.

Now, since I could not justify our claim and in the event it was me who opened this deal with Hanly and we are getting 4% commission because of this, we might just as well get our money and go on with the other deposits.

Find enclosed herewith the pay orders prepared by Te Water (representing Santiago and other Marcos beneficiaries). The original Bank Pay Orders will be issued by the Bank of China upon presentation of Candelaria Santiago in Beijing.

I was requested by the group to hand-carry Santiago's passport photographs, embassy authentication of identify, clear photocopy of letter addressed to principal including my translation) originals of these will be hand carried by her to Beijing. I will be giving the copies to Mr. Handy for submission to Bank of China Beijing. I am supposed to leave this week but I am still immobilized. Were you able to get and or arrange some funds at your end?

If so, I would suggest you come to Hongkong with me, remember, we are getting 4% which is 2.12 B [billion] USD, you can call me now at my new telephone number 829 2563 it was loaned to me by Cely's aunt. I just had it installed yesterday. I am working for the installation of a fax machine but I still need to buy the fax machine unit in Hongkong. Pls call.

My warmest regards to you, Michael, Walter and Gary lets pray together for the early conclusion of this deal so everybody will have money.

Sincerely yours,

Ernie A. Tavaco

The significance of the following writing by Jan Handy, provided to me by Santa Romana's widow, is that it explains where President Marco accepted an offer of $53 billion U.S. dollars (USD) for gold in the Posan Bank, Hong Kong that belonged to Santa Romana's estate.

The following are excerpts from a letter (May 19, 1996) that Brown and Luz wrote to their New York attorney, Eleanor Jackson Piel, in response to attorneys opposing her court filing in New York City of papers showing Luz Romana Brown as the trustee for the estate of Santa Romana:

Mrs. Piel:

To answer the letter they sent you yesterday, I will tell you what I know about this part in as much exact detail as possible and before you take the position as you read this that you need documented proof, I will get this for you as soon as possible.

(1) We both know right after Mr. Sta. Romana's death, when Luz found that her personal accounts in the First National City Bank in Manila could not be taken, because her deposit receipts and savings passport were in the safe deposit boxes in this bank which she was not allowed access to, she didn't have the required filing fees to probate the Holographic Will. (This fee was so high due to the fact that this will listed hundreds of millions of dollars to be paid to various people.) Therefore, her attorneys at the time advised Luz under such circumstances that she had no choice but to file for only the Letters of Administration as she did. (It would be hard for anyone to logically criticize Luz from doing this, especially in a country run by an absolute dictator who was later proved to have been behind a move to steal all these assets. Also, she was a young inexperienced widow simply following her attorneys' advice and instructions.)

(2) To establish this point even more regarding her inexperience and youth, she was also foolish and insisted that her late husband include this Flordelisa not only in his will, but she also listed her in her petition asking to be appointed as the administratrix, because Flordelisa had befriended her at the time and was with her constantly.

(3) Months later, when she was appointed by the Court of First Instance in the City of Manila and she, along with others returned to the First National City Bank, the bank officials first denied that even any safety deposit boxes existed in her late husband's name. However, she always carried a key to one of the boxes that contained the keys to the others. When she presented this in front of the many witnesses with her,

finally the bank opened this box for her. However, despite going to this bank and helping her husband take items from seven additional boxes and place into this particular box, items they planned on taking with them on an upcoming worldwide trip only days before the late Sta. Romana was hospitalized, when this box was opened, all it contained was a Manila newspaper which was dated long after her husband had died and during the time she was being appointed as the Administratrix for the estate.

(4) She turned this newspaper over to the court of First Instance and the last time I personally saw this court file in the court, it was still in the court file on this case.

(5) After this, Luz traveled to New York, and upon a recommendation from Attorney Lubrim, came to your office, accompanied by J.V. Valasquez, to see a Mr. Milton Freedman, who turned her problem over to you.

(6) Approximately two years after this, Luz was contacted by Flordelisa Tanceco, who was now calling herself Flordelisa Sta. Romana and asked for Luz's permission to allow her to be added to the Letters of Administration in the court of First Instance as a co-administratrix, using as an excuse, that while Luz was searching for accounts of Mr. Sta. Romana abroad, she would work in trying to locate assets in the Philippines. This Luz agreed to and Flordelisa was added as such.

(7) I believe it was in 1988, when I first met Luz and went to the court of First Instance in Manila with her. The reason for going because she had been told that her Letters of Administration had been dismissed without notifying her or any of her Philippine attorneys.

(8) When she inquired about this with the Clerk of the Court of First Instance, he only smiled and told her at that time that this was true and told her when this was done.

Luz immediately replied that what he was telling her couldn't be true, because they had gotten an order from the court after that date ordering a bank in Cebu, Philippines to disclose some records.

She then insisted that he get the court file folder. Sure enough, when he did, the order she spoke of was there, along with an unopened letter addressed to one of her attorneys. (Note: Later in 1993, when I saw this file again, they had tried to cover their tracks by showing us a copy of this unopened letter again, only this time, it was opened and they had attached a note to it saying that it had been received by another party and opened by mistake, after which, it was sent back to the court. As God is my Holy wittiness this is true.

At that time, she hired a Philippine attorney by the name of Rene Gasmen, who had been investigating the case because he had been asked to get involved in one aspect of the matter by this Flordelisa. He said that he had discovered not only that Flordelisa's original school records indicated her name as Flordelisa Tanceco, but also he was told that Mr. Sta. Romana's widow (Luz) was still alive and had been the original administrator for the estate.

He continued and informed Luz at the time, that Flordelisa showed him paper work indicating, not only she was the administratrix of the estate and had been appointed by a court in Cabanatuan City in the Philippines, but also in her original petition to the court there, stated that there had never been any other Letters of Administration issued before this. (NOTE: Later we were informed that when Luz went to Cabanatuan and made a fuss over this, that this original petition was changed in the court records omitting the statement of no other Letters of Administration ever existed.)

NOTE TWO: On that visit, Gasmen, myself, and Luz also talked with the late Sta. Romana's brother, who was a judge in Cabanatuan, Judge Mike Sta. Romana, who told us that he had absolutely nothing to do with what was going on regarding Flordelisa and his sister's husband. Another member in the prosecutor's office was there, and that in his opinion, Flordelisa had been ill-advised as he put it. He went on to tell us that Flordelisa, her mother and two brothers had just showed up one day in Cabanatuan when Flordelisa was a young girl and came to the family there and told them that these children's father was Santy.

[Death of Santa Romana's First Wife]

He went on to tell us, that knowing Santy, the family laughed and thought it might be true. However, Santy was not around at the time and they had been there ever since. He also told Gasmen, Luz, and myself, that when Santy did finally show up, it was with Luz, who was the only women he ever introduced them to as his wife, except his first wife Angelian (Compton), the mother of Peter, Roy, and Mary Ann Diaz. (Angelian was killed at the outset of World War II by a Japanese fighter plane and the children were sent back to Pasadena during the war and raised by Angelian's parents.)

NOTE THREE: Obviously, they have manufactured something today. But, at the time that the original Letters of Administration were issued, Flordelisa was asked and couldn't produce one single piece of paper indicating that her or her brothers were even children. Nor, could she produce and marriage contract between her mother and Sta. Romana, because the court and judge asked for it at the time.

Regarding all the court documents relating to judges turning down request by Luz to have this wrong set right, this is true. The first time this happened that I'm aware of was when Gasmen filed a motion to have this done. However, at that time, Luz didn't have the bribe money that Gasmen claimed was required to get the judge to do this, even though it was the proper thing to do.

The second time I know of was, I believe in 1993, when Nori Yamamoto paid a former official of Cory's administration, a Wilson Gamboa, ten thousand U.S. dollars to do this very thing. After a few weeks, Gamboa came back to us and said the judge had agreed, but asked for several thousand U.S. dollars more, which Gamboa smiled and told us was the custom and needed to pay the current judge. NOTE: This is also true, because I was personally there when this happened and I heard and know this to be an absolute fact.

That afternoon, I went to the clerk of the courts office regarding this and threaten to expose the whole thing in the world press. When I did this, the clerk of the court obviously became nervous and admitted to us that everything had been mishandled and went on to tell us that the original order to dismiss these Letters of Administration had come direct from Malaconyang as he put it. (Marcos) He then suggested that Luz either resubmit a request to the current judge, or appeal to a higher court.

NOTE: In the meantime, Luz had given an authority to a Willma Tapalia to act on her behalf, and Willma had managed to get the original Holographic Will returned from another imposter (Tarciana Rodriguez) who had borrowed this will one day from Luz's attorney on the pretence of getting it copied, but who had failed to return it as she promised. (The attorney did at least have enough sense to get Tarciana to sign a receipt stating what she promised to do.) However, she instead had used the original copy of this will to show to another crooked Filipino judge that she was the treasure for the late Sta. Romana, and was able to also get a letter of administration appointing her as the administratrix of the estate as well. (This was who George DePontis first run into and got his authority from.) Willma Tapalia had to pay this Tarciana a sum of money in order to get Tarciana to return this original to her.)

NOTE TWO: Tarciana was the treasurer of absolutely nothing. It was planned before the late Sta. Romana's death to form a Philippine Corporation they intended to call the "Manila Bay Corporation" for the development of additional land reclamation from Manila Bay. However, before this corporation could be legally filled, Mr. Sta. Romana was hospitalized and died.

(9) Willma Tapalia was able to get this will probated, despite objections from Flordelisa.

(10) Then Flordelisa appealed this decision to a higher court, which sense, I understand also turned down this appeal and returned it to the original court for implementation.

(11) Luz then asked her attorneys to cancel the authority of Willma

Tapalia since she was back in the Philippines and appoint her instead. (In my viewpoint, this is the only one the court can truly appoint if that is Luz's desire. Because the will itself states that Luz is to be, not his next in line, but his next in like. (In other words with the same authority as Mr. Sta. Romana upon his death.)

(12) Now we are informed that someone has bought Flordelisa out and yet, are trying to work under her totally improper authority to get Luz dismissed in New York State, by putting forth the same lies that Flordelisa's group had tried to use for years in the Philippines and elsewhere. It should be obvious to anyone knowing the facts what is going on here.

NOTE: It's not the first time this tactic of treating or even perhaps loading up an airplane with crooked Filipino judges to try and paint a fictitious picture has been tried before. This they tried to do in Switzerland. (You hold a letter on Union Bank of Switzerland letter head confirming this.)

NOTE TWO: Obviously these fakes don't know the history well enough to even date the phony marriage certificate correctly. But, I wouldn't advise that you wake this up on this point right now, because they would just run back to the Philippines and print up another one and change some records there again to reflect this.

You hang in there Mrs. Piel. As George laughed and told me the other day, "God bless that old gal." One thing these crooks don't know how to deal with is someone who they can't bribe. "You know, I've told you and wrote for a long time, that the method by which these people operate is to buy, discredit, or kill anyone who they think stands in their way. The banks and the crooks know the truth. (Why do you think they also want you to agree to continue to cooperate with them even if we were foolish enough to go along with this ridiculous offer, which we don't intend to do, should they need Luz to sign off in the future on various banks?)

So, don't worry, I know your problem and I'm trying at this very moment to muster the Calvary to come to your rescue. For sure, they are going to have to kill me, otherwise I fully intend to show the world what crooks all of these people are. (How can Luz be criticized by any proper legal system for doing anything in view of a totally corrupt so-called judicial system that does such things? Let them bring on these judges and let make sure the world judges them instead.)

Kindest Regards

Jim Brown

The following letter was written by Luz's husband to the U.S. Department of Justice in Washington on December 20, 1995. Brown, apparently not realizing the complicity of high-level U.S. personnel in the plundered gold, was seeking help from people in control of the U.S. Department of Justice that were complicit in covering up for the sequestered loot taken earlier from some of the Japanese plunder hidden in the Philippines. He was seeking help relating to billions of dollars of gold bullion that CIA and other government personnel put into Santa Romans name.

December 20, 1995

U.S. Department of Justice Criminal Division
Washington D.C. 20530

Attention: Mr. Donald Foster Deputy Chief,
Fraud Section

Re: Your letter dated December 12, 1995 regarding the estate or Severino Garcia Sta. Romana a/k/a Jose Antonio Diaz

Dear Mr. Foster:

I just returned to the United States after what was originally intended as two week trip beginning the first week of August, 1995. The reason for such a long delay was my constant occupation in gathering additional information and documents relating to the above matter. Of course there is nothing new about this process as I have been involved in doing this for eight years or more.

This trip perhaps was the most productive as far as obtaining firm evidence and I now believe I not only have a clear picture of what happened after Mr. Sta. Romana/Diaz's death, but also have a clearer understanding as to how he operated before his death.

One of the most shocking things I encountered was how the Government of Cory Aquino and now certain elements in the Government of Fidel Ramos have handled the late Sta. Romana/Diaz estate holdings, documents of which Ferdinand Marcos was able to take after the late Sta. Romana's death.

Knowing full well they had no legal claim on these holdings, what they have done and are still doing today is to claim the late Sta. Romana/Diaz never even existed at all and these were just shadow names created by the late Marcos in order to hide his assets.

It's almost beyond description and one of the most flagrant examples of how damn ridicules these government officials could be who formulated and instituted such a strategy in order to steal these Sta. Romana/Diaz assets for their own personal pockets, which is a pretty much accepted and joked about fact even among themselves.

Undoubtedly, there was a basis for a part of this idiotic foolishness which was instituted by Marcos himself, who knowing full well he could not outright take some of the Sta. Romana/Diaz assets in foreign banks. Obviously in some cases, he was able to forge certain documents, backdate others, and by using the power-of- attorney given to him by the late Sta. Romana (for use in the Philippines only, and as one of his attorneys), prior to the late Sta. Romana's death, (which power of attorney expired at the death of the late Sta. Romana), Marcos was able to conspire with certain bankers to change certain certificates of bearer deposits into other names as authorized signatures.

An excellent example of this is a Sta. Romana deposit of gold and cash deposited in Po Sang Bank, Central District, Hong Kong, under account number 681- 11265. We also hold a copy of the original warehouse receipts issued by Po Sang to Mr. Severino G. Sta. Romana and listing his Philippine passport number only. (This is just one of the many examples of the problems the rightful heirs have encountered.)

I've very pleased. Mr. Foster, that you people have now gotten involved. In fact, when I told my wife by telephone last night about receiving not only your letter but also having received a reply from the White House and I also made the comment that perhaps now she had some honest people in America trying to help her. Her immediate reply was, "Good. Perhaps now they can put some of those crooks in jail where they belong."

Sadly, in reality, I'm not sure this will ever be done, because without doubt, you have taken on a puzzle that the greatest of investigative powers might not be able to solve because. It's not only the many years that have passed, but also the huge amounts and the high-powered people involved. There is little doubt in my mind that the roadblocks are firmly in place.

Another problem is, most of the original documents are still in the hands of the original thieves and these thieves are out of the jurisdiction of the F.B.I. Therefore, in order to recover these originals, work must be done in foreign countries which I understand is normally handled by the C.I.A. But this would never work in my viewpoint, because I honestly believe they have been involved all along in a part of the thievery and cover-up.

I will do everything in my power to help you in providing documents and information that I not only hold today but other documents which I have been promised are forthcoming.

I might add in relation to this, in my viewpoint that perhaps reconstruction of information filed with various Federal agencies, which no doubt is accessible to the F.B.I., is most likely absolutely necessary to complete a thorough discovery. Surely there is a record somewhere of Mr. Sta. Romana/Diaz large transfer of funds just prior to martial law in the Philippines.

In the case of First National City Bank, 932 Park Ave., New York, I'm at present looking at a document showing two accounts. Listing one account number as F.N.C.B. account number 430037 and showing a reference code name "Fanerst King Fisher. " The other is an account under the name of Jose Antonio Diaz De La Paz - F.N.C.B. account number 768423, and shows a reference code of Burgst Harbour King.

There is little doubt in my mind that these were originally accounts belonging to Mr. Sta. Romana/Diaz. (Note: To the best of my understanding and knowledge, although he used a variety or account names, in every case that I'm aware of in the United States, he always used either J. Antonio Diaz or Jose Antonio Diaz as the official signatory for all his U.S. accounts.

Also, I believe these particular accounts are accounts that have been tampered with, because it's my understanding and information that both of these code names have to do with the skullduggery which I referred to in my long letter report as the "Purple Ink Document." The name of By-ob-bin, (I'm not sure of the spelling, but will get it for you), is also associated with this transaction.

Please note that there is one other possible name that may show up during your investigation. That of "Luz C. Rambano." This was the maiden name of my wife. The reason for me being able to say this is based on several things which I have been told.

(A) Before his death, the late Sta. Romana/Diaz had my wife sit down and sign bank papers and documents on over forty banks worldwide.

(B) My wife told me that Peter Diaz, Mr. Sta. Romana/Diaz's oldest son once told my wife that she was looking under the wrong name by looking for his late father's accounts under his father's name because his father had changed most of these accounts into her name before he died.

(C) I guess it was in 1990 when I was introduced to a Manila newspaperman by the name of Ray Fajardo; he also had written a small paperback book at the time which he entitled *Marcos' Return—A Challenge to all Filipinos.* When I met this man, he was introduced to me by Mrs. Sta. Romana. (not my wife at the time), who told me she had arranged and given this Fajardo $25,00. She went on to say that Fajardo had been to see Marcos in Hawaii after she had received the taped message from Marcos admitting he had indeed taken the contents of their safety deposit boxes in First National City Bank in Manila after Mr. Sta. Romana's death.

After making these few remarks, she asked Fajardo to tell me himself what he had found out and been told on his trip. At this point Fajardo told me that he had first gone to see Marcos in Hawaii and when he asked Marcos about what my wife claimed, he said the President (Marcos) brought out a letter which was addressed to the Chase Manhattan Bank in New York City instructing them to pay my wife 200 billion U.S. dollars.

He said Marcos told him he didn't know whether this had been paid or not, but Marcos not only gave him a copy of this letter but also a letter of introduction to someone which I don't recall in the main office of Chase Manhattan Bank in New York.

Fajardo went on to say that from Hawaii he proceeded to New York City and did go to the person Marcos had referred him to. He said this person turned him over to a young Rockefeller who was in the legal department of the bank. Once there, when he showed the copy of the letter he said Marcos had given him, this young man told him the reason this order was never carried out was the bank realized by this time that Marcos had nothing whatsoever to say as to who should be paid anything regarding in Mr. Diaz's accounts because there was a new will which had surfaced which left everything to a Luz C. Rambano, which the bank had been unable to locate.

Fajardo then smiled as he proudly told me that he informed this young man that Luz C. Rambano and Luz R. Sta. Romana were one in the same persons.

NOTE: Quite frankly at that time I was far from being impressed with Ray Fajardo, especially after he went ahead to explain how Mrs. Sta. Romana had agreed to furnish him well in excess of a hundred thousand U.S. dollars to print and give away copies of his paperback book which was costing him $14 each to print. (These books couldn't have cost over three dollars each to print if they would have been printed in the U.S.)

NOTE TWO: In retrospect, perhaps there was some truth in what he was saying. I honestly don't know. But if there was any truth to it, there are two things that would seem to be obvious in this. (A) For some reason Marcos obviously did get some kind of control over Mr. Sta. Romana/Diaz's account in Chase Manhattan for a time at least. (B) Obviously, the mistake was recognized and rectified by the bank.

In any event the purpose of this letter was not meant as another long report but primarily to acknowledge the receipt of your letter and to thank you in advance for your kind attention. I also wanted to point out that Mr. Sta. Romana primarily used his American name of J. Antonio Diaz or Jose Antonio Diaz on all his U.S. and even most of his Swiss accounts for signatory purposes.

I also wanted you to know that we are holding many documents and materials which I believe will help in any investigation which we will be more than willing to furnish copies to the F.B.I.

Finally, since I travel a great deal, I think it best to notify the F.B.I., should they request a contact address for me, to correspond with me through my friend, Mr. Waiter Krystof, 10855 Canby Ave., Northridge, CA. 913261. Phone and fax number (818) 363-8336. I speak with Mr. Krystof even when out of the country, every few days, and he always knows basically how to locate me.

In closing, I will inform you that my wife. Mrs. Luz Sta. Romana-Brown, because of all the pressure and aggravation caused over all these years, suffered a paralyzing stroke approximately three weeks ago and no longer can walk or use her writing arm. What we have done to cover any on-going business requirements which might need her signature was to have her execute a notarized, full and absolute power of attorney by using her two thumb prints on a document that gives me absolute and full power to irrevocably perform any and all acts on her behalf as the proper administrator for the estate and on behalf of her personally. These documents are also attested to by the City of Manila Government and the U.S. Embassy.

I hope the truth and some justice can at last prevail in this case and this matter can UP settled by negotiated agreement or otherwise so we may put a end to this matter once and for all.

Thank you again for your help.

Kindest regards.
C.E. Brown

cc: John Hill [attorney in the San Francisco Melvin Belli office]
Luz Sta. Romana-Brown
Eleanor Jackson Piel [attorney in New York City]
Larry Cano

What the above letter indicates was that Brown and Luz were totally unaware of the role played by people in the United States government that sequestered large segments of the Japanese plunder and that Santa Romana, a former OSS and CIA asset, was a gatekeeper in placing portions of gold plunder in secret bank accounts throughout the world.

What should have caught his eye if he had been more aware of the history of the Yamashita Gold was that a co-trustee on some of the bank certificates contained the name Edward G. Lansdale, a well known U.S. military officer and CIA asset. Further, the highly political FBI was not about to help Brown or Luz be recognized on those funds that belonged to the secret group using them for political espionage.

The following are a small *sampling* of dozens of records of bank deposits that I obtained from the widow of Santa Romana related to gold deposited in certain banks. They include Maj. Gen. Eduard Lansdale with a military and CIA background and Santa Ramona with OSS and CIA background:

ASSIGNED SIGNATORY:
- JOSE ANTONIO DIAZ/SEVERINO GARCIA STA. ROMANA
- JOSE ANTONIO DE LA PAZ
- MAJ. GEN. EDUARD LANSDALE

<u>BANK INFORMATION</u>

REFERENCE : Gold bullion certificate (AU)
GOLD DEPOSIT : 250,000 oz of AU-Metal
PER CERTIFICATE : A total of 38 certificates
NAME OF BANK : Regal Bank of Monserrat
Limited at Plymouth, Monserrat, British West Indies
CERTIFICATE OF GOLD DEPOSIT : 0110120330940
OWNER CODE NAME : Ottis C. Cannup
P.O. Box-40116
Tucson, Arizona 85717,
U.S.A.

REFERENCE: : Gold Bullion Certificate (AU)
ACCOUNT NUMBER : 13801 Flat 1140-777-A.U.

Deposit

/s/ JUAN MARIANITO T. STA. ROMANA
No. 1013201918

/s/ RENATO TORRES STA. ROMANA
No. 18201918

WITNESSES:

/S/________________________

/S/________________________________

IRREVOCABLE SPECIAL POWER OF ATTORNEY

ANNEX "B"

ONE THOUSAND TWO HUNDRED (1,200), IN TRANCHES ON ONE HUNDRED (100) METRIC TONS OR MORE

A.	Depository Bank	: Societe De Banque Suisse
		: Swiss Bank Corporation
		: Paradelplatz 6, Zurich Switzerland
B.	Private number code	: A - 112934
C.	Code number:	: 429 - 3284 - 5
1.	S.B.C. CODE NAME	: SEEFLED
	S.B.C. CODE NO.	: 15 - 2504111
	S.B.C. NAME	: SEEFLEDSTRASSE
2.	S.B.C. CODE NAME	: SCHWANMENDICEN
	S.B.C. CODE NO.	: 524 - 402244
	S.B.C. NAME	: WINTERTHURERSTRASSE
3.	S.13.C. CODE NAME	: DELIKON
	S.B.C. CODE NO.	: 399 - 3124521
	S.B.C. NAME	: Schaffhauserstrasse
D.	BANK OFFICER	
	Title	: President
E.	TELEPHONE NO.	: 2251111
F.	DEPOSITORY CODE NO.	: A – 112934

UBS Account	Amount	Code Nos.	Troy Ounce
1. 0ERLIK0N	$ 339M	01-312-4521	(1,695,000,000)
2. SCHWAMENDIN	$ 524M	GEN-01402-244	(2,620,000,000)
3. W I T I K 0 N	$ 185M	01-534-800	(2,425,000,000)
4. ALTSTETTEN	$ 682M	01-621-020	(3,410,000,000)
5. H0NGG	$160M	01-564-435	(8,000,000)

REFERENCE: Gold volume certificate – U.B.S. (38 certificates)
ACCOUNT: Gold deposit (10,000 MT)
Gold Bars Deposited at Kloten Bullion Vault
Union Bank of Switzerland,
Bahnhofstrasse 45 Zurich
- Vault No. 88 RW RP

- ABA Account NOL G725-70367-D U.H.S.
- Private Code No. A112934
- Code No. 429-3284-5
- Master Account No. 7257
- In 200 crates on pallet Nos. 1392 thru1397, Lot Nos. 72413 thrus 72422, marked to contain AU precious metal with J & M Hallmark stamp.

IRREVOCABLE SPECIAL POWER OF ATTORNEY
ANNEX 'A'

J. Antonio Diaz de la Paz/Don Severing G. Sta. Romana

Chase Manhattan Bank, Paseo de Roxas, Makati

Account No.	389678	$ 16	M.
Account No.	3876	$325	M. JOVE
Account No.	432	$ 20	M. MR
Account No.	473	$100	M. JAYVEE
Account No.	---	$350	M. JAYVEE
Safety Deposit Box Account			No. 5002

Suthep Wonsgvorozalee (Sp ?)Manager, Chase Manhattan, Hawaii
Currently, Deputy Manager,
Chase Manhattan, Bangkok

Randolfh N. Earlmann, Jr. -Vice President, N.A.
Miles G. Armstrong "Willie:"-Confidential Trust, Deputy of
Suthep Wongvorozatee

First National City Bank,
Branch San Juan Luna, Branch Office

Daniel T. Jacobsen	--	Vice President
James T. Collines	--	Vice President
Paul Collines	--	FNCB New York, Buffalo
Mrs. Carillo	--	Trust Department
Mr. Fernandez	--	Savings Department

J. ANTONIO DIAZ DE LA PAZ –
Account No. 787632 – US $989M (BIRGETT HARDSBOURKING)

DON SEVERINO G. STA. ROMANA-
Account No. 270093 – Pesos 789M

Hong Kong & Shanghai Banking Corp. No. 1 Des Voeux Rd., Central Victoria, Hong Kong

G.M. Sayer - Chairman
M.G.R. Sandberg Vice Chairman
A.D.A.G. Mosley Manager
J.L. Boyerq - Hong Kong, operations
J. Antonio Diaz/Don Severino G. Sta. Romana
Account No. ______________________________ US $800 M.
Safety Deposit Box Account No. ________________________
(under Tarciana C. Rodriguez)

A.R. Osmund, Deputy Mgr., Trust Dept.

November 30, 1987

II. Chase Manhattan Bank, New York
Address: 1 Chase Manhattan Plaza
New York, N.Y. 10081 U.S.A.

A). MONEY DEPOSIT (US DOLLAR).

1. Total Amount US $6 Million [Six Million U.S. Dollars].
2. Date Deposited: July 1967
3. Agreement of Interest: 2.5% P.A.
4. Account Numbers: 4193006 5505503 "S "
5. Key Code: TY 2012
6. Name of depositor used: Jose Antonio Diaz known aka Severino Garcia Sta. Romana.

B). GOLD (A.U.) Deposit:
1. Total Amount: US$ 3.5 Billion [Three Billion Five Hundred Million]
2. Date Deposited: July 1967
3. Agreement of Interest: 1 % P.A.
4. Metal Account Number: TY 3305X105
5. Name of Depositor Used: Jose Antonio Diaz known aka Severino Garcia Sta. Romana.

Data from one bank statement that is hardly readable is shown here:

Under Date column: 8 MAR 73 [Date could be either 8 or 08]
Under Deposit column: 461,357,316.00
Under Balance column: 461,357,316.00
Under column stating Symbols and oriental figures: CD

A second entry:

Under Date column: 10 MAR 73
Under Deposit column: 35,000
Under Balance column: 461,392,316.00
Under column stating Symbols and oriental figures: CD

U.S. Dollar Sanwa Bank Central
Oriental symbols 916-002358-4

Several of the documents referring to disposition of assets. The following is one of them:

WHEREAS, Te Water warrants and represents that the distribution of all the retrieved funds and /or negotiable bank instruments will be as follows:

10% (ten per cent) to the order of fm Hendy, who in turn will cover all the intermediaries on his sides.

4% (four per cent) to the order of Enna Tavaoo, who in turn will cover Jim Brown.

1% (One per cent) to the order of Manuel Vieira

10% (Ten per Cent) to the order of Adminvest-Comercio E Investimentos Lda. (Te Water's Corporation)

15% (fifteen per cent) to the order of Millora.

10% (Ten per cent) to the order of Reverend Father Rogelio Guibani Cortez and in turn the weekly yield will be deposited in an account in the Vatican Bank, with the following signatories, Jaime L. Cardinal Sin.

10% (Ten per cent) Vatican and Bishop N. Mondejar D.D., Catholic Bishops Conference of the Philippines.

35% (Thirty-five per cent) to the order of CVS (unintelligible writing)

5% (five per cent) to the order of Mrs. Mercedes Evangelists Brinas, Romeo Young, D.C. Medina, Dr. Amelou Reyes.

Hand writing on bottom: *This will be replaced by a Bank Pay Order in the Bank of China upon presentation of CV Santiago in Beijing. Mean-*

while, I need to have for Hongkong to submit all documents relative to this claim: the paying bank is waiting for this information.

This document relates to deposits. Not all the lettering was clear.

Mr. Susumo M. Takahashi CODE; ONGPHIL 2000
Sanwa Bank Limited Metal Acct. No. 681-191-322
Fairmont House Asian stock prop. No. C-1111-137
No. 8 Cotton Tree Drive Fiduiciary C.S. No. C74-8811
Central Hong Kong Trust Serv PH-1010416

Private Code No. 1812955
Sanwa Bank Account No. 916-002358-5
Sanwa Bank Metal Account No. ??1-191-???
Property No. 1111-1?7-4
Fiduiciary Custodial Service No. 074-8811
Code No. 429-3285-5
Code Name: MANUEL DEL ROSARIO

Severino G. Sta Romana, also known as Jose Antonio **D**iaz under the phrases: From father—my Old Man—he often quoted me the following:

"When the work has once began, don't leave it till it's done, Be labor great or small, do it well or not at all. Tis very strange for a man to know how much he has to know in order to know how little he knows. "

USING DIFFERENT NAMES:

1. Severino G. Sta Romana -- Citibank Hongkong
2. Jose Antonio Diaz -- Standard Chartered BNK Hongkong
3. Severino Dela Paz Diaz -- [same]
4. Manuel Del Rosario -- Sanwa Bank Limited Hongkong
5. Benjamin Roque Almonte-- Po Sang Bank Hongkong
6. Inoue Kamashusaki -- Wing Lung Bank Hongkong
7. Ramon Poirrotte -- Hong Kong Bank, Hongkong

Philippine Passport E169724
Manila, March 25, 1991

The following is a record of a certificate of gold deposit by Santa Romana in the Union Bank of Switzerland (the actual bank CD was stolen by Ferdinand Marcos while acting as lawyer for Santa Romana and a trustee):

CANDILARIA VALENCIA SANTIAGO

Union Bank of Switzerland
Union Banque De Suisse
Bahnhofstr. 45
8001 Zurich, Switzerland

SCORPIO—	83 -- JP -- 1140CD – CVS
ZURICH NAME –	NS PNJR RP; KLGZ-5
21392-1-BC:	C-476539
ABA Acct. No.	G-72570367 0- D, USB
Metal Acct. No:	72570367 d
Master Account No.	7257
Vault No.	88 – R.W.R.P.
Location:	Lolten Airport
Bank officer:	President/tel. No. 2341111
Tel.No. Numismatic:	2343049 / PELIKANSTRASSE

Candilaria Valencia Santiago

A July 19, 1995 document from Crown Commodity Holdings, International in the Philippines to Dressner Bank, Singapore, titled Authority to Verify the amount of deposits at that bank under the account names, Ramon Poirrotte and Alfredo F. de Ramos.

CROWN COMMODITY HOLDING INTERNATIONAL
151 SAN JOSE, CALAMBA, LAGUNA

19 July 1995

Hon. Chairman/President
C/o Dressner Bank
Singapore

Authority to Verify

Gentlemen:

This authorizes ________________________ to conduct a probe of the accounts listed herein: To Wit:

Name of Bank: Dressner Bank, Singapore
Private code No.: A1129334
Metal Account No.: 10-583127-333
Account Name: RAMON POIRROTTE/ALFREDO R. DE RAMOS
Client Code: UEB INDUSTRIES MEX
Security Code: 36-90 UEB INDUSTRIES PT. LTD
Fax No.: 65-222959J

Very Respectfully Yours,

Alfredo De Ramos
Passport No. L370283
Owner's Signatory

Republic of the Philippines
Quezon City

Subscribed and sworn to before me this 13th day of July 1995 in the city of Quezon City, Philippines, affiant exhibiting to me his passport No. L370283 issued at Manila on October 15, 1992 and valid.

Ma. Elena R. Castillo
Notary Public

Doc. No. 55	Ptr. No. 231454/1.09.95
Page No. 12	Quezon City
Book No. 1	Until December 31, 1996
Series of 1995.	

A March 14, 1996, document entitled, Special Power to Verify on the letter head of Crown Commodity Holding International, Philippines, showed Maj. Gen. Edward Lansdale and account holder:

10-MAR—96 THU 21145 ATLANTIC METALS CORP +632+8150672 P.01

CROWN COMMODITY HOLDING INT'L
151 BGY San Jose, Calamba, Laguna
Philippines

ALFDREDO R. RAMOS

Crown Commodity Holdings Int'l
151 Orgy, San Jose
Calamba, Laguna
Philippines

March 14, 1996

I. Alfredo R. Ramos, with Philippine Passport No. AA??9456, owner, holder, and seller, acting with full corporate and personal responsibility, hereby appoint Moscha Ciric, German Citizen, passport number 5067803618, owner of Marketing Services located at Hardtrland Str 200, 41167, Monchengladbach, Germany as my true and legal attorney in fact to perform certain acts on my behalf to wit:

TO : Union Banques Suisses (UBS)
Bahnhofstrase 45
8021 Zurich, Switzerland

ATTN: : Hon. Chairman/President
Bank Bullion officer Mr. Martin Wulf/Mr. Alex Wulf

Subject: Authority to verify and perform all deeds and acts necessary for the transaction from Maj. Gen. Edward Lansdale:

Account Name:	MAJ. GEN. EDWARD LANSDALE
Code No:	429-3284-5
Code Client:	A112934
ABA Account No.	: G/2570367-D-UBS
Metal Account No.	:725-70367-D
Master Account No.	: 7257
Vault No.	: 00 RWRP

This special power to verify is valid to check and take all necessary information in my name from the present bank and bank officer.

Other players in the gold scheme

Adnan Kasogi,[11] who was involved in CIA activities such as Iran/Contra, also had gold bullion bank certificates. Two of these certificates in my hand were titled, Obligation certificates, Bank of Note,

[11] Adnan Khashoggi was an arms dealer and businessman, involved in the Iran-Contra affair, the Japan Lockheed bribery scandal, and an associate of President Ferdinand Marcos. The correct spelling is Khashoggi

United Bank of Switzerland, copies of which are at the end.

Admission of the Account's Existence

Santa Ramona's corporate treasurer, Tarciana, appeared at HSBC Bank in Hong Kong to access one of the accounts, providing the necessary account numbers, names, passwords, codes. The bank officer stated that the account did exist.

Santa Romana's daughter, Flordeliza Tan, approached Sanwa Bank in Hong Kong with a passbook showing large cash deposits made earlier, in 1973. The bank denied such an account existed despite having the name, the account number, password, and dates and amounts of prior deposits.

An affidavit by Alfredo Ramos included the statement: "I know the late Don Severino Garcia Sta. Romana, Romana Poirrotte or Jose Antonio Diaz, under the code "From Father My Old Man . . . that once the work has begun, don't leave until it's done, be labor great or small, do it well or not at all."

Soon after his death, Santy's holographic will was probated in Manila, and Tarciana, Luz and Floredeliza were named by the court as legitimate heirs. Luz went to New York City, expecting to gain access to the accounts at Citibank in Manhattan. There she enlisted the help of attorney Eleanor Jackson Piel, giving her Letters of Administration issued by the Philippine court. These had to be recognized by New York courts. Piel proceeded in Surrogate's Court for the issuance of Ancillary Letters of Administration, which would give Luz right of access to his accounts at Citibank, Chase, and Hanover.

While Luz pressed her case elsewhere, Piel wrote letters to the head offices of all the banks concerned, asking about the Santa Romana accounts. Not a single bank replied.

Luz flew to Switzerland, visiting UBS in Geneva with two American friends. According to one of the Americans, Jim Brown: "I sat with Luz and another American . . . while a vice-president told Luz "he wouldn't recommend her trying to claim this account represented, they would not be beyond having her killed first." He also went to tell her, that he wouldn't recommend hiring any Swiss attorneys because the bank would simply buy them off."

Combination of Lansdale Government Positions and Tons of Gold Deposits Showed Secret Side of U.S. Government

The M-Fund was set up solely for affecting Japanese politics and were initially under the control of General Douglas MacArthur. Other funds became known, including the Yotsuya Fund and the Keenan Fund. Initially, it was believed to have been as large as $2-billion. The M-Fund got its name from U.S. General William Fredi Marquat, whose orders were to bring Japanese war criminals to justice, especially those of Japanese Unit 731 that used prisoners of war to conduct various brutal tests using biological and chemical weapons, and surgery on prisoners of war without anesthesia.

The first use of M-Fund was to affect Japanese politics by electing those Japanese that the U.S. wanted elected. After the socialists won elections in the late 1940, the M-Fund made huge amounts of money available to discredit that political party.

Another fund, the Keenan Fund, named after Joseph Keenan on MacArthur's staff, was reportedly used to bribe witness at the war crimes trials. Those trials, in Tokyo, unlike the Yamashita trial in the Philippines, went for several years. Reportedly, witnesses were bribed not to implicate Emperor Hirohito.

Money from the M-Fund was used during the Eisenhower administration in the mid-1950s to have Nobosuke Kishi placed at the head of the Liberal-Democratic Party and then as Japan's new Prime Minister. Ironically, Kishi had signed the prior declaration of war against the United States in 1941 and responsible for some of the worst Japanese atrocities during the Japanese invasions of Southeast Asia. The CIA-favored Liberal-Democrat Party (LDP) was a heavy recipient of money from the M-Fund handled by the CIA.

Sampling of Confiscated Funds Used in Covert Actions

The funds were used as planned, to subvert foreign governments, subvert the political process, and affect the governments of foreign nations. These funds were used to manipulate the political systems in Greece, Italy, Japan and many other countries. I am unknowingly a witness to one such subversive action.

Operation Ajax: One of Many
Subversive Acts Funded by Covert Funds

The CIA, directed by Kim Roosevelt, brought about the downfall of the democratically-elected government in Iran, headed by Prime Minister Mohammad Mosaddegh. That coup d'état on August 19, 1953, brought down the first democratically-elected government in Iran and installed a dictatorship headed by Mohammad-Rezā Shāh Pahlavi. There then followed a brutal U.S.-trained secret police known as the Savak.

That dictatorship continued until February 1979, when the Shah was overthrown and 52 American hostages from the U.S. Embassy in Tehran were held for 444 days. The intrigue associated with the hostages, known as the October Surprise, is detailed in my book, *Defrauding America*, based on information provided to me by CIA people involved with the secret operation. That is another American scandal unknown to most Americans.

I was staying at a hotel in Abadan, Iran, the morning that the revolution erupted and evolved. I was an airline captain for Transocean Airlines flying Muslim pilgrims from throughout the Middle East to the holy cities of Mecca and Medina during the Hajj.

The temporary tangible benefits the United States reaped from overthrowing Iran's elected government was a share of Iran's oil wealth, profits from supplying arms to the unpopular ruler, and controlling Iran's political activities. The blowback consequences of the subversive actions ordered by White House Politicians in the President Dwight D. Eisenhower administration through the CIA, brought down the democratically-elected Iranian leader, temporary replacement with a CIA puppet, followed by a 1979 revolution that put in power an anti-Western Islamic Republic of Iran.

Communication Between Luz Romana and Imelda Marcos

The following letter was sent by Luz's husband to Imelda Marcos (May 16, 1996), attempting to clarify some personal matters:

10855 Canby Ave. Northridge, Ca.

Madam Imelda Marcos (Absolutely Personal)
Congresswoman
% Philippine Congress Manila, Philippines

Dear Mrs. Marcos,

I know of no other way to communicate directly with you. I have made several efforts to do so in the past while in the Philippines, but to no avail.

My first encounter with your problems began several years ago now while I was in Hong Kong on another project and became acquainted with Constantine "Tonti" Rubio, who told me and others that he was mandated by your late husband to sell 36,000 metric ton of gold. I'm not a gold chaser, but I did feel sorry for Rubio and even paid his hotel bill and fed him, his estranged wife Anna Nubla, and one of their traveling companions, while Rubio claimed he was awaiting the arrival of some Japanese with the United Nations who were interested in purchasing this gold.

In time, the Japanese failed to show up and I asked Tonti whether he would like for me to find a buyer for him. He immediately said yes, and I did through Patrick Ma in Hong Kong arrange a buyer who claimed he represented the U.S. Treasury. When I was first told of this, I found it hard to believe because of the press constantly putting out reports regarding how the U.S. Government was cooperating with the newly inserted government of Cory Aquino. (I personally believe President Marcos actually won that election based on what all the people I spoke with told me.)

Patrick Ma I had known for over twenty years and I knew for an absolute fact that the Ma family in Hong Kong was one of the richest long standing families there. Patrick assured me that this person not only did indeed represent the U.S. Treasury, but the Treasury did have a sincere desire to purchase gold which the late President at least had control over at that time.

I'm sure you must remember the incident when we came to Hawaii with Rubio and when he came out and had dinner with you and the President when you were living in that old beach front house. (I should have tried to talk directly with you then, because we have a lot of mutual acquaintances, such as Morris Fisher, Fay Watanobi, Sandy, whom I had known for years, who was at one time Johnny Carson's secretary, etc.)

Prior to this, this alleged government representative confirmed to all of us, after Tonti had first became upset when this man had said twice, after the President left, " that all of you were literally kidnapped against your will and taken to Hawaii. (Later I wrote a book about all of this, but no one wanted to publish it or believe what I was told even after you made the same statement when you were on trial in New York City.) The reason for my writing to you now is, I have continued to be involved in your problems.

At first, it was because I simply didn't like the idea of anyone in our Government having the audacity and power to kidnap another country's Head of State.

Finally, I was promised by this alleged U.S. Government representative, when I told him that I intended to write a book on all that had occurred, if I would hold off for six months and give them time to try and complete a transaction with President Marcos, that if they failed, he would furnish me with absolute proof of the kidnapping. I agreed, primarily because no one wanted to believe me anyway.

I had also been told by these people, that the gold that President Marcos essentially controlled actually belonged to the late Severino Sta. Romana, aka Jose Antonio Diaz.

In time, after interviewing many people, I met Luz Rambano Sta. Romana. For three years after this, I was paid by a very wealthy Japanese who told me that he had confirmed Luz's story as to who she was and what actually had occurred through Ryoichi Sasakawa, who had originally been involved right after World War II in this gold. And that Sasakawa basically told him that what Luz was telling was true. But, after Marcos took all of Mr. Sta. Romana's documents from First National City Bank in Manila and from a private vault Mr. Sta. Romana keep stored at the Philippine National Treasury, right after Mr. Sta. Romana death, that this action gave the banks holding Mr. Sta. Romana's cash and precious metal accounts, in combination with many government agencies the opportunity to steal these assets.

I'm certain you don't know all that happened, nor do your children, because of a copy of a letter I have now allegedly signed by President Marcos relating to one of Mr. Sta. Romana's gold deposits he had on deposit In Po Sang Bank in Hong Kong when he died. (We have had a copy of the gold warehouse receipt in Mr. Sta. Romana's name and showing his passport number for years now confirming this.)

We also now hold solid information that President Marcos sold this gold to Rothschild in France in 1983. However, President Marcos never took the money, after having it deposited in the name of a Mrs. Candelaria Santiago, who I'm told was a cook for him.

There is also another case regarding one of Mr. Sta. Romana's cash and gold accounts which was deposited in Hong Kong in the Sanwa Bank, which in 1983 was moved from Hong Kong to Sanwa's Main office in Osaka Japan. (In this case, we hold several documents listing these accounts in Mr. Sta. Romana's name, including a copy of the original U.S. dollar savings pass book in his name, plainly showing not only Mr. Sta. Romana's name, but his passport number, and the dates of deposits and amounts of these cash deposits.) Plus loads of other copies of documents on other banks in Hong Kong and worldwide listing other Sta. Romana/Diaz accounts.

I was advised day before yesterday of your decision to not go along with a proposed scam to take the Po Sang account which was transferred after President Marcos allegedly improperly sold this gold, now held in the Bank of China. I personally believe that this was a wise move on your part, because the very top people in the Chinese Government have been recently made aware of the circumstances. Besides, they have the original records. However, I'm totally amazed at how people can think they can make up false documents and fool people.

Perhaps, we don't know everything. But I do know that Luz Sta. Romana is not your enemy. I also know that she has been run over by a Mack truck when it comes to any justice at all in this matter, even by her own subsequent governments after you were taken from power.

I have continued to write this story and now I have loads of documents supporting many things she has said and I can assure everyone that it not only can it be published, but we are in the process of doing this and including all the supporting documents.

In 1993, I married Luz and this past fall, she suffered a paralyzing stroke. An interesting note regarding her feelings relating to you personally, she was even thrilled to tell me one afternoon while lying in the hospital that someone told her you intended to pay her a visit. Of course, this didn't happen, and as Luz disappointedly told me later, that was the case, when Marcos promised to come to the same hospital when Santy was dying. To comfort her obvious disappointment, I told her that perhaps, you actually were not informed or didn't know anything about it. She can be rather feisty at times even after having a stroke and replied, "Maybe in Imelda's case you are right." But, that sure was not what happened regarding President Marcos, because on one occasion he even sent his Presidential Security Command, but he still didn't show up.

Never had I asked, desired, or attempted to take matters into my own hands regarding her problems until this happened. Now, I hold her absolute power of attorney to act on her behalf personally and under any authority she still holds on behalf of the estate. I want to see all you come out whole on this thing. I have always advocated this. So, yesterday, I faxed Ernesto Tavaco, who is still playing around with supposedly your number one attorney as to my suggestions as to how to help all of you. The problem has always been, you've always had too many pocket stuffers running interference and we have never had a chance to talk. Therefore, I hope this letter finally gets to you, along with a copy of the fax message I sent to Ernie yesterday.

I also hope, first of all, you actually personally receive this letter, and if you do, you look upon it in the same manner in which it is written. This nonsense for you, Luz, and all your families has gone on long enough. The banks and the crooked governments and government agencies have had their way for too long of a time already. I sincerely hope we can work and fight together. I also hope we can communicate directly, not necessarily all the time through middle people who might mistranslate-anything we should decide together.

Respectfully,

C.E. Brown

A document showing a major figure in the U.S. military and intelligence service as the owner of thousands of tons of gold provides further support for the huge theft of war plunder by a literal secret group in the government of the United States. The following is a retyped copy of the document for easier readability:

SPECIAL POWER TO VERIFY

Alfrldo R. Ramos
Crown Commodity Holding Int'l.
151 Hrgy. San Jose
Calamba, Laguna
Philippines

March 14, 1998

I, Alfredo R. Ramos, with Philippine Passport No. AA—409996, owner, holder, and seller, acting with full corporate and personal legal responsibility, hereby appoint Moscha Ciric, German Citizen, Passport Number 5067803618, owner of Marketing Services located at Hard-trland Str 200, 41169 Monchengladbach, Germany as my true and legal attorney in fact to perform certain acts on my behalf to wit:

TO	: Union Banques Suisses (us) : Bahnhofstrase 45 8021 Zurich, Switzerland
ATTN	: Hon. Chairman/President Bank Bullion Officer Mr. Martin Wulf/Mr. Alex Wulf
SUBJECT	: Authority to Verify and Perform all deeds and acts necessary for the transaction from;
ACCOUNT NAME:	MAJ. GEN. EDWARD LANDSDALE
CODE NO.	: 429-3284-5
??-DE CLIENT	: A112934
Aba Account No.	G72570367-D-UBS
Metal Account No.	72225-70367-D
Master account No.	7257
Vault no.	88 RWRP

This special power to verify is valid to check and take all necessary information in my name from the present bank and bank officer.

For this operation, my representative have full power and authority to do and perform all and every act requisite to carry into effect the authority to verify account up to the total amount of 20,000 metric tons.

At the same time, my representative have full power and authority for necessary contact with potential buyer.

NOTE: Present power to verify is valid up to the total amount of possible transaction and after this is not valid.

First copy of present document, like fax copy will be sent directly on the desk officer in UBS.

Second copy of present document, like fax copy will be sent to our representative.

This cancels and/or supersedes any and all special power to verify on listed account name Maj. Gen. Edward Landsdale issued before the date on this instrument.

Seller will bring all original documents with him at the table top meeting place in Zurich, Swiss, when time comes.

Respectively yours,

Alfred R. Ramos
Passport No. AA-409996

Mar 14, 1996

Subscribed and sworn to before me on this day of March 1996. Affiant Exhibiting to me his Passport No. AA-409996.

DOC. No 256
PAGE NO 53
BOOK No. viii
SERIES OF 1996.

[Note: It is a common practice to sometimes deliberately misspell names.]

CHAPTER FOUR

Myriad Web of Secret Funds

Multiple Secret Funds and Bizarre Twists arose from the scheme to secretly retrieve part of the Japanese plunder. Books could be written about what is known, what is suspected, and what is unknown, about the subsequent disposition of that Japanese loot discovered initially by Santa Romana and Eduardo Lansdale. These included, for instance, the following:

M-Funds for Manipulating Japanese Politics

The M-Fund **was** named after General William Frederic Marquat, the chief of SCAP's Economic and Scientific Section. He acted to conceal the assets and plunder of some of Japan's World War II criminals as part of the plan to have Japan go with the type of government wanted by U.S. leaders. One use of the hidden funds was to control the political process in Japan, and that was called the M-Funds. It reportedly made available over $500 billion U.S. dollars to Japan's Liberal Democratic Party (LDP).

The M-Fund provided bribe money that protected some of the biggest perpetrators of Japan's invasions, plundering, and torture, including those directly involved in Japan's brutal Unit 731 involved in incredible brutality associated with medical experiments. U.S. leaders have kept secret the records of that brutality so as to protect the perpetrators and their involvement in the Japanese plunder. The M-Fund was initially controlled by people close to General Douglas MacArthur.

Rather than encouraging Japan to become more democratic, the M-Fund was used to subvert the political process to manipulate it in the eyes of the U.S. personnel involved in the corrupt schemes involving the Japanese plunder. To do this, the U.S. personnel rewarded and returned to power the people that started the war, those responsible for the extreme brutalities that made the Nazi "Boy Scouts" in comparison. These were also called at different times the Yoshida Fund when Yoshida Shigeru became prime minister and Marquat Fund, used to manipulate and control the postwar Japanese political landscape.

Articles appearing years later in Japan's financial newspaper, *Nikei*, by investigative journalist Takano Hajime described the M-Fund as composed of money gained from the sale of various forms of Japanese plunder.

Another Tokyo reporter, Robert Whiting,[12] wrote, "The Japanese government sold great stockpiles of gold, silver and copper which they had concealed in early 1945 in anticipation of Japan's defeat." The funds were those that should have been used to pay for Japan's war victims, but covert forces in and associated with the United States government kept this information from the American people.

It is believed that control of the M-Fund was lost in the 1960s after President Richard Nixon secretly arranged for its transfer to Japanese politicians in the Liberal Democratic Party in exchange for Nixon's return to Japan of Okinawa. Under control of the LDP politicians, these funds found their way into various financial instruments/bank certificates of deposit. Later, banks that issued some of the certificates of deposit refused to honor them, calling them forgeries, and accusing the rightful holders of them of criminal acts.

The Keenan Fund.

The Keenan Fund was controlled by former Department of Justice criminal division head, Joseph B. Keenan. He was also the chief prosecutor in the Tokyo war crime trials held in Tokyo after the end of World War II. It was originally used to bribe witnesses during the three years of war crime trials held in Tokyo. That included preventing any of the Japanese from testifying about the brutal torture of American POWs in Unit 731.

Yotsuya Fund.

The Yotsuya Fund was controlled by Willoughby and named after a section of Tokyo. Its primary purpose was to manipulate the criminal elements in Japan, including the *yakuza*, and indirectly control the political process through criminal pressure upon politicians.

Unnamed funds looted by U.S. military personnel.

Numerous stories have been told about the discovery of large quantities of jewels and other valuables discovered by U.S. personnel and their subsequent "disappearance."

Japanese Admiral's Plunder

U.S. forces discovered some of the caches of Japanese plunder hidden in Japan, most of which then disappeared. One was the plunder acquired by Japanese Rear Admiral Kodama Yoshio,[13] a Japanese crim-

---

[12] Whiting lived in Japan for many years and wrote several books, describing organized crime in Japan and the corrupt side of the U.S.-Japan relationship. He wrote a weekly column for *Yukan Fuji*.

[13] Also shown as Yoshio Kodama.

inal head, who was helped by the occupation forces to become a key political figure that also cooperated with CIA personnel. Yoshio was involved in Japanese plunder during World War II. He was an indicted war criminal. Charges were dropped against him and he was released after reportedly making an agreement with U.S. Gen. Willoughby that involved turning $100 million to CIA personnel in the U.S. Embassy at Tokyo, to get released from prison and avoid prosecution for war crimes. That money was added to the M-Fund.

Kodama's source of wealth was from hard drugs activities during and after World War II. Kodama used some of the ill-gotten funds to finance the Liberal Democratic Party (LDP), which to this day had heavy support from U.S. politicians.

A *New York Times* article by Tad Szulc stated: 'Kodama had a working relationship with the CIA—Kodama was probably the CIA's chief asset in Japan." Kodama died in 1984. While U.S. leaders were eulogizing criminals such as Kodama, surely, the American GIs that suffered so greatly from the actions of these war criminals now eulogized by U.S. politicians might be somewhat upset. These funds acquired in Japan were only a small fraction of the Japanese war plunder taken from other countries and hidden in various Japanese locations.

Japan's Series 57 Certificates

Out of this spider web of intrigue arose Japan's Series 57 Certificates, given or loaned to Japanese to affect the political process. The recipients were often either Japanese guilty of great crimes against U.S. prisoners or Japanese warlords that could be bought. The funds were used to bring to power Japanese war criminals guilty of some of the most brutal and horrific crimes upon American military personnel.

Understanding Relationship between M-Fund and Japan's Series 57 Certificates

Japan's Series 57 certificates issued in 1983 by Japan's minister of finance, Michio Watanabe with the authority of Japan's Prime Minister Kakuei Tanaka of the Liberal Democratic Party (LDP), were unusual. The Series 57 bonds were issued partly because the M-Funds lacked liquidity and partly to cover the debts incurred by Japan's Liberal Democratic.

It was decided by the Ministry of Finance to replace maturing bonds with unusual Series 57 certificates called Certificates of Redemption. These certificates were unlike any other government bond and called Series 57 certificates because they were issued by the Ministry of Finance in the fifty-seventh year of Hirohito's reign. Reportedly, prior bondholders that were entitled to interest on prior bonds were given cashier checks issued by the Dai-Ichi Kangyo Bank.

The Series 57 certificates were unlike any bonds previously issued by the government of Japan. The public was denied access to them; they could not be traded on the international bond-market; and only the holders of the certificates knew of their existence. In this way, they could be easily called forgeries when presented for payment. And only "favored" holders of them were recognized as holding legitimate bonds for redemption.

Washington politicians and Department of Justice employees supported the scheme perpetrated by Japanese politicians to declare Series 57 certificates counterfeits. The political party in power in Japan, the Liberal Democratic Party, and forces in the U.S. government, planned to address the matter of the Series 57 certificates by calling them forgeries.

Many Deaths Associated with Hiding the M-Funds

Many people associated with the M-Funds had died. These include:

- The death of Prime Minister Sato, the brother of Kishi. Some believe Sato was poisoned during quest with Tanaka for control of the M-Fund in 1975.
- Kodama's publisher and business partner, Harvey Fukuda, died in 1984. He allegedly died in a Japanese hospital of "heart failure" while being treated for cirrhosis of the liver. He knew the dirty part of the funds.
- Aoki Ihei, Prime Minister Takeshita's personal assistant, who knew about the Series 57 certificates.

Tactics by Department of Justice Employees To Prevent Exposure of the Schemes Relating to Retrieved Plunder

Anyone seeking to redeem any of the bank certificates related to the original Japanese plunder became targets for false charges by employees of the U.S. Department of Justice. That involved anyone attempting to redeem Series 57 certificates issued by Japan.

All were involved in the secret plunder retrieval, the M-Fund using Golden Lily plunder, and setting up the Series 57 certificates. The scheme used by U.S. Department of Justice employees to address the problems of anyone in the United States whose actions threatened to expose the Series 57 certificates and the other matters related to them followed the standard pattern used for decades to silence anyone exposing high-level corruption. File false charges against the person, threaten witnesses that undermine the sham charges, pay witnesses that cooperate, and have federal judges cooperate in the schemes. Examples of this are in many of my books, including for instance: *Unfriendly Skies: 20th & 21st Centuries*; *Explosive Secrets of Covert CIA Companies*; *Defrauding America*; *Drugging America*; *Crimes of the CIA-FBI, the Mafia, and al Qaeda*; and *FBI, CIA, the Mob, and Treachery*.

DOJ Personnel Targeting an Elderly Los Angeles Widow

In the early 1990s, one of the targets of federal prosecutors was an elderly and disabled widow in Los Angeles, Barbara Jean Bravender Ah Loo. She was a U.S. citizen and Caucasian that had married a Chinese businessman in Hawaii, Ah Loo, and lived for a period of time in Hong Kong operating a company called Transfield Investments. In 1987, a Japanese by the name of Takahishi Hoshio, approached the company seeking help in redeeming his Series 57 certificates. Their company acquired some of them. Subsequently, Ah Loo died, and his widow moved back to Los Angeles, where she lived on Social Security payment of less than $1000 a month.

Enter a Government Informant Looking for a Target

One of thousands of government informants seeking a target contacted the widow and said he could find a buyer for the Series 57 certificates that she had. It was a trap that included agents of the U.S. Customs, the Secret Service, and Department of Justice employees. Nothing unusual! Included in the group attack were employees of the U.S. Customs Service: Jack Fox, Michael Sankey, and Michael Noonan.

The scheme started with Customs Agent Fox showing the widow a false identification card indicating he was a vice president of a well-known bank. U.S. Customs agent Sankey then appeared, pretending to be a businessman wanting to buy the Series 57 certificates. They arranged for a meeting to be held out of state, which required the widow to cross state lines. In that way, they could build the case into a federal matter where they had control of federal prosecutors and federal judges.

Because the widow, Jean Bravender Ah Loo, could not afford the plane fare, they sent her the plane ticket for the entrapment they had concocted. When she arrived at the destination, she was then arrested and prosecuted. Because she had previously lived in Hong Kong, federal prosecutors argued that she should remain in prison because she might flee the country. In prison, while waiting for trial, exposed to such harsh conditions, the widow's mental condition deteriorated, causing her to be sent to the prison psychiatric ward. Upon arrival there, she was diagnosed with throat cancer—and died shortly thereafter. It was reported that government employees from 16 Secret Service offices were involved by early 1992 in the scheme against the widow.

The Next Target

The next person to be targeted by government employees was Norbert Schlei, a former assistant attorney general under President Kennedy. Norbert Schlei was a lawyer in the Kennedy and Johnson administrations and a key person writing the civil rights legislation. After leaving government, Schlei had a successful legal practice. One of his clients, from Asia, asked Schlei to check on the redeamability of

Japanese Series 57 certificates he possessed.

Schlei's investigation caused him to determine that the Japanese Series 57 certificates were legitimate. He wrote a memorandum to that effect and also the relationship to the M-Fund. His actions threatened to expose a major can-of-worms; that made him a target for government-funded retaliation by Department of Justice employees.

Although Schlei was not attempting to sell or purchase any of the Series 57 certificates, Department of Justice employees used the all-encompassing conspiracy statute to charge him with criminal violations of the financial code. One of Schlei's *former* clients, Takahashi, tried to sell one of his Series 57 certificates through another person, Roger Hill. Government employees, wildly expanding the conspiracy parameters, filed a conspiracy charge against Schlei, claiming he had a relationship with Takashashi, Hill, and the elderly widow, Ah Loo.

Standard DOJ Criminal Tactics

Various agencies of the United States government, including the CIA, collaborated to block Schlei's trial defenses. Similar tactics happen so often that they are nothing new. Among those people who suffered similar fates that are described in my books was Ronald Rewald—the titular head of the covert CIA operation described elsewhere in this book, myself (in the book, *Unfriendly Skies: 20th & 21st Centuries*); and in *Drugging America* and *Defrauding America*.

One witness, Professor Lausier, provided an affidavit showing the validity of Japan's Series 57 certificates that was placed into the criminal trial against a respected lawyer that Justice Department prosecutors were fraudulently prosecuting (a frequent occurrence!).

The fraudulent misuse of the U.S. Department of Justice by DOJ employees was to protect the secrets of the corrupt U.S. and Japanese personnel involved in the myriad schemes associated with the N-Fund arising out of the secret retrieval of Japanese war plunder. The following is a copy of his affidavit:

AFFIDAVIT OF PROFESSOR
EDMOND C. LAUSIER

State of California)
) ss.
County of Los Angeles)

Edmond C. Lausier, being duly sworn, deposes and says as follows;

1. I am an Emeritus Assistant Professor of Marketing in the Marshall School of Business, University of Southern California, and make this affidavit in support of motions I understand may be filed by Norb-

ert Schlei in Unit States v. Schlei, No. 92-49-Cr-T-17(c) in the records and files of the United States District Court for the Central District of Florida, Tampa Division, for new trial and other relief. The facts set forth herein are within my personal knowledge and if sworn as a witness I can testify competently thereto.

2. Beginning approximately five years ago I began what have turned out to be quite extensive studies relating to the origin and validity of a certain type of financial instrument known as a "Certificate of Refund Balance" or "Certificate of Redemption Balance," Series 57, ostensibly issued by the Ministry of Finance of Japan in fiscal year 1982 (Japanese year Showa 57). (For convenience I refer to these instruments hereafter as "Certificates.") It was this type of instrument that was involved in Mr. Schlei's case and was the subject matter of the "sting" transaction which was the principal focus of the case.

3. I began my study of these instruments at the request of counsel to Warren Chiang, defendant in a criminal case pending in Los Angeles, California. I did not testify as a witness in that case, but I had an opportunity to copy and review the documents that had been supplied to Chiang by Saburo Ideno, the named payee of the Certificate which Chiang had purchased from Ideno and which was the subject matter of the offense with which Chiang was charged.

Later I was able to obtain a number of documents relating to the Certificates from Gillian Tett, an investigative reporter for, and Bureau Chief of the *London Financial Times* who is stationed in Tokyo, Japan. Also, I met Mr. Schlei, who initially was able only to provide copies of the documents received in evidence at his trial and to tell me orally what had been told to him by his Japanese clients over the years from 1985 to 1992.

More recently, however, Mr. Schlei has been able to supply a virtual treasure-trove of documents regarding the Certificates which he stated had become available as a result of the release from custody of Toshio Takahashi, a former client, who had previously been a fugitive and unavailable.

Mr. Schlei also was instrumental in obtaining for my use from the Oriental Studies Library of the University of California at Berkeley copies of Japanese government records as to the issuance and retirement of bonds and other obligations in particular years which I had previously been unable to obtain. I have made an exhaustive study of the "Annual Government Bond Summary" published by the Japanese government for all years since its first post-war issuance of bonds in 1966 (Japanese year Showa 41) to the present and am now knowledgeable regarding all bonds issued during those years, including their issuance, maturity, redemption, roll-overs and current maturity.

4. This affidavit is accompanied by Bates-stamped copies of all documents (other than official published records of the Japanese government) which I have reviewed in arriving at the conclusions stated herein.

5. In order to understand the Certificates it is essential first of all to understand that they are not and do not purport to be "bonds," although they have frequently been mistakenly referred to as such in U.S. court proceedings and publications. The Certificates are documents in the nature of receipts which purport to have been issued to the payees upon the surrender by them of Japanese government bonds that they previously held.

The Certificates acknowledge that the payees are due the proceeds of the bonds they have surrendered and state that this obligation is to be satisfied with the proceeds at maturity of 15-year bonds. Seven (7) such bonds issues (actually floating rate notes) thereafter were in fact issued by the Japanese government over a three-year period beginning in 1983. These bonds are unique in that they were the first and only 15-year obligations ever issued by the Japanese government until the maturity of issue #7 in the third quarter of year 2000. These seven issues of 15-year obligations were subjected upon issuance by the Ministry of Finance to restrictions prohibiting their assignment, transfer or conveyance throughout their term.

6. A study of the documents which I have examined shows quite conclusively that the persons who were the recipients of the Certificates, and whose names appear on them as the payees, were previously the holders of Japanese government bonds in the same amounts as the Certificates. Many documents are official certifications of ownership of valid bond issues of years such as 1973, 1975 and 1979.

Some of the bond ownerships are validated by the Tokyo municipal Legal Affairs Bureau as to year of issue, face value of each certificate, number of certificates owned, total amount owned and Custody Number of the issue at the Bank of Japan. Other bond ownerships are verified in official Ministry of Finance correspondence. Also, these records show that the official designated bond transfer agent, Dai-Ichi Kangyo Bank, deposited interest payments to accounts in the owners' names and issued deposit advisories to the bondholders.

7. The documents I have examined show that in 1982, a decision was made in the Ministry of Finance or at an even higher level in the Japanese government to call in the bonds held by certain holders, together with the interest-passbook accounts at the Dai-Ichi Kangyo Bank held by them, and to issue Certificates in exchange for those items. To effectuate these transactions, a precisely orchestrated transfer process was arranged by the Ministry of Finance during 1983 through its desig-

nated transfer agent, the Dai-Ichi Kangyo Bank, with the help of officials of the Liberal Democratic Party of Japan.

The documents include: (a) hundreds of official documents from the Ministry of Finance, the bond transfer agent (Dai-Ichi Kangyo Bank) and the Liberal Democratic Party identifying specific valid outstanding Japanese government bonds to be refunded, and (b) official numbered correspondence during 1983 (Showa 58) directing the refund of those bonds. These documents provide a detailed, undeniable connection between the holders of the bonds so identified (later the payees of the Certificates) and the official transfer process established by the Ministry of Finance and the Dai-Ichi Kangyo Bank.

8. The documents I have examined are so precisely in agreement in innumerable respects with the official published records of the government of Japan—some of which records were not publicly available until after the documents were prepared—that, in my opinion, it is quite impossible for them, or the Certificates that resulted from them, to have been the work of any counterfeiter.

No person outside the government could possibly have had the requisite knowledge to prepare these documents with the requisite degree of accuracy, and indeed, a rather large number of knowledgeable government officials was needed to prepare them. It is, accordingly, my unqualified opinion that the Certificates are not counterfeit. I do not know whether any person has or ever did have rights under these Certificates and I express no opinion on that subject.

9. What was the motive for this recall of bonds and substitution of Certificates for them? I of course do not know. However, I find plausible Mr. Schlei's explanation that the government of Japan grew concerned about the fact that huge sums in verifiably genuine government bonds were held by potentially unreliable nominees, and therefore decided to replace those bonds with the Certificates—a type of instrument previously unknown—which could much more plausibly be repudiated. In this connection, Mr. Schlei points out that shortly after the exchange of Certificates for bonds was concluded, the government arrested, charged and convicted individuals named Aoyagi and Sakamoto of counterfeiting the Certificates. No evidence was presented in these cases, which were based entirely on confessions.

10. A further impetus for pulling back the bonds and issuing the Certificates was certainly supplied by the fact that beginning in 1982 (and continuing for six years thereafter) the Japanese government lacked the funds necessary to carry out its statutory obligations with respect to redemption of outstanding bonds. The government was able to keep its sinking-fund special account from going bankrupt only by making budget transfers and selling its holdings in NTT, Japan's na-

tional telephone company. The government's financial plight was undoubtedly eased by retrieving the outstanding bonds here involved and replacing them with the off-book obligations reflected in the Certificates.

11. The motives underlying the issuance of the Certificates are not my concern and must be left to historians and others. What I can assert with confidence is that the government of Japan conceived the plan and procedure for issuing the Certificates and did issue the Certificates. Whatever the value or enforceability of those Certificates may be, they are not counterfeit.

12. The Dai-Ichi Kangyo Bank checks that were involved in Schlei's trial cannot be as completely explained as the Certificates, since the Bank's records, unlike the government's bond records, are not published. However, it is my firm opinion, based on the documents I have examined, that the checks represent interest that had become due and payable on the bonds prior to their exchange for Certificates. The documents confirm beyond argument, in my opinion, that the checks were in fact issued by the Bank.

Edmond C. Lausier

Subscribed and sworn to
before me this 10th day
of January 2001.

Notary Public in and for
Said County and State

Deidra L. Stauff
Comm # 1201589
Notary Pubic-California
Los Angeles County
Comm. Exp Dec. 11, 2002

A *New York Times* article in March 1995 described acting CIA Director Admiral William O. Studeman stating that the CIA was not about to divulge information on the subject of payola to foreign governments and politicos, which impliedly admitted that these events occurred.

During the trial, government employees under pressure from Department of Justice employees falsely told the jury:

A search of the records of the CIA, the Secret Service, and the National Archives did not disclose any relevant or material documents or information that substantiated . . . that the CIA gave money to employees or officials of the Japanese government, or any political party in Japan. The government searched hundreds of files of CIA paper records dating back to 1948 for any documents that might indicate that payments were made by the CIA to the Japanese government, the Liberal Democratic Party, or individual party members. They also conducted computer searches for Marquat Fund and did not discover any relevant or material documents or information.

That was a lie. But Justice Department lawyers are "immune" from perjury that would put another citizen in prison for the crime of perjury. The naïve jury held Schlei guilty of securities fraud. It is estimated that the trial and corrupt charges cost the taxpayers over $45 million to silence Schlei.

Based on the sham charges, the California Bar Association had revoked Schlei's right to practice law (a decision that was changed in late 2000, but too late). An Eleventh Circuit Court of Appeals in 1997 vacated the conviction on the felony count and remanding the misdemeanor count to the district court for a hearing on Schlei's motion for a new trial

Six Years of Prosecution, Financial Poverty, and Disgrace

Schlei endured six years of prosecution, trials, appeals, during which he was barred from earning any income. His $10 million in assets were lost, causing him to file for bankruptcy. I suffered a similar fate to silence me, which helped make possible the success of the 9/11 hijackings and numerous other tragedies. See *Unfriendly Skies: 20th & 21st Centuries*, for the evidence. Schlei suffered a major heart attack in 2002 and died a year later, financially ruined. Before he died, Schlei was able to clear his name legally.

Terrifying Other Holders of Series 57 Bonds

These prosecutions caused other holders of Series 57 bonds to abandon their claims, or to testify against Schlei to avoid being prosecuted themselves.

Enormous Number of People and Events Had to be "Protected"

Many people and many corrupt events were threatened, and had to be kept from the public at all cost. These included, for instance:

- The enormous plunder acquired by the invading Japanese from a dozen countries from 1937 to 1945.
- The secret retrieval of Japanese plunder by covert groups in and associated with the U.S. government and placement in banks throughout the world, in the names of present and former CIA and other people in covert operations.

- The manipulation of the 1951 Peace Treaty that protected and rewarded Japanese involved in horrific brutalities against U.S. prisoners.
- The horrific experiments on living prisoners by members of the Japanese Unit 731.
- The existence of hundreds of secret bank accounts controlled by people in or associated with U.S. intelligence groups.
- The protection by U.S. personnel, after the end of World War II, of some of the most brutal war criminals responsible for horrific treatment of American GIs during World War II.
- The bribing and undermining of the Japanese political process, using corruptly acquired funds, to manipulate and subvert the political process in Japan to please the wishes of U.S. politicians, CIA and military personnel.
- Using corruptly acquired funds to manipulate and undermine foreign governments throughout the world.
- To protect key people in the United States government involved in the multiple frauds.
- Protection of Japanese politicians that were part of the various schemes.

Other People Targeted to Keep Corruption from the Public

U.S. Secret Service Agent James P. Sena had investigated counterfeiting for the Treasury Department, and during these official duties Sena had examined M-Fund financial instruments in America and Japan. He determined that they were legitimate. With this knowledge, he and two others, Ian Yorkshire of Great Britain and Francis Cheung of Hong Kong, tried to sell several that had a value of $50 million.

All three were then arrested and the Series 57 bonds taken. Then, suddenly, and without explanation, the charges were dismissed with prejudice in November 1995. Prosecutors refused to return the Series 57 certificates they had confiscated as evidence, thereby protecting the hoax and also depriving the holder of the certificate from his investment. This scenario of dismissing charges but refusing to return bank documents worth billions of dollars had become a standard scenario.

Former U.S. Secretary of State Haig
And Series 57 Certificate Redemption

The government of Paraguay had bought one Series 57 certificate from First Hanover Securities in New York City (November 20, 1991) that had a face value of $500 million. Paraguay then requested MIC Debt Readjustment Company[14] to exchange this Series 57 certificate

[14] MIC is an organization backed by the Israeli government, which negoti-

for credit against a debt owed to Japan related to foreign aid. In payment for this service, Paraguay would grant MIC the right to oil exploration and development in Paraguayan territory. MIC chose former Secretary of State Alexander Haig as their negotiator.

Haig Especially Qualified for Piercing the Series 57 Block

Alexander Haig had served under General Douglas MacArthur, Courtney Whitney and Charles Willoughby in Japan, and had knowledge of the financial schemes being perpetrated, including the M-Fund. Haig negotiated directly with former Japanese Prime Minister Takeshita,[15] who was a primary participant in the M-Fund that originated under General MacArthursoccupation of Japan. Before the meeting, the Israeli group, MIC, provided Haig with several documents that provided further proof of the validity of the Series 57 certificates.

After being shown the Series 57 certificate, Takeshita told Haig that the certificate was not legitimate. Haig then presented Takeshita a copy of an insurance contract by the Yasuda Fire Insurance Company,[16] along with several others, making reference to the Series 57 certificates, proving that the certificates were legitimate. Takeshita then reversed his prior denial of the legitimacy of the Series 57 certificate and said this was a delicate matter and he would seek to obtain an answer.

The following day, Takeshita's personal secretary contacted Haig and admitted the legitimacy of the Series 57 certificates, but stated the Japanese government could not purchase it. Haig then replied that the document would be made public. That threat would have a devastating political impact in Japan. Again, the need for further consultation. The following day, the trade was accepted, with the comment, "We are ready to take certain measures on the certificate in question. You must treat this negotiation as strictly confidential. If a similar demand is made by another government, our administration would suffer because we are not prepared for it financially."

The Series 57 certificates were causing serious problems as many inquiries were being received by the Japanese Ministry of Finance seeking to redeem them, for which there were no funds.

Haig's negotiations were undoubtedly known to people in the U.S. Department of Justice. Yet, at the same time that the Series 57 certificate presented by Haig was being accepted as legitimate, the same De-

---

ates adjustments of national debt for governments in Eastern Europe and South America.

[15] Due to scandals, Takeshita had been forced, in January 1992, to resign as prime minister two years earlier, but continued to be a powerful force behind the scenes.

[16] The insurance policy issued in Tokyo was protection during transporting the certificate from the Ministry of Finance.

partment of Justice employees were criminally prosecuting widows and others that had rightful ownership of identical certificates.

There developed an incestuous relationship between Japanese war criminals and U.S. military, intelligence personnel and White House politicians that made a mockery of the sufferings by American POWs. There were many "winners" in the aftermath of horrendous sufferings by American military personnel and American POWs. Kishi, one of the Japanese war criminals, was immensely rewarded, politically and financially, from the M-Fund, He reportedly received about one trillion yen (3 billion dollars) after President Nixon entrusted the M-Fund to him. Kodama was rewarded, Emperor Hirohito was rewarded, to name just a few.

Prime Minister Tanaka had control of the M-Fund for a couple dozen years. Japanese scandals arose from the M-Fund. Japanese Series 57 certificates were connected to the M-Fund, and brought financial and personal misery to many people that had purchased them, or had them forced upon them.

They were issued in ten billion to fifty billion yen amounts and served to park black money from the M-Fund. The issuance of Series 57 certificates was precipitated by the Lockheed bribery scandal that surfaced in the 1970s. That scandal threatened the holders of other Japanese certificates, being the Series 57 certificates. These certificates were not sold to the public, and remained obscured.

Secretive Nature of the Bonds Facilities a Forgery Label

When people owning the 57 Series certificates later sought to redeem them, unless they were favored insiders, the certificates would be called forgeries by the politicians in control of the Japanese Ministry of Finance—controlled until recently by Liberal Democratic Party politicians (LDP).

This tactic, used by the Japanese, was supported by employees of the U.S. Department of Justice, who corruptly charged the legitimate holders of the certificates with a criminal act when they either sought to redeem them, or took actions showing they had a connection to them. Protective media personnel facilitated the fraud upon the people.

An online article published by the University of San Francisco Center for the Pacific Rim and the Japan Policy Research Institute (JPRI)[17] in July 1995, provided more information on the secret M-Fund and the bizarre rewarding of a Japanese war criminal responsible for some horrific acts against American prisoners of war. Some excerpts from that paper follows:

Our interest is in the foreign manipulation of the Japanese political

---

[17] JPRI Working Paper No. 11: July 1995.

process during the Allied occupation and its evolution over the more than forty years since the occupation ended. This issue has not merely historical significance. As Jim Mann has recently put it, "Did you ever want to know why the Japanese government behaves the way it does today—why its politics seem so corrupt, why its political parties are so hopelessly weak? Why Japan never developed a workable two-party system? There are some U.S. government files that could help shed light on those questions." (see "CIA Keeping Historians in the Dark About Its Cold War Role in Japan," *Los Angeles Times*, March 20, 1995.)

Similarly, John Dower (a member of the JPRI Board of Advisers) comments, "We look at the LDP and say it's corrupt and it's unfortunate to have a one-party democracy. But we have played a role in creating that misshapen structure." (see "C.I.A. Spent Millions to Support Japanese Right in 50's and 60's," *New York Times*, October 9, 1994.)

As has frequently been pointed out, the Americans sacrificed the political systems of both Japan and Italy to the requirements of the Cold War. Whether the Americans were right or wrong to do so is a different debate. The costs of their doing so are nonetheless coming due today.

These issues reentered the news last autumn when the *New York Times* published its "C.I.A. Spent Millions to Support Japanese Right in 50's and 60's," by Tim Weiner, Stephen Engelberg, and James Sterngold. This report did not say anything that had not been strongly suspected earlier, but it quoted some important participants, including Alfred C. Ulmer, Jr., the CIA's operations chief for East Asia from 1955 to 1958; Roger Hilsman, the head of Intelligence and Research at the State Department in the Kennedy and Johnson administrations; and U. Alexis Johnson, American ambassador to Japan from 1966 to 1969.

Each acknowledged making or authorizing payoffs to the LDP from 1955 to approximately 1972. In Tokyo the *Sankei Shimbun* reported that on October 10, the day following the *New York Times'* story, Deputy Prime Minister Kono Yohei (whose father, Kono Ichiro, was one of Kodama's closest associates) held an "emergency meeting" with Ambassador Mondale, which the Foreign Ministry later explained was merely a long-scheduled diplomatic appointment (Sankei, November 17, 18, 1994). Both the Japanese and the Americans maintained that the *Times* story concerned old news that had become common knowledge. But the CIA has refused to declassify or allow publication of the files that show what it was doing in Japan in the late 1950s and the 1960s" (*Los Angeles Times*, March 20, 1995).

The record on the Japanese side is not secret at all, even if there are people in Japan who would prefer that it remain private. As a contribution to this continuing inquiry, JPRI is publishing two unusual reports. One is a four-year old memorandum by Norbert Schlei on the "M-Fund" and his unfortunate involvement with it; the other is an essay by a distinguished historian written for the Yomiuri newspapers and reprinted here in English with the newspaper's permission. It is based on information that our author knows but cannot (yet) cite.

The M-Fund is one of the more slippery topics in postwar Japanese history. During the late 1970s and the 1980s, Japanese swindlers used the aura surrounding it and its alleged continuing existence to defraud such companies as Fuji Steel, All-Nippon Airways, and the Tokyo Railroads. Details concerning these cases, as well as the early history of the M-Fund are contained in Takano Hajime, MShikin, Shirarezaru chika kin yu no sekai (*M-Fund: The Unknown World of Underground Finance*) (Tokyo: Nihon Keizai Shimbun Sha, 1980), which is the most important source on the subject. Also relevant is a series of articles in *Asahi Journal*, which were translated into English as "Lockheed Connection: The 'M Fund' Ghost," *Asahi Evening News*, April 19-21, 1976.

It is possible that our author, Norbert Schlei, was trapped by yet another fraudulent misrepresentation of the M-Fund, much like those detailed by Takano. That is an issue before the U.S. Federal courts, although it is unlikely they will ever uncover the full truth of the matter. Schlei is a distinguished American lawyer. He was first in his class at Yale Law School; a former assistant attorney general for Presidents Kennedy and Johnson; deputy to Robert Kennedy in 1962 when troops were sent to Oxford, Mississippi, to integrate the university; and a founding partner of the Los Angeles office of Hughes Hubbard & Reed.

Schlei undertook to represent several dozen Japanese investors in their attempts to get the Ministry of Finance to recognize (and redeem) securities that the Japanese government maintains are forgeries. In his statement to the *New York Times*, Schlei said that the instruments, called "certificates of redemption" and not bonds, "were issued secretly, outside normal channels, to hide or 'park' a political fund in the names of people who would mean nothing to investigators probing into the affairs of former Prime Minister Kakuei Tanaka."

Schlei argues that these instruments were issued in 1982 by the then Minister of Finance in the Suzuki cabinet, Watanabe Michio; and Schlei furthermore says he was negotiating with the Japanese government about them before he was trapped by an American sting operation. For further details, see Rick Bragg, "Stalwart of the Kennedy Justice Dept. Finds His World in Ashes After a Trial," *New York Times*, April 14, 1995; Karen F. Donovan, "The Upending of a Camelot Knight," The *National Law Journal*, April 10, 1995; and 14-page letter to the editor of *The National Law Journal* by Norbert A. Schlei dated

April 12, 1995, on file at JPRI.

Schlei was convicted on January 5, 1995, in Federal court in Tampa, Florida, on charges of securities fraud; and his case is on appeal. Although it is irrelevant to the present discussion, we believe that there are many aspects to the sting operation in which Schlei was trapped that demand review; and we are certain that the Japanese aspects of the case were not properly presented to, or understood by, the jury. But the evidence for the existence of the M-Fund between approximately 1947 and 1972 rests on more than the statements of Schlei's clients.

According to Takano's book "M Shikin," the M-Fund was created out of several different funds that all originally had different names. The "Yotsuya Fund," put together by General Willoughby, the head of G-2 and the CIC, came from black market operations and was used for anti-communist plots. The "Keenan Fund," named after Joseph B. Keenan, chief prosecutor in the war crimes trials, derived from confiscated property. The M-Fund itself, referring to money that Marquat controlled, was initially created from sales of confiscated Japanese military stockpiles of industrial diamonds, platinum, gold, and silver that had been plundered in occupied countries; the sales of shares of dissolved zaibatsu companies; and so-called GARIOA or "counterpart funds," which were accounts of nonconvertible yen derived from the sales in Japan of official American aid imports and authorized imports of such commodities as petroleum.

All three funds were combined into one M-Fund when the occupation ended, and the fund was jointly operated by Americans and Japanese until the late 1950s, when it was turned over to the Japanese by then Vice President Nixon to then Prime Minister Kishi. Schlei's memorandum outlines some of the fund's post-occupation uses and its alleged later history. The amounts involved were very large and were used for industrial projects in rebuilding Japan's economy and later for clandestine activities elsewhere in Asia.

The chief evidence supporting the existence of the M-Fund or something like it, other than circumstances and anecdotes, comes from the life and statements of Kodama Yoshio. For details on his life, see the treatments in David E. Kaplan and Alec Dubro, Yakuza (Reading, Mass.: Addison-Wesley, 1986, part II "The Kodama Years," pp. 41-123); Chalmers Johnson, Japan: Who Governs? (New York: Norton, 1995, pp. 194-97); and Kodama's own two books written while he was an unindicted class-A war criminal in Sugamo Prison from January 25, 1946 to December 24, 1948.

They were translated into English during the 1950s as part of the effort to rehabilitate him—from 1956 on he was the Lockheed Aircraft Corporation's chief fixer and wirepuller in Japan—and were published as *I was Defeated*, Taro Fukuda, trans. (Tokyo: An Asian Publication, 1951), and *Sugamo Diary*, Taro Fukuda, trans. (Tokyo: Radiopress, 1960). The most important Japanese sources are the study by the Mainichi Shimbun's Political Department—Kuromaku Kodama Yoshio (Tokyo: Ertl Shuppansha, 1976)—and Omori Minoru's long interview with him on May 25, 1974 (see Nihon Hokai, Sengo Hisshi [*Japan's Collapse, Postwar Hidden History*, Tokyo: Kodansha Bunko, 1981, vol. 1, pp. 248312).

There is no doubt today that Kodama returned to Japan in 1945 from China as the former head of the Navy's Kodama Kikan (Kodama Agency) a fabulously rich war profiteer. He transferred stolen diamonds and platinum before he went to prison to Hatoyama Ichiro and Kono Ichiro, and the funds these materials produced when sold by Kono, about $175 million, financed the creation of the Liberal Party. The go-between in this famous operation was the Kuromaku Tsuji Karoku, whom the Diet questioned in 1947 about the alleged use of former military and black market funds to influence politics.

There is also little doubt that when Kodama was released from Sugamo on the day after the convicted war criminals were executed, he had been recruited by and was working for U.S. intelligence. On that matter Tad Szulc has written, "Intelligence sources say that Kodama had a working relationship with the CIA from the time he was released from a Japanese prison in 1948"; and another seasoned observer who was also a former SCAP official, Hans Baerwald, comments, "[Kodama's] release from imprisonment allegedly was tied to his becoming an agent of the American intelligence services in general, and ultimately the Central Intelligence Agency in particular." (Szulc, *New Republic*, April 10, 1976, p. 11; Baerwald, Asian Survey, September 1976, pp. 817-18.)

On April 4, 1976, the *New York Times* summarized what Kodama did for the CIA and for Lockheed:

> Last week there was more evidence of the agency's [CIA's] apparently ubiquitous involvement: its officials knew 20 years ago that the Lockheed Aircraft Corporation bribed Japanese politicians in connection with the sale of F-104 fighter planes to the Japanese Government. In a period of 20 years (1956 to 1975) Lockheed paid $12.6 million to top Japanese officials to sell $700 million worth of aircraft. About $1.5 million was spent to win the F-104 contract away from Grumman Aircraft in the late 1950's. It is not known whom the agency told about the bribes. It reportedly did not inform officials of Grumman, or the State Department.

Another service Kodama performed was to counter left-wing protesters by mobilizing "some 50,000 gamblers, street vendors, racketeers, and members of the violent right to take part in the so-called 'Mass Mobilization for Greeting Ike' and to help the police keep 'order' during the presidential visit." Even though Ike ultimately cancelled his 1960 visit because of the storm of protests over renewal of the U.S.-Japan Security Treaty, this effort cost hundreds of millions of yen, "the source of which is still unaccounted for," in John Roberts' words (see John G. Roberts, "The Lockheed-Japan-Watergate Connection: A'Kwantung Army' on the Multinational Front," AMPO: Japan-Asia Quarterly Review, March 1976, pp. 6-15). These funds probably came from the M-Fund; it was available and had been created for precisely such needs. All accounts say that after the end of the occupation, the fund's American managers came from the CIA.

CHALMERS JOHNSON is President of the Japan Policy Research Institute and has authored some twelve books on a variety of subjects including developmental capitalism in Asia and revolution in China. Most recently, Johnson has authored "Japan: Who Governs?" (W.W. Norton, 1995).

Japan's "M-Fund" Memorandum,
January 7, 1991 by Norbert A. Wile'

The subject of this memorandum is Japan's so-called "M-Fund," a secret fund of money of enormous size that has existed in Japan for more than forty years. The Fund was established by the United States in the immediate postwar era for essentially the same reasons that later gave rise to the Marshall Plan of assistance by the U.S. to Western Europe, including the Federal Republic of Germany.

At the outset, the Fund was administered wholly by the U.S. with purely advisory input from Japan. Later, however, control over the Fund was allowed to pass into Japanese hands. Under Japanese control, very serious abuses of the Fund have developed, and it is clear today the Fund has been and is being used in a way that is contrary to the interests of both the United States and Japan.

Such a fund was duly created, utilizing primarily money and property that had been in the possession of the Japanese armed forces at war's end after having been seized during the war in occupied areas such as China, Korea, Taiwan and the Philippines. This wealth, which was turned over to the U.S. at war's end, was not on Japan's books as a nation and was available for use by MacArthur without the need of any public legislative action in the United States. It turned out to be much more substantial in amount than was originally realized. Later, so-called "counterpart" funds—"soft" foreign currencies acquired by the U.S. which could not be converted into dollars—were added.

The new fund was administered by General MacArthur's Headquarters with advisory input from Japanese sources, primarily Prime Minister Shigeru Yoshida. The fund came to be known to insiders as the "M-Fund" or "Marquat-Fund," after an officer named Marquat who was identified with the fund's establishment and early operation. Because of Mr. Yoshida's involvement with the Fund, it has also sometimes been referred to as the "Yoshida Fund." The M-Fund was used not only for the building of a democratic political system in Japan but, in addition, for all of the purposes for which Marshall Plan funds were used in Europe—in effect, the rebuilding of the Japanese economy. Long-term, low-interest or interest-free loans were provided to key Japanese industries such as coal, iron, shipbuilding, fertilizer, electric power, and the like.

In order to make the Fund an even better source of defense funds in time of need, the Japanese negotiators agreed that after the Fund was released to Japanese control, they would add substantially to the amount of the Fund.

[Adding Confiscated American Assets to M-Fund]

The task of adding to the M-Fund, which is believed to have amounted to 12.3 trillion yen (about $35 billion) in 1960, was delegated to Kakuei Tanaka, Finance Minister in the Ikeda Cabinet. The plan was to obtain the necessary amount by selling the Japanese real estate which the government had confiscated during the war from enemy aliens (i.e., citizens of the U.S. and other Allied Powers) who had failed to qualify for postwar restitution.

The Fund has today grown to the staggering size of more than $500 billion. It dominates Japanese politics and is a major force in the Japanese economy. And yet, amazingly enough, it remains a secret fund, unknown to most of the world and to the vast majority of Japanese citizens. Even more amazing, as I discuss below, the Fund is not controlled by the government of Japan or even by the Liberal Democratic Party, but is, rather, the private preserve of a small group of individuals.

Control of the Fund and Resulting Abuses

The exact nature of what Nixon did or intended to do when he yielded control of the M-Fund to the Japanese negotiators in the waning days of the Eisenhower Administration has never been made public. It seems inconceivable that he knowingly "gave" the Fund to Prime Minister Kishi and his associates as individuals, free of any governmental or institutional control. The fact is, however, that beginning with Prime Minister Kishi, the Fund has been treated as the private preserve of the individuals into whose control it has fallen. Those individuals have felt able to appropriate huge sums from the Fund for their own personal and political purposes. The Fund has not been deemed an asset of the nation or subjected to governmental or even institutional control.

The secrecy surrounding the M-Fund and the absence of governmental or institutional controls over it have led to abuses so great as to dwarf any governmental scandal within memory in any part of the world. The litany of abuses begins with Kishi, who, after obtaining control of the Fund from Nixon, helped himself to a fortune of 1 trillion yen (then nearly $3 billion). Kakuei Tanaka, who dominated the Fund for longer than any other individual, took from it personally some 10 trillion yen which he invested through the Union Bank of Switzerland.

Although the people of Japan and the world do not yet know it, the Fund under Mr. Nakasone's control was responsible for the Recruit scandal. So far as the public is aware, the Recruit scandal concerned relatively small sums of money distributed by the Recruit Company to some 200 politicians in order to influence governmental policy. Prime Minister Takeshita resigned because approximately $1.5 million was received by him or his associates as political contributions or in other ways that involved no illegal conduct on Takeshita's part. However, the real abuse underlying these events is that the Recruit Company itself was, in effect, created and financed by the M-Fund to serve Nakasone's personal and political interests.

[U.S. M-Fund Contributed to Murders]

The M-Fund is reported to have been the cause of several political murders. Many people in Japan believe that former Prime Minister Eisaku Sato was murdered, the victim of deliberate poisoning rather than a digestive upset as reported to the press. According to these widely circulated reports, Sato's death occurred at the height of a contest with Kakuei Tanaka for control over the M-Fund. The dispute was, ultimately, settled and a major scandal averted by the payment from the Fund to Sato's widow of a huge death-benefit of 300 billion yen.

In more recent times Mr. Takeshita's assistant, Mr. Aoki, supposedly a suicide, is said to have been assisted by persons having a vital interest in preserving the secrecy of the M-Fund. In the days before his death, Aoki, who was known to have detailed knowledge of the Fund's operations, made the mistake of telling several friends that the Recruit scandal was a minor matter compared to another scandal that was about to become public through his impending testimony.

America's Protected War Criminal: Kishi Nobusuke And the Transformation of U.S.-Japan Relations.

In the book, *America's Favorite War Criminal: Kishi Nobusuke and the Transformation of U.S.-Japan Relations*, author Michael Schaller describes the benefits given to Kishi Nobusuke, who inflicted such great harm upon Americans—by President Dwight Eisenhower and other U.S. officials, and makes reference to the M-Fund. Among his comments:

Evidence in a variety of open and still classified U.S. government documents strongly indicates that early in 1958, President Dwight D. Eisenhower, making what he and his aides earlier called a "big bet," authorized the CIA to provide secret campaign funds to Japanese Prime Minister Kishi Nobusuke—formerly an accused war criminal—and selected members of the Liberal Democratic Party. This fateful decision followed Kishi's June 1957 visit to the United States, where he had addressed both Houses of Congress, thrown out the first pitch at a New York Yankees baseball game, and joined Eisenhower in a round of golf at an otherwise racially segregated country club. In private discussions, the president and Secretary of State John Foster Dulles also gave Kishi a crucial political reward: their pledge to renegotiate the unpopular 1951 security treaty imposed upon Japan as the price of ending the Occupation.

The honors bestowed upon the prime minister could only be described as remarkable, given the fact that as a member of General Tojo's cabinet in 1941 Kishi had co-signed the declaration of war against the United States. As minister of Commerce and Industry and later head of the Munitions Ministry, he had overseen the forced conscription of hundreds of thousands of Korean and Chinese laborers and been responsible for military production. When American Occupation troops entered Japan in August 1945, they arrested Kishi as a suspected Class A war criminal and he spent three years in Sugamo Prison under investigation.

As much as anyone, Kishi represented everything the United States detested about Imperial Japan and had pledged to eradicate. His political resurrection symbolized the transformation of Japanese-American relations during the 1950s. In a literal sense, Kishi's life mirrored Japan's evolution from enemy to ally, the emergence of the Cold War in Asia, and the role played by the U.S. in forging Japan's postwar political and economic structure.

Kishi first came to the attention of American officials shortly before the Pearl Harbor attack when, as a rising star in the Ministry of Commerce and Industry, he struck up a friendship with Ambassador Joseph C. Grew. Grew's admiration was evident in 1942 when, while under detention and awaiting an exchange of diplomats, the ambassador commented on Kishi's offer to release the detained American to play a round of golf. "Kishi has always been one of my highly valued friends in Japan and nothing can ever change my feeling of personal friendship and affection for him," Grew wrote. "That feeling will endure permanently, no matter what has happened or what may happen in the future." This testimonial served Kishi better than he could ever have dreamed.

Final Loss of Political Control of the M-Fund Funded Liberal Democratic Party (LDP) in Japan

In 2009, the U.S.-funded Liberal Democratic Party was ousted and the Democratic Party Japan (DPJ) took political control away from the LDP party. The Prime Minister at the head of the LDP party was Yukio Hatoyama. A major campaign promise that helped gain public support was to force the United States to renegotiate the peace treaty by removing U.S. troops from Okinawa—the island that President Richard Nixon suddenly and without explanation deeded to Japan—thereby reducing U.S. security in the Far East.

Hatoyama had arranged for the United States to move its primary base on Okinawa to a scenic location at the northern edge of Okinawa, which the people objected to; they wanted the U.S. military to be totally removed.

More Intrigue

After becoming Prime Minister, unknown forms of pressure by U.S. personnel caused Hatoyama to backtrack on the promise to bring about the removal of U.S. military forces from Okinawa. The corrupt activities associated with the M-Fund included the U.S. cover-up of the Japanese plunder stolen from other nations and individuals; the retrieval and misuse by U.S. personnel, acting in secret, of part of the stolen plunder; and other corrupt acts arising from the original scheme by U.S. military and intelligence personnel, and White House politicians.

Outrage in Japan and Okinawa at Hatoyama's backtrack on the removal of U.S. forces from Okinawa caused Hatoyama to resign in June, 2010. He was replaced by former finance minister Naoto Kan.

Within days, Naoto Kan stated that the alliance with the United States would remain the linchpin to Japan's foreign policy.

CHAPTER FIVE

Secret Retrieval of Gold By President Ferdinand Marcos

There was irrefutable evidence that Philippine President Ferdinand Marcos had tons of gold and numerous bank certificates of gold deposits and other financial documents. His initial acquisition of the bank certificates of gold deposits occurred after the death of Santa Romana. Marcos had been a lawyer hired by Romana and had been named as trustee to handle matters occurring in the Philippines. He was also a low-level politician.

When Santa Romana died in 1974, Ferdinand Marcos, with the help of crooked Philippine judges and other government personnel, seized the contents of the bank safety boxes that contained dozens of certificates of gold deposits in the name of Santa Romana and the many other names that he used. Marcos was able to change the name of the trustee on some of the bank certificates, showing himself as trustee.

Many of the deposits under the name of Severino Garcia Sta. Romana and José Antonio Diaz de la Paz or Santa Romana used the reference codes, "Fanerst King Fisher" and "Burgst Harbor King."

When Santa Romana's widow sought access to the safety deposit boxes, the bank initially refused to allow this. With legal help, she finally gained access, and found that all of the safety deposit boxes were empty. Her attempts to gain access to the multiple deposits at multiple banks were blocked at every turn. She was told that the accounts that were in her husband's name, for which she was the beneficiary, did not exist, despite the fact that she had the number of the account, the password, and other details that were otherwise unknown. She did not have the actual documents as they had been stolen from the safe deposit boxes by her husband's lawyer, Ferdinand Marcos, but she had copies, and also book keeper records.

President Marcus Used Government Personnel In Search of Japanese Plunder

Over a period of years, Philippine residents started uncovering small quantities of the Japanese plunder. After Ferdinand Marcus became president[18] of the Philippines, he used the power of his office to seize the gold discovered by small-time treasure hunters. He eventually used members of the military to search for Japanese plunder, which required considerable digging in search for the tunnels and caves that were plunder sites.

Leber Group Retrieving Gold for Marcos

Marcos established a group to find, retrieve, and hide the gold, calling it the Leber Group. ("Rebel") The group was composed of military people selected by President Marcos to find and extract the gold. In charge of the operation was General Fabian Ver.

172 Treasure Sites Containing Plunder of a Dozen Nations

Of the reported 172 major plunder sites, Marcos reportedly discovered 30 of them during the 13 years that the operation continued. These sites were discovered with the help of Japanese who had the maps or were involved with the original placement. The first diggings started in March 1973 near Lake Caliraya in Lumban, and then in the vicinity of Lake Caliraya Resort, in Cavinti, Laguna.

Discovery of tunnels

In 1972, a tunnel system was found near the Pasig River that extended from Fort Bonifacio military reservation to Villamor Air Base and Bicutan-Taguig via Fort Bonifacio Army General Hospital. These secret tunnels preceded all the other treasure hunting and digging operations. The soldiers said the gold discoveries made by Marcos, as well as their operations, were the real reasons why he started his strongman rule "in the guise of a threatening rebellion by the alleged newly revitalized CPP/NPA (Communist Party of the Philippines, New People's Army) and Muslim secessionism in Mindanao."

Digging for Tunnels

The 16th Infantry Battalion personnel were used to dig and locate the hidden caves and tunnels. One of Marcos' first treasure finds occurred on April 27, 1973, when backhoes struck several steel cylindrical drums that measured about three feet long and 1.5 feet in diameter and copper boxes, embedded in concrete vaults about 35 feet below the surface. As the backhoe split open the metal drum, gold became visible, each about three inches by two inches by a foot long. President Marcos soon arrived with General Ver by helicopter. Some of the gold bars were coated with black tar, apparently to discourage uninquisitive people that might accidently come upon the gold bars. Several concrete vaults, each six feet long, five feet wide and five feet high, were placed on board trucks by a heavy crane.

Speaking in tagolog, Marcos told the workers: "You will all share

---

[18] Ferdinand Marcus was President of the Philippines from 1965 to 1986.

in everything that's here but you have to wait for the right time." After the treasure in that site was removed, digging then started at several other locations, including in Teresa in Rizal province from 1974 to 1981.

Diggers Tell of 60,000 Tons of Treasure

According to Roberto Caoile, spokesperson of the Forgotten Claimants of Yamashita-World War II Treasures Versus Marcos Estate Inc., different groups were involved with different segments of the recovery. One group dug while another group transported the gold and other treasures, and a third group protected the sites. General Ver's Presidential Guard Battalion guarded the diggers.

The old Central Bank in Intramuros was the storage site initially for the recovered gold until President Marcos ordered the construction of a new gold minting and refining plant for the Central Bank. The recovered gold bars were then remelted and processed to remove markings, such as five star markings from Cambodia; four stars from Sumatra, and three stars from Burma.

Using US-Supplied C-130 to Ship Gold

Gold bars were shipped from the Manila International Airport using C-130 military aircraft after President Marcus declared martial law in 1972, which Marcus predicated on actions of a Huk insurgency group in the Philippines. The shipment of gold bars was witnessed by perimeter security personnel at the airport.

60,000 Metric Tons

One of the workers in the Leber group, Roberto Caoile, stated that their group excavated over 60,000 metric tons of bullion consisting of gold bars and other precious metals, plus diamonds. The treasure sites included Montalban caves in Montalban, Rizal; Montalban Mascat; Sitio Mayagay, Sampaloc in Tanay, Rizal; Fort Bonifacio Tunnel; Fort Bonifacio hospital; Caliraya in Cavinti-Lumban, Laguna; Baras and Teresa in Rizal province; the area of the Manpower and Youth building; Bastion de San Lorenzo in Fort Santiago; Muñoz in Nueva Ecija; Balok bridge, also in Nueva Ecija; site of the Central Luzon State University statue in Muñoz; Sta. Fe in Nueva Vizcaya; Campo 4 in San Jose, Nueva Vizcaya; and San Mateo in Rizal province.

The Japanese had divided the war plunder into major and minor sites, using the Manila Railroad Co. to transport the treasures. Major or minor treasure sites depended on the "suitability, concealment, permanency and location of man-made, built-up areas, mountainous and/or rolling hills, terrain with creeks, rivers, dams, big acacia, mango, camachile or duhat trees that serve as references for future retrieval of said treasure deposits," the soldiers said. Lower ranking Japanese soldiers buried small quantities of gold in small sites under large acacia or mango trees for later retrieval—most of which never occurred.

Caoile reported that at Fort Santiago there were over 100 boxes of treasures that were recovered, buried under the old torture chamber, Bastion de San Lorenzo, near the Pasig River. The gold treasures were buried at or below sea level where the ground temperature was cooler.

Helping to Hide the Gold

Part of the gold that Marcos recovered was hidden through the CIA's Nugan Hand Bank in Australia. When the cover on that CIA proprietary was blown, another CIA front was used: Bishop, Baldwin, Rewald, Dillingham and Wong (BBRDW) based in Hawaii with multiple offices elsewhere. More about this in other pages.

Marcos' First Acquisition of Gold Bars

Ferdinand Marcos' first acquisition of actual gold bars came as he seized gold bars that were the center of dispute between Filipino laborers and former Japanese officers that had returned to where they had hid a gold cache prior to Japan's surrender. Prior to becoming president, and while working as a political aide to President Elpidio Quirino,[19][20] Marcos was working with Japanese sources examining Japanese documents seeking to discover the locations of the Japanese plunder.

One Ton Solid Gold Buddha

Ferdinand Marcus' next experience with Japanese plunder occurred in 1970 as Filipino locksmith and treasure hunter Rogelio Roxas discovered and retrieved from a mine shaft a solid gold Buddha and bars of gold. He had obtained a Japanese map showing a mine shaft in the Benguet mines near Baguio. Upon opening the cave, he found skeletons of American POWs that had been forced to open up the shaft and hide a crate containing the nearly one-ton solid gold Siamese-like Buddha. The cave was then blasted shut, with the American POWs inside.

The Buddha and gold bars were seized from Roxas by President Marcos' soldiers, including Marcos' brother-in-law, Marcelino Barba. He was the husband of one of Marcos' sisters, Fortuna "Baby" Roxas. As the media focused on this theft, Marcos had Roxas jailed and tortured. Witnesses to the theft disappeared.

Starting in the 1970s Marcos sought to sell his tons of gold on the world market. People that examined the gold reported rooms stacked from floor to ceiling with gold bars, more than they had ever seen in their lifetime. But finding buyers for the gold that had a mineral composition indicating that it was Japanese war plunder was difficult.

Help in Locating Other Gold Sites

Marcos had a Chicago psychic, Olof Jonsson visit him at

---

[19] Cline retired in 1973.

[20] Quirino was president of the Philippines from 1948 to 1953. Marcos was president from 1965 to 1986.

Malacanang Palace to help find the Japanese gold sites. At the same time, he hired a Nevada metallurgist, Robert Curtis, to melt down the gold that he had already retrieved and change its characteristics so that it could not be traced to the Japanese plunder. Gold contains characteristics that show where it had been mined. The gold plunder also had to be remelted to meet the standard size required by the London gold market.

Olof did find several gold sites, including one that was a sunken ship. Among the people that Curtis met were Paul Jiga and Ben Balmores, who had been witnesses to several of the burial sites during the war and had some of the burial maps. They represented themselves as Filipinos, but were actually Japanese and had been in the Japanese Navy assigned to Rear Admiral Iwabuchi Sanji, known as the brutal "Butcher of Manila," and Rear Admiral Kodama Yoshio, the person with the ultimate responsibility for the plunder and its shipment to the Philippines.

Marcoses' General Fabian Ver coordinated operations and controlled what Olof and Curtis could see. Both of them were brought to the underground vaults containing stacks of gold bars and both later reported what they saw: gold bars stacked floor to ceiling.

Fearing For His Life, Olof Fled the Philippines

Olof had an intuition that his life was in danger due to what he knew about the location of several of the treasure sites that Marcos wanted to remain secret; he quickly caught a flight out of Manila, warning Curtis of the danger if he remained. Curtis soon followed, taking with him some of the treasure maps. Curtis, a resident of Nevada, then contacted the *Las Vegas Sun* and Jack Anderson, which was followed up with his story.

The *Philippine News* of San Francisco published a detailed story in 1978 about Marcos and the Japanese plunder:

A secret CIA report [1969] on Ferdinand Marcus stated that he had already stolen at least several hundred million dollars. This report was kept secret, only for circulation within a small circle in Washington, but this circle included top officials of the White House, the State Department, and the intelligence community. ... the CIA knew as far back as 1969 that Ferdinand and Imelda had already "stolen funds ranging from not lower than several hundred million U.S. dollars to two billion U.S. dollars."

The CIA was in a position to know. Over the years, CIA agents actively helped Marcos salt money in America, especially in Hawaii. This became abundantly clear during the fraud trial of Ronald Rewald in Hawaii in 1983-85 when it came out that Rewald's investment firm, Bishop, Baldwin, Rewald, Dillingham & Wong, had been set up as a conduit for CIA funds, and as a way of helping Ferdinand Marcos and a variety of Filipino oligarchs to salt black money in America. The CIA had also been funneling Marcos black money out via Australia and Hong Kong through the Nugan-Hand Bank in Australia, which had branches in Manila, Hong Kong, Singapore, and elsewhere till it collapsed in scandal in 1980.

The corrupt and brutal Marcos regime was used by the U.S. secret activities to provide false end-user certificates so as to mask the real destination of weapons shipped from the United States. General Fabian Ver, chief of the Philippines military, signed false end-user certificates, saying for instance that the weapons were being reshipped to Israel. Instead, the weapons went to countries that were on the U.S. blacklist of countries.

In the mid-1970s Marcos became pathologically greedy. He was already a billionaire from clandestinely recovering some of the Golden Lily's treasure. However, the only means he had of selling it was through the CIA or Japan. Both would take the odd sized ingots without the standard paper trail required in the legitimate gold market, but only at a steep discount.

To bypass the CIA and Japan and sell in the open market, Marcos had to have the gold resmelted and the fingerprint from impurities altered so the gold would appear to have a Philippine origin.

By 1975, Marcos had already formed the Leber group (rebel spelled backwards) to uncover the Golden Lily treasure from 34 of the known 172 sites. Due to Marcos's personal fascination with psychics, the group included Olof Jonsson, a psychic from Chicago. Marcos then contacted Robert Curtis, a mining engineer from Sparks, Nevada.

Curtis had developed a process to extract platinum and reclaim more gold from the mining tailings in the Sierras, which made him a moderately wealthy man. He was also an expert at changing the fingerprint of gold bullion. At first, Curtis turned down Marcos's offer to resmelt the gold.

However, Curtis was amazed at the amount of gold that was being discussed in the offer. It was ten times the amount of the average gold that the Philippine mines had ever produced. After several offers, Marcos finally revealed to Curtis that the gold came from Japanese looting during WWII. The idea of recovering Japanese gold fascinated Curtis and he accepted the job, arriving in the Philippines at the end of February 1975.

On March 25, 1975, Curtis signed a contract with the Leber group. As part of his participation, Curtis agreed to supply two smelters. Curtis needed a loan to cover the expenses of the smelters and turned to a previous contact inside the John Birch Society. Curtis had been contacted earlier in the 1970s by Jerry Adams, Robert Welch, Jay and Dan Agnew, and Floyd Paxton. Robert Welch founded the John Birch Society. It was a fringe group on the far right of mostly consisting of wealthy businessmen, far right politicians, ex-military, and intelligence officers. Lansdale was a member.

The members of the Birch Society were also goldbugs. After Nixon allowed citizens to own gold, the Birch Society developed a backdoor through Canada to buy overseas gold and smuggled it into the U.S. through Canada. The Birch Society then used the gold to fund their own private vigilante force. The vigilante force was something similar to a private FBI. The John Birch Society has always maintained some type of blacklist, which is typical of all hard right groups. From time to time, news articles have appeared about the Birch blacklist. Generally, these right wing blacklists receive a wink and nod from the FBI as they view such blacklists as helpful.

Curtis was unaware the inner circle of the John Birch Society knew about the Black Eagle Trust and previous recoveries of gold. They knew because one of the founding members was Colonel Laurence Bunker, who had succeeded General Bonner Feller's position in MacArthur's staff in Tokyo.

The Birch Society arranged the financing for Curtis through Washington State Senator Floyd Paxton and his son. Another participant was Jerry Adams, the head of the Great American Silver Corporation, a company associated with the Hunt brothers. Welch and Congressman Larry McDonald told Curtis that they had cleared the loan personally. MacDonald was the head of the Anti-Communist League before he died in a plane crash. The loan was unsecured except for Curtis's promise to return a 22 percent of his Leber share.

By the time Curtis had opened the first treasure site, the John Birch Society placed new demands on him for additional security for the loan. Curtis offered them the titles to his heavy equipment in Nevada. He also was obligated to give the Birchers the exclusive right to market up to $20 billion of any gold recovered. The Birchers told Curtis that the gold would be sold through Commonwealth Packaging Ltd, located in the Bahamas and owned by Kwik Lok. The proceeds would be deposited in the Nassau branch of the Royal Bank of Canada and finally transferred to a branch in Kelowna Canada. There the money would be smuggled into the U.S. by a key financial expert of the Birch Society.

The sudden demands of the Birch Society were triggered by July 4 and 5, 1975 columns by Jack Anderson, who reported that Marcos was recovering gold with the help of several Americans. Curtis barely escaped from the Philippines with his life.

Later, Curtis learned that Marcos had recovered 22,000 metric tons of gold bullion. Marcos had the treasure resealed without recovering two gold Buddhas and the barrels of gemstones.

While Curtis was still in the Philippines, he learned that the Gold Cartel had offered Marcos a Mafia style deal—either kill Curtis and let the Cartel handle the gold or Marcos would be in trouble. The Cartel refers to the alliance of prime banks, gold companies, and national treasuries (including the Federal Reserve and the Bank of England) that dominate the world gold market. In the end, Curtis was left broke. Johnson Mathey-Chemicals (and a part of the Cartel) now owned his two Philippine smelters.

About the same time, things turned bad for Marcos. Marcos was trying to blackmail the Japanese over the Showa Trust at the Sanwa Bank. The Trust had come from treasures recovered from the Golden Lily. At the time, the Showa Trust was so large that it was generating a billion dollars a year in interest. Exposure of the trust would be embarrassing for both Washington and Tokyo. Apparently, Marcos was successful in his blackmail, as several accounts with his name appeared in the Hong Kong branch of the Sanwa Bank shortly after his negotiating team had visited Tokyo.

In his first year in office, Reagan declared that he would restore the gold standard. Reagan had long standing ties to the Birch Society, dating back to the 1950s. The Reagans were also long time friends with Marcos. To make his plan for a new gold standard work, Reagan needed a large stock of gold. He asked Marcos privately to lend part of his hoard of black gold for his plan. Marcos however, demanded a higher commission than what Reagan was willing to pay.

In combination with Marcos blackmailing the Japanese and his demand for a high commission to Reagan, Marcos had sealed his fate and was shortly removed from office. Once under siege in Manila, Senator Paul Laxalt offered Marcos an ultimatum: forfeit his gold in return for being rescued by the U.S. That evening, after accepting the ultimatum, barges were towed alongside the presidential palace and loaded with gold from the palace. The barges were then towed to Subic. Then Marcos were rescued and taken to Hawaii where authorities seized billions of dollars worth of gold certificates.

Marcos's high flying days playing wild and loose with black gold ended in Hawaii. However, the Reagan administration's interest in the Golden Lily treasure buried in the Philippines continued. In January 1987, Curtis was contacted by Alan Foringer to talk about Philippine treasure.

After meeting Curtis, Alan Foringer and his aide, John Voss, informed Curtis they were with the Nippon Star. The Nippon Star had been formed by General John Singlaub to search for treasure in the

Philippines. Curtis wanted no part of dealing with the CIA or any CIA connected fronts. However, Curtis was then informed by a phone call from General Schweitzer that President Reagan had personally endorsed the Nippon Star and the Phoenix Exploration groups. Reagan couldn't publicly endorse the explorations but had fully briefed the U.S. Embassy in Manila, and the commanders at Subic Bay Naval Base, and the Clark Air Force Base. Others involved in the exploration included Colonel Dick Childress, General Daniel Graham, General Jack Vessy, and Ray Cline.

Curtis reluctantly agreed to meet them in Hong Kong. However, this time he demanded to tape-record the meeting to protect himself. Once again, the John Birch Society was financing the operation. Curtis also discovered that Singlaub had been duped and was using false maps. Curtis had retained the maps for all the sites from his earlier trip to the Philippines. Desperate to dig himself out of a financial hole, Curtis suggested to first try a site on Corregidor. After digging had proceeded for five days, Philippine Army helicopters swooped down and demanded the treasure hunters leave at gunpoint. Curtis then returned home.

Curtis returned the third time to the Philippines as a partner with Charles McDougal, a former Green Beret. Once again, as he was about to strike gold, Curtis was forced to leave the Philippines. Later, his former partners recovered roughly $4.5 billion in gold that Curtis had located.

Further evidence of the Reagan's administration's involvement with recovering Golden Lily treasure comes from a suit filed by Melvin Belli over gold deposits held by Citibank. Belli had concluded that Citibank's John Reed had joined with President Reagan, James Baker, Bill Casey, and Prime Minister Margaret Thatcher to use Golden Lily treasure to finance covert operations by the U.S. and Britain. Belli referred to the plan as "The Purple Ink Document." Unfortunately, Belli died before the case could proceed. However, the case is still pending.

The danger now is that the Black Eagle Trust is no longer fully in the hands of the government. Instead, several far-right groups have access to it and can use it to further their radical agenda. Furthermore, they know more treasure is to be found in the Philippines. Undoubtedly, some of the political shift to the right in the United States since, the 1980s has been funded with parts of the Black Eagle Trust.

A Philippine *Inquirer* newspaper article (1996) in Manila by Rene Espina, the second in the series, was titled, "Marcos" Assets," stated:

Immediately after the departure of Pres. Marcos during the EDSA revolution, forces loyal to then-Sec. Juan Ponce Enrile and Gen. Ramos secured Malacanang Palace. It was then that the "yellow forces" took control of the Palace. While the other buildings in the compound were occupied by the people, the Palace itself where President Marcos and his family lived was off limits to all but authorized persons only. The Marcoses in their haste to depart — via US Armed Forces helicopters— left thinking that the US helicopters would come back for a second trip to pick up the rest of their luggage. Since it did not, at least 24 pieces of Mrs. Marcos' luggage and the Presidents were found at Malacanang [Palace].

As reported by my close friends & AFP officers, to the best of my recollection, at least 16 Louis Vuitton suitcases contained the jewelry of Mrs. Marcos; the rest contained valuable documents.

As the "yellow task forces" proceeded to inspect the private bedrooms of the Pres. And Mrs. Marcos, they found the vault of Mrs. Marcos, which when opened contained some ordinary jewelry, watches and other giveaways and gold coin—mostly special issues of the Phil. Central Bank etc. They also found in her boudoir, pints of perfume and other toiletries, not to mention the famous shoes, Ternos [shoes], and other articles for personal use. In the process of sweeping the Palace for bombs, dogs whose handlers were Americans, were used to sniff for explosives or hidden passageways.

It was during this sanitation drive that the dogs started pawing & barking at what seemed to be a blank wall. Upon closer examination it was found out that there were markings on the floor which indicated that the false wall could indeed be a secret door... the scratches on the floor were caused by the opening and closing of the door.

When the group succeeded in opening the false wall they found out that it covered the steel door to Pres. Marcos/ vault. When it was finally opened, aside from the other valuable documents, the task force found two brown valises full of small diploma-like documents, which upon closer examination proved to be CD's (certificates of deposits) of foreign banks.

The smallest CD denomination was $10 million US dollars. The others were higher. My best estimate would be that such a bag could easily contain anywhere between 250 to 1,000 certificates of deposit. ... let's say 250 CD's times 2 (bags) times a minimum ....

"Soldiers of Fortune"

A 1998 *Philippine Inquirer* article titled "Soldiers of Fortune" described the affidavit signed by 96 members of the 16th Infantry Battalion and 51st Engineering Brigade declaring that between 1973 and 1985 they had recovered over 60,000 metric tons of gold from thirty of a reported 172 Japanese sites in the Philippines. Under President Ferdinand Marcos their recovery of bullion operation was called "Task Force Restoration" and headed by Marcos's head of the Presidential Security Group, General Fabian Ver.

The role of the Task Force Restoration group included massive diggings and excavation and represented to the public as fighting communist insurgency during the period when Marcos declared martial law.

Vatican Involvement in Plundered Gold

Another article in the *Philippine Inquirer* (October 29, 1999) quoted evidence given to the Philippine Senate Blue Ribbon Committee (October 14, 1999) by a former Roman Catholic priest, Marcelino Tagle (former director of the Catholic charity in Manila, Caritas) that he once served as "an adviser to the late President Ferdinand Marcos."

Tagle, the former priest, stated he was an administrator for the estate of a man that "he claimed was the source of the Marcos gold," identifying that person as "Fr. Jose Antonio Diaz." He stated that Father Diaz was entrusted by the Vatican to take charge of Vatican gold buried on the Philippines. The so-called "Vatican gold" was bullion that had been "captured by Hitler" that had belonged to the royal families of Europe and been placed under the trusteeship of the Vatican. The article stated in part:

Tagle added that Fr. Diaz had "assumed several names when he moved to the Philippines." One such name was "Severino Sta. Romana." Tagle stated that Sta. Romana "hired the young Marcos as his lawyer and trustee."

Tagle testified that Marcos, in his capacity as lawyer and chief trustee of Sta. Romana's assets, "had succeeded in isolating the nominees or trustees of the gold certificates from the physical assets—so much so that it is almost impossible to recover them without piecing the various pieces like a mosaic." By abusing his position of trustee, Marcos effectively gained control of Sta. Romana's gold and later, when he had become President, used the "Central Bank to transact the gold."

Catholic secret society OPUS DEI

Tagle's testimony indicated that Santa Romana, a member of the OSS and then a founding member of the CIA, was also a priest and possibly a member of the secret Catholic Opus Dei society. It brings to mind the mysterious death of the pope John Paul in 1978, and the involvement with the Vatican banker, Roberto Calvi, Chairman of the bank, Banco Ambrosiano.

Opus Dei was registered in 1954 as a charitable trust in London, registering as the Sacerdotal Society of the Holy Cross and Opus Dei Charitable Trust. It suddenly became involved as a major player—with huge financial resources—in the Eurodollar market.

As stated in the excellent and highly detailed book, *The Marcos Dynasty*, by Sterling and Peggy Seagrave:

The most frequent reports made by CIA agents in Manila over the years, it turns out, involved secret gold deals by President Marcos. The CIA was keeping a close watch. In some instances the Agency was not just watching, but helping. CIA sources stated that the Agency set up a conduit for the transfer of very large sums of black money out of the Philippines to Honolulu, in gold as well as currency, and was using this to obligate Ferdinand and to keep an eye on his financial transactions.

This was confirmed publicly during sworn testimony in a Honolulu court case, and privately by one of the men directly involved. According to the testimony, the Honolulu conduit was set up for the CIA by Enrique Zobel, a close friend of the Marcoses and of the sultan of Brunei. Rewald got to know Zobel because he ran a polo club in Hawaii, and Zobel was a world-class polo player. Rewald testified that Zobel was (like him) a CIA collaborator, and that through such joint ventures as Ayala-Hawaii, they and the CIA were to "shelter monies of highly placed foreign diplomats and businessmen who wished to export cash to the United States, where it would be available to them in the event of an emergency."

During the same period, we now know that the Sultan of Brunei (another ardent polo player) was lending millions to the Agency as part of the secret Iran-Contra arms deal of Lieutenant Colonel Oliver North, but his money went astray when the CIA mistakenly gave him the wrong numbers for a Swiss bank account.

That the CIA's "secret team" was obtaining millions privately from the sultan reinforces allegations that it was obtaining millions similarly from President Ferdinand that President Reagan did everything short of intervention to keep him in power?

Close Connection between President Marcos and CIA Assets

As I learned from my close friend Ronald Rewald, the titular head of the CIA proprietary based in Honolulu, BBRDW, and from the boxes of CIA documents that he gave me, there was evidence of connections between CIA personnel and President Marcos covering many years. I also received a legal-size box of documents on the relationship from the law office of Melvin Belli.

The CIA boss in charge of BBRDW was General Edwin F. Black, a top aide to CIA director Allen Dulles for many years. I provide more details on this matter in the book, *Explosive Secrets of Covert CIA Companies*. The Seagraves also refer to this in their book, *Gold Warriors*, as they wrote:

Where the gold was concerned, the group Marcos dealt with was a veritable Who's Who of American clandestine operations. Among them were some of the same men fleetingly exposed in the Iran-Contra scandal—a quasi-private military intelligence cell calling itself "The Enterprise" and engaged in worldwide intrigues for the White House involving huge black-bag payoffs. Marcos and Ver themselves were implicated in the Iran-Contra scandal for providing the false end-user certificates that allowed the secret team to divert arms wherever it wished.

Hundreds of millions of dollars were involved in the Iran-Contra arms deals, with collusion among the United States, Israel, the Philippines, and other countries, including the cloak-and-dagger paraphernalia of Swiss numbered accounts, dummy companies, and clandestine ships and planes. But as one of The Enterprise testified, "This is pipsqueak stuff."

The CIA paymaster during this period was Paul Helliwell, sometimes known as Mister Black Bag. He was the chief of intelligence in China during World War II and one of the people moving black money from the recovered Yamashshita gold and other sources, moving it around in shell companies, laundering it.

Secret Funds Used to Subvert Iran's Government in 1953

Part of the retrieved gold was used to subvert the government in Iran in 1953. The CIA's Kim Roosevelt used black money from the retrieved Yamashita gold to fund the overthrow of Mohammed Mossadegh in Iran in 1953. I witnessed that event firsthand as I was staying in a hotel in Abadan, Iran, flying Muslim pilgrims from throughout the Middle East to the holy cities of Mecca and Medina.

Philippine President Ferdinand Marcus

President Marcos sent a letter to Mrs. Santiago (his cook and record keeper) referring to him secretly taking an account belonging to Santa Romana containing 5000 metric tons of gold that Santa Romana had put into Po Sang Bank, Hong Kong. The letter is in the Filipino tagalong language. The tagalog language is the basis of the Filipino national language and a tagalog sentence has few borrowings from English and Spanish, while a Filipino sentence liberally uses English and Spanish-derived words.

OFFICE OF THE PRESIDENT
Of the Philippines
Malacanang

August 8, 1983

TO PERSONAL and----------------

Councilwoman Candelaria V. Santiago Canding:

It's now 2300 past midnight; I studied what you sent me. I write in tagalog for you to understand my instructions, especially things I do not want to be done, this are the following:

1. My letters to you dated April 27, 1983 and July 18. 1983 must be destroyed and not to be returned, the two blank forms with my signatures must be secretly kept, you must not show this to anybody, you are required to place something in it only if something will happen to me as suggested by your trusted advisers, I repeat, my letters must be destroyed because I will deny this, the two blank forms must only be used if something happens to me.

2. If it is necessary my personal Military Aide, not just anybody will fetch you so we can talk, do not mention any authority, and or show my letter to anyone because I will deny this always remember that we will be talking about "projects" because any phone conversation is being bugged and tape, something definitely wrong will happen to me, as President of the Nation if it will be known to anyone I have given you a letter and or authority regarding this, just do not tell this to anybody not even Vic or Teddy, because again I will definitely deny this and declare this to be FAKE: Do not brag, boost or break this secret to anyone, all letters must be destroyed including this one. I strongly suggest you destroy this letter after you and your advisers read this, but first, produce serer copies of this letter erase my signature then sign my name on it, let one of your advisers sign the endorsement give this to your personal trustee to be delivered to me so I know my instruction has been followed. If it is just a Xerox copy I can easily deny this if we fail. I have already somebody to be arrested just in case scandal will arise. There are 16 cases tiled against me and my Government in the International Court of Justice in Hague still pending filed by 16 Nation-Claimants regarding this gold. So just close your lips and I will do the rest.

3. Do not inform anyone you are getting any commission, I have not instructed this; this includes the First Lady, my children, any ministers or Generals because they know nothing about the gold.

4. Do not expect so, much, though I have instructed a big commission to all of you US $4,915,887.00 or a total of $54,074,766.00 every month for 7 to 10 years, this will be divided into three equal parts, one part for you, Carding, the second part to your Advisers and their other companions, the last part to your personal Trustee, do not expect more than this, the computations you gave is wrong, the implementation was based on London price last August, 1984.

Don't ---------give money to my personal -------------, ------------ like you did to those Colonel Nurses you made them "emissaries" to protocol your visits to me, do not follow me nor came to me. I like what you did, since April 21, 2983 you did not come to see me. I am telling you and your Advisers, do not pretend to know something about the gold, you will never understand this, just stay put and keep quiet and I will do the test. Your commission of P 54,074,766.00 monthly is sufficient for everybody it will be delivered to you by your Personal Trustee who contacted the lenders and buyers, implementations will be scheduled within this month or up to four month from today. Again don't tell this to anybody because I will surely deny this, if it is necessary to talk I will have my military aide to fetch you.

6. MY letter dated April 27 and July 18 has been change so you must destroy them, me being the President of the Philippines will implement this time I have appointed four people to secretly implement this deal with your personal Trustee and the buyers-lenders. I also cancelled the authority of the Central Bank and Gov. Laya, so you see it is really hard for you to understand this. However I am telling you of the following:

First, I had already approved the offer of US $53-Billion made by the N.M. Rothschild a Sons Limited Bank and this will be coordinated with 4 offshore banks and 2 or 6 foreign prime banks that I had contacted. You just wait for your groups commissions, Secondly, I have also approved the terms and condition and offers Landmark Trust, Inc. and my signed instructions to the 2 prime banks in Europe or 2 to 3 foreign prime banks in Hongkong will coordinate with Landmark Trust, Inc. Bank anytime this August or September, 1983.

Ask your personal trustee to make a very strong supplemental agreement with Landmark Trust, Inc. As I have already approved the proposed manners of loans and repayments with aurium, including the revolving funds coupled with the bringing of "Machinery-Equipment " in Manila Central Bank Smelting plant to insize each 12.5 kilo bar with the London requirements and standards including the 14 required documents to be done by the Lenders-who-would-be-buyers (?) with guaranteed aurium as repayments as proposed by LANDMARK for which N.M. Rothschild & Son Limited Bank should follow the same, and so with other lenders-buyers from foreign countries. These are the work of your advisers to coordinate with your trustee so the foreign principals will be so guided secretly. Canding, the 6 points that must not be done and other instructions herein musts be follow and everyone must observed this.

Signed: Andy

Your personal trustee is a good and intelligent man. You advisers are also good and sincere you must obey them, Canding.

PRESIDENT OF THE FOURTH REPUBLIC OF THE PHILIPPINES

Bank Offer to Buy 53 Billion USD Gold

In 1983, Ferdinand Marcos accepted an offer of 53 billion USD for a parcel of gold which did not belong to him or the Philippine State. He represented himself as the owner with full power to sell, and persuaded Rothschild Bank to take over the metal. For this they paid him a total of USD $3 billion, which was considerably less than the true value. Jim Handy wrote:

Marcus was very concerned that the transaction should be done secretly because at that time claims had been made through the court of International Justice in The Hague against that particular gold by a number of foreign governments. Marcus knew this. He wrote a letter that if word of the sale got out he would be in serious trouble. The proceeds of the sale were deposited in various banks throughout the world under the eventual control of an account in Posan Bank, Hong Kong.

In accordance with his usual paranoid behavior, Marcus opened the account in Posan Bank under the name of one of his trusted but not very able dependents. In this case it was his companion Miss Candelaria V. Santiago who is known as his loyal cook, some say, secretary, of thirty years standing. He wrote to her partly in tagalog and partly in English, setting out the full situation and asking her not to say a word to anyone but just to sit back and wait for her commission which would be paid by Posan Bank at the rate of over USD 4 million per month.

He explained that he would deny any knowledge of the matter if she told anyone. Even his own wife and family knew nothing. It is not known under which name he made the deposits, but it is likely that is was Miss Santiago who remembers signing documents without knowing what they were.

We were approached by a group of people who showed us the letter from Marcos and gave us a number of the account in Posan. They said that Miss Santiago was visited by two representatives of Posan Bank some time ago who came, she thought, to pay her commission, but she refused to see them.

We have made contact with Posan Bank and are convinced that there is an account in Miss Santiago's name. However, we do not know if she is a sole signatory or if she signs as a trustee.

We arranged for Miss Santiago to come to Hong Kong to meet the Bank officials, but at the last minute, on the day of the meeting, her advisers decided not to let her go into the bank. They wanted to use her power of attorney but in our view that would not be acceptable to the bank.

It is our opinion there is another signature to the account that Miss Santiago is unaware of and that only government intervention can be powerful enough to release the account details and subsequently the funds. .... contacts with the highest levels of the Chinese government. It will then need similar access to encourage the various holding banks to surrender the USD 53 billion which should now be considerably more with almost ten years interest to be added.

We would expect to be appointed officially by the government as authorized agents in the recovery of the funds, receiving for that work a commission of five percent.

Obviously some similar provision must be made to reward the other claimants so they will step aside and help.

As to the use to which the bulk of the funds should be put, we refer you to a paper we have produced which sets out the pros and cons of the various methods and our considered suggestions.

/s/ ______________________________

Jan Hendy

People in Key U.S. Government Positions Assisted in Protecting Marcos' Frauds

Aiding in denying access to these funds were the people in various U.S. government positions that were either part of the original scheme or those covering up for the earlier actions. Federal prosecutors falsely charged claimants with financial fraud when they sought to gain access to the funds.

Numerous books and articles have been written describing how the gold recovered by Office of Strategic Services (OSS) personnel was deposited in banks throughout the world, including Citibank, UBS, Credit Suisse, and others. Some of these names included Severino Garcia Santa Romana.

Declaring Martial Law to Hide Gold Retrieval Actions

Marcos was first elected president in 1965. On September 21, 1972, he declared martial law. In 1983, as his reelection was threatened by the return of his primary political opponent, Benigno Aquino, Jr. To remove this threat, Marcos' General Ver had Aquino assassinated within minutes of deplaning from the China Airline plane that returned him to Manila. That assassination was a catalyst for the People Power Revolution, and in February 1986, facing a revolt, the U.S. military seized Ferdinand and Imelda Marcos and flew them to Hawaii. In *Marcos Dynasty*, the authors wrote:

While he was casting ingots at Johnson Matthey's factory in Quezon City, Ferdinand also devised a scheme to float large loans using as collateral gold bullion that he was as yet unable to get out of the Philippines. This scheme was discovered in November 1983 when U.S. Customs examined a pouchful of documents carried into the United States by one of Ver's agents. The documents described four floors of gold bullion stored beneath a privately owned bank in Manila (Benedictor's Bank). The deal was to be made through an accountant who appeared to have CIA connections in Alexandria, Virginia. The accountant refused to talk, telling Customs the deal involved "national security."

Buddy Gomez, then billionaire Enrique Zobel's right-hand man, said he was asked by Zobel in 1979 to set up a meeting in Hong Kong to arrange the transfer of gold out of the Philippines on behalf of Elizabeth Marcos Rocka, the sister of the president. Most of her gold eventually was moved through branches of the Nugan Hand Bank in Hong Kong and Sydney with CIA help and the participation of a number of wealthy Australians. Her husband, Ludwig Rocka, helped Nugan Hand set up a Manila branch that same year, 1979, in the Magsaysay Building, which included among its occupants a number of CIA fronts. Rocka then shared the office suite with the bank and with a senior American military/intelligence officer who headed that branch. Elizabeth still had $3.5 million in cash on deposit in Sydney when the Nugan Hand Bank collapsed in 1982. Of her precious metals account no record survived the shredder.

After Ferdinand Marcos was removed from the presidential palace in Manila and flown to Hawaii in 1986, and was ousted from being president, Robert Curtis of International Precious Metals in Las Vegas wrote the following letter on October 23, 1987 to then-president Corazon Aquino:

INTERNATIONAL PRECIOUS METALS
5340 WEST EDNA AVE. • LAS VEGAS, NV 89102
INCORPORATED

October 23, 1987

Mrs. Corazan Aquino
President of the Republic of the Philippines Malacanang Palace
Manila, Philippines

Subject: Buried World War II Treasure stolen by the Japanese from countries in Asia and hidden in the Philippine Islands.

Dear Mrs. President:

This letter is being sent to you in the hopes of establishing a procedure for the recovery of World War II buried treasure which was carefully hidden on Philippine lands and surrounding waters. There has been a lot of controversy over whether or not this treasure exists. I am confident that you have ample proof that it does exist,-and that Ex-President Marcos has only been able to recover a very small percentage, even though that in itself was a massive amount.

You may or may not remember me, for we met in Las Vegas briefly in late 1978 or early 1979 when Steve and Presy Psinakis, your late husband and Raul Manglapas discussed the advantages of the release of the Treasure Story for the MFP and the embarrassment it would cause Marcos.

If you do remember me, then you will recall that I headed the LEBER group formed by Ex-President Marcos and in effect recovered two treasure sites in 1975. We now have evidence that a lot of this gold was laundered and sold to several large consortiums in 1983 through early 1986.

It is my belief that Marcos only recovered about six sites, even though he did work on a dozen, or more. As far as I know he only recovered two of these sites after I left the Islands. Those he did from engineering data that I left behind, but he lost the availability of the original Japanese maps, which frustrated him till "the Peoples Revolution" took him out of the treasure hunting business.

I possess photographs and documentation, which I managed to get out of the Islands, along with my life, for Marcos had me on his "hit parade" for a number of years. There were originally 172 treasure locations. I personally possess the information that could effect the recovery of perhaps 45 to 50 of these locations.

With the help of the two living eyewitnesses I could probably increase that number, as I have photographs for all of the sites. I lack only specific information on what location the map actually represents.

The existence of this huge treasure could be a blessing for your country. It could also be a disaster. Presently the Russians, Chinese, and Japanese are attempting recovery plans. Marcos, in all his paranoia of power was aware that this treasure could be the start of World War III. He was also aware the International Precious Metals Cartel was a factor to deal with, if for no other reason than the very existence of that much gold could collapse the value of gold, and bankrupt many countries of the world.

While this is negative thinking, I want to impress you with the fact that all of these factors must be faced. Indiscriminate digging up of this treasure must not be allowed. It must be controlled, kept in absolute secrecy, and very wisely and carefully put into world marketing. i.e.: pre-1939 bars no longer qualify for fair trading in the London, New York, Zurich, and Hong Kong gold markets. These bars must be re-refined, changed in size, and re-hallmarked. The amount of gold recoverable is so large, that it likely will require bartering for other things of value and then the bartered goods resold to realize cash or spendable credit.

I represent a group of HONEST American businessmen who are prepared to make these recoveries for you utilizing their own expense money. We have the information, the management ability and the understanding of worldwide conditions to make it possible to successfully complete this venture. It would be our suggestion to do one or two sites, relatively small in content, to enable us to work out a total organization, both from our end and from yours.

We fully intend to follow ALL Philippine laws as they relate to this treasure. Under international law, the countries that could claim this treasure as their own have lost that ability since the Statues of Limitations are long expired. These treasures belong to the Philippine people. Our intention is to make sure that they get not only their legal entitlement, but have devised a system to enable them to reap additional benefits by the formation of a Philippine-American trust which will be described later.

We are requesting from you and your government, support only in the area of security for our personnel and especially security of recovered treasure once we have successfully completed a site. In other words, we are not asking you to expend any government funds until we have proven that these assets are not only real but that we have the capability to recover them.

The following are some tentative suggestions which you might consider incorporating in some type of formal document:

I. You should designate a representative who has the sole authority to issue permits to search for buried or sunken treasure. You should also appoint a committee to represent the Philippine government which will clearly define the government's role and specify who is responsible for security, transport and storage of the treasure.

II. The permit to search shall be issued for only one site at a time and to one company at a time. Because of unusual circumstances involved in the Bureau of Tourism and the Island of Corregidor with their early plans of restoration of monuments, we would like to request that this first permit be issued to cover all of the sites on the Island. Thereafter, we will revert to issuance of one permit for one site. The group receiving this permit will be responsible for its own financing and shall reimburse the government for any expenses incurred by providing services and/or material to the group. We understand that we are the guests of the Philippine government and that we are subject to all of its laws and will conduct ourselves accordingly.

III. An agreement should then be drawn between this select committee and our group which will define the responsibilities of each. In addition, the government's share of the treasure of each site will be defined. As we understand the law, the government is entitled to 75% of all treasures found on public land and that we must pay taxes on the remaining 25%. This is somewhat inequitable since we are paying our own expenses and since we are setting aside 33-1/3% of our recovery for the Philippine-American trust fund. Perhaps this can be examined. On private property, the government will be entitled up to a maximum of 35% tax, as we understand your tax laws. This would appear equitable, but an private property, we must negotiate a percentage with the land owner, however that is our problem. It is our recommendation that all private sites must likewise have a legal permit and come under the authority of the committee as well as your appointed representative.

IV. The primary role of the committee should be to provide all manner of security. This includes our group in any manner it deems necessary, protection of the site where the search is taking place, keeping unauthorized personnel away from the site and to step up security when recovery is imminent. The latter could involve several hundred men once a sizable site is penetrated and the treasure located. This takes place before a single bar is removed. An officer-in-charge of this security should be appointed in advance and a Standard Operating Procedure (SOP) should be prepared outlining the number of men, the kinds of weapons and their dispersal for every contingency.

V. The committee is to provide transport and security for the transport when the treasure is to be removed from the site to a location for safekeeping and storage. The committee should designate this location as soon as possible and prepare an SOP setting forth the transport,' the location, the space and the security required during transport and on the receiving end to include the number of personnel required for unloading, as well as equipment required for unloading and more importantly, the officials designated to receipt the cargo.

VI. A suggested location would be the Central Bank; providing the security is tight enough and the area is large enough for storage and inventory. It is at this point where a dollar or peso value on all artifacts which includes gold, precious stones, other precious metals, old coins and currency, art effects including statues and possibly paintings. Our group should have the option of removing its percentage in kind once its value has been established, since it has its own refining capabilities and the expertise in getting it into the world market.

VII. Our group will designate a project officer who will be our officer-in-charge in the Philippines. This project officer should be furnished with copies of all SOP's stated in items IV through V above. A very close coordination between our project officer and your committee will insure smooth operation and a successful- mission. That project officer should be subject to your approval.

VIII. Our project officer will be responsible for all of our personnel in the Philippines, both American and Filipino. All of our personnel shall be submitted to your committee for review and approval. This is essential for security matters.

IX. Our project officer will be responsible for establishing a safe house in Metro Manila which will be large enough for proper lodging, feeding and the comfort of all foreign contingencies in our group. This safe house will be at our own expense. It will serve as a base of operations and as such must be provided proper security by your designated committee. In addition, all Filipinos employed at the safe house, which includes maids, drivers, cooks, secretaries, laborers and others, must be screened by the committee and given security clearance.

X. Our project officer will be responsible for obtaining all necessary equipment in the safe house as well as at the projects. This will include, but is not limited to, such items as vehicles, typewriters, computers, security devices, or telephones and radios, outside illumination for the safe house and sites and communication equipment between the safe house and the sites. We would appreciate any assistance your logistics people have in this regard to save us running all over the Island.

XI. Our project officer will be responsible for obtaining other necessary equipment to ensure a successful operation at the recovery site. This will include, but is not limited to, blowers, jack hammers, gas masks, acetylene torches, pumps and other heavy equipment required to dig. We will appoint an equipment officer who will prepare SOP's for maintenance of all equipment and will be responsible for such maintenance and care.

XII. The handling of demolitions is a highly technical and well trained occupation. We feel we must rely upon your trained military and/or- other demolition experts on sites where explosives have been placed and the danger exists. Your committee must be able to supply us on demand with the necessary personnel and equipment to accomplish a safe removal. Before a recovery, the expense will be borne by us. After a recovery, the expense will be borne by you.

XIII. The committee should designate an inventory control officer and our group should designate an inventory control officer who together will inventory the cargo in terms of size of bars, barrels of precious stones, and art effects. The treasure will be measured, weighed or counted on the site. No value determination will be made at the site. Appropriate containers will be supplied and the cargo sealed in the presence of both inventory control officers and the project officers. All four must sign the inventory sheet which should be in four copies, one to the committee, one to the group and one retained by each of the inventory officers. Scrambler telephone and radio communications from the site after recovery are mandatory.

XIV. At the recovery site, in addition to the aforementioned security:

1. All laborers and management personnel must be screened and searched at the start and end of each day.
2. The project officer must insure that adequate messing, toilet facilities and rest facilities for inclement weather are available.
3. The project officer must insure that adequate first aid be available and an SOP must be prepared in the event that medical evacuation is necessary.

I realize, Mrs. President, that this has been a lengthy introduction. I must point out, however, that this is only the tip of the iceberg that will require many hours of your committee's deliberations in order to achieve a perfectly run operation. There is no room for mistakes. We cannot have press coverage, radio and television exposes, or other unauthorized public relation type releases. In a free press situation, I imagine this can be difficult which will mandate our choosing the right people to be associated with, both from your side as well as our own. Marcos was able to achieve this by holding a gun to their heads. We are not proposing this but it emphasizes the need to select our personnel carefully and fining them for any unauthorized breaches. You will have to tell me how we can contain a whole town should we select such a site and in this area I will need assistance from your mayors and governors of various provinces who must likewise be secured.

I hope that after reading this we can have early communications to establish that which we are suggesting. We are open to any suggestions and will appreciate your prompt consideration.

Sincerely yours,
International Precious Metals
Robert H. Curtis
President and
Chairman of the Board

Curtis Filing Federal Lawsuit Against Ferdinand and Imelda Marcos

On March 21, 1992, Robert Curtis filed a federal lawsuit[21] at Las Vegas against the estate of Ferdinand Marcos and Imelda Marcos. Las Vegas attorney Carl E. Lovell, Jr. filed the action. The following are some of the statements made in the original complaint:

(1) Fraud in the inducement;
(2) Fraud and misrepresentation;
(3) Breach of contract;
(4) Breach of covenant of good faith and fair dealing;
(5) Outrageous conduct;
(6) Conversion against all defendants;
(7) Constructive trust;
(8) Negligent infliction of emotional distress;
(9) Intentional infliction of emotional distress;
(10) Punitive damages;
(11) Accounting:
(12) Attorney's fees;
(13) Declaratory relief and damages.

At the time this cause of action accrued, Plaintiff was completely disabled due to (1) the fraudulent and intentional concealment of the actual recovery of treasure by Defendants, and each of them; (2) Defendant's powerful stature, especially in the Philippines where any action for remedies would not have been possible, certainly before 1984, and probably would still be a risk; and, the fact that Defendants, Imelda Marcos, did not, until April 4, 1990, formally admit in a court of law that she and Ferdinand Marcos had recovered Japanese gold allowing Plaintiff to now seek his remedies for denial of his contractual share and for the tortious acts against the Plaintiff. Decedent, Ferdinand

---

[21] U.S. District Court Case No. CV-S-92-332-LDG-RJJ.

Marcos, did admit in a taped conversation to two Agents of the Central Intelligence Agency in mid-1987 that he had, indeed, recovered Japanese treasures. In addition, Imelda Marcos, in late 1991 and early 1992, admitted to the world press that the source of their wealth was the "Yamashita Treasure" and several of her relatives have made similar admissions to the press.

In January, 1992, a highly placed Philippine Government Cabinet member confirmed the fact that the Defendants were successful in 1975 and has affidavits from a former Governor and a Marcos military man who transported the treasure to the Marcos home after Plaintiff Robert H. Curtis was forced out of the country for fear of his life. This information was made public on television.

Furthermore, Plaintiff Curtis has obtained additional proof of the recoveries from other of Defendants' employees, agents and associates including photographs of some of the bullion being moved and inventoried.

Sometime in December, 1974, Plaintiff, Robert H. Curtis, received a telephone call from a Mr. Norman Kirst, who allegedly was a representative of Defendants Ferdinand and Imelda Marcos, whereupon Mr. Kirst told Plaintiff Robert H. Curtis that Ferdinand Marcos, the President of the Philippines, wished to engage the services of Mr. Curtis. Plaintiff Robert H. Curtis than told Norman Kirst that he was indeed flattered and honored, but because of the personal commitments of Mr. Curtis, as well as the increasing demands of business operations, he could not entertain any thought of an additional burden at that time.

The next day Mr. Curtis once again received a telephone call from Norman Kirst who was in the presence of Ferdinand Marcos and the Malacanang Palace in the Philippines. Mr. Kirst reiterated the request of Ferdinand Marcos, and Plaintiff Curtis again rejected this offer. Defendants Marcos then personally took the telephone and told Mr. Curtis that one of Marcos' friends, Jose Figueroa, President of Costa Rica had informed them that Plaintiff Robert H. Curtis was a chemist and metallurgist who had developed two interesting processes: First, a process for higher yield from any particular ore, and Second, to alter the composition of gold bars and recast them with any desired metallurgical "fingerprint." Defendant Marcos went on to explain that this was a most important undertaking and a "chance of a lifetime" and that Plaintiff Curtis should truly weigh such a proposition and he encouraged Mr. Curtis to come to the Philippines as his personal guest. Mr. Curtis once again told President Marcos that he was honored and flattered, but just could not undertake any new project at this time.

The very next day during a heavy snowstorm in Reno, Nevada, Plaintiff Robert H. Curtis arrived at work only to find Norman Kirst standing in that heavy snowfall in a tropical suit (after a 12,000 mile flight), whereupon he attempted to induce Mr. Curtis to consider the Marcos' offer or at least come to the Philippines for a week-end at the palace as the personal guest of President Marcos. If Mr. Curtis again chose to reject the offer, fl he would be returned to the United States. Plaintiff Curtis, after weeks of continuing telephone calls and correspondence, finally did relent, partly because of curiosity, and, partly because of courtesy to President Marcos. Of course, Plaintiff Curtis was now entirely intrigued by the prospect of recovering large World War II treasure which he was now told was the real reason he was wanted in the Philippines.

During the lengthy ensuing negotiations with Mr. Kirst, it was negotiated that Plaintiff Robert H. Curtis was to "process" up to 2000 tons per week of gold bullion, meaning to refine old gold at 99.5% purity to 999.5% purity. It was explained that gold at a purity of 99.5% purity is not marketable as bullion in today's marketplace; and, for that service, President Marcos would pay twenty percent (20%) per ounce when gold, at the time, sold for $55.00 per ounce!

Plaintiff Curtis was told a tale of World War II (WWII) treasure of astounding proportions, a "treasure" which was "gathered" by the Japanese military forces and secreted in the Philippines. In 1975 (thirty years after WWII), there was still a question of ownership and the World Court Statute of Limitations would not prevent suit or claims until November, 1985. Therefore, President Marcos knew he must remove the clear evidence of title in respect to hallmark and recorded number and establish a logical explanation for the presence of large amounts of gold. Plaintiff Curtis initially rejected the entire proposition primarily on a premise of non-belief, Plaintiff Curtis was literally overwhelmed with offers and correspondence of every sort until at long last Plaintiff Curtis consented to travel to the Philippines and meet with President Marcos.

Upon arrival in the Philippines, Plaintiff Curtis was entertained on a grand scale. However, there was an involved private conversation lasting 6-7 hours with President Marcos at the Malacanang Palace wherein President Marcos attempted to convince Curtis of the reality of the Japanese treasure and continued with many meetings, boat rides and tours. During those days following, Plaintiff Curtis was shown authentic Japanese maps; taken to more than 45 actual treasure sites and shown the applicability of those maps for those treasure sites and how they related thereto; met actual eyewitnesses to the Japanese burial of gold; and, was finally taken into a very large storage area with gold bars stacked from floor to ceiling more than 10 feet high, with aisles with barely enough room to pass. Here was irrefutable evidence of Japanese treasure with oriental markings which the trained eye of a professional could easily identify to be of that claimed time and place.

Plaintiff Curtis was also shown a golden Buddha, weighing in excess of one ton, which had a head that unscrewed revealing a chamber about the size of a large urn that Defendants Marcos said was recovered from a site. The chamber had been full of diamonds and other precious stones.

Plaintiff later saw a picture of the stolen Buddha of one Rogelio Roxas, which makes them believe this is one and the same.

Plaintiff Curtis was impressed and truly convinced that the Japanese WW II treasure did exist and that Marcos held the key to future recoveries. Based on these unique experiences and the presentation of undeniable evidence by President Marcos and his appointed associates in respect to gold bars actually recovered by Marcos, and, the incredible treasure that remained to be recovered by the use of those said maps, eye witnesses and engineering diagrams, Plaintiff Robert H. Curtis was induced to seriously consider a contractual relationship for recovery of the WWII treasure stolen and secreted by the Japanese.

An attorney for Robert H. Curtis advised Curtis that a 30 year Statute of Limitations claimed by President Marcos was effective to bar any claim to the treasure from the previous owners and that no laws had or would have been broken. However, the real rub here was that this documented booty or treasure amounted to as much as one-third (1/3) of the entire wealth of the world, and would have far reaching effects with the potential to affect the balance of world power and economy which might well escalate into WW III. Even the Japanese claimed title to that treasure as their separate property, and were stopped by President Marcos from retrieving it.

On or about March 25, 1975, Plaintiff, as a member of the eleven (11) member Leber Group (rebel spelled in reverse), entered into a contract with President Marcos for the recovery of the various treasure deposits. It was originally proposed on or about March 5, 1975, that where either Government or private property was involved, fifty percent (50%) of the entire cache would go to the Leber Group and fifty percent (50%) to President Marcos through a foundation named the Philippine Foundation, Inc. However, after due consideration, President Marcos decided differently and on March 25, 1975, signed a different contract. Marcos insisted that Plaintiff Robert H. Curtis direct all recovery efforts for this Japanese maps and engineering diagrams and planned both a sunken Leber Group and Plaintiff Robert H. Curtis was given the authentic treasure ship recovery and a buried land location recovery.

In addition, President Marcos insisted that Plaintiff Curtis dismantle his refractory plant in Reno, Nevada, and ship it at great expense by boat to the Philippines. He assured Curtis that this was needed to reprocess more than 6,000 metric tons of gold already recovered, as well as to handle the future recoveries of the Leber Group. To do this, Plaintiff Curtis had to effectively bankrupt his Nevada Corporations, for he cut off any possibility of income, as well as he was forced to borrow money from The John Birch Society, which would have devastating effects on him and his companies later.

In addition, Plaintiff Curtis had to agree to build a refinery in partnership with United Drug Company, which would also launder this gold, and provide cover to disguise where this gold was coming from since this refinery would have new chemical processes which would enhance the abilities of the Philippine mines to increase their output, in this way pretending that the new process was the cause of the greatly expanded gold output.

Under the terms of the final "Leber Contract," each Party thereto was to receive one eleventh (1/11) of the Leber share with the Philippine Government receiving nothing. President Marcos assured them, especially Plaintiff Curtis, that his share of "anything recovered" would be under "Presidential protection" and held for his direction whatsoever and wheresoever. He also assured him that no Philippine taxes would be paid. If they had been paid, security would be breached.

Plaintiff CURTIS returned to the Philippines whereupon Plaintiff Curtis chose a water recovery of the Japanese cruiser Nachi as the first site. This sunken ship was easily located the first day (with the help of Philippine divers) which eventually yielded six (6) billion United States Dollars ($6,000,000,000)1

This was at a time when the price of gold was $65.00 per ounce and at current values this same gold would have a worth of approximately Forty-Two (42) Billion United States Dollars ($42,000,000,000)1 This figure does not include a barge full of silver pesos and dollars of undeterminable value which also was recovered.

The second site was to be a cache buried at a location outside a provincial town called Teresa, designated as Teresa II. Teresa II was described on the Japanese maps as containing seven hundred and seventy-seven billion yen, mindboggling even at 1942 currency rates.

Now enters the green giant known the world over as greed. The Nachi site recovery was deceitfully and insidiously delayed and interrupted, probably with a Marcos planned theft for himself of the total six (6) billion in gold, which forced Plaintiff Curtis to shift efforts to the Teresa II. After months of digging approximately 130 feet, on July 5, 1975, Plaintiff entered into the tunnels of Teresa II and reached the target which later allowed President Marcos to recover treasure worth eight (8) billion United States Dollars, knowing full well there was an additional nine (9) billion Dollars in the tunnel system.

A number of things had occurred which had been engineered by President Marcos. A "leak" allegedly resulted in a newspaper article by Jack Anderson of the Washington Post which appeared in the United States, wherein the recovery attempts were revealed; and unknown to Plaintiff, the International Gold Cartel had "approached" Marcos with a Mafia-type "offer"—either kill Curtis and let the Cartel do the business of distribution, or, he (Marcos) would be in trouble."

In point of fact, the Teresa II excavation was successful and treasure was recovered worth at least eight billion United States Dollars ($8,000,000, 000) (at $65.00 per ounce) but Plaintiff was not allowed to return to the Teresa II site. Earlier, Johnson and Matthey had opened a refinery at Quezon City evidencing the Cartel presence which Marcos had promised Plaintiff he would not allow under any circumstances. The planned "double-cross" on the Teresa II site was put into motion which was also the case with the heavy cruiser Nachi site.

Now Olof Jonsson, a Swedish born American Psychic and member of the Leber Group had a premonition of impending danger which was so overwhelming Jonsson warned Plaintiff Curtis and he left by plane the very same day.

Plaintiff Curtis, still confident with the Marcos agreement and the "Presidential protection" so lavishly touted by Marcos, suddenly found himself and his partner standing in their own graves in an American war cemetery with a .45 caliber automatic at their heads. Quick thinking on the part of Curtis admonished the special assassin to consider the fact that he (Curtis) had long ago secreted copies of the original Japanese maps in the United States and had destroyed the originals. Certainly, killing Curtis would eliminate further recovery. It worked.

Marcos searched Curtis's rooms and belongings and soon found that the maps were, indeed, missing; and Plaintiff Curtis and his partner were reluctantly released. In point of fact, the maps really were at the hotel where Curtis had hidden them; however, because Curtis found it necessary to return to the United States, thinking he might want to work on the maps, he had made complete photographic copies which truly were in the United States.

Plaintiff and his partner quickly returned to the hotel and definitely and completely burned the original maps as life insurance.

Defendants Ferdinand Marcos and Imelda Marcos, in an attempt to induce Plaintiff to enter into the contract for recovery of the Japanese booty of WW II, fraudulently and falsely represented to Plaintiff with intent to deceive him that:

- Each site recovered after the signing of the Leber contract would be shared with the Leber members pursuant to the terms of the March 25, 1975, agreement; and in fact other sites were recovered using the engineering drawings of Plaintiffs that they left behind. Some of these known recoveries are: The 6 finger site at San Agustin Church, the Airvent site at Fort Bonafacio, the Rizal monument site at Fort Santiago, the remaining treasure sites at Teresa II and the tunnel system below General MacArthur's Headquarters at Fort Bonafacio. President Marcos worked on other sites, but it is unknown if he was successful, but it is possible that these other attempts were successful and that could be proven during discovery. For example, there is evidence that the Anchor site in Calatagan Bay was successful.

One of many documents showing the tens of tons of gold that President Ferdinand Marcus had offered for sale, indicating his discovery of parts of the huge hidden Japanese gold plunder was a May 3, 1983, document that is reprinted here:

Office of the President
Of the Philippines
Malacanang

HIGHLY CONFIDENTIAL

May 3, 1983

THE FOREIGN BUYERS/FIDUCIARY BANKS

Kind attention: Mr. Daniel W. Swihart
Buyers' attorney-in-fact
Engineering Construction Co. Ltd.

Subject: Scheduled presentation of bank drafts
And other Banks instruments, etc.

Gentlemen:

Below are very, very and strictly classified and confidential and in the name of "CODED ONE" of the Fourth Republic of the Philippines thru his most trusted woman in the sales of these Hot test commodity by the name of Konsehala Candelaria V. Santiago, we wish to inform you of the following:

1. That either May 11 or 12, 1983 you and your buyers' bank officials may present personally to the prime local servicing bank designated by

"CBRP" thru "CODE ONE", the banks drafts original copies of unconditional irrevocable hard several copies of banks guarantees with "verifiable signatures" of said prime banks for the buyers, for the total sums as payments for the 716.045 pieces of 12.5 kilos each bar, 4x4x16, 24 carat, fineness 999.9% with complete export documents and clearances and with specifications of good London delivery;

2. That prices as approved by "PN-1518254" will be US$ 442.00 per troy ounce conditioned that US$400.00 net for "CBRP"/Konsehala C.V. Santiago/assignee", and US$30.00 per troy ounce for "R.B. Marasigan/R.B.Maralet/assignee" (or US$22.00 per troy ounce VIPS': 6?50 securities/ with prime banks guarantees/tax free thru PN-1518254 name: US$11.50 per troy ounce for "Ramon B. Marasigan/RBMaralit/P.A. Pascual/PN-1518254.

3. That upon presentation of banks drafts, etc. cited in No. 1 to personally ?? PN-1518254, Secret-seller's prime local servicing bank will confirm au-stock(?) and all about everything to your buyers' banks abroad.

Any secret documents you'll receive from us, don't xerox it or show it to any one except your concerned buyers/banks, or else we'll cancel the sales of 716.045 pieces with you—without notice.

By the authority of "Code One/K-CVS"

CHAPTER SIX

View From Inside the Philippines

This chapter provides a view of the Japanese gold plunder from the eyes of people in the Philippines. Philippine investigative reporter and author of *The Marcos Legacy Revisited: Raiders of the Lost Gold*, Erick A. San Juan[22], published in the Philippines in 1998, described during an interview with a prominent civic leader and political activist what his investigation had uncovered:

Question: From your direct knowledge, what events or conversations with certain personalities indicated foreign complicity in the EDSA Revolution and its connection to the Marcos gold? Who were the gainers and why?

Answer. During the latter stages of the Marcos regime, I came to be friends with James Brandon Foley [Note: I am constrained to break my pledge to preserve the anonymity of my sources because without any attribution to an authoritative source, this revelation will be nothing but hearsay. My apologies. I sincerely hope he will understand, given the situation I am in and the position I have taken.

A political officer, another term for CIA agents at that time of the U.S. Embassy. We used to go out and date several women, sometimes to discos, and the like. Our favorite hang-out was the Hyatt Regency. In between socials, Jim and I would engage in frequent brain-storming at his private apartment at the Seafront. On one particular night, he disclosed to me that there was a secret operation plan to oust Marcos, and that men like Jose Concepcion of RFM and the Ayalas were being used as conduits to access the smooth flow of funds to finally bring an end to the Marcos authoritarian government.

---

[22] His credentials included a political activist, prominent civic leader, journalist & weekly contributor to newspapers & Philippine radio. He provides answers to some of the questions as seen from the perspective of Philippine citizens close to President Ferdinand Marcos:

[Cardinal Jaime Sin]

Cardinal Jaime Sin involvement was to draw a large crowd of supporters and sympathizers in the event that a blocking force was needed. Sin is an expert in the Antonio Gramsci-type of Marxism. This was confirmed by Dr. John Coleman in his expose "The Violation of the Christian Church," where he stated that Sin's Radio Veritas speaks out Communist propaganda in 13 languages all throughout Asia, "using Liberation Theology to destroy the moral fiber of the large number of Catholics. Sin believes in the Marxist principle that "Religion is the opium of the masses." He exploited this tactic to the hilt and succeeded in what is now called "people power" mass action. As acknowledged by Coleman, "Cardinal Sin of the Philippines worked diligently to overthrow the government of President Marcos. He was ably assisted by a former executive of the World Council of Churches, Jovito Salonga. Salonga was brought back to the Philippines under escort of the U.S. State Department." (CDC Report, October 1988)

In Coleman's estimation, Salonga was to take Mrs. Aquino and this Protestant will cut a deal with the Marxist New People's Army (NPA). Although this did not materialize because of Salonga's poor health, Coleman was still partly correct. Another fellow Protestant filled in his shoes (Fidel V. Ramos) and has quite successfully negotiated peace with the Communists.

Q. What events preceding Marcos announcement of the snap election proved that he was under American pressure? Why do you think he acceded to the "request?"

A. Everything really hinged on the Marcos gold bars. The Trilateral Commission, through its chairman David Rockefeller, and member George Schultz, were convinced that they had been conned by President Marcos. This being so, the Trilateralists did everything to pressure him, to destabilize his one-man rule, cut his source of funding, and even blackmail him (the Dovie Beams affair). A part of the globalists' notorious activities were documented by David Smith of the U.S. based *Newswatch* magazine, in August 1987:

Representatives from Indonesia and the Philippines went to Jonathan May (ex-World Bank head) and stated that agents from the Chase Manhattan Bank and other banks said they would "forgive" the loans and interests if the following were met:

(1) Eliminate their National Currency;

(2) Dollar-denominate their new money system;

(3) Use a debit card system instead of a currency system;

(4) Give the bankers perpetual rights over all natural resources.

Ferdinand Marcos of the Philippines refused to accept, and was deposed very shortly thereafter.

Marcos eventually gave in to the globalists' proposal for a snap election, using veteran "ambush interview" expert Ted Koppel of CBS. Clever as he was, Marcos did not reveal to the Americans that prior to his interview with Koppel he had already conducted a secret survey of the electorate. Despite thc adverse media hype launched against him, Marcos was confident of a re-election.

However, Jim Foley (who was later transferred to Algiers), disclosed that the real agenda was not the snap election; rather, it was to persuade Marcos to sign a document attesting to the fact that his gold bars and other precious metals deposited at Fort Knox and other depositories of the world would be under the guardianship of the Trilateral Commission, and a certain percentage would be given to the Philippine Government in the form of an investment loan from the World Bank.

The document was subsequently hand-carried by. U.S. Ambassador-at-Large Phillip Habib, which Marcos refused to sign. The Filipino head of state felt that the war loot (which was remolded into gold bars bearing the Central Bank seal) must be given to the Filipino people.

Q. How was the American's influence exerted during the snap election? Was there American involvement in the walkout of the computer workers?

A. First, there was the barrage of disinformation launched by *Newsweek*, *Time* and other publications regarding the illicit love affairs of both Marcos and the First Lady (e.g., George Hamilton), the incurable ailment of the President, and the public confidence in Namfrel and distrust in the Comelec. Then came the walk-out of the computer workers at the PICC. These were all part of the U.S. scenario during the snap election.

Most of the computer workers were promised visas and immigrant status to the U.S. Some of them, I understand, took advantage of this rare opportunity.

Q. Did any of your contacts know about the outbreak of the mutiny at EDSA?

A. Both Jim Foley and Norbert Garrett, CIA Station Chief, U.S. Embassy, predicted a bloody confrontation in the event that Marcos stubbornly decided to stay in Malacanang. The Presidents only saving grace was the signing of the document brought by Habib.

Q. Who were pressuring Marcos to give in and leave? Is there any, credible evidence that this happened?

A. The pressures came from both U.S. and Philippine sources. On the American side, there was Philip Habib. He was joined by U.S. Ambassador to the Philippines, Stephen Bosworth, Richard Armitage, Michael Armacost,[23] Rep. Stephen Solarz, Norbert Garrett (CIA Station Chief in Manila), and Joseph Mussomelli (Anti-Fraud Section, U.S. Embassy). Senator Paul Laxalt, as you probably know, was the guy who spoke to Marcos on the phone and told him to "cut and cut cleanly." Lines to Washington were kept busy by calls coming in from Lawrence Eagleburger and Henry Kissinger. Later on, I was told that operating funds came in from Maurice "Hank" Greenberg, through dollar grants from the C.V. Starr Foundation of New York. Greenberg is a powerful member of the B'nai B'rith. Others like Higdon, Brzezinski and Generals Pike and Allen of JUSMAG also formed part of the American initiative to oust Marcos.

On the Philippine side were assets like Joe Concepcion, Jobo Fernandez, Cesar Zalamea, Jaime Ongpin, and Alex Melchor. Journalists, likewise, were used for their media hype.

Q. Could you elaborate more on Habib's role in the events that followed?

A. As I have earlier stated, Habib was sent by the Trilateralists to the Philippines to pressure Marcos into signing the document prepared in the U.S. It contained provisions of equal sharing of the gold bars among different countries (through their banker's in the Commission), transshipped by Marcos to Fort Knox and other depositories under a top secret operation plan coded "Tuna Highway." Initially, Marcos was supported by the Commission to implement martial law in 1972, and was even provided with a martial plan.

Plant to Convert Plundered Gold

Along with it came a minting plant, installed at the Central Bank premises by Thomas de la Rue Ltd. of London, and a smelting plant with which to convert the war booty into new gold bars. The plan was executed by trusted generals of Marcos who diverted some portions of the shipment to other destinations aside from Fort Knox. This was covered by a prescription period (November 1945 to November 1985) in accordance with international law. After this 40-year period, it was to be declared "finders keepers." Some countries who felt conned by these agreements pursued their claim at the International Court of Justice, to mature in 2005.

Had Marcos chosen to sign the document, he would have remained

---

[23] Michael Armacost was a member of the National Security Council (NSC) responsible for East Asian affairs under the Carter administration from January 1977 to July 1978. He was U.S. Ambassador to Japan fro 1989 to 1993 and Under Secretary of State for Political Affairs from 1984 to 1989. He was Ambassador to the Philippines from 1982 to 1984 during the period of unrest in the Ferdinand Marcos presidency.

President for life. In the process, he would have received the distinction of being "the best President we ever had." In addition, the Philippines' share could have paid our external debt of, at that time, $24 Billion, plus a comprehensive Marshall Plan for industrialization. (To date, our external debt has zoomed up to $47 Billion, according to the latest BSFI figures.) Instead, he chose the hard way, and very badly miscalculated. He wanted to regroup his forces in the North, but was flown to Hawaii instead.

Q. Were there contacts between the Military camps and the Embassy and/or Washington during the four days at EDSA?

A. Definitely. It has always been standard operating procedure for our military officials to "keep the line open" between them and the defense attaches of the U.S. Embassy. Most of our top ranking officers have been nurtured in U.S. military schools. Some were even granted immigrant status in the U.S. while serving the Armed Forces of the Philippines (AFP). Their families were granted entry to the exclusive clubs of the American government such as JUSMAG, Seafront, Clark Air Base, Subic Base, Camp John Hay, etc. There they could avail of clubhouse facilities, golf courses and other amenities.

After EDSA, most of the renegade Marcos generals migrated to the U.S. These are the ones who never resisted the Aquino-Ramos-Enrile-Sin forces.

Q. Why didn't Marcos move during the first hours of the mutiny when there were very few people around the camps?

A. Marcos was sternly warned not to harm the people at EDSA. Otherwise, Malacanang would be targeted by the U.S. military sources. Thus, Marcos took the backseat and relied on the group of then Col. Rolando Abadilla to finish the job for him. You see, Abadilla's elite force from the MISG (Military Intelligence and Security Group), together with a SWAT team, successfully penetrated Camp Crame, disguised as Ramos supporters. As soon as Marcos was confronted about this by his Chief-of-Staff, General Fabian Ver, the president simply advised the latter to relax, as Abadilla was in the process of arresting Defense Secretary Juan Ponce Enrile and his cousin, Fidel Ramos, whom the president underestimated as a gutless individual. Marcos never imagined that Abadilla would have a change of heart. Abadilla was the prime suspect as the chief operator of Aquino's death at the tarmac.

Q. How do you connect Cardinal Sin with the American plan?

A. Cory Aquino was instructed by Cardinal Sin to seek refuge in a Cebu convent. As the fireworks were about to start, Cory was to install her revolutionary government in Davao with the assistance of the RAM forces and her NFIA sympathizers. This alternate plan vas likewise designed by the CIA, with Col. Voltaire Gazmin given the role of securing

Cory in Cebu. This plan was totally discarded when Marcos peacefully left the Philippines, due to the insistence of Cardinal Sin, who was backed up all the way by the Vatican and the U.S. State Department. Cory ended up being the sole titular head.

An article by Donna S. Cueto in the *Philippine Inquirer* (October 28, 1999) stated in part:

HONOLULU—Former President Fidel Ramos, Sen. Juan Ponce Enrile and a late congressman were each allegedly gifted with $1 million worth of gold bars by the late dictator Ferdinand Marcos before he died in 1989. This is part of the can of worms that businessman Enrique Zobel plans to open during his deposition today before the Senate blue ribbon committee, according to sources close to the tycoon.

Apart from Ramos and Enrile, the late Ilocos Sur Rep. Floro Crisologo was allegedly also given gold bars worth a million dollars. Aside from giving independent confirmation on the Marcos gold, Zobel, 72, is also expected to relate how Marcos accumulated much of his wealth during martial law using contingents of soldiers. Their main function was allegedly to dig up and transport gold and other treasure.

"It must be remembered that Zobel was a close confidante of the Marcoses, not only at the height of their power but also during the dying days of Marcos himself," Sen. Aquilino Pimentel Jr. said here yesterday. According to one source, Zobel will also relate how two relatives and officials of former President Corazon Aquino allegedly offered deals in which they wanted a cut of the Marcos wealth. They are former congressmen Emigdio Tanjuatco and Francisco Sumulong, said the source.

Zobel, a paraplegic after his polo accident in Spain in 1991, is expected to independently confirm the existence of around $35 billion worth of Marcos gold certificates. Zobel made the estimate in 1992 based alone on the certificates which Marcos showed him in Honolulu in 1988, when the late strongman allegedly tried to borrow $250 million from the businessman to pay the accumulated salaries of Marcos loyalists. Marcos allegedly showed the gold certificates to prove to Zobel that he could pay back the desired loan.

Zobel's estimate places the Marcoses' wealth much higher than the reported $13.2-billion "I. Arenetta" account at the Union Bank of Switzerland. Zobel's testimony will revolve mostly around events before 1991 and will not touch on the $13.2-billion account, according to former Solicitor General Francisco Chavez. Senate panelists are scheduled to take the deposition of the wheelchair-bound business magnate at 2 p.m. Wednesday at the Philippine consulate here.

Marcos met with Zobel before he became extremely ill. The deposed president allegedly expressed a desire to set up a foundation or trust fund to eventually transfer at least 75 percent of the Marcos wealth to the Filipinos. Only around 10 percent would remain with the family. Former first lady Imelda Marcos was aghast at the idea and wanted to raise the share to 15 percent, the source said. The meetings on the foundation were the subject of a series of interviews with Zobel published in the Inquirer in 1992.

What happened to gold? Most of the gold bars and other treasure dug up by the soldiers were allegedly re-minted at the Central Bank. From 1983 to 1985, Tamaraw Security Services allegedly transported some of the gold bars via Cathay Pacific and American President Lines. Tamaraw was owned by the late Fabian Ver, Marcos' closest military adviser and former Armed Forces Chief of Staff. The bars were reportedly shipped to Johnson and Matthiey's, a renowned gold assayer.

The sources said Zobel would talk about how Marcos gave a total of $3 million worth of the gold to Ramos, Enrile and Crisologo. The three, they said, were suspected to have had secret accounts in Swiss banks like the Marcoses. Ramos was the military vice chief of staff and Enrile, defense minister, when they turned against Marcos in 1986 in the People Power revolt that ousted the late dictator.

Before he died, there were also officials of the Presidential Commission on Good Government who allegedly approached Zobel regarding a deal to recover the Marcos wealth, offering him a share if he revealed what he knew. But the PCGG officials all allegedly wanted a cut of any recovered wealth. Even former PCGG Chair Magtanggol Gunigundo once allegedly offered 5 percent of recovered Marcos assets to Zobel for his cooperation and information on the secret Marcos accounts. Zobel has a document of the supposed agreement, signed by Ms Marcos—but not by Gunigundo.

According to the sources, Zobel also has a European contact who holds information on where other Marcos deposits are stored. This second witness, however, will not be able to testify, although the Senate was originally planning to take the deposition of both Zobel and this witness in Hawaii.

Once Zobel finishes his testimony—other witnesses, including some of the soldiers who supposedly dug up the gold for Marcos in the 1970s—are expected to agree to testify at the Senate hearings. Chavez yesterday clarified that Zobel was not his witness but a resource person of the Senate.

Pimentel, who arrived here yesterday, said the Senate would pursue any substantial leads supplied by Zobel, particularly on the Marcos gold deposits. But Pimentel also said that unless Zobel's testimony included the location of the deposits, the Senate would still have a lot of work to do. If Zobel confirms the gold, the Senate committee will have gathered only 50 to 60 percent of the evidence it needs, according to Pimentel, head of the blue ribbon committee.

"We're just building the database" on the Marcoses' hidden wealth, Pimentel said. "Number one, even if Zobel says something about the gold bars, the next question is where are these now? Who keeps the gold certificates or the gold bars?" he asked.

Pimentel said that, if necessary he would expand the investigation to include other personalities if doing so would help the senators get to the bottom of the Marcoses' secret wealth. He said he wanted to build a "solid" wall of evidence with which to confront Swiss authorities, enough to pursue the recovery of Marcos assets through diplomatic negotiations.

"The Swiss would become accomplices or co-conspirators (in money laundering) if they continued to deny the existence of these Marcos accounts and gold deposits even if there were solid and corroborating evidence presented to them," Pimentel said.

Solicitor General Ricardo Galvez, who also arrived here with Pimentel, yesterday said that happy days were over for Ombudsman Aniano Desierto, who had dismissed at least 27 behest loan cases against the Marcoses and their cronies. Galvez said a Supreme Court decision overturning the Ombudsman's ruling on one of the cases meant that Desierto could no longer dismiss such cases on a technicality. Desierto in 1997 and 1998 dismissed most of the behest loan cases on the grounds of prescription—that the government had filed the cases belatedly, or 10 to 15 years after the loans were made. If it could be proven that Desierto had violated the Constitution, Galvez said, this could lead to his impeachment.

Vatican Involvement in Gold Plunder

An article in the *Philippine Inquirer* (October 29, 1999) made reference to Vatican involvement. The article stated in part:

DAVAO CITY—A former Catholic priest here claims to have evidence that the alleged Marcos gold horde is composed of World War II "Yamashita gold and Vatican gold." Ex-priest Marcelino Tagle of Bataan, a former director of Caritas Manila and one of the nation's "Ten Outstanding Young Men" in 1967, said in a recent interview that the nation "should benefit" from the Marcos gold, which he estimated at "10 trillion dollars." Ten trillion dollars is 10 times more than the gross national product of China in 1998; around 127 times more than the GNP of the Philippines last year; and almost 10 times the combined worth of the world's 200 richest known billionaires in 1999. "I am ready to substantiate and defend my claims for the benefit of the Filipino people," Tagle said when told that his claims were preposterous.

The former priest said he once served as an adviser of the late President Ferdinand Marcos and administrator for the estate of another man whom he claimed was the source of the Marcos gold. But because Marcos was allegedly able to gain control of the gold certificates and cover the paper trail, according to Tagle, "it is almost impossible to recover them without piecing the various pieces like a mosaic." Tagle said the gold certificates and bullion were deposited in at least 15 countries.

[Vatican Involvement]

How the Vatican and Yamashita treasure reached the Philippines is a story that, he claims, involves two of the century's most influential personalities—Adolf Hitler and Gen. Douglas MacArthur. Tagle said the Vatican gold included "gold bars captured by Hitler (which belonged) to the royalties of Europe of which the Vatican was the trustee." It also included "royal gold" which the British reportedly shipped to Singapore for safekeeping in the event that Hitler would conquer all of Europe. Tagle said the Vatican entrusted the treasure to a certain Fr. Jose Antonio Diaz, who assumed several names when he moved to the Philippines.

[OSS operative Santa Romana Hired Marcos as Lawyer]

One of his aliases, according to Tagle, was "Col. Severino Sto. Romana." Tagle said Sto. Romana hired the young Marcos as his lawyer and trustee. He said the Sto. Romana gold was "actually more than the Marcos gold, about $50 trillion, but this treasure is tied up with the Marcos gold." Tagle, co-administrator of the Sto. Romana estates, said the Yamashita treasure was recovered through the help of MacArthur and Yamashita's wife. But an estimated 400,000 metric tons from both the Marcos and Sto. Romana gold, he said, "are still in the country, hidden in caves."

The heirs of Sto. Romana were unable to recover the assets "for lack of original documents and (because of the) nature of the accounts (which required) full cooperation of nominees and trustees constituted by the late President Marcos."

Appearing before the Senate blue ribbon committee on Oct. 14, 1997, Tagle said Marcos, as lawyer and chief trustee of Sto. Romana, "succeeded in isolating the nominees or trustees of the gold certificates from the physical assets—so much so that it is almost impossible to recover them without piecing the various pieces like a mosaic."

Tagle went into exile in the United States in September 1969 because the Marcoses were displeased about his leading a protest against graft and corruption in the Bureau of Customs. He resigned from the priesthood and married. He is now chair and chief executive officer of International Consultex Inc., a New York-based mining, consultancy and engineering firm.

The Senate is conducting public hearings on the Marcos wealth, revolving around a $13.4-billion Swiss bank account once allegedly kept by Irene Marcos Araneta. Former Solicitor General Francisco Chavez is presenting the evidence. "Chavez knows what he is talking about," said Tagle, adding that the Marcos wealth was so huge that even Marcos' widow Imelda did not know its exact worth.

Tagle proposed a "seven-point solution" to the problem of recovering the Marcos wealth: Create a Global Trust Fund to "secure, recover and distribute the assets of Marcos in an out-of-court settlement." Have "banking groups lend money to the Trust using the gold certificates and physical assets deposited in the lending banks, for a period of 15-20 years."

[Carolyn O. Arguillas, Chief, PDI Mindanao Bureau, with a report from PDI Research.]

Another article in *The Philippine Inquirer* (October 29, 1999), written by Donna S. Cueto, focused on the gold hidden by President Ferdinand Marcos, including in the Vatican and the U.S. Treasury:

Honolulu—There is allegedly around $100 billion worth of Marcos wealth stashed all over the globe, including US Treasury and Federal Reserve notes, as well as assets being kept by the Vatican. So testified business magnate Don Enrique Zobel, who yesterday appeared before the Senate blue ribbon committee at the Philippine consulate here to "open a Pandora's box."

[U.S. Treasury and Plundered Gold]

"This is the first time the US Treasury has been mentioned as a depository of at least a portion of the Marcos wealth," said Sen. Aquilino Pimentel Jr., head of the investigating panel, after Zobel's four-hour long testimony. The businessman also showed the committee a photocopy of what he said was a $161-million US Treasury note in Marcos' name. "It's in the name of Mr. Marcos. It looks like this $161 million is being held by the US Treasury until now," Pimentel said.

Sen. Juan Flavier, a member of the investigating committee, said he believed the document was authentic. "The credibility of Don Enrique Zobel is of the highest order," he said. "I've known him for 30 years. He's a leading industrialist and banker, and a man whose integrity has always been at the highest level," Flavier said.

Zobel testified that Marcos in 1988 had shown him gold certificates worth around $35 billion, deposited in several countries, including Switzerland, Portugal, the United States, the Vatican City, Spain and the Solomon Islands, among others. Zobel estimated that the Marcos fortune would reach $100 billion "between gold, assets and dollars, (and judging from) over-all comments of even banker-friends." Zobel, who was paralyzed from the neck down after a polo accident in 1991, said he had nothing to gain by making his claims.

"I'm 72 years old. I won't last much longer," he said in a rasping voice. "So I feel I would like to contribute something to the Filipino people." Zobel testified that former President Fidel Ramos, Sen. Juan Ponce Enrile, the late Fabian Ver and the late Rep. Floro Crisologo were each given by Marcos $1 million worth of gold bars each. Marcos told Zobel they were "loyal" men when he gave them the gold bars. The businessman said Marcos paid Ramos and the other officials in gold bars to discourage aggressive pursuit of his assets. He did not provide other details about the alleged bribes.

Zobel said he first talked to reporters seven years ago about his discussions with Marcos but was dismayed to see that the government did not investigate his claims. Much of his testimony yesterday first appeared in a series of interviews published in the *Inquirer* in 1992. Pimentel said this was the first time that Zobel revealed what he knew under oath before a government body, and that his testimony now acquired "far greater significance."

The senator said Zobel's testimony had a "cumulative effect" and would help the committee gather evidence to compel the release of still-hidden Marcos assets. "The importance therefore of Zobel's testimony is that it strengthens our resolve to press the Swiss bank authorities to return the Marcos assets," he said.

Asked by Pimentel why he thought it took until this year for a government body to question him, Zobel said: "I don't know, but an educated guess is the government doesn't want the Filipino people to know the truth." He also said Marcos did not want his wife Imelda and children to know the extent of his wealth.

According to Zobel, when Ferdinand "Bongbong" Marcos Jr., learned about the gold deposits, he allegedly blurted out in Filipino: "Why didn't our father tell us about this?"

"The way I saw it, he never knew that his father had that much money or that much gold," Zobel said.

He spoke at length about revelations made to him by the late strongman Ferdinand Marcos in 1988, one year before he died. He said that he had received information that part of the Marcos wealth also came from Nazi gold brought by the Japanese to the Philippines during World War II. He said Marcos told him that most of his gold was composed of "Yamashita treasure" and gold bars he bought at $20 each from soldiers.

[U.S. Treasury Involvement]

Zobel presented a copy of the US Federal Reserve Note or Treasury Deposit apparently placed by Marcos in the amount of $161 million. He said the note was renewed several times. "And this only involved one certificate," said Zobel. The US Treasury Note bore the name of the depositor "Mr. Ferdinand Marcos" and had the transaction No. 65089793422199675.F.L. The certificate was marked "International V.A. Trusty Dollar Transaction."

[Borrowing Money While U.S. Sequestered Him in Honolulu]

Marcos had sought to borrow $250 million in the fall of 1988, saying the money was needed to pay the accumulated salaries of his staff of 300 in Hawaii, Zobel said. He said he never intended to loan Marcos any of the money, but asked Marcos how he planned to repay it. Marcos produced a "thick folder" containing gold deposit certificates amounting to more than $35 billion, based on the prevailing market price of $400 per ounce, Zobel said. "I felt they were authentic. There was no question about that," he said. "I scanned through the (certificates). I was openly interested in the (number of) ounces and the location, and the locations were all over the world," he said. "You name any country in the world. They even had the Solomon Islands. And of course, Switzerland," Zobel said.

Zobel said he found it very curious that a day after Marcos told him about the gold, two senior officials of the National Bank of Saudi Arabia contacted him and told him to tell Marcos that they would buy the strongman's gold at a 40-percent discount. Zobel said he communicated their offer, but Marcos said he would only agree to sell at a discount of 30 percent. The bankers then left.

"The (US) government really got mad at the situation. They didn't want Saudi Arabia to get that gold since it was enough to finance a war," according to Zobel. He said the money was enough to pay the Philippine government's debt. He said that if the interest alone were distributed, Filipinos would each receive $2,000.

A one-time Hawaii resident who now lives in Spain, Zobel, wearing a white barong, was strapped to a wheelchair throughout the hearing. He had difficulty speaking, and a secretary had to position a microphone whenever he spoke to amplify his words.

He later thanked the Senate for hearing him out. "I'm extremely satisfied that the Senate blue ribbon has finally asked me questions because before they (people in government) never even wanted to talk to me about it," Zobel said. "I felt it was my duty to reveal this to the Filipino people, particularly now that economic situation is very bad," he said.

Zobel expressed readiness to testify in the other Senate hearings, particularly to accompany two other witnesses who had been waiting for Zobel to testify. One of them was a certain Dra. Pascual, a doctor of the late President. The Senate will also take the deposition of Australian investigator Reiner Jacobi, who first exposed the alleged $13.2-billion "I. Arenetta" account in the Union Bank of Switzerland. Pimentel also said the evidence the Senate had gathered so far also showed that the Marcos gold underneath Kloten Airport was still in Switzerland.

Asked if he had received threats before his deposition, Zobel said he had gotten calls threatening that his children in the Philippines would be kidnapped. He said two people had flown in to Hawaii on the alleged instructions of the Marcoses or their allies. He named the two as a certain retired Army Captain Luga, and public relations man Bobby Dacer, whom he called "a usurer paid by the administration to confuse the issue."

The testimony of an Australian investigator revealed account numbers for sequestered gold by one of Ferdinand's daughters was reported in the *Philippine Inquirer* (November 4, 1999) by investigative reporter Donna S. Cueto and an international monitoring network that kept track of the huge quantities of plundered and sequestered gold:

Australian investigator Reiner Jacobi will reveal new account numbers under new names in new banks to trace what happened to Irene Marcos Araneta's alleged $13.2-billion account, according to former Solicitor General Francisco Chavez. The lawyer also spoke yesterday of an "international monitoring network" which studies "movements of the Marcos gold and other accounts." Jacobi will divulge the "final piece of evidence" to link the account to the daughter of the late strongman Ferdinand Marcos at the "appropriate time," Chavez said.

The evidence will include proof of the transfer of certain accounts under Client No. 885931, he said. Chavez also said other witnesses, aside from Jacobi, would "unload very vital evidence" of the gold hoard and of the Araneta account. At least three witnesses are expected to be called this month to corroborate industrialist Enrique Zobel's testimony regarding alleged Marcos gold deposits which he valued at $35 billion. One is the leader of an alleged group of soldiers in the 1970s whose main work was to dig gold and other buried treasure for the Marcoses.

Chavez said he wanted Jacobi to be the final witness in the Senate's investigation of the alleged Marcos hidden fortune, so his evidence would not be "diluted." The Senate blue ribbon committee is scheduled to take Jacobi's deposition in Australia this month. Most of the funds under the account held by Marcos foundation Sandy Anstalt, including the "I. Arenetta" account, were allegedly transferred from the Union Bank of Switzerland.

On March 10, two days after Jacobi's lawyer filed a case against the Presidential Commission on Good Government in the Sandiganbayan and the same day that it was reported in the *Inquirer,* the account was allegedly "muted." That was when transactions on the account stopped, Chavez said. The account was allegedly collapsed on April 30. Sources said that all but one dormant sub-account under the mother account were closed or transferred. "If they think we have no eyes or ears, they are mistaken," Chavez said.

[Standard UBS Complicity]

Sen. Aquilino Pimentel Jr., chair of the blue ribbon committee, said the Senate would use the admission of UBS official Hans Peter Bauer to compel the recovery of Marcos deposits. "We could use this official's admission to push diplomatically, upon instruction of the President, further recovery of the Marcos wealth at UBS," he said. Bauer, the bank's chief internal watchdog, made the admission on Sept. 16 at a conference on economic crimes and money-laundering in Cambridge, England. Bauer made the disclosure before some 500 bankers and other conference participants. He said, however, that the bank denied any knowledge of the $13.2-billion account.

Solicitor General Ricardo Galvez, who attended the conference, said Bauer had admitted "dealing with the Marcoses" when the late dictator was still "not projected in a bad light." It was not clear what time frame Bauer was referring to.

[Philippine Troops Digging Up Japanese Plunder]

Apart from Roberto Caoile, the alleged leader of the troop that dug up portions of the Marcos gold, the other expected witnesses are Dra. Lourdes Pascual and Teresita Gillego, the anesthesiologist and the private nurse, respectively, of the late strongman. Caoile has formed a group called the Forgotten Claimants of Yamashita-World War II Treasures Versus Marcos Estate Incorporated, composed of soldiers from the reactivated 16th Infantry Battalion in the 1970s who allegedly dug up gold and gemstones for Marcos. Their story was the subject of an *Inquirer* special report which came out in January. They were allegedly part of Task Force Restoration, purportedly organized by then Armed Forces Chief of Staff Gen. Fabian Ver. Their main task was allegedly to conduct "massive diggings and excavations" under the cover of fighting insurgency in the countryside.

The Big Hawaiian

There is also a possible fourth witness, Larry Mehau, Marcos' former Hawaiian security officer. Mehau, who now works for Zobel, will supposedly corroborate certain parts of Zobel's testimony. Mehau, nicknamed "Big Hawaiian," allegedly saw Marcos show a thick folder of gold certificates to the businessman. Pimentel Jr. said Mehau was willing to come to the Philippines to testify. He said the bodyguard told him that he saw one gold certificate indicating $2 billion worth of deposits. Pimentel Jr. said the testimony of industrialist Enrique Zobel was very important because it was the first time that someone who had first hand information and who had access to Marcos before he died had testified at the Senate hearings.

Chavez said, "There is truth to Mr. Zobel's claim about the existence of Marcos gold certificates but their valuation at $35 billion was the result of estimation based on certain assumptions. I would not rely on the accuracy of this figure," Chavez said.

Pimentel and Flavier are themselves two of the most respected, honest and credible lawmakers around. So, what are the Filipino people to make of Zobel's fascinating revelations? Zobel has put the Marcos fortune at $100 billion--$35 billion in gold and the rest in foreign currency deposits and other assets. That is P4 trillion in depreciated pesos and it dwarfs even Imelda Marcos' claim in an interview with the *Inquirer* that her family's fortune amounted to P600 billion. It's a truly mind-boggling amount even to the Filipinos who can count beyond what it costs a family to have three square meals a day.

[Where did the gold and other wealth come from?]

The difficulty stems from the basic question of where Marcos got—or stole—all that wealth. This leads us to the favorite story of Imelda and the Marcos loyalists: Marcos made his fortune by discovering the treasures of Yamashita and later through very savvy gold trading in the international market. Zobel, in fact, has a duplicate of a gold certificate worth $161 million belonging to Marcos. If indeed this was the source of his immense wealth, then Marcos was not only the richest man who ever walked this earth but also the smartest and the luckiest businessman the world has ever seen, a reputation no one has heard about.

In a *Philippine Inquirer* article (November 5, 1999) the paper referred to the seizure by U.S. Customs at Honolulu of Marcos' Gold certificates:

Imelda Marcos yesterday promised "my family will cooperate" with the government to recover gold certificates allegedly seized by US customs authorities in 1986 [when the U.S. forcibly removed them from the palace in Manila and placed them in Honolulu]. She confirmed the claims of an *Inquirer* source who said that "more than $100 billion" [was seized]. "The Filipino people, not the Americans, are the rightful beneficiaries of whatever the amount the US government would be returning to us," the former first lady told the *Inquirer* yesterday in a phone interview. "My family will cooperate with the Estrada administration's efforts to reclaim the assets," she said.

"I won't sue US"

Marcos denied a report in another paper which claimed she was planning to sue US government officials for withholding the Marcos assets. In an official statement which she signed and issued before the *Inquirer* interview, Marcos said: "I have not issued any statements on any plan to sue officials of a foreign country or relating to the ongoing investigation of the Senate blue ribbon committee." Sought for clarification, Marcos said she did not want to cause any legal skirmishes that might hamper efforts to recover the gold certificates. "With the help of the government, we might be able to recover the gold certificates without having to be confrontational about the issue," Marcos explained.

The *Inquirer* source had said there was an agreement that the gold certificates, allegedly seized at Hickam Air Force Base when the Marcoses fled to Hawaii, would be returned once US authorities approve the proposed development projects. The sooner the gold certificates were reclaimed, the former first lady said, the earlier the projects could be implemented. Marcos said she would divulge the details of the infrastructure and livelihood projects "at the proper time." She lamented that for as long as the money allegedly remained in the hands of the Americans, the Filipino people would continue to wallow in poverty.

"Kawawa naman ang mga kababayan natin kung patatagalin pa natin ang paghihintay. Hindi mga Amerikano ang dapat makinabang sa mga gold certificates na iyon (Pity our countrymen if we prolong the wait). It shouldn't be the Americans who benefit from those certificates," she said.

Because of the recent admission of a top official of UBS, Chavez said the Senate could pursue a money laundering case against the Swiss bank which is suspected of hiding billions in Marcos deposits. The admission of Hans Peter Bauer that UBS had dealings with the Marcos family "means UBS has been lying to the Philippine government from 1986 to the present when it insisted it held no Marcos deposits," Chavez said. "UBS has given ample ground for prosecution, at the very least for the filing of charges of money laundering," he said. Chavez said he would file a motion urging the Senate to pursue a criminal case against the bank.

"Shift in posture"

Solicitor General Ricardo Galvez said Bauer's statement was a "significant shift in the posture of UBS which had consistently denied having transacted business with the Marcoses."

By Christine Herrera, Cathy C. Yamsuan and Donna S. Cueto, with a report from Martin P. Marfil.

Promissory note from Ferdinand Marcos to Enrique Zobel

In 1988, while Ferdinand Marcos was under literal house arrest in Honolulu after being flown from the presidential palace in Manila to Hawaii and separated from the hundreds of bank deposits throughout the world by the United States and cooperating banks, Marcos lacked funds to pay his bills. He asked Enrique Zobel, who was also spending time in Hawaii, to loan him money. Zobel agreed to do this, and the contents of the first page of the legal document appears below:

PROMISSORY NOTE

This is in consideration of two hundred fifty million dollars (US $250,000,000) which I now ask to be advanced to me by Don Enrique Zobel personally or through any bank representing him. Both parties shall consider these advances as a loan from Don Enrique Zobel., the party of the first part and the borrower, President Ferdinand E. Marcos as the party of the second part. I impose the condition that the U.S. Two Hundred Fifty Million Dollars (US $250,000,000) to be loaned to me through Upperrock Corporation Limited, Hongkong be actually delivered to AC # 47-299-0870-7 Standard Charter Bank Treasury Deposit Unit, 10th Floor, Edinburgh Tower, The Landmark, Hongkong.

In consideration of this loan, I hereby promise to deliver Three Million Ounces of gold (99.99% purity) within three years after I return to the Philippines although the parties may contact for any other times and places of delivery. The individual accountability as maybe finally agreed upon by both parties shall be binding, upon the same when approved and signed by each individually through their signatures.

October 17, 1988.

Don Enrique Zobel President Ferdinand E. Marcos

Ferdinand Marcos never returned to the Philippines; he died in Honolulu on September 28, 1989, of kidney, heart and lung ailments and was interred in a private mausoleum in Hawaii.

Another of many documents relating to tons of gold deposited in banks throughout the world:

October 31, 1992
Confidential & Exclusive Offer
To:
Thru: Araceli J. del Rosario

Gentlemen:

Upon your compliance with the loan Protocol in favor of our principal, the Beneficiary, the undersigned and other trustees commit to transact immediately the sale of the following commodity in favor of your buyer:

Commodity	Gold bullion in bars of 12.5 kilograms, with fineness 999,5/better, 24 karats, with complete documents, free and clear of any encumbrances prior to or at time of sale.
Quantity	Out of an available quantity of 350MT, an initial. quantity of 50MT is being sold to your buyer in exchange for your compliance with the Protocol; however, we reserve the option to sell more to your buyer depending on our principal's satisfaction with your buyer's performance.
Price	LMER second fixing on the day of signing, less gross incentive of five percent (0%) distributed as follows: 3% net to buyer , 1% to buyer's negotiators, and 1% to seller's negotiators.

Implementation procedure:

1. Buyer's bank officer to verify the following commodity coordinates:

Seller's bank	UBS Zurich, Switzerland
Quantity	350 MT up to 2,450 MT
Place of storage	Kloten Airport
Vault No.	88 RW-RP
ADA Account No.	G72570367-d-UBS
Metal Account No.	7257
Master Account No.	70367-D

2. After verification of commodity, seller and buyer to sign contract of sale in Hong Kong.

3. Sellers's bank to confirm the commodity for sale to buyer's bank.

4. Buyer's bank to confirm funds availability.

5. Seller's bank to set window time for the lifting of the first 25MT, to be followed by another window time for the next 25MT. [Metric tons]

Mobilization fund:

> As agreed with Mr. [redacted], a mobilization fund of $ 15,000 to $40,000 will be provided for transport and hotel expenses of the seller's party for trips abroad of people involved in the transaction. This mobilization fund will be derived from the 5% facilitation fee on the loan Protocol and will be paid by the Beneficiary from the $10M loan proceeds.

We are ready when you are ready.

Very truly yours,

/s/ ______________________ 11/8/92
CONFORMED BY:

/s/ ______________________________

The following power of attorney from Imelda Marcos related to YAB-42.

SPECIAL POWER OF ATTORNEY

Know All Men by These Presents:

I, Imelda Romualdez Marcos, of legal age, Filipino citizen, and with postal address at __________________________________ do hereby name, constitute, and appoint Dr. William C. Bryant, likewise of legal age, American citizen and with postal address at 1425 S. Brookhurst Blvd., Fullerton, California 92633, U.S.A., to be my true and lawful Attorney-In-Fact, for me and in my name, and stead, to do and perform the following acts and things, to wit :

To act in my and my legal heirs behalf concerning any and all businesses related in anyway to "YAB-42". To ask, demand, claim, sue for, recover, collect any and all sums of money, debts, value of-whatever nature or kind as may now be or may hereafter become due, owing, payable or belonging to me, and to have, claim, sue and to take any and all lawful ways and means for the recovery thereof, by suit, attachment, compromise or otherwise;

To make, sign, execute, and deliver contracts, documents, agreements, and other writings of whatever nature or kind, with any and all third persons, concerns, or entities, upon the terms and conditions acceptable to my said Attorney-In-Fact;

All properties shall be placed in Trust with the Los Angeles Church Loan Corporation, 1425 Brookhurst Blvd., Fullerton, CA 92633 U.S.A. serving as Trustee and I as Trustor. Whatever is required to reactivate the program known as "YAB-42" or to create another procedure is at the total discretion of Dr. W. C. Bryant acting for Los Angeles Church Loan Corporation. However, any and all related activities performed by my Attorney-In-Fact shall be coordinated properly with my Trustees and/or duly authorized representatives, Messrs. Luis Tabuena and Roberto M. Paredes, all of legal ages Filipino citizens and with postal address at 1001 San Marcelino St., Ermita, Manila, Philippines and under no circumstances violate these terms and conditions.

To delegate in whole or in part any or all of the powers herein granted as conferred, by means of an instrument in writing, in favor of any third party or person/s whom my said Attorney-In-Fact may select and/or choose.

Hereby giving and granting unto said Attorney-In-Fact full power and authority whatsoever necessity or requisite or proper to be done in and about the premises as fully to all intents and purposes as I might or could lawfully do if personally present, with power of substitution and revocation, and hereby, ratifying and confirming all that my said Attorney-In-Fact shall lawfully do or cause to be done under and by virtue of these presents.

In witness whereof, I have hereunto set my hands and affixed my signature, this ____ day of April, 1992, in the City of Manila, Republic of the Philippines.

Affiant
Signed in the presence of:

Salvador Bareng and Roberto M. Paredes
Witness Witness

Acknowledgment:
Republic of the Philippines)
: s.s.
City of Manila)

Ferdinand E. Pviarcos

The following copy of a letter suggested a plan to retrieve bank accounts and transfer them to another bank and another account holder.[24]

February 21, 1192

Yoshinobu Ohyoma
Shinji Hare

Dear Ohyams-san/Hars-san,

I have been authorized by Romeo to disclose to you the details of our proposed project for your clear understanding.

In this connection, please take note of the attached document showing the procedure of transferring accounts from Zurich-Switzerland and others like Geneva, Switzerland and London, England .... into the Philippines.

Background:

At present there are around 137 accounts secretly deposited abroad mostly in Zurich; others are in Geneva and others are in London.

This big volume of deposit has been the object of the Philippine Government's recovery efforts since Cory Aquino became President in February 1986. But the banks abroad would not reveal any information concerning the secret deposits as it would violate their Bank Secrecy Laws.

There is a great need for us to use a bit portion of the -money deposited in said countries, to enable us to finance the political campaign of bur chosen candidates this coming May 11, 1992 National and Local elections. But obviously, the money cannot be withdrawn and remitted into the Philippines as easy as ordinary accounts due to the continuous monitoring of the Philippine Government.

In view of this, we have to use a cover by adopting a very sure procedure recommended by top international financial experts hires for this purpose.

Procedure or Transferring Secret Accounts

STEP 1

1. Mama shall appoint Mr. John Dos as trustee to act as her author-

---

[24] This letter appeared in the book, *Marcos Legacy Revisited: Raiders of the Lost Gold.*

ized signatory for the transfer of accounts from Zurich to free countries recommended like Hongkong, Bahamas and Austria.

2. Mama shall provide her trustee with the information needed so the trustee can proceed with the transfer of funds; such as

e) Bank Name and Address

b) Name of Bank Officer

c) Secret Code Account Numbers

3. Mama shall contact and inform the Bank Officer that she has given her trustee the required signatory authority to be able to effect the transfer of funds from Zurich to Hongkong, Bahamas and Austria.

4. Mama shall appoint a set of new trustees composed of three (3) persons, who will act independently of each other, to open separate accounts for and in her behalf in the following countries:

a) Mr. A.B.C. shall open an account in a Bank in Hongkong

b) Mr. D.E.F. shall open an account in a Bank in Bahamas.

c) Mr. G.H.I. shall open an account in a Bank in Austria

All accounts opened by these three (3) trustees in Hongkong, Bahamas and Austria shall receive the fund transfer/remittances from Zurich arranged by her first trustee Mr. John Doe. Once the funds have been transferred to Hongkong, Bahamas and Austria, the second step shall then be adopted.

STEP II

1. Mama shall appoint a set of new trustees composed of three (3) persons who officially represent three (3) foreign dummy corporations based separately in Hongkong, Bahamas and Austria, namely Mr. JKL, Mr. M.N.O. and Mr. P.Q.R.

2. Mama shall then individually instruct the three trustees to open individual accounts under the name of their respective corporations in the same Banks in Hongkong, Bahamas, and Austria where Mr. A.B.C., Mr. D.E.F. and Mr. G.H.I. maintain their respective accounts.

3. Mama shall then give the following instructions:

a) For Mr. A. B.C. to issue an order of payment in favor of Mr. J.K.L.'e corporate account in Hongkong.

b) For Mr. D.E.F. to issue an order of payment in favor of Mr. M.N.O.'s corporate account in Bahamas.

c) For Mr. G.H.I. to issue an order of payment in favor of Mr. P.Q.R.'s corporate account In Austria.

Once the corporations of Mr, J.K.L., Mr. M.N.O. and Mr. P.Q.R. have received the funds, Step III shall then be followed:

STEP III

1. Mama shall then give fresh instructions to her new trustees:

a) Will instruct Mr. J.K.L., who is an officer of a foreign dummy corporation in Hongkong to open and make deposit under Foreign Currency Deposit Unit (FCOU) account at the Rizal Commercial Banking Corporation (RCBC) in Manila and transmit foreign currency thru wire transfer.

b) Will instruct. Mr. M.N.O. who is an officer of a foreign dummy corporation in Bahamas to open and make deposit under FCDU account at the Bank at the Philippine Islands (BPI) and transmit foreign currency thru wire transfer.

c) Will instruct Mr. P.Q.R. who is an officer of a foreign dummy corporation in Austria to open and make deposit under FCDU account at the Philippine Bank of Commerce (PBCOM) and transmit foreign currency thru wire transfer.

Once the funds have been transferred at the three (3) Philippine Commercial Banks under FCDU accounts, step IV shall than be adopted.

STEP IV

1. Mama shall select three (3) local dummy corporations to act as borrower of funds from the following banks where the FCDU accounts have been deposited:

a) Local Corporation D-1 shall apply loan at the Rizel Commercial Banking Corporation (RCBC).

b) Local Corporation D-2 shall apply loan at the Bank of Philippine Island (SP1)

O) Local Corporation D-3 shall apply loan at the Philippine Bank of Commerce (PBCOM).

2. Mama shall than give this following instructions to her three (3) trustees:

a) For Mr. J.K.L. to give instruction to the lank Officer of Rizal Commercial Booking Corporation (RCBC) to approve and grant this loan application of Local Corporation D-1 using his FCDU account as collateral security.

b) For Mr. M.N.U. to give instruction to the Bank Officer of the Bank of the Philippine island (SP1) to approve and grant this loan application of Local Corporation 0-2 using his FCDU account as collateral security.

c) For Mr. P.Q.R. to give instruction to the Bank Officer of the Philippine Bank of Commerce (PVCOM) to grant the loan application of Local Corporation D-3 using his FCDU account as collateral security.

Once the loan applications of the throe (3) Local Dummy Corporations have been granted, Step V can then be applied.

STEP V

1. Mama shall than appoint her final trustee (Mr. RCP) and shall in-

struct him to open a new account at an Off-Shore Bank based in Manila.

2. Mama shall than give instructions to the three (3) Local Dummy Corporations to release their loan Proceeds based on schedule.

3. All the lorn proceeds acquired and released by the three (3) local dummy corporations shall then be deposited under One Mother Account opened and maintained by RCP.

4. RCP will then disburse funds as instructed by Mama.

******** END********

The authority given to me by Romeo to disclose this information to you regarding our proposed project only Indicates his whole hearted trust in you and your ability to keep under wrap confidential matters.

With respect to your participation in this project which is very important and crucial at this point including our sharing conditions shall be discussed to you in person, by Romeo himself.

Finally, I just hope that you will give this matter your first priority attention by coming to Manila as soon as possible.

Please send your reply upon receipt of this letter at Fax Nr. 832-3485 Phil. Plaza.

Regards,

Freddie

The "Freddie" that signed the above letter was identified as Freddie Johnson in a letter that he wrote to Shinji Hara of Tokyo, Japan on January 6, 1992. Portions of that letter follows:

January 6, 1992

Mr. Shinji Hara
Tamaki Bldg., Shinjikuko
Shinjukuko, Tokyo, Japan

Dear Shinji,

We just spent quite a long holiday season and during that time I took the opportunity to write you this letter hoping that it would help you better understand our real intention regarding our project proposal.

Since the arrival of Mrs. Marcos and party here in the Philippines last November 4, 1991 from New York I had the occasion of discovering many hidden information not known to many people. Since the Marcos family were kidnapped by the Americans and brought to Hawaii by force sometimes in February 1986, many questions were left in the minds of Filipino people which remain unanswered up to this time. Questions like, how much wealth have been acquired by the Marcoses during their 20 year rule in office? How those wealth were acquired? Where are these wealth being kept or deposited? And to whom these wealth are intended for?

My close association with Roger, the spokesman of Mrs. Marcos, had helped me discover the reality of this hidden wealth, the manner of their acquisition, to whom these wealth are intended for, and the great plans and visions of the Marcos family for the Filipino people. [Their contempt for the Filipino people was shown by the decades of hidden wealth; not until imminent death did Ferdinand Marcos think of the Philippine people!]

Imelda Marcos object of Harassment by Cory Government

The life of Mrs. Marcos for the last almost six years had been characterized by so many struggles. After her family's forced exile in Hawaii, the death of her husband, the late President Marcos, her eventual acquittal of the RICO criminal charges in New York, the Cory government does not relent on putting continued pressure to make Mrs. Marcos life more difficult and miserable.

And as if to show its last ditch effort to humiliate and limit her movements, several tax cases and other charges had been filed by the Cory government in local courts—thus preventing her from withdrawing her deposits abroad. It is a fact that in Mrs. Marcos is now temporarily living on the generosity of friends who regularly give provide her moral and financial support.

Our Project Proposal

Going back to our project proposal, actually, our proposed project is not all there to it. But it is just a beginning or a first important step to open the door for a wider business opportunities that will surely come simultaneously after this. What Roger actually plans to do is to bring Mr. Ohyama closer to the heart and attention of Mrs. Marcos so that when the right time comes he can get the first priority in all our big business undertakings.

Please take note that Roger Peyuan personal preferences for Mr. Ohyama to be our permanent partner in all our business dealings. He feels it is in our way of returning favor to Mr. Ohyama for his valuable financial help he extended way back in 1985. He wants, in other words, to work with Mr. Ohyama on a "Give and Take Basis."

And so, as I took pain in preparing that letter, I just hope that you will take the patience interpreting and explaining this offer to Mr. Ohyama.

Finally, we expect that by January, 1992 Mr. Ohyama can come to so we can hold serious discussions on more important business matters. Remember, time is of the essence.

With warmest personal regard,

Freddie Johnson

Letter relating to proposal for gaining access to bank deposits:

ROGER C. PEYUAN
5 East 80th Street, New York, NY 10021
TEL: (212) 249-7782 249-7647
FAX (212)-861-4472

Fax No. (03) 3372-9633
November 28, 1991

Mr. Yoshinobu Ohyama
Tamaki Bldg.
2F 5-6-2 Nishi Shinjuku
Shinjikuko, Tokyo

Dear Ohyama-san,

I and Freddie Johnson discussed many things about you. Of course, we can never forget the days when we undertook a project that never pushed through due to the unfortunate incident in EDSA which everybody knows, that was more than five years ago.

But the most important thing is that we were able to maintain mutual trust and respect among each other. And so this time, we are again confronted by a new situation much different from before. I do hope and believe that this will provide us the occasion of recovering many things like lost time, efforts and opportunity including of course your previous investments.

And this is of course the main subject of our concern which we would like to discuss with you privately in person.

For this reason, we would like to invite you to come to Manila for an important discussion on a very important confidential matter that will touch mainly on the prospect of advancing our mutual business interests.

In the meantime, we requested Mr. Mitsutoshi Minowa to deliver to you our message (picture of Madame Imelda Marcos and our letter) which we sent this morning thru DHL. We also authorized Mr. Minowa to discuss with you initially about our plans.

We do hope that you would be able to come to manila at the soonest time possible.

With warmest personal regards to you and to Ambassador Sazaki.

Sincerely,
(SGD) Roger C. Peyuan
Spokesman of
Mrs. Imelda R. Marcos

(SGD). Freddie Johnson
Special Assistant to
Roger C. Peyuan

Note: Please acknowledge receipt of this letter thru FAX Nr. (63-2) 521-34-13 & (63-2) 521-52-75
Attn.: Roger Peyuan or Freddie Johnson Japan

The following is a request for funding the scheme to gain control of bank deposits being withheld by banks. The plan provides still more support, which is hardly needed, to show that Japanese plunder did exist:

December 9, 1991

"FOR YOUR EYES ONLY"

Dear Ohyama-san

We would like to invite your serious attention to our business proposals which we cannot discuss over the phone.

Actually, there are two kinds of projects which we are working right now and both of which projects have 100% chance of success.

First Project:

The first project is a very sensitive one as it is strictly confidential in nature. This involves solid assets in big volume deposited under secret accounts in Switzerland which is the subject of our recovery efforts.

I was given specific instructions by Mama to work on this immediately and I was also given the authority to invite somebody whom I can trust to help me in this effort. And I want you to know that you are the first person in my mind whom I can trust because you are close to my heart and also, I feel I have an obligation to help you recover your previous investments way back in 1985.

Plan of Action:

At this point, we are in the process of screening and selecting purely trusted personnel to be sent to Switzerland "to serve as our base. Once the selection process has been completed, they shall be immediately sent there purposely to conduct confidential negotiations and to receive our specific instructions from time to time mostly regarding transfer of accounts from one bank to another.

Ultimate Objective:

Our ultimate objective in doing this is for us to be able to release our assets in a manner that will be free from any kind of detection. Once this is successfully accomplished, then we can begin to payback and help in return our friends who have been very kind, helpful and supportive to us especially during these days when we are facing a crisis situation.

Logistical Support:

But to succeed in this undertaking, we are badly in need of logistical support in the form of cash in order to finance the whole operation. Our rough estimate on the cost of this project is ranging from between US $250,000 to US $ 500,000. Once this amount is raised, then we can immediately execute all our plans and be able to finish it in a more expeditious manner.

Fund Utilization Program Or
Schedule of Expenditures:

Actually, the utilization of the proposed budget is divided into two stages:

1st stage: Initially, we are so much concerned on how to raise US $250,000' immediately or before December 20, 1991. Said amount shall be used by our personnel for travelling expenses, allowances, foods, hotel accommodations, payment for the services of foreign legal and technical payment and other miscellaneous and incidental expenses.

2nd stage: The other US $250,000 shall be used as stand-by fund and could be raised even on a staggered basis as the need may arise. Said stand-by fund shall be used for our contingency operation.

Timetable:

Our timetable is that we have to start this project on or before December 20, 1991 by all means. The purpose of setting this schedule is for us to be able to finish the whole project before the end of February 1992. But assuming that we have all the fund resources already on stand-by intended for the operation, then we are more than confident that we can finish the project even earlier than scheduled.

If I may tell you, we have also many other bigger plans ahead like playing a big role in the coming elections of 1992. We are also committed into helping many people in the electoral contest. But all this we cannot do without first succeeding in our first project.

Areas of Cooperation/Participation:

It is in this particular area where I would like to seek your participation or cooperation by way of financing the whole project. Your important help at this stage shall be very much appreciated and that such assistance, which shall be considered as your personal investments, shall forever be acknowledged.

Return of Investments and Other Considerations:

Once this project has been successfully completed, all your investments that have been put up in this project shall be immediately returned. With respect to your benefits and or other consideration, "Just name it and you shall have it". All I can say is that we are a decent people who know how to pay debts of gratitude to people like you who have been very understanding and helpful to our cause.

Collateral Security or Guarantee:

If in case you may be interested in securing collateral security or guarantee from us inconsideration of your investments, we are more than willing to comply with such a condition. In fact, one of the reasons why we are inviting you to come to Manila, aside from discussing this matter, is for you to see proof of our hard assets which we are willing to use as collateral.

Finally, I think that what we need at this point is mutual trust and cooperation with each other and the positive belief that we can succeed in our common undertaking.

Meantime, I have authorized Freddie to communicate and coordinate with you and Mr. Shinji Hara from time to time regarding this project. I also requested him to send you complete documents pertaining on second project thru DHL with complete and clear explanations.

So long, best regards and I will be waiting for your immediate reply.

Sincerely,

Romeo

CHAPTER SEVEN

Covert CIA Financial Operations in Pacific

Years before writing this book I had written about covert CIA operations throughout the world, including within the United States, and especially in the Pacific. Many of the people in those covert operations were also the same people involved in the Japanese plunder activities. The books containing that earlier information include *Explosive Secrets of Covert CIA Operations, Defrauding America,* and *Drugging America.* A partial reference is made here to that information.

Nugan Hand: CIA Operation in Australia

A primary covert CIA money laundering operation in the Pacific area was Nugan Hand Bank with headquarters in Sydney, Australia, and branch offices throughout the Far East, Europe, and the United States. Nugan Hand Bank was incorporated in 1976 in the Cayman Islands, a popular money-laundering location.

Nugan Hand Bank was a replacement for the CIA's Mercantile Bank and Trust Company and Castle Bank & Trust, incorporated in Nassau, Bahamas. Earlier, the IRS, unaware of the CIA connection, started to conduct an investigation of Castle Bank and Trust Company, but was quickly halted by powerful people in government. That publicity resulted in the CIA replacing it with the Nugan Hand Bank.

The Nugan Hand offices were involved in laundering drug money from the Golden Triangle drug producing area. Secondary functions for these covert CIA companies were arms sales and funding covert activities, such as undermining governments and funding assassination squads. Nugan Hand was comprised primarily of people with ties to the U.S. intelligence community. The primary partners were Francis Nugan, Michael Hand, and Maurice Bernard Houghton.

Vast amounts of money were hidden in assets and financial holdings throughout the world. Either to appear as a legitimate international investment operation, or to defraud people out of millions of dollars,

Nugan Hand took deposits from individuals throughout the world. That money would be lost by these investors when the CIA's cover was blown. When the cover for this CIA-related operation was blown, these funds were quickly moved to other CIA proprietaries, inflicting financial losses upon the investors and depositors. Many of the individuals putting money into the CIA's Nugan Hand Bank were military personnel, who eventually lost everything they deposited.

Exposing Fraud in CIA's Nugan Hand Bank

Nugan Hand's cover was blown on April 11, 1980, by a reporter for *Target*, a Hong Kong financial newsletter. That exposure required the CIA to shut down the operation and destroy evidence of its CIA links. It was further exposed as a CIA operation in an Australian government report. That report strained the American and Australian relationship that had existed since the 1970's when the government headed by Prime Minister Gough Whitman found that U.S. secret activities were taking place on bases in Australia. Although joint operations with Australia had been approved, those covert operations were a complete surprise to the government there.

Officials in the Labor Government were outraged upon learning that even their country's Foreign Ministry was unaware of these operations. One base was used as a key ground control station for satellites and an early warning system, code named Casino. It was used to serve as a link in the Defense Support Program against Russian ICBM Attack on the U.S., its sister station located in Colorado.

During an Australian Royal Commission investigation into Nugan Hand Bank in 1980, it was discovered that the former—or sheep-dipped—former U.S. military and CIA personnel have been engaging in drug dealings, drug-money laundering; arms shipments; other financial crimes; arranging the sale of a spy ship to Iran in a secret deal; and that it was a CIA front.

The Whitman government went public with much of this information, resulting in a stern warning from Washington against further CIA exposure. At the same time, a spy working for TRW in California, whose job it was to monitor clandestine messages in what was known as the "Black Box," passed CIA secrets to the Russian KGB. This information showed how CIA funds were being used to influence labor unions in Australia against the Whitman Government.

According to the Australian report, Nugan Hand Bank and its CIA agents supplied arms to Africa, including 3,000 weapons and 10 million rounds of ammunition. These were shipped from a U.S. Company in the United States to Task Force 157. It appeared that a spy ship might have been sold to Iran at about the same time. It was estimated that over 100 proprietary companies might have been tied to the Nugan

Hand CIA operation.

Secret Navy Intelligence Operation: Task Force 157

Of the 16 intelligence units within the United States government was the U.S. Navy unit called Task Force 157. It was a top secret intelligence unit located in Alexandra, Virginia, and formed in 1970. The unit consisted of multiple companies or proprietaries located throughout the world.

The primary function of Task Force 157 was spying on Soviet activities. Under contract for Task Force 157 was former CIA operative Edwin Wilson. Internal problems caused the termination of Task Force 157. Wilson had also been a part of Nugan Hand covert financial operations.

Also a part of Nugan Hand was Theodore Shackley, second in command of all CIA covert activities. Shackley had been involved in the covert actions against Cuba's Fidel Castro. Shackley had a reputation within the spy agency as a ruthless man who would go to extremes to accomplish his goals. While stationed in Saigon as CIA Chief, a Special Forces unit asked their CIA liaison officer what they should do with a double agent they discovered. Shackley ordered him killed, as he had done to an estimated 250 political prisoners in Laos. The Australian report identified Shackley as a key figure in the Nugan Hand operations.

Another CIA agent was Donald Beazley, president of Nugan Hand Banking Group International. He later became president of City Bank in Miami. Beazley, according to the Australian Report, played an important part in the purchase of London Capital Securities Ltd. a.k.a. Stonehouse Bank. All were tied to A.P.I. Distributors of Houston, Texas. They helped Wilson sell 20 tons of plastic explosives to Qaddafi. Thomas Clines was also tied to Shackley and was a highly ranked CIA veteran of over 30 years. Beazley purchased the London Bank for $300,000 in travelers' checks bought by Bernard Maurice Houghton, a Nugan Hand executive in Australia and a veteran CIA agent.

Another figure Major General Richard Secord, later of Iran-Contra fame, having just left his post as Secretary to Casper Weinberger, introduced Houghton to Shackley and Clines. Houghton ran Nugan Hand operations in Saudi Arabia, collecting large deposits in cash that were converted to traveler's checks and taken out of the country. The Australian report estimated it at approximately $10 million dollars. Some checks were later tied to the London Bank purchase.

According to the Australian Report, Shackley and Hand had a longstanding relationship. The report finally concluded that it could not say why or who killed Frank Nugan. Michael Hand was smuggled out of Australia by CIA operatives after Nugan's death, and fled the country before he could answer any investigators questions.

The Australian report tied Nugan Hand Bank to Lt. Gen. Leroy Manor, Chief of the Pacific Command in the Philippines, and Edwin Black, a former high-ranking intelligence officer and assistant Army Chief of Staff. Both men served as Nugan Hand Bank Presidents.

Australia's complaints that the U.S. Intelligence community refused to cooperate in their investigation fell on deaf ears. The Report also said the CIA lied repeatedly to them. Admiral Bobby Ray Inman, former Deputy Director of CIA, stated on at least two occasions that any additional investigation by Australia would result in exposure of "a range of dirty tricks against foreign governments."

Francis Nugan was one of the most visible players in the Nugan Hand operation. He was an alcoholic with a reputation for talking too much, a trait that threatened to expose the CIA's role in the operation. Assassins killed Nugan,[25] leaving his body in a car alongside a lonely road outside of Sydney, Australia. A bolt-action rifle was found alongside the body, and the scene was made to look like a suicide.

An unspent bullet remained in the firing chamber of the bolt-action rifle. For an unspent bullet to be in the chamber after firing the shot that was instantly fatal, someone, other than Nugan, had to manually operate the bolt handle. Nugan obviously did not do this. The bullet had killed Nugan instantly, blowing away much of his skull and scattering it throughout the car. There were no fingerprints on the gun, indicating that whoever fired the fatal bullet wiped the fingerprints from the rifle.

The only identification on Nugan's body was a calling card apparently overlooked by the killers, belonging to William Colby, former Director of the Central Intelligence Agency, with a meeting date written on the back. Colby was legal counsel for Nugan Hand. He also had connections to the Wall Street law firm of Reid & Priest, suggesting that this firm was a front for the CIA or a CIA proprietary.

Immediately after Nugan's death, the CIA removed the funds from the various Nugan Hand offices and laundered them into other CIA operations. Misinformation commenced immediately, denying that the CIA had any connection to the rogue bank, despite the many intelligence agency officers in the operation.

Before Australian authorities started an investigation, Michael Hand disappeared, along with most of the Nugan Hand records. Although the media reported that Hand had disappeared, leaving no trace, two of my CIA sources had been in contact with him after he fled Australia. Hand secretly surfaced in Iran, followed by his participation in CIA Central America drug trafficking.

---

[25] January 27, 1980.

Hand disappeared as Australian authorities sought to question him about Nugan's death, the Nugan Hand Bank operation, and the disappearance of approximately one billion dollars from the bank. Hand first went to Thailand under CIA cover and then showed up in Florida and the Caribbean area. One of my deep-cover CIA contacts, Trenton Parker, told how he and Hand had worked together in the early 1980s. Parker's CIA faction was interested in discovering Hand's operation, and Parker met Hand in Jamaica on February 2, 1980. They then worked together on Operation Interlink[26] and Operation Anacondor. Parker's CIA activities are detailed in my *Defrauding America* book.

Parker said that Hand and Vice President George Bush were in frequent contact after Bush became vice president, and while Australian authorities were searching for Hand. Parker stated that CIA Director William Casey frequently met with Hand in Panama in the early 1980s concerning arms sales and drug trafficking.

Parker stated that he and Hand took over one of the drug trafficking operations for the CIA in Central and South America. He said that Hand's experience in developing the Golden Triangle drug operations for the CIA made him useful in expanding the drug operations from Central and South America into the United States.

Like most CIA-related operations, Nugan Hand Bank relied upon a pattern of fraud and deception. Large amounts of currency were moved in and out of various countries, including Australia and the Golden Triangle areas.

Michael Hand was a Green Beret and a colonel in the U.S. Army, assigned to the CIA. Earlier, Hand was handling the CIA's drug business and laundered the money from the Golden Triangle area of Asia. In the 1960s, the CIA transferred Hand from the Golden Triangle assignment to Teheran, where he set up the secret police for the Shah of Iran. (I was an airline captain flying into and out of Iran, and residing in Iran, at approximately that same time, flying Muslim pilgrims to the holy cities of Mecca and Medina during the Hajj.)

The Nugan Hand affair received considerable media attention in Australia, but the mainstream media in the United States said virtually nothing about the CIA operation and its implications. Australian authorities conducted numerous investigations, but in their final report they whitewashed the Nugan Hand affair. The CIA had an ongoing relationship with Australia's Security Intelligence Organization (ASIO), which probably played a role in the cover-up of Nugan Hand.

One of Nugan Hand's CIA assets who suffered a fate similar to

---

[26] Operation Interlink was a covert CIA operation to raise funds for covert operations. See the book, *Defrauding America*, by Rodney Stich.

Nugan was John Fredericks; he and his bodyguard were killed (July 28, 1991) in Australia.

Staffed by the CIA

Most of the management personnel of Nugan Hand Bank were intelligence community personnel. When Nugan Hand shut down, most of them moved to other CIA operations. These players, with a long CIA and military intelligence background, moved into other covert activities.

Covert CIA Companies Staffed by Military and Other Insiders

Most covert CIA companies have been staffed at higher levels by former military and other government personnel, but mostly military. They are either retired personnel, or sheep-dipped from their prior positions. The various worldwide offices of Nugan Hand Bank had the following personnel:

- Adm. Earl Yates, chief of U.S. strategic planning for Asia and the Pacific. He was president of Nugan Hand Bank. Yates had been commander of the aircraft carrier, John F. Kennedy. He retired (or was sheep-dipped), from the Navy in 1974 and became president of Nugan Hand Bank in 1977.
- Michael Jon Hand, CIA operative, former Green Beret, vice-chairman and part owner of Nugan Hand Bank.
- Gen. Edwin F. Black ran Nugan Hand's Hawaii office.
- Paul Helliwell was a CIA asset heavily involved in drug money laundering.
- Gen. Earle Cocke, Jr., ran the Nugan Hand Washington office and headed the American Legion.
- William Colby, retired Director of CIA, was the lawyer for Nugan Hand Bank.
- Dale Holmgren headed flight services for several CIA airlines and ran Nugan Hand's Taiwan office.
- Robert Jantzen, CIA station chief in Thailand, was Nugan Hand's officer in Thailand.
- Gen. Leroy Manor, chief of staff for U.S. Pacific Command, ran Nugan Hand's Philippine office.
- Walter Macdonald, former deputy director of CIA for economic research, was a consultant to Nugan Hand.
- Theodore G. Shackley, top clandestine officer at the CIA, had numerous dealings with Nugan Hand.
- Gordon (Billy) Young, CIA asset, represented Nugan Hand in the Golden Triangle drug zone of Southeast Asia.
- George Farris was a military intelligence specialist working in the Hong Kong office of Nugan Hand.

- Guy Pauker was an advisor to Henry Kissinger.
- Edwin Wilson, a CIA operative, had frequent dealings with Nugan Hand Bank.
- Thomas Clines, a CIA operative and deputy to Major General Richard Secord in the Iran-Contra arms network, had frequent dealings with Nugan Hand. After Nugan was killed, and before Australian authorities started investigating the bank, Clines rescued Houghton from Australia.
- Walter McDonald, former Deputy Director of the CIA, became a business consultant to Nugan Hand.

Massive Cover-Up of the CIA Operation

Many people holding check-and-balance responsibilities covered up for the Nugan Hand scheme. These checks and balances included the oversight agencies in Australia; the Reserve Bank in Australia that had responsibilities over Nugan Hand; Citicorp, which traded securities with Nugan Hand; taxing authorities in Australia, who were familiar with Nugan Hand's operation; the accounting firm that certified the Nugan Hand records; U.S. Consul General in Australia who knew of the CIA operation; the Premier of Australia, who had offices adjacent to Nugan Hand; Irving Trust Company, the correspondent bank for Nugan Hand in the United States; Corporate Affairs Commission in Australia that stonewalled requests for information; prominent Australian lawyers who worked closely with Nugan Hand; Australian Department of Commerce, who had considerable information about Nugan Hand's activities; Australian intelligence agencies that worked with U.S. intelligence agencies, and who knew about the rogue operations, and others.

After Nugan's body was found, intense activities were initiated to destroy evidence linking Nugan Hand Bank to the CIA. Retired three-star U.S. General Leroy J. Manor (formerly chief of staff for all U.S. forces in Asia and the Pacific), who had been head of Nugan Hand's Philippine office, tried to have the wire services block the reporting of Nugan's death. Recently retired Rear Admiral Earl P. Yates (formerly chief of staff for strategic planning for U.S. forces in the Pacific and Asia) flew to Australia to direct the shredding of documents. Yates was president of Nugan Hand, and lived near CIA headquarters at Langley, Virginia. Michael Hand joined in the shredding. Maurice Houghton and his lawyer, Michael Moloney, also arrived. Hand threatened lower-level employees, stating if Maloney's orders to sanitize the files before the law arrived weren't followed, "terrible things would happen; your wives would be cut up and returned to you in bits and pieces." (*Wall Street Journal*, August 24, 1982.)

Two in a series of *Wall Street Journal* articles (August 25 and 26,

1982) described Nugan Hand Bank as a drug and arms-related operation, staffed by CIA and military personnel. The articles stated in part:

> Nugan Hand bank was deeply involved in moving funds about the world for big international heroin dealers...U.S. servicemen are big losers in failure of Nugan Hand Bank.

Australia Blocking Investigation

Australia's Royal Commission on Drugs found so much evidence of drug and drug-money trafficking by the CIA operation that it recommended a separate Royal Commission be appointed just for the bank's operations. But Australia's intelligence agency, ASIO, blocked an investigation, reflecting the common practice of intelligence agencies protecting each other rather than their own country. U.S. officials stymied every attempt by Australian authorities to obtain information about Nugan Hand Bank.

During its investigation, the Royal Commission found that drugs were flown into a landing strip by former Air America pilot K.L. "Bud" King and Michael Hand. The strip was on a real estate development promoted by U.S. singer Pat Boone and financed by wealthy shipping magnate D.K. Ludwig. King, who also worked for the Boone-Ludwig project, whose testimony could have been very damaging to Nugan Hand and U.S. officials, died mysteriously in a fall.

Australian authorities connected Nugan Hand not only to drug and arms transactions, but also to contract murders, of which there were several associated with Nugan Hand's demise. Australian lawyer John Aston and his law firm were found to represent Nugan Hand and various drug traffickers, and the law office was used as a drop point for money to be secretly deposited and moved by Nugan Hand.

The Australian investigations left no doubt that Nugan Hand management was heavily involved with drug dealers, including Khun Sa, the Golden Triangle's biggest opium producer.

Culture of Lies

One of the most pervasive traits of CIA-related companies is the lying by government officials, including those at the CIA, the State Department, the Defense Department, and elsewhere in government. Throughout these pages, in scandal after scandal, government officials "assured" the public that government officials were not involved. And the public swallows these denials, hook, line and sinker.

U.S. officials "assured" Australia's Prime Minister Malcolm Fraser that the United States had no connections to Nugan Hand Bank. These "assurances," given routinely to Americans by their government, were, of course, lies. Vice President George Bush, while visiting Australia, also gave his assurances that the CIA wasn't involved with Nugan

Hand Bank. In Australia, the CIA worked secretly with ASIO to topple Australia's Labor government led by Prime Minister Gough Whitlam.

Hand's death, and the sudden publicity focused on Nugan Hand Bank, caused its liquidation in April 1980. With its demise, the CIA company concentrating on arms and drug sales and money laundering had to be replaced with another company. That company is described in following chapters.

Nugan Hand Bank and the Sultan of Brunei

Nugan Hand bank conducted extensive banking business for the Sultan of Brunei, who was reportedly one of the richest individuals in the world. In one instance, the Sultan of Brunei provided $10 million for the Enterprise's subversion of Nicaragua. Oliver North, National Security Council staff member, gave the wrong account number in a Swiss bank and the $10 million ended up in someone else's bank account.

Among Firms Tied to Covert CIA Companies

The accounting firm of Price Waterhouse audited the books of Nugan Hand for several years, and gave it a clean bill of health, thereby covering up for the CIA activities. That same firm audited the books of other covert CIA companies, covering up for financial irregularities, and provided the same clean bill of health.

Citibank and Its Many Ties to Covert CIA Activities

Over the years as covert CIA operatives described their activities to me, several stated that they had ties with, or their superiors obtained for them positions with Citibank. Many years ago one of my first major CIA connections, Gunther Russbacher, described his placement with Citibank. More recently, a former FBI agent, Richard Taus,[27] described to me how military and covert operation officials provided him a position with Citibank after he left the Army and after returning from a covert trip to Central America and before being hired by the FBI.

Nugan Hand Ties to Major Banking Figures in U.S.

The Washington, D.C. office of Nugan Hand was headed by former Brig. Gen. Erle Cocke, Jr., who, along with former Admiral Earl Yates, was listed in papers filed with the U.S. Secretary of the Treasury as the principal offices for Nugan Hand in the nation's capital. The purpose of the filing was to register the Washington, D.C. office of the Nugan Hand bank. In his position with Nugan Hand Bank, Cocke received a monthly salary and other perks. Cocke had an office in Washington, D.C., and Bernie Houghton used it for carrying out Nugan Hand business. Cocke[28] also operated the public relations, lobbying, and consult-

---

[27] I describe Taus' experiences in *Defrauding America* and also the book, *The FBI, CIA, the Mob, and Treachery*.

[28] Cocke served as national commander of the American Legion during

ing firm of Cocke and Phillips that had its offices in Washington, D.C.

It was believed that Cocke and Phillips International, of which Cocke and Gen. Eugene Phillips were the principals, was and is a covert off-the-books CIA company. That company had connections to Nugan Hand Bank and to another covert CIA company, Associated Traders Corporation.

A lawsuit filed in the late 1980s against Associated Traders Corporation caused CIA Director William Webster to seek a court order placing a secrecy lid on the case. Syndicated columnist Jack Anderson, in a series of articles, accused Associated Traders Corporation of various CIA activities, involving military weapon sales and money laundering. Cocke was alleged to be involved in that company.

Project Hammer and Brigadier General Cocke

Cocke was heavily involved with highly secret project called Project Hammer, a covert and complex money-moving operation involving banks throughout the world. In April 2000, shortly before he died of pancreatic cancer, Cooke[29] gave a sworn deposition stating many facts about Project Hammer and his involvement in CIA and complex financial operations.

Cocke testified that Project Hammer was started by some unknown people in high government positions, that much of the money was diverted into covert activities, and that it was started as a secret program to repatriate dollar assets from several prior decades, starting with World War II. This also involved much of the gold bullion hidden in the Philippines by the Japanese during World War II. Cocke testified:

> *It was mainly to bring monies back to the United States from all types of activities, both legitimately and illegitimately. Not that they were in the smuggling business per se, but they were all in the arms business; they were all retracing dollars of one description or another that had accumulated all through the 40s and 50s. And that probably is as broad a definition as I can give you. All kinds of nationalities were involved, and all kinds of people became involved.*

Everyone In On the Act!

Cocke was asked if various agents of the U.S. government were involved, to which Cocke replied:

---

the last 1940s and early 1950s, a director at Delta Airlines, and operated the Nugan Hand office in Washington, D.C.

[29] Earle Cocke came from a family of bankers. His father was president of Fulton National Bank that became part of Bank of America. Later, the father was president of the American Bankers Association and then chairman of the FDIC.

Yes. Obviously the CIA, the FBI, the national security agencies of all types, and the Pentagon in the broadest sense; and the Treasury, Federal Reserve. Nobody got out of the act; everybody wanted to get in the act.

Citibank Closely Involved With CIA Covert Activities

Included in his sworn testimony was that Citibank was the main bank involved, especially the New York and Athens offices, with many other banks acting as correspondent to Citibank, and that Citibank was the disbursing bank.

Additional Information Concerning General Cocke

During 2005 I received several e-mails from a person who worked with General Cocke before Cocke's death in 2000. He confirmed some of the statements I made in *Defrauding America* and *Disavow*. The person, who was still in covert activities, identified himself only as "Clark." The following are some of the statements he made in his emails to me:

I have attached a copy of my credential which were authorized by General Cocke. There were only seven of us and we were known as the seven deadly sins. We were his best-kept secret. This card was issued a few months before he passed away in April of 2000.

Cocke had a Special Operations Team that was formed in the early 80s. This team was not part of the government per se. It was made up of ex-military guys such as myself. If the General wanted something done that had to be kept secret from everyone, he called on what he called "his Team." I was the Team Commander so I knew most of what went on.

Most everything that went on with General Cocke was highly secret. I knew he had secret meetings with many of the presidents.

Cocke was one of the most powerful and feared men in Washington, D.C. Although he was behind the scenes, he was calling the shots. He did a lot of secret banking all over the world for the government and died a very wealthy man.

Cocke would provide me with passports from other countries as well as U.S. passports under different names. He and several others ran everything. Admiral Turned and two other Generals, one army and the other Air Force, were all part of the group that was headed by Cocke. The General and his group needed his own people with no influence from the outside; therefore he formed a Special Operations Team, which was sometimes just called "The Team." Basically, the Team didn't exist to anyone other than Cocke and his group and I'm not sure how much the group even knew about us. If we showed up somewhere, the story was we were never there and we don't exist. Just like Area 51 a few years ago.

It was not part of the Special Operations Command and was basically an entity of its own made up of ex-military personnel. His reasoning for using ex-military guys was, if something went wrong they could deny our existence completely and prove we were not on military payroll. I had to sign a secrecy agreement with Cocke and I still keep those secrets.

I was in charge of the team for Cocke and still have the team together. Some of the members have changed, but the team still exists. Shortly before the General passed away, he told me to keep the team intact because we would be called upon again to continue working for different government agencies to serve our country.

Cocke would provide me with appointments with other governments as Trade Attaché or Ambassador at Large or military attaché that would allow me to move freely in and out of other countries using diplomatic passports, therefore never showing an exit stamp on my U.S. passport.

When I would ask, "Who do I say I work for if questioned," his response was, "When it's not convenient for you to say you work for CIA then you say D.O.D., When it's not convenient to say you work for D.O.D., and then say CIA, but you always work for me and I will keep you out of trouble."

Anything and everything we did was secret and clandestine. Nothing was ever over.

Hope this is helpful to you.

Thank you again for your response. It is a pleasure knowing you are providing the American people with the truth. Everything I have been seen written by you is truth.

God Bless You,

Clark.

In a May 28, 2005 e-mail from the same person, providing additional information about General Cocke, he stated:

> *All I can tell you about those operations is, I secretly worked for General Cocke Jr. from 1972 until 2002. I do know, what your book says, is true.*
>
> *God bless you,*
>
> *Clark*

In another e-mail, he stated:

I don't think it's very safe to talk about most of the things I am aware of. I am fully aware of how easy it is for the government to make people disappear when they don't like what you are saying. My under-

standing is that the only reason you are 82 is because if they made you disappear it would add credibility to your books, which would make people realize you are telling the truth. So for you, your books are like an insurance policy.

I am presently working with a member of the president's roundtable, John P. Curry, ex-military, ex-Company. He was also a secret advisor to four presidents and at one time almost killed General Westmoreland with his bare hands. John is around 70 years old. I'm sure if you ask your company contacts about John Curry you will get many stories. John and I have formed a partnership and we are working on several secret projects now.

Clark

In another email relating to Cocke and the procedure for hiding huge quantities of money, he stated:

I can tell you from the days of JFK, Erle Cocke was responsible for setting up ways to hide large amounts of money all over the globe. This money belonged to Senators, congressmen, and high ranking White House officials up to and including the President during each changing administration, up to the time of the General's death in April of 2000. Which means, the General worked for every president from JFK to GW Bush to find ways to hide and launder money for the government or government agencies such as the CIA.

There was a Navy Captain and also Admiral Stansfield Turner, ex CIA director, who were close to the General and often had lunch or dinner with him to discuss business. Meetings were often held at the Mayflower hotel.

He also was the key negotiator who set up the ownership of the HSBC bank[30] *by the CIA among other well-known world banks. The Special Operations Team, known as the SDS (Seven Deadly Sins) were there to escort documents, currency, bank instruments and gold on behalf of the General. Our other function was to eliminate any person or entity that threatened the success of the mission by any means necessary.*

According to the General, everything he did was sanctioned by the White House, which is why he could and did provide us with many different passports and identities. The General would set us up with diplomatic appointments for other countries, which would allow us to move freely throughout the world, allowing us to carry or ship just

---

[30] HSBC Bank has over 100 million customers in 79 countries, with branches in the United States, Asia, China, Brazil, and Hong Kong. It was originally an Asian bank until it took over the Midland Bank in the United Kingdom in 1992.

about anything from one country to another under diplomatic protection.

When I received the appointment to Gambia as Ambassador-At-Large and Trade attaché, it was the General who wrote the letter of recommendation. Also, when I was appointed Consul General for another African country, it was the General who pushed my papers through at the State Department.

From what I have been told by the General, he would orchestrate the secret ownership of world banks. He told me the public perception of ownership is one thing but the reality of who really owns or controls the bank is something else. When the General died in April of 2000 he was one of the owners of Bank of America and worth millions.

The above statements are true to the best of my recollection. If you have specific questions, feel free to ask. If I can answer them, I will. I will not go against the CIA. As you well know, they will end my life.

Clark

In a February 27, 2006, e-mail:

One of the things that General Cocke told me he helped set up was a secret wing at Leavenworth. If the government wants you out of the way, a team will extract you from your home and you will be taken directly to Leavenworth where you are put in front of a panel of four Naval officers who will read you the charges against you.

If you piss off the wrong person, your life as you know it will be over. I would be very careful about what you say regarding the CIA; that is very dangerous ground. They have unlimited funding and work outside the law as you well know. I personally believe the country is beyond repair at this point.

I wish you well,

Clark.

In response to my comments about one of my contacts, Steve Crittenden, the former head of a secret CIA airline, and whose covert activities are extensively described in several of my books, he provided me related information. For instance, he described having recently flown loads of gold from the Philippines to the United States:

> *I did many of those trips to Manila, negotiating deals to bring back C-130s and C-131s with gold bars. Most of them went back to Atlanta or a private airstrip in Florida, the last one of those trips was a couple of years ago because it was after the death of General Cocke, and I was very concerned about doing the trip with new people involved, especially ones I had never met or worked with. On one of the trips I got into a hand-to-hand situation and I was*

cut on my left leg all the way to the bone about 11 inches long. It was not pretty and I also took a bullet in my left knee on one other occasion.

In 2002, Stephen Crittenden, the former head of a covert CIA airline, was flying a load of bank certificates from Manila to Lexington, Kentucky, having chartered a Lockheed 1011 jet solely for that purpose. Department of Justice personnel arrested him upon arrival in Lexington, charged him with having financial forgeries, and Crittenden was sentenced to seven years in prison.

That operation had similarities to the Japanese plunder located in the Philippines, and to other companies holding bank CDs in Lexington that were part of the Japanese plunder schemes. For some reason, Crittenden, who had been very open with me for years on covert activities, suddenly ended communications.

Irony of the Gold Shipments

During the late 1940s, Transocean Airlines, based in Oakland, with extensive operations throughout the world, was hauling a load of gold, having departed Clark Air Force Base in the Philippines for Wake Island. Enroute, the aircraft lost two engines, and to maintain altitude, the crew threw the gold overboard.

The captain was a very likeable guy, a Texan, Rand Reid. I also was a captain for that airline, and we would joke with him about having dumped an entire load of gold into the ocean and a year later he invests in a gold mine.

The *Saturday Evening Post* in 1950 ran a three-series of articles on the unusual airline, calling the series, "The Daring Young Men of Transocean Airlines." Ernie Gann, the author of numerous books and movies based on the books, including *Island in the Sky* and *The High and the Mighty* was a pilot for Transocean Airlines. As long as I am alive, I have a web site about the airline: www.transoceanairlines.com.

CIA Starting A Replacement Financial Operation Based in Honolulu: BBRDW

As the Nugan Hand operation was coming under suspicion, the CIA started in 1979 another covert operation based in Honolulu with offices throughout the world. That covert operation was called Bishop, Baldwin, Rewald, Dillingham and Wong (BBRDW) and used many former military and intelligence personnel. By the end of 1980, BBRDW began setting up offices in such former Nugan Hand locations as Hong Kong, Taiwan, Indonesia, Singapore, New Zealand, London, Paris, Stockholm, Brazil, Chile, and Australia.

The offices were staffed with over 30 CIA agents, including some of the same high-level people that operated Nugan Hand Bank: Gen. Edwin Black; Gen. Leroy Manor; Adm. Lloyd Vasey; Adm. Earl Yates; Walter McDonald; Maurice Houghton, and others. It is common for military personnel to be sheep-dipped into the CIA and other intelligence groups. The CIA made Ronald Rewald the head of the covert CIA office in Honolulu.

Covert Funding for CIA Proprietaries

Part of the covert funding for BBRDW came from other CIA-related companies. Money usually came in response to fictitious bills sent by BBRDW to covert CIA companies, such as law firms and public relations firms, for work that was never done. These companies were located in California, Virginia, Hong Kong and Paris.

BBRDW was active in numerous covert CIA activities, including:

- Supplying arms to Taiwan, India, and other countries, which was unlawful under federal law, but carried out under CIA orders.
- Setting up banking and trust companies for CIA money laundering.
- Secretly acquiring Japan's secret plans for the Japanese High Speed Surface Transport (HSST) by paying a $27,000 bribe to a Japanese businessman.
- Targeting foreign political, military and business leaders whose funds were placed in accounts alongside money obtained through clandestine CIA operations.
- Funding worldwide CIA operations, including assassinations.
- Soliciting private investors in order to appear like a legitimate international investment concern, commingling their funds with those of the CIA.
- During the Falklands War, Rewald traveled to Chile and Argentina under cover of playing polo, obtaining intelligence information for the CIA.
- Targeting foreign political, military and business leaders whose funds were placed in accounts alongside money obtained through clandestine CIA operations

Innocence in an Area of Corrupt Activities

Rewald was director and chief operating officer of BBRDW. In an e-mail to me he stated:

> *I didn't run all the covert operations that were tasked through that cover [BBRDW]. That's why they had compartmentalization. We had 22 covert CIA agents working out of that cover in Honolulu alone, not to mention seven other offices worldwide. I didn't know what everyone was doing, nor did I give orders to all of them. I can only speak for myself and the operations I was assigned to do.*

His CIA handlers, including Welch, Kindschi and Richardson, directed many of the covert CIA operations. Many of the details of the company's local and foreign operations were kept from Rewald. He was kept uninformed about the more lurid activities carried over from the Nugan Hand operation.

Meeting Enrique Zobel and Sultan of Brunei

Among the people that Rewald met and socialized with were Enrique Zobel and the Sultan of Brunei, both extremely wealthy people with Southeast Asia. Enrique Jacobo Emilio Zobel was a prominent Philippine businessman, the chief executive of the Ayala Corporation and in frequent contact with President Ferdinand Marcos, and aware of Marcos' financial holdings. In 1990, Zobel[31] established the Enrique Zobel Foundation, which focuses on social and economic development projects in Calatagan, Batangas.

Sultan's Offer to Have Rewald as Partner in Business Venture

Rewald knew he needed headquarters' assistance on this one, and he knew they would be only too happy to help. The Sultan asked Rewald to please look into the matter and let him know when he had reached a conclusion. Rewald assured him he would.

Zobel introduced an idea he had recently been considering. Ayala Corporation, of which he was Chairman of the Board, had an investment in Sotogrande, Spain. It was a magnificent polo real estate development and he thought the potential was very high indeed. He felt that it was wrongly purchased by Ayala and needed personalized care. He also thought it was a wonderful investment to personally enjoy.

Signing Contract for Joint Venture: Sultan and Rewald

After more very informative conversation, Tim Holzer buzzed Rewald and said that he had the corporation papers prepared if the new partners wanted to sign them. Rewald told him to come right over. In less than fifteen minutes, Zobel and Rewald signed the papers and established Ayala of Hawaii. Rewald, Zobel and the Sultan all shook hands. They all knew that they would be seeing a lot more of each other.

Zobel's Knowledge of Ferdinand, CIA and Gold Plunder Matters

As stated in other pages, Zobel testified before a Philippine panel, as reported in The *Philippine Inquirer*, describing his frequent contacts with President Ferdinand Marcos and his knowledge of the Yamashita gold and President Ferdinand Marcos' hoard containing tons of the gold and the certificates of gold deposits in banks throughout the world.

---

[31] Zobel died on May 17, 2004. His son, Iñigo Zobel, carries on his extensive business interests.

Procedure for Communications with CIA Headquarters

Rewald knew the routine, so he knew Rardin went straight to the vault and started transmitting the report to Langley. Information is always sent to CIA headquarters in two parts; one transmittal includes cryptonym of source or agent and is for internal use only. The other pages list the text. Every report has an address line that gives its destination, followed by a slug line, which directs the way the report is to be disseminated within the CIA. In almost all cases, material is transmitted electronically and stored in computers.

Each communication has designed levels of importance: from Critic, Flash, Immediate, Priority, and Routine. The first two are rarely used other than war or crisis time. Most reports go to Directorate of Intelligence, marked Routine, and they use it to prepare estimates and other memos through the National Intelligence Council and will likely shape the future of the world's events. Other cable traffic is used to receive and report on assigned missions and operations.

Sultan of Brunei Transferring $7 Billion

Within the year the Sultan of Brunei transferred seven billion dollars into two U.S. financial institutions that were recommended by Ronald Rewald. The new Ayala Corporation operation in Hawaii enabled Rewald to develop high-level political and economic sources in the Middle East. He had cultivated Saud Mohammed of the United Arab Emirates, a powerful member of OPEC, and entered into joint ventures with him.

BBRDW CIA Bank Accounts in Foreign Locations to Facilitate Money Laundering

Offshore accounts for BBRDW were opened in New Zealand and the Cook Islands with the help of Richard Spiker and Reuben Taylor, a director of South Pacific Trust Corporation (and a BBRDW consultant). These accounts were opened specifically to launder CIA operational funds. A secret branch BBRDW office was opened by the CIA in New Delhi, India, leasing the former Russian Embassy building.

State Department and Drug Smuggling

While Rewald was head of BBRDW, he was asked by Richard Armitage, from the State Department, to use BBRDW for laundering drug money from CIA operations. Rewald responded that the company did not have expertise in these areas and he didn't want to get involved in them. Rewald's CIA handler, Richardson, later told Rewald that CIA people in BBRDW and its subsidiaries *had the expertise* to handle these matters, and made reference to former Pan American pilot Ned Avary. At a later time, Rewald learned that Ned Avary, General Hunter Harris, and Richard Armitage, were involved in these areas. I describe more details of Armitage's involvement in CIA drug smuggling in *Drugging*

America and *Defrauding America.*

Honolulu TV Reporter Disclosed BBRDW Irregularities

In 1983, a Honolulu television reporter broadcast irregularities that she had discovered about BBRDW. Her broadcasts caused Washington CIA and Department of Justice personnel to concoct a scheme to prevent BBRDW as being seen as a covert CIA operation. The scheme is described in great detail in *Explosive Secrets of Covert CIA Companies*, and consisted essentially of the following, with the cooperation of a federal judge and U.S. Department of Justice personnel:

- Charge Rewald with conducting a sham financial operation.
- Block the introduction of CIA documents showing it to be a CIA operation.
- Block the testimony of CIA personnel willing to testify for Rewald.
- Refuse to allow famous San Francisco attorney Melvin Belli to represent Rewald, and instead, assign to him for defense a young just-graduated lawyer with no trial experience.
- In the process occurred the suspicious death of a potential CIA witness who was killed shortly before he was to testify, while piloting his small plane from a private airstrip near Santa Rosa, California.

Prison Sentence Resulting from Corrupt Federal Judges, Federal Prosecutors, CIA, and Other Key Government Personnel

The corrupt acts of key people in the federal government and a gullible jury resulted in Rewald being sentenced to a long prison term. The trial and the CIA involvement had received worldwide attention—except in the United States where U.S. media people and media corporations did their usual cover-up. Prison was especially hard for Rewald due to a physical injury he received from his involvement in polo matches with Enrique Zobel. (Zobel also received a serious polo injury in 1991.)

Ronald Rewald was finally granted a pardon after ten long years in prison. The corrupt DOJ prosecutors, CIA personnel, and the federal judge that assisted in the criminal cover-up, were never prosecuted!

Upon his release, Rewald turned over to me three legal-size boxes of CIA documents, in addition to one similar box of documents released to me by the Melvin Belli office in San Francisco.

Explosive Disclosures of CIA-Funded Bank Accounts for High-Level Officials

Deeply imbedded in these documents was an envelope labeled "Lawyer-Client information." The envelope contained a sheet typed by Rewald listing the names of certain U.S. politicians for which BBRDW funded secret bank accounts. The information in this envelope included information from Rewald's confidential "Green Book" that the CIA sought to get. The information listed high-level people with secret CIA-funded accounts. The names on the left side of the notes were the aliases Rewald used to identify the people on the right for which there were secret bank accounts opened and funded by the CIA through BBRDW.

Irwin M. Peach	Vice President George Bush
Mr. Bramble	Vice President George Bush
Commander Quinstar	General Hunter Harris
Mr. Apan	Robert W. Jinks
Mr. Grey	Robert Allen
Farrah Fawn	Jackie Vos
General Shake	Arnold Braswell[32]
Mr. Branch	Richard Armitage[33]
Mr. Denile	CIA Director William Casey[34]
Slimey Affirm	CIA Legal Counsel Stanley Sporkin[35]
Captain Perjury	Ned Avary
Attorney Doright	Robert Smith

General Hunter Harris:

General Hunter Harris was commander in chief of Pacific Air Forces. In 1964 he became commander of the Pacific Air Forces, Hickam Air Force Base, in Hawaii. He "retired" in 1967, or was sheep-dipped into the CIA, and later joined BBRDW. He died on March 5, 1987, shortly after the cover was blown on the CIA proprietary.

General Arnold Braswell:

He was in the U.S. Army and his highest rank was Lt. General. In the book, *Drugging America*, I made the following reference to him.

Arnold Braswell was commander-in-chief of U.S. Pacific Air Force (CINCPAC). Rewald's notes also indicated that fictitious names were used to hide money for Philippine President Ferdinand and Imelda Marcos, among others. Richard Armitage was U.S. Assistant Secretary of Defense and reportedly heavily involved with drug trafficking while in Vietnam. William Casey was Director of the Central Intelligence Agency. Stanley Sporkin was legal counsel for the CIA, and then a federal judge in Washington, D.C. In this capacity, he unlawfully dismissed one of my federal actions seeking to expose the government

[32] Arnold Braswell was Commander-in-Chief of U.S. Pacific Air Force (CINCPACAF).

[33] Richard Armitage was U.S. Assistant Secretary of Defense and reportedly heavily involved with drug trafficking while in Vietnam.

[34] William Casey, Director of Central Intelligence.

[35] Stanley Sporkin was legal counsel for the CIA, and then a federal judge in Washington, D.C. In this capacity he unlawfully dismissed one of my federal actions seeking to expose the government corruption in which he was involved.

corruption in which he was involved.

These notes, written by Rewald over ten years earlier when he was head of BBRDW, provided additional evidence of U.S. officials hiding their money in secret bank accounts overseas. The accounts were in financial institutions in Hong Kong, Switzerland, and the Caymans.

Information on another sheet that I found in Rewald's papers revealed activities engaged in by CIA agents embedded into BBRDW and its various subsidiaries. These are the activities in which Rewald refused to get involved, including CIA drug trafficking.

These notes revealed other activities that I hadn't known about earlier. While Rewald was hospitalized in Honolulu, sources kept him informed of some activities being taken to remove and hide the funds from BBRDW and subsidiary accounts. General Hunter Harris called President George Bush to alert him that the cover on BBRDW had been blown, and wanted instructions as to how to proceed. CIA head, William Casey, then called Robert W. Jinks, and told him to work with Robert Allen. Jinks was then ordered to proceed to Texas to get bank account numbers and then go to the Cayman Islands where the accounts were located.

Rewald's notes indicated that someone from CIA headquarters at Langley, or an associate of Robert Allen, eventually went to the Cayman Islands and moved BBRDW funds to another offshore country. Robert Smith, who wasn't directly involved in the money transfer but aware something was going on, learned that a General in Texas was to give Robert Jinks bank account information and that he, Robert Smith, was to go to the Caymans to retrieve the hidden money. General Arnold Braswell was to assist in this removal, but because of stress and his drinking problem, he was too unreliable and was not used.

Similar efforts were being taken to remove funds from BBRDW and subsidiary accounts in Hong Kong and Switzerland. About this time, funds were being received from secret arms sales and Rewald said that Ned Avary diverted these funds away from BBRDW.

While these events were taking place, Robert Allen sought to force Jackie Vos to disclose the whereabouts of the Green Book that listed these accounts so as to destroy the records.

Forbes Magazine Reported Similar Financial Irregularities

Former senior editor of *Forbes* magazine, James Norman, had reports (*Media Bypass*, February 1996) that a secret group in the intelligence community, outraged at what was going on, infiltrated bank money transfer systems and discovered large quantities of money sequestered in overseas bank accounts for government figures. One of these people was allegedly Vincent Foster, President Clinton's personal attorney, who made a number of one-day trips to Switzerland to conduct bank activities.

Richard Armitage:

Armitage was associated with the CIA and during this period he was involved with the CIA's Phoenix Program while the U.S. invaded Vietnam. That program killed a reported 20,000 to 40,000 people suspected of not supporting the invasion of their country. He worked with the office of the U.S. Defense Attaché in Saigon. After the United States withdrew from Vietnam, Armitage worked for the U.S. Department of Defense in Washington, and served in Iran until November 1976, after which he moved to Bangkok and operated an import-export business. In 1980, Armitage was a foreign policy advisor to President-elect Ronald Reagan, and then became Deputy Assistant Secretary of Defense for East Asia.

Armitage was confirmed by the U.S. Senate for Deputy Secretary of State on March 23, 2001. He was a close associate of Secretary of State Colin Powell, dating back to their days in Vietnam. In this position, he urged military action against Iraq. According to Pakistan President Musharraf, after 9/11, Armitage demanded that Pakistan cooperate with attacks upon Al Qaeda or the United States would consider Pakistan an enemy and "bomb it back to the stone age." Armitage left his government post in February, 2005.

Stanley Sporkin:

Stanley Sporkin was a Washington, D.C. lawyer in 1960 and 1961, and from 1961 to 1981 he worked for the Securities and Exchange Commission. From 1974 to 1981 he was director of the Division of Enforcement from 1974 to 1981. He was general counsel for the Central Intelligence Agency from 1981 to 1986. He was appointed by President Ronald Regan to a federal judge in the U.S. district courts in the District of Columbia in the later part of 1985. He retired from the courts on January 15, 2000. Thereafter, he became a member of a private consultancy called Gavel Consulting Group.

Admiral Earl Yates:

Admiral Earl Yates was involved in the U.S. strategic planning for the Far East and president of Nugan Hand Bank. In my prior book, *Explosive Secrets of Covert CIA Companies*, I wrote the following about Yates:

> The CIA staffed many of its covert CIA companies with former military personnel. (Or military personnel sheep-dipped into the company position.) This was especially evident in the covert CIA companies described within these pages, starting with Nugan Hand Bank.

Far Eastern Economic Review had the headline, "A Former Admiral Commands Our Private Bank," and described the role played by Adm. Earl Yates. The article stated in part:

> When Admiral Yates exchanged the gold stripes of an admiral for the pin stripes of a banker, he brought added strength to Nugan Hand International Private Bankers. He brought the experience of a man who administered the office that controls a powerful navy. He brought the executive experience of a man that controlled the careers of tens of thousands of men.

Another of the high military personnel with Nugan Hand was General Leroy J. Manor. (He had been involved with Marcos in negotiating a ten-year lease for the Clark Air Force Base in the Philippines. Manor was part of the team investigating the failed rescue of the 52 American hostages in Iran.)

General Edwin Black:

General Edwin Black had possibly the most extensive intelligence background of the people at Nugan Hand Bank and BBRDW. He started under Allan Dulles and Richard Helms, both of whom became CIA directors. He was a member of the National Security Council in the Eisenhower administration; he was a member of the team associated with the negotiations for U.S. military bases in the Philippines in 1956. He was in charge of U.S. Army troops in Vietnam during the U.S. invasion. He died in Honolulu in 1985.

Gen. Black[36] was another military officer who was sheep-dipped into covert CIA operations. Black headed the Nugan Hand office in Honolulu. He was also a key person in the Pacific Forum, a Honolulu-based organization in the 1970s.[37] He was quoted in a series of articles appearing in the *Wall Street Journal* as being involved in the Nugan Hand Bank. He operated the Nugan Hand office in Honolulu, until the bank folded in 1980. Black shifted from the CIA's Nugan Hand Bank to BBRDW Bank in Honolulu that had branches in the same Far East locations as the former Nugan Hand Bank.

Admiral Lloyd R. Vasey:

While serving in the Pacific, he helped supervise the withdrawal of U.S. forces from Vietnam. He also ran the Pacific Forum, which some say was a CIA front operation. He was part of the CIA's Nugan Hand Bank operation.

---

[36] Black was in the Office of Strategic Services (OSS) during World War II, and then became part of the CIA.

[37] Gen. Edwin Black commanded the deployment of army troops in Vietnam in the early days of the Vietnam War. He died in 1985 after he was shown as being involved in another covert CIA company in Honolulu.

Brigadier General Erle Cocke:

Cocke was associated with the CIA Nugan Hand Bank, and operated Cocke and Phillips International out of the same offices as Nugan Hand Bank. He later became a director at Delta Airlines and then a national commander of the American Legion.

Fictitious Names for Secret Bank Accounts for President Marcos

Rewald's notes also indicated that fictitious names were used to hide money for Philippine's President Ferdinand Marcos and his wife, Imelda. Rewald wrote these notes over ten years earlier while he was head of BBRDW. They provided additional evidence of people in high-level U.S. positions facilitating the hiding of secret bank deposits for Marcos obtained from the Japanese gold plunder—and what he had stolen from Santa Romana—another CIA asset.

Cooperation of U.S. Bankers in Drug-Money Laundering

In one of my other books I describe the testimony by CIA agent Felix Rodriguez[38] revealing details of the many U.S. banks cooperating in CIA money laundering and the use of special representatives. Among the banks he named were "Citibank, Citicorp, Bank of America, First National Bank of Boston," and the competition among U.S. banks to receive the drug-money. These are the same banks that cooperated with the placement of the gold and funds associated with the retrieved Japanese plunder in the Philippines. And also the banks that cooperated by declaring bank certificates of deposits to be forgeries—without fear of consequences from U.S. regulators.

Describing the power of the drug cartels in Colombia, Rodriguez testified that the cartels owned airlines, soccer teams, radio and TV stations, newspapers, and "politicians." Rodriguez described how Colombia's M-19 kidnapped "one of the Ochoa women [Leona]," how the individual drug traffickers merged into a group, and formed its own army of 2,000 people. This testimony coincided with what other CIA assets had stated to me, including Gunther Russbacher, Trenton Parker, Russell Bowen, and others.

Rodriguez testified that drug proceeds were used to fund the contra fighting. In the book, *Drugging America,* I wrote the following:

Richard Brenneke[39] was asked during a congressional hearing: "Let's take a payment from Mr. Reale in cash, and follow the procedure

[38] Felix Rodriguez was a Central Intelligence Agency officer involved in the Bay of Pigs invasion of Cuba with ties to the Iran-Contra affair to the George H.W. Bush. He was testifying before Congress.

[39] Richard Brenneke was a CIA agent during the Iran-Contra affair, and testified in a congressional hearing.

step-by-step as you know it for the transmittal of that money from the Gotti organization to the Central Intelligence Agency."

That money was delivered to us in cash. There were occasions where there were wire transfers, but the generally followed method was cash. That would be stored in the aircraft on its return trip to Panama. Once it reached Panama, we would put it into a bank account, which at that time was in the Banquo de Panama.

And the account name was the initials, IFMA, which was a company that I set up in Panama City in 1970. The money would be subsequently and almost immediately transferred to Spain or Liechtenstein. From there it went to Monte Carlo, and the ultimate destination was Zurich or Geneva. But in any case, Switzerland.

"The money was given to you by the agent for the Gotti Organization?"

Yes sir. And there were other people besides the man that I've named.

Providing Detailed Records

Brenneke supplied the investigators with telephone records of that and other calls, providing further credibility to his statements. He identified the names of the CIA accounts that he had set up, offering the incorporation papers that were filed "in the late sixties and early seventies." Brenneke testified that he personally transferred money out of one account and into others. He testified that he discussed the money transfers with CIA employees Robert Kerritt and Robert Ellis.

Returning to questions about how the drug money from the Gotti crime family went into the CIA accounts, Brenneke explained:

I set up, in 1969 or 1970, a number of corporations in Panama City. Those corporations in turn opened bank accounts. Those bank accounts were accounts that I would normally use in the course of my business with the CIA to transfer money into the accounts, and from there to transfer them into specific accounts in Spain or, as I say, in some cases other countries in Europe. The ultimate destination was Switzerland, where those funds were. I knew where they went, because I'm the person who went in and gave the order to the banker to move them.

[Secret CIA Bank Accounts Overseas]

"And you had an arrangement with the CIA to organize those banks for the CIA, to open the account?"

That was what I specialized in doing. I laundered money there. When I was first recruited by the CIA, which was in 1968, 1969, all we were doing was selling mutual fund stock offshore.

"Name the banks [in which accounts were] opened for the CIA."

Panama City, Banquo DeMexico. At one point we were using a Citibank correspondent down there whose name escapes me. We had a man on-site who worked for us, as well as worked for Ron Martin, a man named Johnny Mollina. John would spend a lot of his time in Panama City and worked in one of the banks that we used. I set up more than one account in Madrid that was used.

I set up an account in Brussels at Bank Lambert that was regularly used. I set up accounts at Credit Suisse, a Swiss bank. And Bank of Credit & Commerce, commonly referred to as BCCI. Also, a bank that no longer exists called Bank Hoffman. I set up a bank in Panama City on behalf of the mutual fund company I worked for so that I could ultimately control how the transfers were handled.

"And you organized a bank in Panama for the CIA?"

I organized it for the company I worked for. It was subsequently used by the CIA, and it was used by members of the organized crime families. The bank was called U.S. Investment Bank. It really existed in Panama City. You could actually go in and open a check account there.

[Crime Family Money Laundered by CIA Operative]

"And the money that you got from the Gotti organization that you put on the airplane [in Arkansas] and returned to Panama on the next trip, you personally took to a bank in Panama City?"

Yes, I did. Let's take Banquo DePanama, the Panamanian National Bank down there, as an example. I would go in and meet with, for instance, Johnny Mollina. John worked for one of the banks down there. I think it was Citibank that he worked for at one time. In any case, I would go in. I knew the bank officers by name. And I would provide them with directions as to how the money was to be transferred and where to transfer.

That is, it was to be transferred by cashier's check and courier to Madrid in a specific account there, or it was just wire transferred to Madrid as a transfer of funds from IFMA, a Panamanian corporation, to IFMA's affiliates in Madrid or Brussels at Bank Lambert. They needed to know that. And then I would have to tell them at the other bank that money was coming into that account.

"So you would notify the CIA bank, or the bank having the CIA account in Spain or in Switzerland?"

Yes, that the deposit had been made in Panama.

"How would you notify them?"

Generally by telephone. And they would be told that...there were a variety of codes that were used, but the message was very simple. You're going to receive money in this account. The money will probably stay in the account anywhere from 24 to 72 hours, at which time it will be transferred out of that account.

[Bearer Bonds to Launder Drug Money]

"Did you ever utilize bearer bonds for the purpose of laundering money?"

Sure. It was handled in two ways. When U.S. Investment Bank was active in Panama it would issue bonds, no names on them, which was common. It's common in Europe. It's common in Central and South America. And those bonds actually belong to the individual that is carrying them, as, for instance, the stock in IFMA belongs only to the person who happens to have it in his hand at that moment. You lose it, you lose your money.

"And what would you do with the bearer bonds?"

The bearer bonds would be taken generally by courier, in some cases to Banquo DeMexico in Mexico City and transferred from there or sent from there by their couriers. By 1986, it was getting uncomfortable in Panama, and so some of the Venezuelan banks in Caracas were used. The same procedure was followed, though.

The money would be deposited into an account; you would walk into the bank, for example, and sit down with the Vice President or Managing Director of the bank. You were clearly a large depositor and a large customer of that bank. And you just simply explained that you wanted to deposit the money in this bag, and he would just kindly go ahead and do so for you.

[Drug Trafficking Controlled from Washington]

"Mr. Brenneke, under whose direction were you working in order to carry out the function of depositing the money from the sale of the drugs to the New York crime family?"

"Bob Kerritt, an officer of the Central Intelligence Agency in Washington, D.C."

Protesting the CIA Drug Involvement

Brenneke described his adverse reaction to discovering the CIA involvement in drug smuggling into the United States and the CIA's involvement with drug money laundering. In answer to a question, Brenneke testified:

When I found that we were bringing drugs into the United States, and that we were receiving money which was being put into accounts which I knew to belong to the United States government, as I'd set them up specifically for that purpose, I called Mr. Don Gregg, who was a CIA officer with whom I was acquainted, and complained about the nature of what we were doing.

Office of Vice President and President, and CIA, In Drug Trafficking and Drug-Money Laundering

Donald Gregg worked closely with George Bush when Bush was director of the CIA, and became his national security advisor when Bush was vice president of the United States. Bush later nominated Gregg to be Ambassador to South Korea. When asked about Gregg's response to Brenneke's concern about the drug trafficking, Brenneke testified:

I was told that it was not my business what I was flying in and out of the country. That I was hired to do specific things, and if I would do those things and not pay any attention to anything else, we would all be very, very happy. I didn't like that. He said shut up and do your job. I subsequently talked to Mr. Gregg on a number of occasions as well as to other people in the vice-president's office to voice my concern over the use of drugs, importing drugs into the United States.

Criminal and Subversive CIA Drug Smuggling Known Throughout Government

The overwhelming evidence of drug smuggling into the United States by people in or associated with the CIA, described in my books, *Defrauding America* and *Drugging America*, and scores of other books on the matter, clearly showed that government employees in the Department of Justice knew and were covering up for these major crimes against the United States and the subversive nature of it.

Further, with the United States having 16 intelligence groups, obviously, they knew of the criminal and subversive activities and became complicit in the crimes by covering up for them.

CIA Role in Looting Banks

Brenneke testified about the criminal charges made against Heinrich Rupp concerning looting the Aurora Bank in the Denver area, saying "that was common in our line of work with the CIA." When asked if Brenneke ever complained to CIA director William Casey about these activities, Brenneke replied:

Yes, I did on a number of occasions. And Mr. Casey's telephone logs would reflect phone calls to me, made to me in Lake Oswego, which was at that time the location of my office.

Testifying About Israel's Role in Drugging America

Brenneke testified about Israel's involvement in the drug smuggling operations, and that he had gone to Israel "because I tried everybody in the U.S. Government first, and they sure as hell weren't going to help" shut down the operations.

"Do you have any knowledge of the money coming from the Gotti organization being used for any other purposes, other than depositing in the bank accounts for the CIA?"

> *Sure. We had to run the operations at Nella, for instance. The training facilities at Nella had to be paid for. Nella was a training base for military and paramilitary folks from south of the border; Mexico, Panama.*[40] *The base was operated by the Central Intelligence Agency.*

Brenneke identified CIA agent Terry Reed as one of the flight instructors at a small airport in Arkansas at Nella Airport. Reed co-authored the book *Compromised* with John Cummings, describing the drug trafficking and money laundering in Arkansas and Mexico, and involving Arkansas personnel, including Governor Bill Clinton and some of his staff.

Moving CIA and Organized Crime Drug Money Back into the United States

"Did you establish an account in the United States to get that money back into this country?"

> *Yes, I did. I established an account at Brown Brothers Harriman in New York City around 1980. That's a bank in New York City.*

"How do you know that the money you picked up and that you received in Mena from the Gotti organization, and took to Panama, wired to bank accounts in Europe, came back to the United States?"

> *I ordered the transfer of funds.*

"And to whom did you report these actions?"

> *I reported them to Don Gregg, Bob Kerritt, Bob Ellis and from time-to-time other people. I not only have notes, I have letters that I wrote to some of these people. Copies of these letters were submitted to congressional investigators.*

---

[40] Nella Airport consisted of a small airstrip north of Mena that was used by the CIA for paramilitary and military training of personnel from Mexico and Central America, and used for training Contra pilots, during the Contra subversive activities.

Arkansas Attorney General's Attempt to Discredit Evidence

Chad Farris, Chief Deputy attorney General for the State of Arkansas, tried to discredit Brenneke:

> *"Why would you care about the use of drugs as part of this CIA plan? If you were so concerned about the use of drugs in the operation because of the reasons you've described, why did you continue to take part in the operation; what do you hope to achieve by testifying here today; what's the purpose of your testimony, to you personally?"*

These were rather stupid questions. Brenneke had repeatedly objected to the CIA drug trafficking and working with organized crime. Quitting an uncover operation of this nature gets people killed! Brenneke was testifying because he was asked to testify, something that other members of Congress had avoided doing earlier.

Bank Records and Documentation Corroborating Brenneke Testimony

Brenneke clearly testified, without hesitation, times, dates, places, and either telephone logs or notes that he made of conversations with his CIA handlers in Washington. Brenneke testified to, and provided the Congressional investigators with writings that he sent to his CIA bosses in Washington complaining about the CIA role in drug trafficking and drug-money laundering and its operation with major crime families in the United States. He provided the investigators with copies of bank records, corporation papers, and detailed testimony, wherein there could be little doubt that his testimony was true.

No Perjury Charges Filed Against Brenneke by DOJ

No perjury charges were ever filed against Brenneke for this testimony about the CIA drug crimes. If his testimony was perjured, Justice Department prosecutors would have immediately filed criminal perjury charges against him, as they did once before when DOJ employees tried to cover up for George Bush' s involvement in the scheme known as October Surprise. It would have also been a responsibility for congressional questioners to charge him with perjury if they felt his testimony was not true.

Important Ramifications

Despite the gravity of the testimony, revealing criminal and even subversive activities by key people in government, and the use of powerful government offices in the subversive activities, members of Congress, Department of Justice personnel, and the media, became complicit in the criminal and subversive conspiratorial, acts by covering up for them. That continued and protected the underlying corruption in government who's many tentacles inflicted, or caused or allowed to be inflicted, all types of grave harm to national security and the lives of the public.

DOJ's Prior Sham Perjury Charges
To Cover Up for October Surprise Operation

Brenneke testified about the Justice Department's sham perjury charges against him for testifying in a 1988 federal court trial in Denver concerning CIA operative Heinrich Rupp. Brenneke testified that he saw George Bush and Donald Gregg in Paris during the period of October 18, 19, and 20, 1980, which was a key point in the "October Surprise" operation (which is detailed in the book, *Defrauding America*).

Brenneke stated that in the Denver proceedings Justice Department attorneys offered him a plea agreement; plead guilty to perjury charges concerning his testimony about seeing Bush and Gregg in Paris and he would not receive any prison time or fine. Brenneke refused to commit perjury for DOJ personnel and refused to cover up for Bush's role in October Surprise. Brenneke went to trial and fortunately for him, the jury was smart enough to recognize the sham charges by the DOJ prosecutor. The jury found Brenneke not guilty.

Brenneke was involved in many other CIA activities. Tape recordings made of telephone conversations between Brenneke and Russbacher, in my possession, described their role in other CIA operations, including Operation Gladio, which sought to destabilize the Italian government in the 1950s.

Brenneke had given a speech at the University of Arkansas in 1991, which was videotaped, further describing the involvement of government personnel in drug smuggling into the United States.

Testimony by IRS Investigator Bill Duncan

William Duncan was an investigator for the Internal Revenue Service and spent several years investigating drug-related activities in Arkansas and the role played in these activities by Governor Bill Clinton, the Arkansas Development Finance Authority, Dan Lasater's brokerage business, and the Stephens' financial powerhouse. Duncan had functioned in the capacity of congressional investigator for the Subcommittee on Crime, and discovered the involvement of Arkansas officials and the CIA in drug trafficking and drug money laundering. Duncan was a criminal investigator for the U.S. Treasury Department from 1973 through 1989.

In addition to what Duncan stated to me, I received a transcript of his congressional testimony, marked Confidential, given to a Joint Investigation by the United States Congress and the Arkansas State Attorney General's Office in June 1991. Duncan testified that one of his assignments was to "investigate allegations of money laundering in connection with the Barry Seal organization, which was based at the Mena,

Arkansas airport." Duncan testified in detail about the drug-money laundering he uncovered, involving the CIA, and how attorneys with the Department of Justice repeatedly blocked investigations and prosecutions.

Pattern of Justice Department Obstruction of Justice

Duncan found, as I had in the past, that Justice Department attorneys routinely covered up for major corruption involving high-level government personnel. Duncan testified about the tactics used by Justice Department employees to protect the CIA and the people working with the CIA in drug trafficking and drug-money laundering.

DOJ Blocking Testimony About CIA Drug Smuggling in Arkansas

Duncan testified that important witnesses were not called by the U.S. Attorney to testify before the Grand Jury; that important witnesses with valuable information were not allowed to present it, being limited literally to giving their name, address, phone number, and type of employment. Duncan testified that the vice-president of Union Bank in Mena, Gary Gardner, wanted to testify about the CIA money laundering and how Justice Department prosecutors blocked his testimony.

Duncan testified that he gave U.S. Attorney Asa Hutchinson in Fort Smith, Arkansas, the names of 20 witnesses for the grand jury investigation, all of whom had direct knowledge and evidence of drug-money laundering. Of the three witnesses called by the U.S. Attorney, Duncan testified that two of them were angry because the U.S. Attorney refused to allow them to give meaningful evidence to the grand jury.

Referring to the huge profits received by the CIA from the drug trafficking, the affidavit continued:

Edwin Wilson explained that the profit from the sale of narcotics was laundered through a series of banks. Wilson stated that over 70% of the profits were laundered through the banks in Panama. The remaining percentage was funneled through Swiss banks with a small remainder being handled by banks within the United States.

I understood that some of the profits in Panamanian banks arrived through Israeli Couriers. I became aware of that fact from normal conversations with some of the embassy personnel assigned to the Embassy in Panama. Wilson also stated that an associate whom I don't know also aided in overseeing the laundering of funds...Wilson indicated that most of Operation Watchtower was implemented on the authority of [CIA Thomas] Clines.

CIA Proprietary

According to Victor Marchetti, a former CIA agent and author of *The CIA and the Cult of Intelligence*, there are basically three types of

CIA operations. One, known as a Proprietary, a concern that has been designed by the CIA to provide some type of needed service. The proprietary was wholly owned by the CIA itself, but was disguised to appear to the public as a privately owned business.

The CIA hires, and can fire, the heads of proprietaries, although for all practical purposes the proprietary conducts its own financial affairs with a minimum of oversight from Langley. If a proprietary were in need of funds for some reason, such as expansion, it would request funds from the CIA. Therefore, a proprietary tends to take on a life of its own. Several have grown too big and too independent to be either controlled or dissolved by CIA headquarters. Nugan Hand, most likely was also a proprietary, although some might consider it an "independent".

CIA Proprietary or "Front"

A second kind of CIA operation, Marchetti pointed out, was a simple front. A front is an organization whose purported business is a sham and is kept in place solely to provide a cover for covert CIA activities and involved agents.

Independent Asset

The cover of the third kind, Marchetti explained, is literally an independent organization that is closely allied to the CIA, not only ideologically, but also with many former or present CIA people working for it or running it. The organization has mutual goals with the CIA. An example cited by Marchetti was Interarms Company, the World's largest private arms dealer. It was run mostly overseas. Nugan Hand may have been more of this third kind than a proprietary.

Proprietaries are dangerous because they are hard to control and relatively easy to expose. Proprietaries are all used to provide covers, to launder money, and to serve as "cut outs" for highly clandestine operations. This means a direct link to the CIA and a problem for "plausible deniability." A paper trail to CIA headquarters at Langley almost always remains, no matter how much is shredded or hidden away, or how many lies are told by the Agency or government officials.

Project Hammer

Project Hammer consisted of a covert operation using funds from various sources to fund covert activities against foreign countries—and within the United States. The source of funds came from sources with various names. These included the Yamashita Gold, the Golden Lily plunder, Black Eagle Trust, the Marcos gold, and the Durham Trust. People from several of the U.S.' covert operations, mostly CIA, staffed the Project Hammer operation. Between 1945 to 1947, enormous quantities of gold were secretly retrieved from caves and tunnels in the Philippines under the direction of U.S. covert personnel and shipped to banks throughout the world. One name for these funds was Black Eagle Trust.

To keep the retrieved plunder a secret, U.S. officials insisted that the Japanese did not plunder the nations they brutally occupied. A fantasy the literal secret government expected the uninformed and uninquisitive American public to swallow.

CHAPTER EIGHT

Culture of Major Banks

The conduct of U.S. and foreign banks of fraud involved with the certificates of gold deposits is in line with other conduct that is little known by the uninformed person. The *New York Times* published an article (October 10, 1997) referring to the Union Bank of Switzerland's withholding funds deposited by holocaust victims prior to being sent to the Nazi extermination camps. The article, by David Sanger, titled, "New York Punishes Swiss Bank Over Nazi Gold," stated:

New York City quietly administered a major sanction against the Union Bank of Switzerland last week by barring it from participating in a billion-dollar bond offering, a move meant to underline disapproval of the way the bank has responded to the investigations into dealings with Nazi Germany, city officials said yesterday.

The action by New York City's Comptroller, Alan G. Hevesi, was immediately criticized by the State Department, which is attempting to coax Swiss banks to make larger contributions to humanitarian funds for Holocaust survivors and their heirs.

Stuart Eizenstat, the Under Secretary of State for economic affairs, said in an interview from Egypt yesterday that New York's action could "further inflame passions in Switzerland" and insisted that "confrontation with the banks will achieve far less than cooperation."

Nonetheless, Mr. Hevesi, who is running for re-election with only token opposition next month, said he would not let Union Bank profit from expanded dealings with the city while its top Swiss officers remain unapologetic for the bank's response to the widening Nazi gold investigations.

New York's action was prompted by a routine request by the city for bids from global banks to handle a $1.075 billion revenue anticipation note, money that the city borrows in anticipation of receiving state and Federal aid for education and welfare expenditures.

The winning bidder was a syndicate of banks led by UBS, which

Wall Street experts said would have garnered nearly half of the $1 million fee New York ordinarily pays for "letters of credit" from the banks.

"We were faced with the decision of whether to go ahead and do business as usual, or send a message to Union Bank of Switzerland," said Mr. Hevesi, who led the protests earlier this year when the bank dismissed a guard who revealed that the bank's archivist was shredding World War II-era documents, but refused to dismiss its honorary president, who said he thought a Jewish conspiracy lay behind American-led revelations about the banks. "We decided it would be sending the wrong message to accept the bid," said Mr. Hevesi, who added that the Giuliani administration "had no objection" to excluding UBS.

So before the winning bid was announced, Mr. Hevesi's office approached the second bank in UBS's syndicate, Morgan Guaranty Trust Company, and asked it, Mr. Hevesi said, to "reconfigure the team of banks to exclude UBS." It immediately complied, city officials said, replacing UBS with National Westminster Bank of Britain and Societe Generale of France.

The chief operating officer of UBS Americas Region, Richard C. Capone, who met with Mr. Hevesi late last month in an effort to avoid the sanction, was traveling yesterday, and the company said he was not available to discuss the issue.

But in a statement, Mr. Capone said: "We respect the position of the Comptroller even though we do not agree with it. We are proud of the fact that the Swiss banks are working extremely hard and providing leadership in resolving the World War II dormant account issue fairly, and with sensitivity. We understand it is an emotional and complex issue, and we are committed to understanding the truth and doing what is right." Mr. Capone also noted that his bank aided the city "in its darkest hour" during the 1975 fiscal crisis. For months now, New York City and the State Department have been sparring over sharply differing approaches in dealing with the Swiss.

[Death Threats for Exposing Bank's Looting of Holocaust Money]

Mr. Hevesi, whose family included a number of Holocaust victims, has repeatedly pressed Swiss firms to declare how much they are contributing to the Holocaust funds and has criticized UBS in particular for its continuing refusal to release copies of the documents rescued by the guard. Those documents apparently include records of "forced sales" of properties held by Jews in Germany.

Revealing Citibank's Involvement With Project Hammer General Earle Cocke

General Erle Cocke, a lawyer and banker, served in the U.S. military and intelligence services during World War II, Korean invasion, and Vietnam invasion. That included working for Gen. Douglas MacArthur during the Korean and Vietnam War and under General Westmorland during the Vietnam War. As a banker, he served as Alternate Executive Director of the World Bank during the early 1960s. He was also a commander of the Knights of Malta. For his services, Cocke received several medals including the French and Belgium Croix de Guerre, and the Légion d' honneur from France,

Cocke was associated with Project Hammer, and in April 2000 he gave a deposition answering questions related to the project. He testified about the black money from the retrieved Japanese plunder. Referring to the dozens of accounts at Citibank, he was asked, "Would they have been in control of Mr. Reed?"

Probably not all because there were so many different participants involved, and in different locations, countries, that I would say no, he did not have complete control, but everybody recognized it wouldn't be settled until it got to him.

Question: "And these were, you say, accounts for various people around the world?"

"yes."

Question: Produced as a result of what?

Most of them figured that greed in particular was mighty high. And, if they put up this amount of money, then I am going to get this kind of money coming back. That's the way practically all of it was. I hate to use the word "sole", but "present" might be a better word.

Question: "Were these accounts for the benefit of people who had engaged in some kind of trading program?"

They were all to get in the trading program. I haven't found anybody that didn't go in wanting to increase their income and their greed in the highest bracket if they could possibly put up money.

Question: "What I am understanding from you is that whatever these individuals, corporate entities, or even government...they believed, apparently by putting these funds with Citibank as part of this effort, they would then receive later down the road a pay-off?"

That is correct.

Question: "As a result of Citibank's management of these funds, is that fair to say?"

Yes, basically the whole trading bloc in a nutshell.

Question: "Who created Project Hammer?"

I don't know, but it had to be someone at a "pretty high level. The original structure had obviously got way out of proportion as time went by.

Question: "What government agencies were involved with Project Hammer?"

Obviously the CIA, the FBI, the national security agencies of all types. The Pentagon in the broadest sense, and the Treasury, Federal Reserve. Everybody wanted to get in the act.

In response to a question of what banks were involved, Cocke stated:

I am sure that every big bank in every major country at some stage of the game had some of this pass by them. They had a chance to refuse, or they had a chance to take it up.

When asked about Citibank's involvement, Cocke stated they were the primary bank, including,

Citibank of New York, in both their Athens, Greece, office and in their New York City office.

Cocke stated that Citibank Vice President John Reed was a coordinator. Shortly after revealing this information, Cocke died of pancreatic cancer. His impending death may have prompted his decision to reveal this highly sensitive information.

Misuse of U.S. Department of Justice in the Scheme's Cover-Up

A standard practice used for decades to silence or discredit anyone exposing high-level corruption is to have federal prosecutors charge the person with a fabricated crime, especially a conspiracy. I report an endless series of this tactic against good Americans trying to expose high level corruption, especially revealed in the books:

- *Defrauding America.*
- *Drugging America.*
- *Unfriendly Skies: 20th & 21st Centuries.*
- *Crimes of the FBI-CIA, Mafia, and al Qaeda.*
- *FBI, CIA, the Mob, and Treachery.*
- *Explosive Secrets of Covert CIA Companies.*

Huge Bank Profits by Declaring Bank Certificates to be Forgeries

Banks throughout the world, including such U.S. banks as Citibank, enjoyed huge multi-billion dollar profits by declaring bank certificates provided by heirs to be forgeries. In some cases, the banks where the huge deposits were made transferred the gold and other valuables to off-shore nations, thereby immune from legal attacks in the United States.

The history of money laundering by these banks, some examples being in my other books such as *Defrauding America*, is a culture that makes denial of bank certificates a normal practice.

The primary heirs named by Santa Romana were his wife, Luz Rambano, one of his daughters, Flordeliza, and his accountant, Tarciana Rodriguez. Even though they had the names, the account numbers, codes, amounts, keys to bank safety deposit boxes, they were repeatedly blocked by almost every bank that they approached, as well as agencies of the U.S. government. They faced a huge conspiracy to block any action that could reveal the existence of the funds that were part of the secret scheme involving the Japanese war plunder. Several bank officers did initially admit that the accounts existed, but their admissions were later contradicted by other bank officers.

Multiple Parties Engaged in Blocking Heirs Access to Funds

Multiple parties with multiple reasons blocked the heirs from gaining access to the accounts throughout the world, as if they were acting with each other's protection. These included, for instance:

- The banks that stood to gain millions and even billions of assets by declaring their own bank certificates to be forgeries and denying the existence of account numbers, account names, account codes.
- The literal secret group acting both inside and outside the U.S. government that had multiple reasons for assisting the banks in denying the existence of the gold and other valuables on deposit in the banks:
    - Regain access to the funds that were placed in the names of straw depositors.
    - Prevent information from being known about the secret scheme involving the retrieval of portions of the Japanese plunder.
    - Prevent the other actions from becoming known that were part of the scheme: protecting some of Japan's war criminals responsible for horrendous harm to American POWs; providing money to one of Japan's political parties to control the Japanese political process.
    - Prevent disclosure of the multiple bizarre elements of the scheme, such as the secret retrieval of part of the Japanese war plunder; the need to return the plunder to the nations from which they were taken by the Japanese; the M-Fund used to undermine foreign countries; prevent exposure of the many people in key government positions that were complicit in the schemes or their cover-ups; reveal the existence of covert CIA companies; protect careers and reputations of key people in the U.S. government;

Threats Also Part of the Blocking Tactics

In addition to the blatant universal block by the banks were the threats to people whose actions threatened the scheme and the schemers. Christophe Meili, an employee of UBS, revealed the fact that UBS was destroying records showing bank accounts for Holocaust victims. In 1997, he was a student working a temporary position as a security guard at the Zurich office of UBS when he discovered a pile of records waiting to be shredded. He took a sampling of the records and provided them to the Hebrew Congregation of Zurich.

When the documents and shredding were publicized, UBS fired him from his job. UBS president Robert Studer responded: "This issue of so-called unclaimed Jewish money in Swiss banks rears its head again and again. For us, it is no issue at all. The problem was thoroughly discussed after the Second World War and we conscientiously investigated then what money in our bank might have belonged to Holocaust victims because we wanted to settle the question once and for all. For us the case is closed."

Switzerland Death Threats

In Switzerland, Meili, his wife, and children, received dozens of death threats for revealing the criminal and morally bankrupt actions of Swiss bankers. The death threats forced them to move to the United States, where they received asylum. A congressional committee investigating the financial aid given to the Nazi by Swiss banks had Meili testify. Senator Anthony D-Amato called Christophe Meili a hero.

In Switzerland, international publicity forced Swiss prosecutors to open an investigation into the matter, which ended with no action taken.

Former Head of CIA Covert Airline Sentenced to Prison Using Standard Department of Justice Silencing Tactics.

The former head of a covert CIA airline, Steve Crittenden, of whom I write about in *Defrauding America* and *Drugging America*, was charged with holding forged financial documents when he hired a Lockheed 1011 jet to fly to and from Manila and arrived in Lexington, Kentucky to deliver them.

Justice Department prosecutors, with a long history of cover-up of high-level corruption, arrested Crittenden, and after a court trial, sentenced him to five years in prison.

Coordinated Lies for the Masses

Many people and many stories have surfaced to deny the facts. None of these lies given to the masses address such facts as:

- It is a known fact that the Japanese plundered the riches of a dozen nations that were invaded from 1937 to 1945.
- An official explanation for the whereabouts of this plunder of a

dozen nations has never addressed these matters.

- The hundreds of records of bank accounts, listing names, account numbers, codes, present amount of the gold and other deposits, and the loading and weight receipts.
- The tons of gold certificates that did exist in the name of Ferdinand Marcos that have not been denied shows the existence of tens of tons of gold for which there is no other explanation other than the Japanese plunder hidden in caves and tunnels in the Philippines.

Methods Used to Cover Up The Plunder and the Secret Retrieval

Among the methods used by U.S. personnel to cover up for the schemes associated with the Japanese plunder—and to protect the schemers—included for instance:

- The design of the Japanese peace treaty that was signed at San Francisco in 1951 that gave Japan immunity against law suits by victims of the Japanese wartime brutality.
- Hiding the fact that much of the initial Japanese plunder was shipped to Japan and was hidden somewhere in the country.
- Quickly holding a military trial for Japanese General Yamashita in a form that prevented him from revealing the hiding of the Japanese plunder in the Philippines and then quickly putting him to death by hanging.
- Protecting some of the Japanese responsible for the worst atrocities.
- Assisting banks in criminally depriving heirs of the gold and other valuables in accounts that legally belong to them.
- Standard practice by U.S. media people and media corporations of withholding information, or providing disinformation, when the natures of corruption by key government personnel exceed a certain level.
- Putting a myth label on the actions for which there is overwhelming evidence, but which the uninformed and uninquisitive American people gullibly accept.

In my books, *Defrauding America* and *Drugging America*, many former government agents and other insiders have provided me information on the use of banks by CIA and other personnel in laundering drug and financial fraud money. Among these banks were Citibank, Castle Bank, Nugan Hand Bank, BBRDW, and others. Only after reading about these practices and realizing that top personnel at many banks engage in such corrupt activities can the massive frauds in the financial sectors that brought about the 2008 financial implosion be better understood. I write about this latest segment of bank misconduct in the book titled *America's Housing and Financial Frauds*.

The shenanigans at another bank, BCCI—sometimes called the bank of crooks and criminals—with heavy involvement of CIA personnel, provides additional understanding into the banking world.

BCCI, Bank of Crooks and Criminals

One of the world's largest banking scandals, inflicting huge financial losses on thousands of people worldwide, surfaced in the media in 1991. This was the Bank of Credit and Commerce International (BCCI). As could be expected, it had heavy ties with CIA and related personnel, terrorist organizations, drug traffickers, and any other crooked financial transaction shunned by most other banks. It financed terrorist activities, financed drug trafficking deals, and defrauded depositors.

Following a standard pattern, Justice Department officials and the various divisions including the FBI and other government agencies kept the lid on the worldwide criminal activities of the bank. It wasn't until law enforcement agencies in Europe and a state prosecutor in New York City prepared to file charges that the bank's corrupt operations were shut down in the United States.

BCCI was a private bank operating in over seventy countries, including the United States. At one time BCCI had over 400 branches in 78 countries and assets of over $20 billion. Its holding company was based in Luxembourg and its principal operation in London. The primary bank supervisor for BCCI was Luxembourg Monetary Institute, the central bank of Luxembourg.

The BCCI scandal was related to other criminal activities including BNL, Iraqgate, Iran and the Iran-Contra affair, among others. BCCI and BNL both played a role in the Iraqi armament buildup, during which funds provided by U.S. taxpayers were forwarded by the Atlanta branch of Italy's Banca Nazionale del Lavoro. There were numerous cross-dealings between the banks. BCCI used its international connections to fund loans to BNL, which funded the Iraqi weapon buildups, which then required the U.S. taxpayer to fund much of the Persian Gulf War.

Cover-Up of the Bank of Crooks and Criminals

Millions of people throughout the world lost billions of dollars, made possible by the cover-up actions of officials in foreign countries and in the United States. Part of these losses would not have occurred had officials and lawyers in the United States not engaged in criminal activities, including cover-up, misprision of felonies, obstruction of justice, aiding and abetting the criminal activities. Congressional committees, Justice Department personnel, the FBI, and the CIA, all knew about the corrupt BCCI operation for years.

Source of Startup Funding

BCCI commenced operations in Pakistan in 1972, with much of its funding provided by Bank of America and the CIA.[41] Bank of America claims that it sold its BCCI interest in the early 1980s, but records indicate that the bank continued to control much of BCCI's operation until shortly before BCCI was shut down. In the early 1970s, CIA operative Gunther Russbacher described to me how he transferred sizable amounts of CIA funds into the bank for the start-up operations.

Made to Order for CIA Activities

The CIA knew about BCCI's activities, finding this mindset suitable to its own operations. If, for argument, the CIA had not been partners in the corrupt BCCI activities, its world-wide network of operatives and assets should have discovered the BCCI activities that brought about the world's worst banking loss. BCCI was custom-made for the covert and corrupt activities of the CIA, the Mossad, drug dealers, and terrorists. My CIA contacts, including Russbacher, told how CIA operatives used the bank to launder money from CIA enterprises. These included drug trafficking proceeds, the looting of savings and loans, funding unlawful arms shipments, financing terrorist operations,[42] undermining foreign governments, and other covert activities.

Manipulating U.S. Checks and Balances

Investigative reports indicated that BCCI was able to manipulate the spy agencies of numerous countries, including the U.S., Israel, China, Saudi Arabia, and Pakistan, among others. BCCI was supplying funds for terrorist organizations such as Abu Nidal. BCCI rigged international commodity markets that permitted certain insiders to make hundreds of millions of dollars in profits, offset by the same amount lost by depositors. BCCI was laundering drug money for drug cartels throughout the Americas, Europe, and the Middle East.

Bank of America Involvement

Bank of America was heavily involved in BCCI from the date of its inception in 1972. It put up an initial cash investment amounting to 25 percent of the stock, which was later increased to 45 percent. (Some argue that Bank of America had a 60 percent interest.) Bank of America and the CIA had a major ownership in BCCI at that time.

Bank of America loaned money to people to buy stock in BCCI, possibly as fronts, making Bank of America's interest considerably

---

[41] The author's CIA informants described how they diverted funds from secret CIA bank accounts in Europe to BCCI in 1972. CIA operative Gunther Russbacher informed me that while he was in Afghanistan he placed a large amount of CIA money into BCCI.

[42] The Abu Nidal terrorist group and others obtained funds through BCCI, which helped to bring about the Pan Am 103 tragedy and others.

higher. Three out of seven members of BCCI's board of directors were former senior executives at Bank of America, some of whom were on leave from BofA.

A class action lawsuit[43] filed in San Francisco courts[44] by a class of defrauded BCCI depositors charged that Bank of America officials had considerable control over BCCI and had more knowledge of its illegal operations than previously disclosed. The lawsuit charged that Bank of America had a major ownership interest and control in BCCI, and that Bank of America loaned millions of dollars to BCCI front men so that they could unlawfully purchase financial institutions in the United States. The suit charged that five Bank of America officers were either on BCCI's board of directors or helped manage the bank. One of them, P.C. Twitchin, allegedly approved all BCCI loans over $5 million.

The suit charged that in 1978 Bank of America hired the son of Pakistani General Zia for a position, even though he was completely unqualified, solely to bribe important Pakistani officials. The suit charged that through a correspondent banking relationship with BCCI, Bank of America continued to conspire with and aid and abet BCCI activities until the summer of 1991. The suit charged that the wrongful acts of BCCI could not have been accomplished without the active and knowing assistance of Bank of America.

The president of an Atlanta Bank controlled by BCCI was a Bank of America official, adding to the evidence that BofA had heavy interests in the activities constituting the world's worst banking fraud. Bank of America had a symbiotic relationship with the "Bank of Crooks and Criminals," which continued years after the criminal activities became public. Bank of America made large profits from its relationship with the rogue bank. But fearing that its direct ownership in BCCI could be embarrassing, Bank of America officials started selling (1977) its interest in BCCI, lending money to front men to acquire these interests.

"The mother of all scandals," stated syndicated columnist Jack R. Payton in the *San Francisco Examiner*,[45] as he wrote of the BCCI affair. "Top BofA Alumni Filled Major Posts at BCCI," was another headline in the *San Francisco Chronicle*. The article named top executives of Bank of America who filled high-level positions at BCCI.

Another *San Francisco Chronicle* article was entitled, "BofA, BCCI Dealings Hit $1 Billion-Plus a Day." Bank of America was a crucial repository for large infusions of cash needed by BCCI to keep its

---

[43] Filed by the San Diego law firm of Milberg Weiss Bershad Specthrie & Lerach.

[44] *San Francisco Chronicle*, with the column headed, "Lawsuit Links BofA to BCCI."

[45] October 9, 1992.

worldwide financial empire afloat. The article stated that the transactions continued throughout the 1980s, long after BCCI's corrupt activities were known to thousands of people.

According to a *San Francisco Chronicle* article quoting a Congressional source, Bank of America did not sever ties after BCCI's corrupt activities became common knowledge. The Congressional source added that as late as March 1990, Bank of America kept two of its accounts open with BCCI's Miami office, two years after the Miami office had been indicted and was widely known for alleged money laundering deals involving drug money for former Panama dictator Manuel Noriega, among many others.

Bank of America Kept BCCI in Business

Without these financial transactions from Bank of America, BCCI would have occasionally run out of funds. Bank of America was instrumental in permitting BCCI to continue stealing depositors' money. Without this help the corrupt activities of BCCI would have been discovered years earlier.

The author of numerous books on financial institutions[46] told how Bank of America's $1 billion daily money transfer was strange and unusual. He estimated that the deposits were a Ponzi game probably involving letters of credit, which banks use to handle foreign trade payments. Mayer wrote that a great deal of BCCI sham activities were in bogus letters of credit.

Bank of America sold some of its stock to a BCCI subsidiary called International Credit and Investment Company, making a $27 million profit on the transaction. That same company, ICIC, has since been identified as the BCCI entity that handled some of BCCI's most notorious deals. These included fraudulent insider loans that were never repaid.

Congressman Frank Riggs asked the House Committee on Banking, Finance and Urban Affairs to investigate Bank of America's ties to BCCI, stating in a letter to Congressman Henry Gonzalez, chairman of the Committee, that there is "very clear evidence" that Bank of America had links to the scandal ridden BCCI. In his letter to Gonzalez, Riggs wrote, "I believe that the links that have already been found between BCCI and BofA are of such far-reaching implications that a hearing is needed now." Riggs continued, "It troubles me that BofA continued to handle as much as $1.3 billion of BCCI deposits per day even after BCCI was indicted for money laundering in 1988."

Riggs pointed out that there existed a close financial relationship between Bank of America and International Credit and Investment

---

[46] Mayer.

Company (ICIC), a BCCI subsidiary in the Cayman Islands. Riggs added, "We know that Bank of America, a founder of BCCI, also provided a start-up loan to ICIC. We also know that BofA later sold its BCCI holdings to ICIC and provided financing to ICIC for the purchase. BofA made more than a 600 percent profit off this transaction."

Bank of America Money Laundering

Bank of America was fined $7 million in 1986 for 17,000 separate acts of money laundering.[47] Bank of America's name surfaces throughout BCCI's sordid history. Despite the widespread knowledge by U.S. banking and intelligence agency personnel of the BCCI criminal activities during its two decades of corrupt operations, Bank of America officials, who controlled much of the BCCI operation, claimed they knew nothing about the corrupt unlawful activities.

Unlawful Acquisition of U.S. Banks and Savings and Loans

BCCI, as represented by Clark Clifford and Robert Altman, tried to convince U.S. regulators in the 1970s to allow BCCI to purchase a bank holding company. When U.S. regulators refused to allow this purchase that was barred by U.S. law, BCCI then loaned money to people who bought shares in American banks, including Financial General Bankshares, Inc.

When BCCI secretly sought to acquire in 1978 Financial General Bankshares, Inc., the stockholders of Financial went to court to block a takeover attempt, citing questionable activities by the BCCI front men. The stockholders requested supporting documents from Bank of America. To keep the BCCI activities from the public, from the stockholders, and from the government, Lawyers Clark Clifford and Robert Altman threatened to sue Bank of America if the bank produced the requested documents.

Bank of America officials then refused to produce documents that would otherwise expose these activities.[48] With the help of powerful U.S. law firms willing to subvert U.S. laws and interests, BCCI was able to violate U.S. banking laws, engage in a pattern of criminal activities, and inflict billions of dollars of harm to people throughout the United States and other countries. But U.S. taxpayers came to the rescue, and are now paying the price for these corrupt acts heavily involved with U.S. officials and law firms.

After secretly and unlawfully purchasing Financial General Bankshares, its name was changed to First American Bankshares. Altman was rewarded by being named president of the holding company and

---

[47] *Time*, October 7, 1991.
[48] *San Francisco Examiner*, September 22, 1991.

given stock that eventually netted him several million dollars profit, in addition to his monthly compensation. Many politicians were also paid off handsomely. When billions are stolen it is possible to pay well for those helping in the scheme. They all played the part of the amiable dunce, claiming they did not know First American Bankshares was controlled by BCCI or that the criminal activities existed.

Many law firms and lawyers, including Clifford and Altman, fraudulently hid these covert ownerships that were harming U.S. interests. Clifford, chairman of First American Bankshares, said he didn't know of any ties to BCCI, in spite of the fact that his law firm represented BCCI; he was Chairman of BCCI front companies, and was the main U.S. Attorney for BCCI in the late 1970s. Clifford was frequently called the number one fixer in the Democratic Party.

First American Bank in New York was part of the BCCI operation. BCCI secretly acquired First American's parent, First American Bankshares of Washington, D.C., in 1983. Federal law restricted the operations of BCCI's offices, prohibiting BCCI from accepting deposits in the United States. This restriction was violated, causing many depositors to lose their deposits. BCCI secretly acquired Independence Bank in Encino, First American, and invested in CenTrust in complex financial deals that were difficult to detect. BCCI acquired various U.S. banks including First American Bank in Washington with its many branches; National Bank of Georgia.

Saudi Arabia Involvement

The biggest and most prestigious bank in Saudi Arabia, National Commercial Bank, was implicated in the BCCI scandal. District Lawyer Robert Morgenthau, County of New York, brought a fraud indictment against the largest banker in Saudi Arabia, Sheik Khalid bin Mahfouz, charging the Saudi bank with failing to report purchases of stock in Washington's largest bank holding company, First American Bankshares, which was illegally and secretly controlled by BCCI. The purchase of the stock was financed by loans from the Saudi bank to people acting as fronts for BCCI. The Saudi bank loaned money to BCCI in a manner that permitted BCCI's illegal operations to continue.

Canadian Involvement

Canadian politicians were also implicated. When members of Canada's Parliament were forced to investigate BCCI activities, they learned that the former deputy commissioner of the Royal Canadian Mounted Police (RCMP), Henry Jensen, who had supervised the BCCI investigation from 1987 to 1989, had gone to work for BCCI as a paid consultant shortly after his retirement.

Canadian officials refused to cooperate in the Inslaw investigation. Canadian officials have been charged with covering up sensitive facts relating to the Arrow Airlines DC-8 crash at Gander that killed 248 American GIs under suspicious circumstances. Arrow was a CIA front company.

Congressional Hearings

A BCCI insider, Abdur Sakhia, testified at a Senate Foreign Relations Subcommittee on Terrorism, Narcotics and Internal Operations about events that he had seen as a BCCI officer. He described a July 1988 meeting at the Washington offices of Clifford and Warnke, at which Clifford joked to one of the BCCI officers: "Welcome aboard. We will tell more lies now." Sakhia testified to meetings at which Altman and other senior BCCI executives referred to secret agreements under which BCCI retained control of Independence Bank of Encino. Clifford and Altman have consistently denied knowledge of any relationship to BCCI. Sakhia told how the CIA used BCCI for money transfer in the Iran-Contra affair.

Former federal budget director Bert Lance in the Carter Administration testified before Congress (October 23, 1991) that he was convinced the CIA recruited the founder of the Bank of Commerce and Credit International to use the bank for CIA purposes.

Acting director of the CIA, Richard Kerr, testified to the Senate subcommittee (October 26, 1991) that the CIA knew in 1985 that BCCI had secretly gained unlawful control of Washington's largest bank holding company.

Savings and Loans and BCCI

The savings and loan debacle had numerous connections with the BCCI scandal. Savings and loan figure Charles Keating served on the board of a Bahamas-based investment company, Trendinvest Ltd., along with Alfred Hartmann, who was a director of BCCI. Reports given to me by CIA sources state that the Keating group, among others, moved hundreds of millions of dollars into offshore bank accounts and trusts. Lawyers at the law firm of Alvarado, Rus & Worcester, representing over 15,000 investors who were defrauded by the Keating group, stated: "It was clear to us back in 1989 that Mr. Keating had been involved in significant movement of cash offshore."

Two failed savings and loans, CenTrust Savings Bank in Miami and Viking Savings in Santa Monica, California had direct or indirect connections to BCCI. Viking Savings and Loan was secretly acquired through money provided in part by California Democratic State Senator Alan Robbins, who contributed $900,000. Robbins allegedly obtained the money from BCCI Independence Bank of Encino, California. Viking was acquired by Michael Goland, a pro-Israeli candidate. Goland used money to mount a 1984 Senate campaign against Republican Charles Percy, who Goland felt was anti-Israel, a common reaction for any member of Congress who incurs disfavor by Israel.

BCCI had a secret and illegal 28 percent ownership in CenTrust Savings Bank. CenTrust's failure will cost the American taxpayer over $2 billion. CenTrust was run by David Paul, a major fundraiser for the Democratic Party and a close friend of Senator Kerry, who investigated the BCCI scandal, and to this day hasn't taken any significant action. Senator Kerry was chairman of a key campaign committee for Senate Democrats in the late 1980s, while Paul was the chairman of the committee's fund-raising arm. Ghaith Pharaon, a Saudi Arabian financier, openly acquired a 28 percent stake in CenTrust, acting as a front man for BCCI.

A BCCI front purchased the Bank of Georgia in 1977, in which former budget director during the Carter administration, Burt Lance had a substantial financial interest. Lance sold his shares in National Bank of Georgia to Saudi businessman and BCCI front man Ghaith Pharaon, who then sold them to First American Bank Holding Company in Washington, D.C., another secretly controlled BCCI operation.

BCCI had tentacles in other criminal activities including Iraqgate and the bank primarily owned by the Italian government: Banca Nazionale del Lavoro (sometimes referred to as Bank Lavoro, or BNL for short). Both of these scandals implicated high U.S. officials.

BCCI, Bush, and Clinton

One of the men behind the founding of BCCI was Jackson Stephens who headed Stephens, Inc, located in Little Rock, Arkansas. Stephens, Inc. was a large U.S. investment bank with numerous hidden connections, including one with Harken Energy, to obtain the oil drilling rights off Bahrain. George Bush, Jr., was a consultant and member of the board of directors of Harken, before the oil-drilling contract was signed. Stephen's firm helped secure a loan from a BCCI affiliated Swiss bank for Harken Energy.

Bill Clinton's involvement in the BCCI affair was shown in a February 1992 article[49] under the headline "Clinton and BCCI." The article reported that the Clinton campaign had a $2 million credit line from a bank with connections to BCCI. The credit line was from Worthen National Bank in Little Rock, Arkansas, controlled by Little Rock billionaire Jackson Stephens and managed by Curt Bradbury. Stephens was involved in the 1970s deals in which BCCI unlawfully acquired Washington's First American Bank.

Stephens' links to BCCI were reported in an *Arkansas Democrat* article (December 1991) titled "Reports link Stephens to BCCI." The

---

[49] The article first appeared in the *New York Times*, and reported in the *Wall Street Journal*, February 10, 1992.

article stated that an employee of Stephens acted as chairman, president, and chief executive officer of Worthen National Bank. In addition, the article stated that in 1977, Stephens, Inc. assisted BCCI to unlawfully take over First American Bankshares. Another *Arkansas Gazette* article (August 1991) entitled "Little Rock on the BCCI route to power," stated in part:

Curt Bradbury, then a financial analyst for Stephens, Inc., and now chairman and chief executive officer of Worthen National Bank of Arkansas, provided [a BCCI officer] research about Financial General, including a copy of its latest annual report. Financial General was the parent company of the National Bank of Georgia, the bank run by Bert Lance [longtime crony of former President Jimmy Carter].

It was the purchase of Financial General and the National Bank of Georgia that evolved into First American Bankshares, operated by lawyer Clark Clifford in Washington.

An article in *Spotlight*[50] tied Democratic presidential candidate Clinton to the BCCI scandal and charged that the mainstream press was concentrating on Clinton's extramarital activities and his draft dodging during the Vietnam War while ignoring Clinton's involvement in the BCCI scandal. The article referred to *New York Post* writer Mike McAlary's reporting of the connections between Clinton and the BCCI mess. Money allegedly came from Arkansas billionaire Jackson Stephens, who reportedly brokered the transaction that enabled BCCI to gain unlawful and covert control of two U.S. banks, First American Bankshares and the National Bank of Georgia.

Houston oil consultant Michael Ameen, who was on the payroll of the U.S. State Department as a consultant, was highly instrumental in working out the Bahrain deal. Ameen had close contacts with a major BCCI shareholder, Kamal Adham, who was also a former chief of Saudi Arabian Intelligence.

Many Links

Alfred Hartmann, a Swiss banker, was a BCCI director and chairman of its Swiss unit, Banque de Commerce et Placements S.A., or BCP for short. Hartmann was also chairman of BNL's unit in Zurich, Switzerland, known as Lavoro Bank. Hartmann was vice chairman of a joint-venture institution in Geneva called Bank of New York-Inter Maritime Bank. Hartmann was involved in the BCCI and BNL banks and in the Bank of New York-Inter Maritime Bank. An officer of Bank of New York, Bruce Rappaport, also had close ties to the CIA and the Mossad.

---

[50] March 2, 1992.

Profits for Sabotaging America's Interests

Many lawyers, public relations firms, members of Congress, and others made handsome profits at the expense of the American taxpayers and the thousands of depositors who lost their life's savings.

Carter, while President of the United States, owed money to a bank with connections to BCCI and was bailed out along with his banker friend, Bert Lance, by Pharaon. Pharaon first loaned $3.5 million to Lance through BCCI and then bought control of Lance's bank for an additional $2.4 million.[51] Several days later President Carter approved the sale of F-15s to Saudi Arabia. BCCI paid for former President Jimmy Carter's trips around the world after he left the White House.

BCCI wrote off a $160,000 loan to an Atlanta consulting firm operated by Andrew Young, former mayor of Atlanta.[52] The loan had been made by National Bank of Georgia, which had been acquired by BCCI front man Ghaith Pharaon. Young had served as U.S. ambassador to the United Nations during the Carter administration. Enlarging on his many trips to Africa, Young promoted BCCI to individuals and governments in Africa and Central America. Mayor Young received a retainer for introducing Third World leaders to BCCI. A former BCCI official provided about $11,000 in travel accommodations to Reverend Jesse Jackson.

White House aide and lawyer Ed Rogers went to work for a BCCI front man, Kamal Adham, in October 1991. Adham was a front man in the illegal purchase of Washington's First American Bank. In a press conference, President Bush denied knowing Adham, although the facts indicated otherwise. Adham was head of Saudi Arabia's spy agency while Bush was head of the U.S. Central Intelligence Agency. Despite Rogers' young age, 33 years, and his lack of legal experience, BCCI offered him $600,000 up front for two years work plus expenses to leave his job as White House aide and assistant to chief of staff John Sununu. He obviously wasn't being paid for his legal knowledge, but for his political contacts with the Bush Administration.

Rogers, a young lawyer who had never practiced law and had relatively little experience, stated on his application to register as a foreign agent that he had been hired for his legal expertise. The two most probable reasons for Rogers to be hired by a mastermind in the BCCI web were (a) either for his influence in the White House, or (b) with the urging of the White House to facilitate the various covert activities between President George Bush, other White House officials, or the CIA.

Abu Dhabi's role takes on political dimensions because the ruling

[51] The Jack Anderson syndicated column.

[52] Wall Street Journal September 3, 1991.

family of Abu Dhabi contracted with a firm operated by President Bush's deputy campaign manager, James Lake, to handle public relations. That firm has been paid over $1 million over a twelve-month period to have the U.S. media define Abu Dhabi as a victim of the scheme to illegally gain control of banks in the United States. Abu Dhabi was uncooperative in providing documents and refused to allow any of its citizens to testify. Lake was sitting in on White House campaign strategy meetings while also providing information to Sheik Zaved bin Sultan al-Nayhan,[53] who controlled a major portion of BCCI's shares.

Public Relations Firm's Sellout of U.S. Interests

BCCI hired a public relations firm led by prominent Republican Robert Gray and Democrat Frank Mankiewicz, which was paid fees of $50,000 a month while it spread false information to Congress and the public protecting BCCI. The accounting firm responsible for inspecting BCCI, Price Waterhouse, received a $600,000 loan from BCCI.[54] An employee of Price Waterhouse, who audited the financial statements of BCCI and covered up for the irregularities, received over $100,000 from a BCCI affiliate within two years after leaving the accounting firm. The same practice continued as private auditors (hired by those looting the savings and loans, and receiving exorbitant salaries) kept the lid on the corrupt activities.

San Francisco lawyer Henry Fields and the law firm of Morrison & Foerster were used by BCCI front man, Ghaith R. Pharaon, to obtain regulatory approval for the purchase of Independence Bank of Encino, California. Fields assured regulators that Pharaon would be the sole owner of Independence. But Pharaon signed an agreement putting 85 percent ownership of the California bank in the hands of a BCCI subsidiary. Immediately after the California bank changed hands, Pharaon hired another Morrison & Foerster lawyer to be on the board of directors of Independence Bank.

Many lawyers in the United States and overseas were involved in the complex activities of BCCI, and not a single one spoke out, typical of their role in almost every scandal stated in these pages.

CIA Connections

The CIA provided part of the startup funding for BCCI. It moved large amounts of money through BCCI during its entire operation. Former CIA Director Richard Helms tried to arrange for the purchase of First American by BCCI and failed. Clark Clifford then sought to arrange the purchase using BCCI front men, obtaining U.S. regulatory approval based upon Clifford's false representations.

---

[53] Sheik Zaved bin Sultan al-Nayhan was president of the United Arab Emirates.

[54] *Wall Street Journal* article by Peter Truell.

Jeb Bush

One of President Bush's sons, Jeb Bush, had numerous dealings with BCCI and was frequently in BCCI's Miami office. Jeb Bush's company invested in real estate with a company controlled by a BCCI customer, who was later sent to prison for defrauding BCCI and other banks.

Bribery Was Everywhere

BCCI had a bribery list of U.S. elected public officials. Reference was made to this list during Congressional testimony (September 13, 1991) before the House Banking Committee, which was chaired by Representative Henry Gonzalez. One method reported for conveying bribes to members of Congress was through the Chicago Commodity Exchange, Chicago Board of Trade, Chicago Board Options Exchange, and the Chicago Mercantile Exchange. Money was put into commodity exchange accounts overseas under the name of a particular member of Congress. Periodically the Congressman would be informed that there was money in his account, and he was then advised how he could withdraw it if he wished. Huge amounts of cash were brought into Chicago to orchestrate this scheme.

People in Control of Both Political Parties Implicated

As in many of the scandals mentioned in this book, both political parties were implicated, receiving large financial contributions or bribes from the illicitly operated bank. As in the savings and loan scandal, members of Congress were handsomely rewarded for either looking the other way or obstructing any investigations. The key to continuing the corruption and harms inflicted throughout the world by BCCI was bribing U.S. and other officials.

Senator Orrin Hatch (R-Utah), the senior Republican on the Judiciary Committee, was one of hundreds of Congressmen who received money from BCCI officials. He was more openly protective of the BCCI corruption. Senator Hatch issued a glowing endorsement of the Justice Department's plea bargain settlement with BCCI's money-laundering operation in Tampa, Florida, which was a slap-on-the-wrist settlement blocking further investigation into high-level BCCI corruption. It also prevented investigation of Hatch's involvement with BCCI.

Although BCCI pled guilty to several dozen felony counts, Senator Hatch said in his Senate floor speech, "There was no systematic money laundering uncovered in the BCCI case." Hatch has extolled "senior management, directors and shareholders of BCCI for the responsible way" they behaved. This probably reflected the mindset of U.S. Congressmen (and Congresswomen).

Senator Hatch's speech had been prepared by the same BCCI cutouts that perpetrated the sham against the American people: Washington lawyer Robert Altman and his law office. Immediately after giving the unusual speech defending the crime-infested bank and those who made the crimes possible, Senator Hatch placed a telephone call to BCCI's chief executive officer, Swaleh Naqvi. Hatch requested a loan for his business associate, Munzer Hourani, a Houston businessman.

In another instance, Senator Hatch's office misused his senate office trying to protect BCCI against drug money laundering charges. When the media exposed this attempt, Hatch sought to divert attention from himself by blaming a former member of his staff, Michael Pillsbury. Pillsbury had represented Senator Hatch by seeking a more favorable outcome in the 1989 money laundering indictment in Florida against BCCI officials. Hatch sought to sidestep blame by asking the Senate Ethics Committee to investigate his former aide.

Senator Hatch was involved with a part owner of BCCI, Mohammed Hammoud, a front man for BCCI in First American Bankshare purchases. Hammoud's loose talk about the BCCI operations threatened politicians and crooks worldwide, possibly causing his May 1990 death under mysterious circumstances in Geneva, Switzerland. The insurance company refused to pay death benefits because the corpse was four inches shorter than shown on Hammoud's last physical examination.

Senator Hatch was one of the senators to whom I sent evidence of these various scandals and who refused to receive my evidence. It is understandable that a member of Congress already implicated in one or more scandals or criminal activities would refuse to receive evidence of other criminal activities. The same argument can surely be applied to each of the other senators and representatives who refused to receive the testimony and evidence of our group of whistleblowers.

One of the infamous Keating-Five senators from the savings and loan scandal, California Senator Alan Cranston, intervened on behalf of BCCI.[55] Cranston wrote a letter to the Federal Home Loan Bank Board at the request of David Paul, owner of BCCI-related CenTrust Savings Bank[56] of Miami, requesting relief from regulatory actions, while simultaneously receiving political contributions that are usually bald-face bribes. Senator Cranston repeatedly intervened on behalf of the biggest crooks in the savings and loan debacle while refusing to receive my evidence of massive criminal activities. He also intervened on behalf of the crooks in the world's worst banking scandal. That same scenario applied to many other members of the Senate and House.

Congress *Forced* to "Investigate"

The media attention over BCCI's activities forced Congress to con-

---

[55] *Los Angeles Times*, October 7, 1991.

[56] About one fourth of CenTrust's stock was owned by BCCI before it collapsed.

duct an "investigation." The Senate Foreign Relations' Subcommittee on Terrorism, Narcotics and International Operations, chaired by Senator John Kerry (D-MA), conducted an investigation. At the same time, Kerry received financial contributions from BCCI's front man David Paul, of Florida's CenTrust (a U.S. financial institution unlawfully affiliated with BCCI). CenTrust failed, costing the American taxpayer over two billion dollars. CenTrust Chairman, David Paul, arranged for BCCI to invest $25 million in CenTrust bonds in 1988, and then repurchased the bonds two months later. The intent was to make CenTrust temporarily look healthier than it really was. This temporary financial support further substantiated the BCCI-CenTrust relationship.

The bribe to Kerry, or whatever one wishes to call it, may be the reason that the Senate Committee did not request the appointment of an Independent Prosecutor despite the serious corruption uncovered by the committee investigators. Many members of Congress were involved in the scandal, which also helped to eliminate any desire for an Independent Prosecutor.

Cover-Up of Very Serious Crimes Ignored by the Senate Committee

Senate investigator Jack Blum unsuccessfully sought to have Congress act on the alarming disclosures that he had uncovered. When much of the criminality focused on corrupt members of Congress, other U.S. officials refused to delve into those areas. In desperation, Senate Investigator Jack Blum quit his Senate investigative function and tried to get Justice Department officials to act. After being stonewalled there, Blum sought to interest Manhattan District Lawyer Robert Morgenthau in the scandal that had tentacles in New York.

The overwhelming evidence that Blum presented resulted in Morgenthau obtaining a grand jury indictment (July 29, 1991) against BCCI and two cutouts, Clark Clifford and Robert Altman. They were charged with engaging in a multi-billion-dollar scheme to defraud depositors, falsifying bank records, concealing illegal money laundering, and engaging in larceny. Even after the indictment, Justice Department officials refused to produce requested documents. By July 1991, Morgenthau had enough evidence to indict Clifford and Altman. They were charged with bank fraud and with receiving $40 million in bribes from BCCI as part of a conspiracy to give BCCI control of several banks in the United States.

The Senate Report

The committee issued a nearly 800-page report (October 1, 1992), accusing BCCI of using political insiders to commit fraud upon the United States on a global scale. The report stated that there exists "an elaborate corporate spider-web with BCCI's founder, Agha Hasan

Abedi and his assistant, Swaleh Naqvi, in the middle." The report stated that BCCI's *modus operandi* throughout the world, including the United States, was bribery and subversion of government officials.

The report stated that BCCI "systematically bribed political figures around the world." Senator Hank Brown, a member of the Senate committee, stated at a news conference, "We found it was BCCI's overpowering use of the nation's political insiders like [former Defense Secretary] Clark Clifford...that permitted BCCI's secret expansion in the United States."

The report described an international operation that would exceed SPECTRE, the fiendish "Special Executive for Counter-intelligence, Terrorism, Revenge and Extortion," found in James Bond novels and movies. Senator Kerry said "BCCI constituted international global crime on a level that boggles the mind." The report criticized U.S. bank regulators, the CIA, and the Justice Department, and offered a scathing portrait of political influence, international bribery, and inaction by agencies having the duty to act, becoming the catalyst for one of the biggest financial frauds in the world's history.

The report listed the financial contributions or bribes paid to various members of the U.S. Congress, including former Senator John Culver (D-Iowa) and Senator Orrin G. Hatch (R-Utah). The report severely criticized two lawyers, Clark M. Clifford, a former Cabinet member and adviser to various Presidents of the United States, and his protégé, Robert A. Altman, who have been charged with taking bribes from BCCI in exchange for hiding BCCI's ownership of First American Bankshares, a Washington holding company of which Clifford was the chairman.

Senator Hank Brown (R-CO), who was the subcommittee's ranking minority member, substantiated the fact that BCCI's financial contributions were so extensive that "there was not a single committee of this Congress that wanted to conduct a complete, thorough investigation."

The report stated that while Senator Hatch and Mr. Pillsbury, a former State Department official, worked on behalf of BCCI to halt investigations, Senator Hatch was requesting BCCI to lend $10 million to a business associate with whom the Senator was in partnership.

The report stated that BCCI used political insiders such as former Defense Secretary Clark Clifford and members of Congress to commit fraud on a global scale. It told how BCCI paid members of Congress, lobbyists, and lawyers to obstruct the investigation into its terrorists and drug-money-laundering activities. The report implicated Democrats and Republicans, lawyers and lobbyists, public relations firms, Congressional staffers and former senators.

The report treated with kid gloves Senator Hatch's frequent attempts to protect BCCI and to obstruct criminal investigations while receiving BCCI money. The report tried to make Senator Hatch's aide the scapegoat and recommended that the aide be "investigated" by the Senate Ethics Committee. The activities of lawyer and former Senator John Culver (D-Iowa), were stated, in part:

> *Sen. Culver's role in lobbying Congress to assist BCCI was more significant than had been publicly understood, and .he provided valuable advice to BCCI on how to handle Congressional attempts to investigate the bank.*

Despite the gravity of the crimes depicted in the Senate report, much remained to be learned when the Senate committee discontinued its investigation and issued its report. CIA officials refused to produce hundreds of documents that it had on the BCCI operations, in which the CIA itself was involved.

Refusal to Request Independent Prosecutor

Despite the many unanswered questions concerning involvement of U.S. officials, the Senate committee refused to request appointment of an *independent* prosecutor. To do so would have implicated many members of Congress in both major political parties. When questioned by reporters as to whether he would request appointment of an independent counsel, Senator Kerry replied, "There already is an independent counsel, Bob Morgenthau." That answer was a farce.

A county district lawyer has a limited budget, and has neither the funds nor the authority, nor the responsibility, to investigate a complex scandal with international implications of the magnitude of the BCCI scandal. The authority of a local county prosecutor is obviously inadequate to investigate the national and international aspects of the BCCI scandal. Morgenthau's yearly budget for prosecuting *all* criminal acts in Manhattan was approximately $50 million. Independent prosecutor Lawrence Walsh, for instance, spent over $40 million just to determine who was lying to Congress in the Iran-Contra affair.

Hundreds of Tips, and the Usual Justice Cover-Up

Federal agencies received hundreds of tips for over ten years detailing BCCI criminal activities. Federal agencies, including the FBI, Justice Department, Drug Enforcement Administration, and the Internal Revenue Service, had thousands of investigators, many of whom knew about the corruption for years, and no action was taken. As in every other scandal, Justice Department officials blocked corrective actions.

An initial investigation in 1989 by Justice Department officials into BCCI's secret ownership of First American had been abruptly canceled, protecting the criminal elements within BCCI, powerful Washington law firms, members of Congress, Bank of America, and others.

Former BCCI officers informed the Senate committee that they believed the Justice Department's cover-up and failure to properly investigate BCCI was due to BCCI's extensive connections with the CIA and other U.S. intelligence agencies. An investigation would expose the unlawful Iran-Contra arms flow, the drug trafficking into the United States from throughout the world, CIA money laundering from its covert domestic proprietaries, bribing of U.S. officials, especially members of Congress, and God knows what else.

The BCCI scandal would most likely have slowly drifted away and become worse, if it had been left up to those in charge of the U.S. Department of Justice and Congress. It would be one more major scandal kept secret from the American public. But a persistent investigator, Jack Blum, went to a County Prosecutor in New York when Congress and the Justice Department stonewalled the matter, and convinced a 73-year old County Prosecutor, Robert Morgenthau, to prosecute BCCI and the crooks associated with it. Soon after commencing the investigation, Morgenthau encountered the obstruction of justice tactics by Justice Department lawyers, who wanted to keep the lid on the scandal.

Over a Decade of Ignoring Informants

Thirteen years before BCCI was seized in 1991, an American bank examiner, Joseph Vaez,[57] warned in a memo that BCCI was rife with bad loans and that the bank used front men to disguise fraudulent transactions. The memo described the incestuous lending and ownership arrangements with affiliate companies in offshore havens, the practice of almost limitless lending to favored customers, and other serious banking irregularities.

The memo referred to the ICIC Group, a Cayman Islands affiliate that the Federal Reserve called BCCI's alter ego, and estimated that it controlled 70 percent of BCCI, and that BCCI's front men operated through ICIC. Vaez testified before a Senate subcommittee[58] concerning the memo, which mysteriously disappeared from the government files. Vaez then produced his copy of the document. The Senate committee then requested the original from the comptroller's office, which refused to produce it. The committee then subpoenaed the document.

Assistant Secretary of Intelligence at the State Department, Douglas Mulholland, testified about another hidden memo on BCCI. In January 1985, while he was special assistant for national security to the Secretary of the Treasury, he received an unusual report from the CIA relating to BCCI. Mulholland further testified that the CIA forbade him from discussing the memo on the basis of national security.[59]

---

[57] Vaez was an examiner for the Office of the Comptroller of the Currency testifying before a Senate subcommittee.

[58] *New York Times*, February 20, 1992.

[59] The "national security" label is routinely used to prevent the disclosure

A CIA telex message from CIA Director Richard Helms was entered into the Senate hearing record showing the CIA knew of the BCCI activities a decade before the scandal surfaced. The telex related to the wording of an agreement to grant power of lawyer to a Washington law firm relative to a transaction involving Financial General Bankshares of Washington, D.C., later renamed First American Bankshares.

House "Investigation"

The House also conducted an "investigation" into the BCCI scandal. Representative Charles Schumer chaired the House committee, and the report was for all practical purposes a cover-up. Congressional investigator and cover-up artist Lawrence Barcella helped persuade Senator Orrin Hatch to give a speech on the Senate floor praising BCCI.[60] This is the same Barcella who in 1992 engaged in a cover-up of the House October Surprise "investigation." Barcella also helped to conceal a covert CIA operation supplying military equipment to Libya's President Colonel Moammar al Kadhafi, after its cover was blown, by charging CIA-operative Edwin Wilson with a federal crime for carrying out CIA operations.

CIA Deputy Director Robert Gates reportedly stated in 1988 to the head of Customs, William von Raab, that BCCI stood for the "Bank of Crooks and Criminals International." Yet, the CIA continued to deposit and launder funds in BCCI, covering up the criminal activities that would defraud people all over the world who had put their money into the bank.

In the 1980s, U.S. Customs Commissioner William von Raab unsuccessfully tried to get the Justice Department to act on the serious federal violations committed by BCCI. Raab testified to Senate investigators that in 1988 he told Gates of the drug money laundering at BCCI, and that Gates refused to proceed with the information. Raab did not know, apparently, that the CIA was *itself* laundering drug and other illicit money through BCCI.

BCCI officer Nazir Chinoy tried to provide information to federal prosecutors about covert arms deals involving BCCI and the CIA.[61] Instead, Justice Department officials indicted Chinoy, and in that manner, the CIA drug smuggling was again kept under wraps.

Justice Department officials were put on notice during a 1985 federal heroin investigation that money was being laundered in BCCI's Independence Bank of Encino in California. The Justice Department's DEA and the Treasury Department's Internal Revenue Service learned of the BCCI connection and the drug money laundering, and did noth-

---

of information on internal misconduct by government officials.

[60] *Newsweek*, August 26, 1991.

[61] San Francisco *Daily Journal*, November 13, 1991.

ing about it. To do so would have exposed the CIA and bribing of federal officials. Tape recordings of a BCCI officer talking to an undercover investigator included the following statement:

> *Now we are trying to extend our operations into the United States, we have offices in New York, Atlanta, Miami, Houston, and San Francisco, also we have acquired some local bank which we take over very shortly.*

Kidder, Peabody & Company notified federal regulators from 1978 through 1981 that it was helping BCCI acquire an interest in First American Bankshares, Inc, while First American was telling banking regulators that First American had no connections to BCCI.[62] This information was prepared by Martin Siegel, showing that BCCI was behind the ownership change involving First American, the largest bank holding company in Washington. After the acquisition was approved in 1982, Kidder renewed its registration as an agent for BCCI, working in connection with the acquisition of First American. No reference was made on the application form that Kidder was working with the front men.

Seeking to circumvent the block by Justice Department officials, U.S. Customs officer Robert Mazur wrote to Senator John Kerry (D-Mass.), chairman of the Senate Subcommittee on Terrorism, Narcotics and International Operations, complaining about the cover-up within the Justice Department and Customs. Mazur wrote:

> *Tons of documents were not reviewed...and the CIA put a halt to certain investigative leads into a 1988 Florida inquiry that led to the indictment of BCCI officers in Tampa. We had drug traffickers, money launderers, foreign government involvement, Noriega and allegations of payoffs by BCCI to U.S. government political figures. I will not elaborate on who these U.S. government figures were alleged to be, but I can advise you that you don't have all of the documents. Some were destroyed or misplaced.*

Senator Kerry refused to release the letters written by Mazur, but those who have seen them state they were political dynamite, exposing serious misconduct by many members of Congress. Dozens of members of Congress received political contributions or bribes from BCCI and its unlawful outlets in the United States, including the chairman of the investigating committee, Senator John Kerry, who received the highest reported amount of contributions. Kerry also failed to recommend appointment of an independent prosecutor into the BCCI scandal.

---

[62] *Wall Street Journal*, September 10, 1991.

In testifying before the Senate committee,[63] Mazur testified to the following facts: (1) that his group discovered hundreds of leads indicating gross misconduct by BCCI officials; (2) that Justice Department officials refused to send investigators who were needed to follow through on the leads;[64] (3) that the leads indicated large political payoffs in the United States; (4) that BCCI was financing unlawful arms transactions; (5) that BCCI secretly owned U.S. banks, and other federal violations; and (6) that Justice Department officials blocked exposure of these matters in numerous ways, including refusal to provide additional personnel, refusal to grant permission to obtain testimony outside the United States, and by reaching a plea bargain with BCCI before higher-ups were implicated.

Mazur further testified that he resigned from the U.S. Customs Service[65] because of his frustration at the cover-up by Justice Department officials and within the Customs Service. He described the discovery of BCCI's money-laundering activities in Tampa, Florida, and the political payoffs, along with the secret ownership of U.S. banks.

Justice and CIA Caught Red Handed

Feisty Congressman Henry Gonzalez's (D-TX) persistent investigations and demands for documents exposed the cover-up by Justice Department and CIA officials. Each of them had reported to Congressional committees that every document in their files pertaining to BCCI had been released to the Congressional investigative committees. These statements were proven false after the CIA inadvertently released sensitive documents disproving the statements. Media attention and charges of cover-up created a crisis situation, each of the two agencies blaming the other for cover-up.

Acting CIA Director Richard Kerr testified to the Senate committee on November 11, 1991, revealing that between 1983 and 1985 the CIA had sent several hundred reports to government agencies, including the Justice Department, chronicling BCCI's illegal activities. Justice Department officials had lied to Congress, stating initially they did not have any other documents. Thereafter, Justice Department officials sought to have CIA officials explain the discrepancy by lying, but without success.

Retaliating Against FBI Director

Congress and the media demanded that an independent prosecutor be requested to investigate the Justice Department and the CIA. FBI Director William Sessions assured Senator David Boren (D-OK) that the FBI would investigate the conduct of Justice Department officials.

---

[63] November 21, 1991.
[64] *Los Angeles Times*, November 22, 1991.
[65] Resigned in April 1990.

This statement was an unprecedented threat to his bosses in the Department of Justice, and who were implicated in several major scandals. Two days after Boren announced Sessions' intention to the press, U.S. Attorney General William Barr announced an investigation of Sessions for ethic violations.

The basis for the investigation of the FBI head? Sessions used government telephones for private business, allowing his wife to ride with him on government aircraft on a space available basis, and installing a security fence at his home to protect government secrets. Big deal! If applied in the same manner, this charge could be leveled at major segments of the federal and state governments.

Recognizing the phony and retaliatory nature of the charges, Senator Boren was among the Congressmen who charged Justice Department officials with trying to obstruct justice by threatening the Director of the FBI with phony charges.[66]

It was ironical that while Attorney General William Barr was engaging in widespread cover-up and obstruction of justice of many of the crimes described within these pages, he sought the removal of the FBI Director on these sham charges.

President Clinton Assisted in Cover-Up

Clinton had already played a key role in obstruction of justice relating to the vast CIA drug trafficking near Mena, Arkansas, while Clinton was governor of that state. After Bill Clinton became president and appointed Janet Reno as U.S. Attorney General, the two of them carried out Barr's previous plan to remove the Director of the FBI who constituted a threat to government corruption. Without allowing Sessions to defend against the obvious sham charges, Reno and Clinton removed the FBI Director.

The lapdog press eulogized this removal and said nothing about its relationship with Sessions' intent to investigate Justice Department corruption.

It is estimated that the BCCI corrupt practices cost innocent depositors from $5 to $15 *billion* in losses. Over a million depositors in 69 countries, including the United States, lost all or most of their savings and deposits. Part of BCCI's losses will be paid by the U.S. taxpayer through the losses of secretly owned savings and loans and the stockholders in the U.S. banks secretly owned by BCCI. The Independence Bank of Encino, California,[67] a BCCI bank, caused losses of $130 to

---

[66] Very few government employees have not used government phones for private calls. Many government employees, including myself, used government aircraft for flight experience which concurrently had an element of private use attached.

[67] Independence Bank had fourteen branches in the Los Angeles area.

$140 million. The American public, who will pay the tab, insures these losses.

U.S. investors in the bank-holding company secretly acquired by BCCI lost large sums of money. First American Bankshares paid $225 million to acquire National Bank of Georgia in 1985, receiving only $90 million from its 1992 sale after the BCCI scandal broke. The $135 million difference is a loss to the U.S. investors who owned part of the bank holding company.

Central banks and governments of Third World Nations will lose billions. These losses could have been prevented if the CIA or any of the other U.S. officials had performed their duties instead of engaging in felony cover-up. And the same goes for the members of Congress who also covered up. Of course, the same goes for each and every one of the other corrupt activities described within these pages.

Vatican Bank Scandal

Similar to the deaths of informants in other scandals such as Inslaw, Chapter 11 corruption, and October Surprise, witnesses and informants to the BCCI scandal were killed or mysteriously died. The 1988 death of a New York City lawyer, Cornelius Ahearn, is believed due to the fact that he knew too much about the links between the BCCI scandal and the Vatican Bank scandal[68] of the 1980s.

White House Involvement

The White House had numerous tentacles to the BCCI scandal, and through its control over the Justice Department blocked or greatly reduced action against BCCI for years, despite knowledge of the bank's criminal activities. President Bush's deputy campaign manager, James Lake,[69] simultaneously worked in 1992 for the main owner of scandal-riddled BCCI.[70]

Lawyer Ed Rogers, the right-hand assistant to President Bush's Chief of Staff, John Sununu, signed a lucrative employment agreement with a BCCI participant, Sheik Kamal Adham, the former chief of Saudi intelligence. Adham was at the heart of the BCCI bank swindle.

At the same time, the U.S. Attorney General and his Justice Department were blocking prosecution of BCCI. It was an interesting connection, to have a top-level campaign adviser for President Bush representing a major owner of the corruption-riddled renegade bank while the Justice Department was blocking prosecution of the multiple

---

[68] The Vatican bank scandal surfaced in 1982, following the collapse of Calvi's Milan-based bank. The Vatican settled law suits for $250 million.

[69] Lake worked as a senior communications adviser to the Bush campaign, being promoted on February 27, 1992 to deputy campaign manager for surrogates, advance and scheduling.

[70] *Associated Press*, February 28, 1992.

crimes involved in the BCCI scandal.

British Cover-Up

It was the English government that first acted to shut down BCCI in 1992 when the scandal became public. BCCI was chartered in Luxembourg but actually operated primarily in England under British regulators and investigators. The Bank of England and other British checks and balances knew about BCCI corrupt activities for years, and covered up. England's security agencies, MI5 and MI6, surely knew what was going on, and did nothing.

British media attention forced an "investigation," conducted by Lord Justice Bingham, who issued a report in October 1992. The report did nothing to prevent another BCCI, and did not delve into those responsible for the world's worst banking scandal. The report described BCCI's performance as "a tragedy of errors, misunderstandings and failures of communication." It wasn't a misunderstanding, nor failure of communication, that permitted BCCI to engage in world-wide money laundering, financing terrorists and drug cartels, threats and murders; it was criminal cover-up by every check and balance.

The people sabotaging their own country's interest were not only in the United States. The Bank of England reported (September 28, 1992) that it would seek a probe into allegations revealing that several of its employees took bribes from BCCI. It subsequently issued a whitewash report, stating that no evidence was found of bad faith, duplicity, cover-up, or conspiracy by British subjects in the BCCI corruption. The Bank of England entered into an arrangement with the bank's principal owner, Abu Dhabi, and under this agreement, important records and witnesses were allowed to leave England. In that way, those in England who aided and abetted the BCCI scheme escaped exposure.

Justice Department Cover-Up

"Something fishy is behind this government's reluctance to prosecute aggressively the well-connected predators of BCCI," stated William Safire in his November 1991 syndicated column.

Until January 1992, high Justice Department officials blocked an investigation into BCCI corruption, according to the testimony of a former U.S. Attorney in Miami, Dexter Lehtinen.[71] He testified that in 1991, when he was building a case against BCCI, Justice Department officials in Washington blocked court orders to obtain documents from foreign countries concerning BCCI corruption. Lehtinen also testified that in late August 1991 he received a phone call from a high Justice Department official who said he was calling on behalf of Acting Attor-

[71] Testified on May 14, 1992, before the Senate Subcommittee on Terrorism, Narcotics and International Operations.

ney General William Barr. The official said that Barr wanted him not to seek an indictment against BCCI. Congress also assisted in this cover-up by refusing to approve Lehtinen's temporary U.S. Attorney position to a permanent position, causing him to resign.

Members of Congress demanded in 1992 that Attorney General William Barr request the appointment of an Independent Prosecutor to investigate BCCI. Barr refused to do so. He had earlier refused to appoint a congressionally requested independent prosecutor in the Inslaw matter, in the Bank of Lavoro matter, and in the Iraqgate matter.

The prosecution of BCCI on the money-laundering charge was not initiated by the Justice Department but on the initiative of local Customs Service agents. Justice Department officials had sought to block that prosecution, but this proved difficult due to media attention, Justice sought to limit the scope of the investigation by reaching a plea agreement allowing BCCI to ensure that the evidence collected during the investigation wouldn't be used against BCCI in any future federal charges.

One of Many Reasons for Justice Department Cover-Up

Before William Barr came to the Justice Department, he was a lawyer with the Washington law firm of Shaw, Pittman, Potts & Trowbridge. This law firm represented BCCI for several years. A partner in the law firm, Kenly Webster, was representing a former BCCI chief executive, Swaleh Naqvi, who had been indicted by a Manhattan grand jury on fraud, false accounting, money laundering and other charges. Naqvi had also been indicted in Tampa, Florida, on similar charges. Barr's former law firm also represented B. Francis Saul II, a director and powerful shareholder in Financial General Bankshares, Inc. Financial later became First American Bankshares, a covert BCCI operation.

Further, Barr had been legal counsel for the CIA, the same agency that was heavily involved with BCCI corrupt activities. He was CIA counsel during the time that George Bush was Director of the CIA. Barr appeared with CIA Director Bush in hearings before Congress.

Attorney General of the United States Involved in Drug Offenses?

Terry Reed wrote in his book, *Compromised*, that William Barr was a lawyer for Southern Air Transport, to whom Reed routinely reported for coordinating arms shipments from Arkansas to Central America and drug shipments on the return flights. Reed wrote that he knew Barr during the 1980s as Robert Johnson.

Miami lawyer James F. Dougherty II, representing an insurance group that had sued BCCI, appealed directly to Attorney General Richard Thornburgh (December 1990) when evidence surfaced that BCCI was planning to destroy or move records of its corrupt activities. No response was received.[72]

Justice Department officials blocked the testimony of two key witnesses before a Senate hearing on BCCI,[73] who would have exposed not only BCCI's criminality but also the cover-up by Justice Department and CIA officials. Robert Mazur, who headed the Customs Service's investigation of BCCI in Tampa, and an assistant U.S. Attorney, Mark Jackowski, had sought to file charges against BCCI, but Washington officials blocked the investigation.

Justice Department officials shut down an investigation into the BCCI ownership of First American Bankshares in October 1989, allegedly so that it could focus on another probe. But when that probe was completed, Justice Department officials never went back to the far more serious matter of illegal ownership of First American Bank Holding Company. It wasn't until the Manhattan prosecutor started exposing the BCCI corruption and the Bank of England seized control of BCCI that Justice Department officials showed signs of life. At that point Justice Department officials had to do something. Some reports state that as many as twenty percent of the members of both houses of Congress received bribes from BCCI.[74]

Although known for years, the corruption surfaced in September 1991. BCCI accomplished its corrupt activities by bribing prominent citizens and high government officials throughout the world, including the United States.

Top law firms and public relation firms in the United States fronted for the rogue bank, secretly enabling it to operate in the United States. Members of Congress, the CIA, Justice Department, and other U.S. government agencies were responsible for the continuation of most if not all of the criminal activities described in these pages. The mentality of BCCI suited to a "t" much of the criminality by U.S. officials.

BCCI secretly and unlawfully owned several American banks in violation of federal law. Included in these banks secretly owned by BCCI were First American Bank of the District of Columbia and its 43 branches in New York City.

U.S. authorities had known of BCCI's corruption and looting of deposits for years. Dozens of informants notified Justice Department officials and members of Congress of the corrupt activities. But, as in every other scandal within the federal government, nothing was done to stop BCCI's corrupt activities until the scandal broke (July 1991) in England, causing the bank to be closed.

---

[72] *Daily Journal*, October 21, 1990.
[73] New York Times October 2, 1991.
[74] *Spotlight*, October 21, 1991.

Hundreds of Ignored Warnings

Before the bubble burst on this racketeering operation, depositors lost billions of dollars, wiping out the life savings of many people, especially those in undeveloped countries. Insiders, including drug traffickers[75] and the CIA,[76] had advance notice of the pending collapse and took their money out before BCCI collapsed.

Just prior to the Justice Department crackdown on the BCCI secretly owned bank in Tampa, forewarned drug dealers made a run on the bank, withdrawing over $10 million.

Front men such as former Defense Secretary Clark Clifford and Robert Altman acted as cutouts or front men to cover up for the unlawful BCCI ownership. In 1979, lawyers Clifford and Altman deceptively acted to permit BCCI to unlawfully acquire ownership of First American Bankshares in Washington, D.C. Clifford was a lawyer and veteran power broker in Washington, and he was a pillar of the Washington Beltway establishment.

Other U.S. financial institutions were later acquired through lawyers acting as BCCI front men, or with their connivance. These included Independence Bank in Encino, California, and CenTrust Savings in Miami.

The Atlanta branch of BNL loaned or pledged nearly $5 billion to Iraq between 1985 and the summer of 1989.

Jack Blum, who initially learned of the criminal activities while an investigator for the Senate, believes that both Republicans and Democrats blocked an investigation because members of their own parties were responsible for covering up early warnings of the criminal activities. The same can be stated of the 1980 October Surprise scandal and the many others within these pages.

Prominent Washington figures made the BCCI scandal possible. There were numerous members of Congress; prominent lawyers Clifford and Altman; former Treasury Secretary John Connally, who bought a Texas bank with BCCI front man Ghaith Pharaon; former Atlanta Mayor Andrew Young, who borrowed money from BCCI and never paid it back; Ron Brown, chairman of the Democratic Party, a partner in the Washington law firm of Patton, Boggs and Blow, which received $1.3 million in fees from BCCI, later joined President Clinton's Washington staff.

In February 1992, a federal grand jury indicted David Paul, the former chairman of CenTrust Savings Bank in Miami, on fraud charges. The charges arose from a $25 million securities deal involving an

---

75 New York Times October 28, 1991.

76 Statements made to me by CIA informants.

investor linked to BCCI. Also charged were Ghaith Pharaon, reportedly a front man for BCCI, and William Christopher Berry.

The Usual Congressional Bribing

BCCI penetrated the U.S. financial system through American law firms and lawyers who helped inflict upon the United States and other countries great financial harm and aided and abetted the drug-money laundering, financing of terrorists, and other unlawful activities. They turned their legal expertise against the United States for profit.

Crimes Aided by Jury Members

The trial of lawyer Robert Altman as part of the largest bank fraud in the nation and the world's history occurred in 1993 in New York City. Altman, with his boyish smile of innocence, was accompanied throughout the trial by his attractive wife and former television star, Lynda Carter. She was a popular sideshow to the trial.

The jury, composed of many unsophisticated people, some of whom couldn't be expected to balance their personal check books, were confronted with complex matters, compounded by the usual misrepresentation of legal counsel. On August 14, 1993, the jury acquitted Altman of the charges, proving again that crime pays, especially when cloaked in complex legal activities.

The outcome of a jury trial by unsophisticated jury members is similar to playing a slot machine. There are those jury members who believe everything the prosecutor says, assuming that *surely* an innocent person would not be charged if the facts were not true. There are the jurists who are influenced by legal chicanery that tricks the jury. There are those jurists who are influenced by the look of innocence, such as displayed by Oliver North and Robert Altman.

The BCCI corruption was effectively covered up by New York jury members, followed by the cover-up of President Clinton's Justice Department. It remained for foreign countries to prosecute and punish many of those who played key roles in the BCCI debacle.

Independent Counsel Versus Special Counsel

There are vast differences between an "independent counsel" (or independent prosecutor as they are sometimes called) and a "special counsel." A special counsel is selected by the U.S. Attorney General, works under Justice Department officials, and submits a report to the Justice Department. If Justice Department officials are implicated, the most obvious expectation is that it will be a cover-up. The Attorney General's selection of the special counsel will be almost sure to obtain that result.

An Independent Counsel or Independent Prosecutor, on the other hand, is selected by a panel of three appellate judges in the District of Columbia, following a request by the U.S. Attorney General. The Attorney General considers the request for an independent counsel following the request by a majority of the House or Senate Judiciary Committees. But even an independent counsel has its limitations. The person appointed by the federal appellate judges is often inexperienced, and may have a cover-up agenda.

Citi Bank and CIA

Since I first started hearing from many people in the government's covert operations that name Citibank frequently arose, indicating a close relationship between covert operations and the bank. There are numerous references to Citibank, the CIA, and money laundering in the books, *Defrauding America* and *Drugging America.* In one book, *FBI, CIA, the Mob, and Treachery*, former FBI special agent Richard Taus described his transition from a military pilot during the Vietnam War, his time spent in covert operations, his subsequent employment with Citibank, and then his transition to an FBI agent.

History of Citibank

Citibank is part of Citigroup. It started in 1812 as the City Bank of New York, and later became First National City Bank of New York (FNCB). It is a contributor to the Federal Reserve Bank of New York. Following its merger with the First National Bank, the bank changed its name to The First National City Bank of New York. In the mid-1970s, First National City Bank and its holding company First National City Corporation were renamed Citibank and Citicorp, respectively. Citicorp and Travelers Group merged in 1998.

Vatican Bank Corruption

The hundreds of Catholic priests and thousands of criminal sexual crimes they repeatedly committed, protected at virtually every level of the church up to and including the Vatican and the popes, should not expect the conduct of the Church's bank, the Vatican Bank, to be any less lawless. The lawlessness of the Vatican Bank has been detailed in various books, including *In God's Name: An Investigation into the Murder of Pope John Paul I.* That book detailed a pattern of financial frauds and murder during the 1980s.[77]

The Vatican Bank is located in Vatican City. It does not have any shareholders. It has a chief operating officer reporting to a group of cardinals, and in turn, to the Pope. The Vatican Bank invests in foreign companies.

The Vatican Bank was exposed in a major financial and political scandal that involved the murder of Pope John Paul I and others. Involved was the 1982 collapse of the bank, Banco Ambrosiano at a loss

---

[77] Other books included *Unholy Trinity: How the Vatican's Nazi Networks Betrayed Western Intelligence to the Soviets; Genocide in Satellite Croatia 1941–1945;* and *The Vatican's Holocaust,*

of $3.5 billion to the Vatican Bank.

Archbishop Paul Marcinkus was the head of the Vatican Bank from 1971 to 1989. After Banco Ambrosiano declared bankruptcy in 1982, Marcinkus was under consideration for indictment for his role as an accessory to the conditions preceding the bankruptcy filing. Marcinkus avoided indictment and trial in the Italian courts because of his diplomatic immunity as a member of the sovereign nation of the Vatican.

During this period in the 1970s and 1980s, a financial advisor in the Vatican Bank, Michele Sindona, with a questionable past, was responsible for heavy deposits from drug money laundering of the Gambino crime family. The Vatican Bank reportedly received a 50 percent fee for the money laundering.

The deposits were made through a shell corporation called Mabusi, and assisted by a banker at Banco Ambrosiano, Roberto Calvi. Calvi and Sindona were members of the P2 Lodge.[78]

Pope John Paul I's suspicious death, after becoming Pope in 1978, was preceded by instructing the Cardinal Secretary of State, Jean-Marie Villot, to investigate reports of misconduct at the Vatican Bank. That action resulted in his suspicious death within 33 days of taking office.

Vatican Bank, Banco Ambrosiano and Money Laundering

Father Paul Marcinkus headed the Institute for Religious Works from 1971 to 1989. When Banco Ambrosiano went bankrupt, Marcinkus was indicted in that year and named an accessory in the $3.5 billion collapse of Banco Ambrosiano. Banco Ambrosiano reportedly was laundering drug money for the Sicilian Mafia with the help of a Masonic lodge called P2. On the basis of being a citizen of the sovereign nation of the Vatican, Marcinkus had diplomatic immunity against being tried by an Italian court. He eventually moved to Sun City, Arizona, where he died on February 21, 2006. *The Godfather, Part III,* was a 1990 film portraying the Vatican Bank as a central element in the Vatican Bank covert activities.

During those proceedings, Roberto Calvi of Banco Ambrosiano was believed involved in the murder of Gérard Soisson, a member of a financial clearing house, Clearstream. Evidence indicated that Calvi's death resulted from the decision of the ruling council of the Sicilian Mafia, the Cupola.[79] They viewed Calvi as a liability.

---

[78] Propaganda Due, or P2 was a Masonic lodge operating legally in Italy from 1945 to 1976 and then illegally from 1976 to 1981. It was involved in multiple criminal activities, including the collapse of the Vatican-affiliated Banco Ambrosiano and the murder of Roberto Calvi. The group was sometimes referred to as the shadow government or a state within a state.

[79] The Cupola is a Sicilian Mafia commission that decides on important

Secret Convey of Funds from Croatia to the Vatican

A report issued by the US State Department in 1998 stated that the Nazi Croatian treasury[80] was unlawfully transferred to the Vatican Bank and other banks after the end of World War II. The Vatican has refused to open its wartime records to support its denial.

An earlier top secret report[81] by U.S. Agent Emerson Bigelow (*The Bigelow Report*), quoted reliable sources in Italy that confirmed evidence already obtained by the U.S. Army's CIC[82] intelligence personnel. That report stated that Croatian officials had sent 350 million confiscated Swiss francs to the Vatican Bank "for safekeeping", a sum largely in the form of gold coins. During the transfer to the Vatican, British soldiers at the border between Austria and Switzerland seized 150 million Swiss francs.

Reflecting the somewhat unholy nature of the Vatican Bank dealings, it reportedly was involved in moving covert funds for the United States to the Contras during the covert Iran-Contra operation.

A number of class action lawsuits were filed against the Vatican Bank. These lawsuits accused the Vatican Bank and Franciscan Order of laundering assets taken by Nazi concentration camp, financing ODESSA,[83] and the ratlines.[84] One lawsuit, *Levy v. CIA*, filed under the U.S. Freedom of Information Act, sought the release of U.S. intelligence agency files relating to a reported Vatican spymaster, Father Krunoslav Draganovic.[85]

---

matters and settles disputes within the Mafia members.

[80] Just as the Japanese were doing, the Germany looted the assets of the countries that it invaded and deposited the gold and other treasures in cooperating banks in other countries, including Croatia, receiving currency in return to finance its war machine.

[81] The U.S. Treasury report dated On October 21, 1946, was declassified in 1997.

[82] The U.S. Army Counter intelligence Corps (CIC) was existed in World War II and during the Cold War. Its function was later taken over by the U.S. Army Intelligence Corps in 1961 and, in 1967, by the U.S. Army Intelligence Agency. Its functions are now performed by the United States Army Intelligence and Security Command and by the Defense Intelligence Agency.

[83] ODESSA was an organization of former Nazi SS members established toward the end of World War II, seeking to avoid being captured and prosecuted for war crimes by going to South America and the Middle East.

[84] Ratlines referred to the smuggling of Nazi war criminals out of Germany and Austria at the end of World War II.

[85] Krunoslav Stjepan Draganović was a Croatian Roman Catholic priest reportedly one of the main organizers of the group, referred to as ratlines, that aided Nazi war criminals to escape from Europe after the end of World War II. He died in 1983.

A class action lawsuit, ***Alperin v. Vatican Bank,***[86] was filed in the federal courts at San Francisco in November 1999 against the Vatican Bank and Franciscan Order by plaintiffs consisting of Holocaust survivors and other concentration camp survivors. The district court dismissed the action in 2003 on the holding that it was a political question. But the Ninth Circuit Court of Appeals reinstated the lawsuit in 2005. The lawsuit involved claims under the Alien Tort Claims Act (ATCA)[87] and the Foreign Sovereign Immunities Act (FSIA).[88]

The lawsuit was dismissed in 2007 on the basis of sovereign immunity, based upon the Vatican being considered a sovereign nation.[89] That was done despite the fact that the lawsuit was not against the Vatican City but against the Vatican Bank. The U.S. Supreme Court refused to hear the case in January 2006.

Vatican Involvement with Japanese Gold Plunder

In other pages, reference is made to OSS and CIA operative Santa Romana, his retrieval of portions of the Japanese gold plunder in the Philippines, and his role as a priest in the Catholic Church.

Big Bank Culture Surfaced in 2008 Financial Implosion

The flagrant corruption throughout the financial system in the United States that imploded in 2008 resulted in the culture also seen in these pages. My book, *America's Housing and Financial Frauds* provides many more examples of how people pay the price for this corrupt culture and endemic cover-ups.

The following is a letter sent by Washington attorney Robert A. Ackerman describing what he discovered about the banks' refusal to admit the existence of deposits by Santa Romana to the administrator of his estate. The letter shows that Ackerman was unaware of the culpability of key people in the government of the United States and their complicity with the banks.

ROBERT A. ACKERMAN

---

[86] 104 F.3d 1086 (9th Cir. 1997), 284 F.3d 1114.

[87] The Alien Tort Statute (28 U.S.C. § 1350; ATS, also called the Alien Tort Claims Act (ATCA) reads: "The district courts shall have original jurisdiction of any civil action by an alien for a tort only, committed in violation of the law of nations or a treaty of the United States." This statute allows U.S. courts to hear human rights cases filed by foreign citizens for conduct committed outside the United States.

[88] The Foreign Sovereign Immunities **Act** (FSIA), Title 28 §§ 1330, 1332, 1391(f), 1441(d), and 1602-1611, establishes when a foreign sovereign nation may be sued in U.S. courts and the procedures for service of process and attachment of property for proceedings against a Foreign State.

[89] President Ronald Reagan recognized Vatican sovereignty in 1984.

ATTORNEY AT LAW
1250 FOURTH STREET. S.W. NO. 504 W
Washington, D.C. 20024
(202) 554-2908
January 9, 1991

Following is a description of the efforts of George J. DePontis (hereinafter "D"), with whom I am cooperating, to retrieve large sums originally delivered in Gen. Lansdale's Philippine days to a now deceased agent, Severino Santa Romana, DOB 2/29/1901, died 1974. You may see some angles in this matter—which I have overlooked.

1. Summary. D is a 45 year old (approx.) Miamian who has been drawn to politics since working in the 1968 Hubert Humphrey Florida campaign. He worked for Claude Pepper, who was his mentor, operated a political consulting PR firm in the early 1980's, now publishes a magazine for disabled persons ("Ability Magazine"), advises an opposition party in the Bahamas to Pindling for which he is a registered agent, and advises the general minister of the People's Democratic Party now holding power in the Turks and Caicos Islands.

D contacted Ray Cline recently for financial or other support in an effort to retrieve large sums of money out of 174 odd bank accounts in 40 countries including USA/NYC set up by former agent Santa Romana under various aliases and names of corporations controlled by him.

D is working on behalf of a Philippine lady who was a close coworker of the dead agent and her two Philippine lawyers. Ray Cline referred D to me in mid-December. I agreed to work with D on a contingency basis and have been in telephone contact with him and the Philippine lawyer who has been his prime point of contact.

The Philippine lady, Tarciana Rodriguez, has interest and apparent legal authority to claim the funds, either as personal representative of the dead agent's estate which she is seeking a Manila court to name her, or as treasurer of some of the corporations which she already is.

D would like me or someone to contact intelligence authorities for possible help in retrieving money from the NYC and other accounts. I have declined to do so, noting my style is to have no direct contact with such governmental arms (while bringing to bear whatever general experience I have in such matters as a former Justice Dept. attorney, etc.)

I agreed to work with the Philippine lawyer to:

1. get some money for me if I can contribute to success in retrieving some funds, and 2. possibly broker an agreement between the Philippine claimant and the USG under which most of any money belonging to the USG would go back to it with suitable finder's fees going to each person concerned. D has provided the account number, name in

which the account is held, and other specifics on a Citibank NYC account thought to hold large amounts of bullion, cash, and 9 safe deposit boxes originally established by the dead agent in a Manila bank branch taken over in the meantime by what is now Citibank.

2. Referral by Ray Cline. Enclosed is a copy of a memo I banged out quickly for my own purposes on Ray's initial Dec. 12, 1990 phone call to me (complete with typing errors, etc. - hopefully my hieroglyphics are intelligible.). Also enclosed are copies of a follow-up Dec. 13 letter Ray wrote me enclosing a Dec. 13 fax from D to Ray describing the project. D beat me to the punch and called me from Miami before I got up to calling him, about Dec. 16. In a long telecom he explained the pot of gold he was working to get. Thus was provided the following information.

3. D first heard of the project through William H. Bancroft of Ohio (who D says is not very important in the matter now). The central figure was a Philippine national, Severino Santa Romana (AKA Jose Antonio Diaz, AKA J. Antonio Diaz, AKA Mateass Connea, AKA Severino Pena Garcia de la Paz, AKA Jose Almonte, AKA Santy) who died in 1974. Santa Romana was recruited by CIA while a student in the USA. From a wealthy wife who predeceased him, Evangeline Compton, he inherited much money. He womanized a good bit. He owned several companies, namely, DPB Enterprises, Diaz and Poirotte Enterprises, Crown Enterprises, Goleen Enterprises, DNP Enterprises, and Cooley Enterprises.(N.B.- the key Citibank account on which we are targeting as described below is "owned by" Diaz and Poirette Enterprises).

Santa Ramona had about 176 accounts in 42 countries in his name under the various aliases above or in the name of his various companies. Included are accounts in Hong Kong (with the Hong Kong and Shanghai hank and the PRC controlled Busan Bank), Malaysia, NYC, Switzerland (Union Swiss Bank, Geneva, and City Bank, Geneva), Luxemburg, Lichtenstein, Monaco/Monte Carlo, Puerto Rico, and Brazil. What I infer was his devious nature is seen in the fact that one of the corporations (I believe DNP or Diaz and Poirrette Enterprises) was "registered" in Monte Carlo.

Santa Romana is said (by whom is not clear) to have known George Bush. (D also noted that he himself has had some contact in Florida with Jeb Bush, a son of George, who is active in Florida real estate.)

Santa Romana's long time trusted assistant, Tarciana C. Rodriguez, was named as one of 14 beneficiaries in his holographic will. Although he died in 1974, the estate has not yet been settled. Tarciana is represented in a court considering the will by Manila attorney Justo G. Trazo (referred to as "Tony" by D) who practices with Caesar R. Estonillo.

Trazo has pending a motion to have Tarciana named as administrator in Case No. M-1885 before the Regional Trial Court of Markati in Cebu ("Markati" is phon. in a telecon among Trazo, D. and me - but cf. the nearby island of Marbata, which I noted later in the atlas). If she is named, Tarciana would have authority to demand payment of all accounts in Santa Romana's name. (An interesting legal question, which I defer for the moment, is whether this would include authority to demand payment of accounts held by Santa Romana under one of his aliases. My current sense is that Philippine law would control the answer. Note that the Citibank account discussed below is in the name of "Jose Antonio Diaz". Apart from her authority as personal relative of the estate, Tarciana is the "national treasurer" of the deceased agent's DNP Enterprises and of his Diaz and Poirette Enterprises corporation, the latter of which "owns" the Citibank account in the name of Jose Antonio Diaz.*/

D has been in frequent telephonic contact with Manila attorney Trazo, who appears to be his primary source of information on the project. He has not yet been in touch with Tarciana, although he has a power of attorney from Trazo, who in turn holds a power of attorney from Tarciana. Just what these powers provide I have not seen and cannot say. D anticipates soon having a telephone conference among him, me, Tarciana, and probably Trazo as well.

On about Jan. 3, 1991 D set up a three way telephone conference among Trazo, D, and me. (He would have set one up earlier, but I deferred until I had received the documentary information in D's Dec. 19 letter to me, so I could have a firmer grasp of what I might be discussing). On Jan. 3 I summarized for Trazo my background (ex cold warrior, 6 years in Justice Dept., in private practice since 1971, once worked for Ray Cline). Taro noted his (studied at University of San Carlo, took Philippine bar exam in 1958, passed bar in 1959, began practice in 1960, had been a secretary to a Congressman in Cebu, is now president or a corporation, the head of a construction company, and owns a hotel in Cebu City).

He summarized the probate court action: there have been 3 hearings; Tarciana's petition to be appointed administrator has been published as required by law; there are possible other claimants for the function of administrator of the estate (who may be descendants of Santa Romana - I missed something here); the other possible claimants have not appeared in court at hearings, however, an "are in default". Tarciana petition remains pending and may be granted.

[Footnote in original document] */ That the account is in the name of Diaz and is "owned" by the corporation does not make sense to me and discords with American practice, as I have noted to D. Possibly the explanation is that the account was originally opened in the Philippines which used such a practice. If so, I do not understand its implications. To be clarified.

I stated to Trazo an excellent suggestion made earlier that day to me, namely, that Tarciana transmit to banks holding deposits in the name of corporations for which she can act a modest (perhaps $200.00) deposit. I added a suggestion that in doing so she request regular transmission to her of statements on the accounts, thus setting the stage for a subsequent action to withdraw funds therefrom. Trazo liked the idea and apparently will discuss it with Tarciana. I noted that if a U.S. bank refused to comply with such a demand by her where her authority is clear, she could then sue the bank for conversion and probably get a judgment (with me as her U.S. attorney, presumably). Then action could be taken to attach the account.

Trazo and I exchanged addresses and telephone numbers. I provided my fax and telex numbers to facilitate direct, timely communication, with information and copies of all communications to go to D), since, I stressed, "it is his case". Trazo is at 3 Mayapis Street, Marietta-Romeo Village, Sta. Lucia, Parsig, Metro Manila (apparently his law office with Ceasar Estonillo). He was calling from his sister's house with telephone 992336. It may not always be reachable there at that number.

D raised the question of a fee for me. I suggested a contingency arrangement under which I would get perhaps $ 2,000.00 out of the first funds to be recovered with my help and a percentage (now undefined) of later recovery. No agreement was reached thereon; Trazo will apparently discuss this with Tarciana. I noted I would give the case priority in any event pending further developments.

D noted he expects to go to the Bahamas (where he is the registered representative of an opposition party to Pindling) and hopes with the help of his contacts there to get funds from an account or accounts Sanata Romana had there, which might provide some funds to support further effort.

<u>NYC Accounts</u>. D had previously provided information on two key NYC bank accounts, as follows:

a. Citibank. The account is in the name of "Jose Antonio Diaz", and the principal owner of the account is "Diaz and Poirotte Enterprises", a corporation of which Tarciana is "national treasurer".

D provided: the account number, the tax umber pertaining to the account, the Identification Code for the account (which is Santa Romana's birthdate), a Codename pertaining to the account.

D did not provide an "opening code" used with 9 lock boxes presumed to be in the account, which has been memorized by Tarciana. (Presumably, thus she has to come to NYC to enter the lock boxes.) The account is thought to contain bullion, the 9 lock boxes, and speculatively, some cash. Tarciana has not paid rental charges for the lock boxes since martial law was declared in the Philippines. Originally the account was opened with the First National City Bank of Manila, of which a James Collin was manager. Collin is now nowhere to be found. The manila branch was taken over by what is now Citibank. Presumably the lock boxes and the supposed bullion have been transported to NYC. D advised me that he had recently spent the better part of one day on the telephone with Citibank, NYC which disclaimed any knowledge of such an account. Regarding possible escheat to the state of N.Y., D gave the address of the appropriate office as State of N.Y., Office of State Controller, Albany, N.Y., c/o Betty Powell. Bureau of unclaimed Property. D will contact that office for any trace.

My present best thought on how to examine/obtain the account's contents is: first, disregard the bank disclaimer of knowledge of the account over the phone; emphasize properly stated and authorized dealings on paper (which can serve as evidence in a possible later conversion action); have Tarciana acting on behalf of Diaz and Poirotte Enterprises send a $ 200.00 check to Citibank for deposit in the account giving account number and name; have Tarciana request Citibank to send regular bank statements to her as treasurer of Diaz and Poirotte Enterprises; scrutinize the statements to clarify the name in which the account is held, ascertain that charges have been deducted if any for rental of the 9 lock boxes presumably in the account and now located in NYC.

If Tarciana has by that time been granted letters of administration for the Santa Romana estate by the Philippine court, have her in that capacity request a statement of the balance and transfer to her for the estate of same providing documentation that Jose Antonio Diaz was a name used by Santa Romana and (new thought, not yet suggested to D or Trazo, she having documented to the Philippine court, as she should be doing now, that Santa Romana had used Jose Antonio Diaz and the other aliases noted above) she to present to Citibank documentation in court records that Santa Romana and Jose' Antonio Diaz were the same person. Comment: under American law, and presumably under Philippine law as well, there is nothing illegal in a person's using an alias so long as it is not used for fraudulent purposes; it was not so used here.

Should Citibank refuse to deliver to Tarciana in response to her demand made as personal representative of the estate the contents of the account, she should sue Citibank in New York State for conversion and should prevail and get a judgment for the accounts contents. This would require a local NYC lawyer (whom I could select and oversee) but would not be a complicated or difficult case, if we do our preparatory work now properly. Comment: I note happily that the statute of limitations should be no problem since the conversion action "does not accrue" until the bank has refused to comply with a demand for delivery of the balance.

Further comment: it is doubtful that court action would be necessary if we take care to see that Tarciana's demand is made with proper' authority and properly documented for the record. It is in the atmosphere that the culinary people have a close working relationship with Citibank. But the bank's attorneys will monitor this closely to see that the bank is not exposed to suit. They will not allow such exposure just to maintain good relations with culinary people who might (D speculates) encourage Citibank not to deliver the account's balance. The bank's attorneys are responsible for covering Citibank's anatomy, and they can be counted upon to do so. Finally, should Tarciana not be granted letters of administration of the estate, we should examine what authority to demand payments she might have as treasurer of Diaz and Poirrotte Enterprises. Her getting bank statement: may help clarify this.

b. Chase Manhattan. This account is in the name of Severino Santa Romana. It is a bullion account. D provided me the account Number and a "Reference Code". The bank officer concerned is/was Randolph Earman. The confidential trust officer was Miles Armstrong.

Tim Tyler and Billy Guererra (sp?) D noted that an earlier, unsuccessful effort had been made by these two to get the pot of gold. The names are unknown to me.

Possible Approach to Dante Fascell. D spoke early on of the possibility that, if nothing else works, he might contact Rep. Dante Fascell for help in clarifying the matter and obtaining the funds. My sense is that this is not an active possibility at present. (And I do not see how this would help in any event. All that excellent, highly experienced congressman would do is refer the matter to the appropriate USG executive department authorities to look into. My guess is that, unless the above is a total fabrication, which I do not think it is, governmental authorities are already familiar with at least some of the above.)

D's Contacts With Miami Police and FBI. D noted early on that he had discussed the matter with a friend in the local police and also with an FBI person he knows. I commended him for doing so, noting the advisability of covering the anatomy to protect against misunderstanding of what he (and I with him now) are doing.

The Widow Lansdale. I advised D that after Gen. Lansdale died I had been in touch with his widow, Pat Lansdale, a Philippine resident in Virginia, and reviewed his will. I provided her address from the file which I retrieved (2008 Lorraine Ave., McLean, Va. 22101 as of early 1987.) I noted I would contact her to see whether she knew anything of Santa Romana. I now have her current tel. No: (---------), and plan to contact her. D noted he had been in touch with the author of a biography of Gen. Lansdale who might contact the widow. Hopefully this may produce some confirming or additional information on Santa Romana,

Newspaper Editorial Mentioning Santa Romana. D is eager to obtain, as he mentioned in the three cornered telecon with Trazo, a copy of the August 31, 1990 Manila Inquirer, an editorial of which mentioned Santa Romana. Trazo knew thereof, D reminded him to send a copy. I also to check that issue at the Library of Congress, which I offered to do. This would be welcome information on Santa Romana from a source other than Trazo/Tarciana.

As to the accounts other than the Citibank one noted above, would generally favor the following approach:

1. Identify each and every account in all of the 40 odd countries held in the name of a corporation for which Tarciana can act, e.g., DNP Enterprises and Diaz and Poirrette Enterprises for which she is treasurer. By "identify" I mean assemble in the hands of D and myself such specific information.

2. Trazo and Tarciana to determine in each such case whether any bank statements can be found in corporate files. If so, copies thereof to go to D and me.

3. Giving priority to accounts in the U.S.A., Tarciana to send a check of perhaps $ 150.00 to deposit in each account, acting in her corporate capacity and requesting regular transmission of bank statements to her and check blanks, if she does not already have such, D and I to monitor each such action closely and keep good records.

4. Proceeding first as to accounts in the U.S.A., Tarciana then to write a check on each account for about $ 3,000.00 payable to the order of the corporation; or later checks to be written by Tarciana. D and I to monitor each action closely.

5. If the bank does not honor the check/ when presented, legal action to be instituted against the bank for conversion, with me acting as attorney for the corporation. I to select and oversee local counsel in cases in jurisdictions in which I am not admitted to practice, i.e., California (Wells Fargo), Puerto Rico (City Bank, San Juan).

6. Proceeding thereafter against accounts outside the U.S.A. or Philippines (and keeping in mind that non-U.S.A. countries may not have the clear law of conversion which obtains everywhere in the U.S.A.) Trazo and I jointly to select and oversee local counsel to institute suit for conversion against those banks which fail to honor checks written by Tarciana when presented. I have contacts with reliable private investigators or local lawyers in some overseas areas which may be useful in selecting reliable, cost effective attorneys to handle any

actions against banks which prove necessary (London, Caracas, Oslo, Tokyo, etc.)

7. When and if Tarciana is granted letters of administration of Santa Romana's estate, she would request each bank holding an account in any name used by him to provide information on the balance and them demand payment to her as personal representative. I note again for emphasis the importance of getting evidence before the probate court of Santa Romana's use of every name in which it appears an account may be held and, if possible, having the court in granting her letters of administration specifically refer to each alias and authorize her to collect assets held under that name. This could solve a lot of problems where accounts are held under an alias.

Action By Imposters To Acquire Contents of Malaysian Account. Somewhat out of order, I note that D mentioned an effort currently underway by a certain person claiming to be the son or other descendant of Santa Romana to get assets of one of the accounts in Malaysia. No other details currently available, but D knows more about it and I hope to learn more of it.

I write you this rather comprehensive summary because:

a. I need to summarize and record the matter for my own purposes anyway;

b. Your background in Philippine matters in-the Lansdale time may well enable you to recognize (or not to recognize) some of the names and transactions involved. I find the matter fascinating and will continue to work with it (assuming some firm contingency arrangement can be agreed on). It just does not seem to me to be a total fabrication, although continued checking will throw further light thereon. And if it proves to be true that considerable sums involved should go back to the USG and its taxpayers, it would be interesting to help work out an arrangement for getting such done, with finder's fees to all concerned, including me.

And if the USG could help in retrieving the pot of gold, that would be nice. In any event, it would be foolish of me not to give you a chance to look at this matter from the standpoint of your background in Philippine affairs during the time period concerned. Thus I send you this for any comment you care to make. (Terry and the Pirates, anyone?)

Enclosures: Enclosed are:

a. My home grown, uncorrected memo on Ray Cline's 12/12/90 call.

b. Ray Cline's 12/17/90 letter to me.

c. The 12/13/90 letter by D to Ray Cline, which was sent to me.

d. The 12/19/90 letter by D to me.

e. A brochure entitled "project Masters -News Clips" which D sent to me.

Truly,
Bob
Robert A. Ackerman

Famed San Francisco attorney Melvin Belli filed a lawsuit[90] for conversion of bank deposits, in the California courts at San Francisco on March 11, 1994, showing Luz Rambano Santa Romana as Plaintiff and Citibank, Chase Manhattan Bank, Hong Kong Shanghai Banking Corporation, Bank of America, Wells Fargo Bank, and John S. Reed, CEO of Citibank, as defendants. The complaint stated in part:

Plaintiff is the widow and successor in interest to the estate of Severino Santa Area, a/k/a Jose Antonio Diaz. Plaintiff's late husband was a multi-billionaire who passed away in 1974, leaving plaintiff as the heir to his bank accounts at defendants' banks. These accounts represent large amounts of cash and gold bullion which decedent had deposited in said banks, and include the accounts mentioned hereinafter at defendants' banks. Plaintiff will amend this complaint to include additional a defendants, and additional accounts, as these are ascertained.

Plaintiff, the rightful and legal heir to these accounts, demanded that defendants turn these accounts over to her, which are her personal property, Plaintiff is entitled to the possession of the following property:

- Accounts 787632, 224461, 77236, 0033516 and 48278 representing cash deposits in the name of Jose Antonio Diaz at defendant Citibank N.A.
- Account 270093 representing cash deposits in the name of Luz C. Rambano at defendant Citibank N.A.
- Accounts MR-432, JOVE-3876 and JAYVEE-473 representing cash deposits in the name of Jose Antonio Diaz at defendant Citibank.
- Accounts in the name of Jose Antonio Diaz representing gold bullion deposits using the code names of "Bridgett" and "Harbor King" at defendant Citibank I.A.
- Accounts 389-618, 13087 and 131187 representing cash and gold deposits in the names of Jose Antonio Diaz and Crown Enterprises at defendant Chase Manhattan bank N.A.
- Account 306-14-87-7 using code name VHMSRS CROWN repre-

---

[90] Superior Court of San Francisco, Case No. 955366,

senting gold deposits in the name of Jose Antonio Diaz at defendant Chase Manhattan Bank

- An account representing cash deposits in the name of J. Antonio Diaz using customer identification number 0000001246137 at defendant Hong Kong Shanghai Banking Corporation, Ltd. 11. The above-mentioned property has a value in excess of $20 billion U.S dollars. As these accounts are interest-bearing and are accruing interest, plaintiff will amend this complaint to reflect the value of the accounts at the time of trial.

12. Despite the fact that the above-mentioned property belongs to plaintiff, who is entitled to possession of it, defendants have refused to turn over to Plaintiff the aforementioned personal property, and have converted the same to their own use.

13. In 1971, Mr. Santa Romana/Diaz opened an account at First National City Bank, now defendant Citibank, at the Manila, Philippines office. Plaintiff accompanied him and the sum of $43 million U.S. dollars in cash was deposited in the presence of bank officer James J. Collins. The transaction was unusual in that the cash was in small denominations and it took six (6) days for bank personnel to count it. On April 6, 1893, Collins had his deposition taken in New York City and denied that he was ever involved in establishing this account. Collins denied that the transaction ever took place, and stated that he did remember Severino Santa Romana coming into the bank on one occasion in 1971 "talking about borrowing some money for some venture."

14. All of the aforementioned tortious conversion of plaintiff's personal property by defendant banks was done in concert with and in furtherance of a conspiracy with the Trilateral Commission, an international organization which controls banking and finance around the globe, and with government officials in different countries, including the United States. Defendant John Reed, the Chairman and Chief Executive Officer of defendant Citibank has spearheaded Citibank's conversion of the gold bullion which was owned by plaintiff's late husband and rightfully belongs to plaintiff. Defendants Reed and Citibank have systematically sold and are selling said gold bullion to buyers and converting the sales proceeds to their own use. Plaintiff will amend this complaint to include additional information as it is ascertained.

Learn How This Culture Affected All Americans

Learn how this bank culture affected the American people and the nation in the early twenty-first Century. Read my *America's Housing and Financial Frauds*.

CHAPTER NINE

Another M-Fund Intrigue: Five Star Trust

Among the multiple accounts that were part of the scheme to hide the retrieved plunder were multiple accounts in banks throughout the world in the name of Five Star Trust. The intrigue related to Five Star Trust arose from the diversion of some of the plundered gold secretly retrieved by U.S. personnel in the Philippines shortly after the end of World War II and the M-fund, which were further split into other covert funds.

Marion Horn reportedly purchased at discount, in October 1983, a certified certificate of cash deposit issued by the Mitsui Bank in Tokyo from a Japanese national, and owner of record, Soichi Mr. Soichi Iizuka, the original owner of record. The U.S. Embassy in Tokyo issued a certification confirming and certifying that the CD was issued by Mitzui Bank and that it was a legitimate, genuine, legal, authentic and assignable document. At the end of this chapter is a caveat about Marion Horn.

The primary signatures and attestors on the CD were two bank officers of Mitzui Bank in Japan: Eiji Usuyama, assistant manager of the Ginza branch in Tokyo, and Akira Mishima, assistant manager of the Jueon Branch, and Mr. Takashi Takahashi, an attorney who was reported to represent the Liberal Democratic Party.

A U.S. Embassy person authorized to authenticate such signatures acknowledged and placed a seal on the CD stating that the signature and pictures of the bank officers were genuine.

As payment for the discounted CD, U. S. Mortgage and Trust Company issued on November 7, 1983, a sight draft payable to William Sim Meng Lyang in the amount of $500 million. That payment was made to the escrow department of Chase Manhattan Bank, Singapore, in escrow account number 4051100-92. More information in the following pages.

I started communicating with a person that purchased one of these accounts, Marion Horn, and through him and other sources I acquired numerous documents relating to funds that were used to manipulate the Japanese political process. Horn was a business man that had acquired at a large discount certificates of gold deposits from the Mitsui Bank in Tokyo. These certificates were held in the name of Five Star Trust at various banks with the account number of 405100-92.

As encountered by prior owners or heirs of bank funds originating with the U.S. secret retrieval of bank funds, Horn encountered repeated obstacles to gaining access to the funds, similar to what the heirs to Santa Romana's black accounts experienced. With one addition.

Horn was not only denied access to the financial certificate that he legally purchased, but was also falsely charged with financial fraud, alleging that the certificate of bank deposit that he had on the Mitsui Bank was a forgery. The certificate was seized and he received a federal prison sentence. Several of my other books show this to be a common tactic used by employees of the U.S. Department of Justice to silence someone exposing high-level corruption, or retaliation for attempting to do so.

One of the Five Star Trust bank certificates of deposit was issued by the Mitsui Bank in Tokyo. How that bank gained access to such a huge amount of gold and money is not clear, and Horn refused to provide me with an answer.

Question of Where the Money Came From for Politically Connected Mitsui Bank to Issue the Five Star Trust CD

Reportedly, a large amount of the M-Fund was secretly made available in 1960 by Vice President Richard Nixon to the leaders of the Liberal Democratic Party (LDP) in Japan. That fund enabled the Liberal Party to remain in control for many years. It is believed that the Five Star Trust issued by Mitsui Bank in Tokyo was in some way connected to the M-Fund that was made available to the Liberal Democratic Party many years earlier.

CIA General Robert Ferrera and Five Star Trust

One of the many people who became involved with the bank certificates of deposits was General Robert Ferrera, who had ties to the CIA. Ferrera was a trustee of Five Star Trust. Life does not go well for anyone that is a danger to exposing the greatest bank heist in the world's history. A *Los Angeles Times* article (July 12, 1985) stated under the heading, "Death of a Mystery Man," the following:

> Elements of International Intrigue Surface After "Routine" Crime. On the police blotter, it is a robbery-murder of the sort that happens with dismaying regularity in Los Angeles these days: an 82-year-old man trussed up and dead of a heart attack, his fourth-floor apartment ransacked, valuable gold heirlooms taken.
>
> But to his brother-in-law, it has the unsettling look of a Graham Greene spy story. He finds it odd that a former Navy intelligence

man—decorated by the governments of Spain and Mexico for hush-hush services rendered during World War II, an American liaison officer to Britain's Lord Mountbatten of Burma, a decoding expert who visited such wartime hot spots as Saipan and Tinian, and who even years later made mysterious strips to Mexico and Europe, usually with a bodyguard, a man cautious and secretive—was killed in his own apartment with no sign of forced entry.

The body of retired Cmdr. Stuart P. James was found stuffed under the kitchen sink of his mid-Wilshire apartment nine days ago. His brother-in-law, Robert Ferrera, [former CIA] found the body when he delivered James' Social Security check and the retired Navy man did not answer the elaborate secret knock that he had insisted his acquaintances use since he was mugged out front six months earlier—a coded knock that he changed every few months as a security protection.

In a green attaché case usually hidden in the closet, the intruder found and stole:

A large gold medal, possibly the Order of the Aztec Eagle, awarded to James by Mexican President Miguel Aleman in 1947, for exceptional services of an unspecified nature. Another large gold medal, this one from the government of Spain, presented in 1946 for unknown wartime services rendered.

Ferrera believes that James, a "very, very careful man" who wouldn't even open the door for probate attorneys when his brother died not long ago, may have been done in for something he knew, not something he owned.

There is "plenty of reason to believe it was not just robbery," said Ferrera, who had first met the man that his sister, Irma, would later marry in the South Pacific in 1942.

Sensitive Information

"He'd known sensitive U.S. information—he thought it was sensitive," Ferrera said. He traveled often to Mexico, where he held honorary dual citizenship, and was invariably protected by "bodyguards supplied by the U.S. Embassy or Mexican government," Ferrera said.

"He kept saying he had to make one final trip to serve his country," said Ferrera, who said James was still afraid of things he had done when he was young—that people may (still) be angry about.

Numerous Legal Opinions Showing the Accounts Legitimate

Marion Horn spent large sums of money over the years paying investigators to obtain evidence showing his certificates of deposits to be valid. Some of the writings relating to these investigations follows.

A November 22, 1985, letter from Washington D.C. attorney

Willard C. McBride to J.R. Horn, president of U.S. Mortgage and Trust Company with offices in Lexington, Kentucky provided a legal opinion on the validity of a bank certificate of deposit No. 405100-92 issued by the Main Branch of Mitsui Bank, Ltd., main office, Tokyo, Japan.

WILLARD C. MCBRIDE
ATTORNEY AT LAW
THE FEDERAL BAR BUILDING, SUITE 1100
1815 H STREET, N.W.
WASHINGTON. OC 20006
(202) 293-7818

November 22, 1985

Mr. J. R. Horn, President
U. S. Mortgage and Trust Co., Inc.
870 Corporate Drive Suite 201.
Lexington, Kentucky 40503

Re: Legal Opinion Concerning Title to
Certificate of deposit No. 4051100-92
Issued by the Main Branch of Mitsui
Bank, Ltd., Head Office, Japan.

Dear Mr. Horn:

This is in response to your request that I give you my legal opinion as to the title to the above Certificate of Deposit No. 4051100-92.

It is my opinion that the U. S. Mortgage and Trust Co., Inc. holds legal title to Certificate of Deposit No. 4051100-92 in the amount of 318 Billion Japanese Yen, issued by the Main Branch of the Mitsui Bank and the Government of Japan on August 1, 1977, Reference Number 118-65; and as such, the U. S. Mortgage and Trust Co., Inc. should be entitled to the interest on, the said Certificate of Deposit at the rate of Five Percent (5%).

This opinion is based, inter alia, on the following events and circumstances:

According to documents in my possession, on November 7, 1983, the depositor (or holder and owner) of the said Certificate of Deposit, Soichi Lizuka, 2-26-12 Ohara, Setagaya-kee, Tokyo, Japan, made a Deed of Assignment and Bill of Sale to the U. 5. Mortgage and Trust Co., Inc. Included in this instrument, which was attested to under a notarial seal, appears this statement addressed to the Mitsui Bank and the U. S. Mortgage and Trust Co., Inc. signed by Soichi Iizuka (owner):

This letter is to inform you that as of this 7th day of November, 1983, I Soichi Iizuka do hereby sell, assign, unconditionally, irretractably and irrevocably transfer all rights, title and ownership of C. D. # 4051100-92 to U. S. Mortgage and Trust Co., effective said date as per validation by the United States Embassy and two (2) Bank Officers of the Mitsui Bank, Ltd. in Tokyo, Japan dated October 19, 1983 and made a part of this Deed of assignment and Bill of Sale.

The validation referred to immediately above was made in the office of the United States Embassy in Japan, and was done in the following fashion:

A statement was prepared containing all of the pertinent information concerning the Certificate of Deposit (its number, issuing bank, name and address of the depositor (holder), the amount of the deposit (318 Billion Yen), interest rate, etc.). Thereafter, the following statement was made:

"This is to confirm and certify that the above mentioned Cash Deposit Certificate is issued by Mitsui Bank, Limited Head Office Japan."

This statement, as well as the entire description of the Certificatc of Deposit was then signed by Eiji Usuyama and Akira Mishima, both as Assistant Managers of the Mitsui Bank, Ltd., and by the attorney for the bank, Takashi Takahashi. It was also signed by Soichi Iizuka, the depositor (holder). Thereupon, Frances T. Lide, Consul of the United States in the Embassy, attested to the signatures of the above parties. And, inasmuch as the entire proceedings was to establish the genuiness of the Certificate of Deposit, Ms. Lide in effect attested to the proper identity of Eiji Usuyama and Akira Mishima, or that they were indeed Assistant Managers of the Mitsui Bank. Having done so, she thereafter placed a Ribbon Seal of the United States on the document.

With regard to the signature and Seal placed on the instrument by the United States Consul, Frances Lide, and that to which she attested, representatives of the State Department add support to the proposition that Ms. Lide established the identity of the persons whose signatures she witnessed.

John Binette, 60 Adams Street, Biddeford, Maine 04005 told me this account: He said that at the request of you, J. R. Horn, he visited the State Department and talked to a woman whose name he will look for in his records and give me, and a man by the name of Tim Hamilton. He told me that both the woman and Tim Hamilton told him that in witnessing and attesting to the signatures on the validation document, that Ms. Lide must necessarily have established to her complete satisfaction that the parties, Eiji' Usuyama and Akira Mishima, were indeed Assistant Managers of the Mitsui Bank, Ltd.

If this were so, with Ms. Lide's signature and the Seal on the document as proof thereof, the Certificate of Deposit was indeed genuine and certainly valid. Mr. Binette is providing me a sworn affidavit with respect to that recounted above.

That related hereinbefore is important to bear in mind inasmuch as on or about November 17, 1983, the Singapore government seized this Certificate of Deposit alleging the same to be a forged document. A receipt was issued to the U. S. Mortgage and Trust Co., Inc. on November 21, 1983 by Chai Yong Song, an official of the Singapore Government. As far as is known, the Certificate of Deposit is either in the possession of the Singapore government or has been returned to the Japanese government.

The U. S. Mortgage and Trust Co., Inc., has filed a claim against the United States Department of State seeking the return of the Certificate of Deposit on the grounds that it is a valid document and properly belongs to the U. S. Mortgage and Trust Co., Inc. But, in the event that the document was a forgery, the corporation will claim huge damages from the United States for the tort committed by the United States through its Consul at the United States Embassy, Frances Lide.

Inasmuch as the evidence is quite overwhelming that the Certificate of Deposit is genuine and valid, it would seem that the United States Department of State will exercise its power and demand the return of the Certificate of Deposit. For it must realize that not to do so, it (or the United States Government) will be required to pay huge damages to the U. S. Mortgage and Trust Co., Inc.

I could list other documentary evidence and oral testimony in support of the validity and genuiness of the Certificate of Deposit and that the U. S. Mortgage and Trust Co., Inc. properly holds title to it, but it is my view that the account related herein attests to the same.

Yours truly

Willard C. McBride

A legal letter to McBride from the U.S. Department of State:

United States Department of State
Washington, D.C. 20520

Certified Mail
Return Receipt Requested March 21, 1986

Willard C. McBride, Esq.

The Federal Bar Building, Suite 1100
1815 H Street, N.W.
Washington, D.C. 20006

Dear Mr. McBride:

I refer to the administrative tort claim filed by U.S. Mortgage and Trust Company, Inc. dated August 2, 1985 under the Federal Tort Claims Act, 28 U.S.C. § 2672 et seq. and 22 C.F.R. § 3.1 (1985). The claim seeks $700,500,000 in damages arising out of the alleged negligent or wrongful action of the U.S. Embassy in Tokyo in reversing and setting aside its "validation" of a $1.2 billion Certificate of Deposit on October 19, 1983.

Under the provisions of the Federal Tort Claims Act, the Secretary of State is authorized to consider and administratively settle tort claims arising as a consequence of the negligent or wrongful act or omission of any employee of the Department acting within the scope of his employment.

The U.S. Government is liable to the claimant under the Act in those circumstances in which a private person would be liable in accordance with the law of the place where the act or omission occurred (28 U.S.C. § 2672). The Act of August 1, 1956, extends the tort claims authority of the Secretary to claims arising in foreign countries in connection with the Department of State operations abroad (22 U.S.C. § 2669(f)). In brief, the claim as submitted to the Department makes the following allegations.

In the fall of 1983, the President of U.S. Mortgage and Trust Company, Inc. ("USMT"), Mr. Marion J.R. Horn, negotiated for the purchase of a certain Certificate of Deposit from its holder, Mr. William Sim. As an apparent precondition to negotiations, Mr. Horn required that the original certificate be presented by its owner of record, Mr. Soichi Iizuka, for "validation" by the U.S. Embassy in Tokyo.

On October 19, 1983, Mr. Iizuka and three other individuals met with consular officer Frances T. Lide at the Embassy and presented to her a document entitled "Certificate of Cash Deposit" for "validation." Ms. Lide notarized the signing of that document, using the standard procedures of a notary public.[1/] The claim asserts that in so doing Ms. Lide "certified" that the Certificate of Deposit is "a legitimate, genuine, legal, authentic and assignable document ... (and) ... is issued by Mitsui Bank Limited Head Office Japan."

Upon receipt of the "validated" document, Mr. Horn and the Secretary and Vice-President of USMT, Mr. Burns, concluded it was authentic and actively pursued its acquisition, traveling first to New York and then to Singapore. On November 17, 1983, Singapore police authorities arrested the participants to this transaction, alleging that they were attempting to cash a fraudulent certificate of deposit. The Singapore police seized and retained all original documents pertaining to the transaction.

In the context of the ensuing investigation, the U.S. Embassy in Tokyo informed the Embassy in Singapore on December 15, 1983, that, based on statements of an official of the Mitsui Bank, Ltd., Mr. Yasushi Yoshimura, the certificate of deposit was a forgery. Conceding that Consul Lide "did sign it", the Embassy concluded that, "given that the basic document which the explanatory affidavit covers has proved to be fraudulent, the question of the genuineness of the consular notarial now appears to be immaterial."

The claim characterizes this statement by the U.S. Embassy in Tokyo as "an attempt to remove its liability' by reversing and setting aside its earlier "validation" of the certificate, and alleges that this was a wrongful or negligent act "so as to allow the claimant to recover damages for claimant's reliance on the original validation." The claim argues that "the procedures used by Lide cannot now disprove the genuineness of the documents", and that the procedures used to safeguard against fraud were defective. It places special emphasis on the fact that Consul Lide failed to retain a copy of the notarized document. In sum, it asserts that the Embassy "cannot claim fraud as a defense to its validation of a document when its own procedures to safeguard against fraud were themselves defective. . . . (T)he Embassy's own act [proved] the genuineness of the document and the Department of State cannot now prove [its] fraudulent nature". Claimant seeks .damages of $700,000,000 for lost profit and $500,000 for expenses in furtherance of the transaction, including approximately $100,000 paid as earnest money.

1/ See 22 C.F.R. S92.[2].

Our review of the evidence submitted on behalf of U.S. Mortgage and Trust Company, Inc. and of the results of the Department's own investigation leads us to conclude that the central allegation of the claim is incorrect. Ms. Lide did not validate the authenticity of the certificate of deposit; that could only have been accomplished by the issuing bank, here the Mitsui Bank, Limited. Rather, Ms. Lide performed the simple notarial act of administering an affirmation; i.e., she affirmed that those who signed the document were as they identified themselves to be on the basis of documents customarily used for identification purposes. Indeed, under the relevant regulations, that was the only function she could legitimately perform.[2/] Nothing she placed on the document purports to indicate otherwise.

Moreover, Ms. Lide properly followed the requisite procedures for administering an affirmation. Under the pertinent regulations in effect at that time, consular officers were required to do the following[2]/:

1) Check the identification of the signatories,

2) Maintain a Record of Fees as a registry of official acts,

3) Sign and seal the notarial certificate and fasten the pages of the document, and

4) Include a jurat.

In signing the jurat, Ms. Lide attested to the fact she had checked the identification of the signatories and that an oath was given to the individuals. Ms. Lide used reasonable diligence to verify the identities of the signatories. In the December 15, 1983 telegram from Embassy Tokyo to Embassy Singapore (attached as Exhibit 7 to the Claim), Ms. Lide stated that she was certain that appropriate identification, showing the name and a photograph, was presented for each person who signed.

Consular receipt #9247 in her Record of Fees, dated October 19, 1983, registered that "general notarial service" was provided to a "Takahashi' as was required. (Mr. Takahashi accompanied Mr. Yoshimura to the American Embassy and was one of the signatories to the document entitled "Certificate of Cash Deposit.") Attached hereto is a copy of the telegram reporting the Embassy's search of its consular receipts.

To the extent that claimants relied upon Ms. Lide's acts as a "validation [which] made the whole thing 'real', that reliance was misplaced. A notary public is not a guarantor of the truth of the statements made in a document which he/she notarizes. Consular officers are specifically cautioned not to certify the validity of a document in a foreign country.[4]/

2/ See 7 FAM 812 (1961); 22 C.F.R. S 92.4(a) (1983).

3/ See 7 FAM 814.1, 815.2, 823.1, 823.4 - 823.6-2, 831.3, 831.4 T1961).

4/ See 22 CFR 592.41(e).

In addition, the December 15 telegram from the American Embassy in Tokyo did not purport to "reverse" anything. It merely noted that in view of the invalidity of the document itself, the question of the genuineness of the consular notarial appeared to be immaterial. Since there had never been any validation, there was nothing which could be reversed or set aside.

As to the issue of retaining a copy of the notarized document, we do not find that issue to be relevant. Specifically, we cannot agree that if a copy had been retained, then there would be a definitive answer to everything." Moreover, there was no requirement that a copy be retained. The practice is that only records of foreign governments or important documents recording such events as births, deaths or marriages are copied and maintained. The reason for this practice is the fact that literally thousands of documents are notarized each year at embassies such as the one in Tokyo.

For the foregoing reasons, we have concluded that the procedures utilized by the Embassy were in accord with established procedures and that no negligent or wrongful act or omission was committed by any employee of the Embassy acting within the scope of employment giving rise to liability towards the claimant. Accordingly, the claim must be and hereby is' denied. This denial is final since the claim arose in a foreign country in connection with Department of State operations abroad (28 U.S.C. § 680(k) and 22 CFR § 31.18).

Sincerely,
David P. Stewart
Assistant Legal Adviser
Office of International Claims
and Investment Disputes

The following was the other letter indicating the validity of the bank certificate of deposit No. 405100-92:

WILLARD C. MCBRIDE
ATTORNEY AT LAW
THE JUDICIARY PLAZA
SUITE 200
450-5TH STREET, N.W.
WASHINGTON. D.C. 20001
(202) 293-7818

January 12, 1987

J. R. Horn, President
U. S. M. T., Inc.
821 Corporate Drive, Suite 200
P..0. Box 22184
Lexington, Kentucky 40522

Re: Legal Opinion Concerning Title to Certificate of Cash Deposit No. 4051100-92 issued by the Main Branch of the Mitzui Bank, Ltd., Head Office, Japan In The Amount Of 318 Billion Japanese Yen.

Dear Mr. Horn:

You have asked me to give you my legal opinion as to the title to the above Certificate of Cash Deposit No. 4051100-92 in the amount of 318 billion Japanese yen. On November 22, 1985, I gave you my written legal opinion regarding this matter. But since then, I have received other evidence which adds considerable support to the opinion I gave you on November 22, 1985 to the effect that the U. S. Mortgage and Trust Co., Inc., now U. S. M. T., Inc., holds legal title to the above Certificate of Cash Deposit. That which follows, then, should be considered my updated legal opinion to this date (January 12, 1987).

In my opinion the U. S. Mortgage and Trust Co., Inc., now the U. S. M. T., Inc., holds legal title to Certificate of Cash Deposit No. 4051100-92 in the amount of 318 Billion Japanese Yen, issued by the Main Branch of the Mitzui Bank and the Government of Japan on August 1, 1977, Reference Number 118-65; and as such, the U. S. M. T., Inc. should be entitled to the interest on the said Certificate of Cash Deposit at the rate of Five Percent (5%).

This opinion is based, inter alia, on the following events, circumstances and evidence:

According to documents in my possession, on November 7, 1983, the depositor (or holder and owner) of the said Certificate of Cash Deposit, Soichi Iizuka, 2-26-12 Ohara, Satagaya-kee, Tokyo, Japan, made a Deed of Assignment and Bill of Sale to the U. S. Mortgage and Trust Co. Inc., Mitsui Bank denied the existence of the Certificate of Cash Deposit and said it must be a forged document. The Singapore government then seized the Certificate of Cash Deposit. A receipt was issued to the U. S. Mortgage and Trust Co., Inc. on November 21, 1983 by Chai Yong Song, an official of the Singapore Government.

As far as is known, the Certificate of Cash Deposit must have been returned to the Japanese government by the Singapore government. A claim has been lodged with the State Department by the U. S. Mortgage and Trust Co., Inc. inasmuch as its agent, Frances Lide, purportedly established the correct identity of the bank officers who certified that the Certificate of Cash Deposit was indeed issued by the Mitsui Bank.

The U. S. Mortgage and Trust Co., Inc. is undoubtedly the owner of the Certificate of Cash Deposit. The question is whether or not this Certificate is a forged document or is valid. Evidence demonstrating its validity follows:

Frances Lide's Attesting to the signatures of the bank officers. As indicated earlier, Frances Lide, Consul of the United States Embassy in Japan attested to the signatures of the two bank officers, Eiji Usuyama and Akira Mishima, or in effect, satisfied herself that they were indeed whom they purported to be. And she placed a United States Seal on the document.

Further evidence in support of the proposition that Frances Lide did establish the true identity of the two bank officers which would tend to show the validity of the Certificate of Cash Deposit comes from John Binette as found in an Affidavit executed by him on March 11, 1986. This Affidavit is in my possession. In examining into the above matter on behalf of-the U. S. Mortgage and Trust Co., Inc., Mr. Binette stated, among other things in his Affidavit:

In February, 1984, I visited the Singapore Embassy, and made inquiry concerning the Certificate of Deposit that had been seized by the Singapore police. Aman at the Embassy said he could not, or would not, tell me anything, but to inquire at the Department of State. I then telephoned Inspector Chai Yong Song of the Singapore police and inquired of him concerning the Certificate of Deposit for 318 Billion Yen that had been seized.

He said that the Attorney General of Singapore had closed the case, and that the Certificate of Deposit was impounded by a court order; that thereafter, in February 1984, I then went to the Department of State, the Hong Kong desk, Room 5206, Telephone 632-3276 and spoke with Tim Hamilton.

I inquired of Tim Hamilton just what the signature of Frances T. Lide, Consul of the United States Embassy, together with the Seal, signified on the Validation Certificate. He told me that Frances T. Lide was certifying that the persons who signed the document were whom they purported to be. Namely that Eiji Usuyama and Akira Mishima were indeed Assistant Managers of the Mitsui Bank, Ltd. And that the signatures appearing on the Validation Certificate were their signatures, and similarly with respect to the attorney for the-bank, Takashi Takahashi; and that Tim Hamilton told me that the Validation Certificate was a good and valid validation.

<u>The Evidence of John Burns</u>. An affidavit was also executed by John Burns who was very much Involved in matters concerning the Certificate of Cash Deposit. In his Affidavit (as did John Binette in his), Mr. Burns stated that he knew his Affidavit would be presented to the U. S. State Department in connection with a claim by the U. S. Mortgage and Trust Co., Inc.

Thus, both Mr. Burns and Mr. Binette realized, in making their statements in their Affidavits, that the same would go to the U. S. Government; and they both knew that they subjected themselves to criminal prosecution if they made a false statement to a U. S. Government agency. (See United States Code, Title 18 Section 1001.). It may be of interest and helpful to recount some of the things Mr. Burns related concerning the acquisition of the Certificate of Deposit (or the Deed of Assignment and Bill of Sale to the U. S. Mortgage and Trust Co., Inc.) and that which happened subsequently. In substance, Mr. Burns stated:

> That through other contacts he and you (Mr. Horn) were able to obtain a bona fide buyer of the C.D., and that the buyer was a brokerage firm of substantial capabilities in New York City; that he was informed by the buyer that in order to consummate the transaction, the original document must be certified at the U. S. Embassy, or that there must be a certification of the C. D. signed by two bank officers (which was done as described earlier where Ms. Lide attested to the proper identity of the two bank officers, Eiji Usuyama and Akira Mishima).

That a while after the certification of the C. D. was done, Mr. Sim called him from Singapore and informed him that everything was in order; that he and you (Mr. Horn) went to Singapore; that after making a trip to Hong Kong with Mr. Siochi Iizuka (the holder of the C. D.), all met in Singapore again; that all documents were prepared, and the Japanese seemed fully satisfied that the U. S. Mortgage and Trust Co., Inc. had the ability to purchase the C. D, the sale was consummated and. a written Bill of Sale and Deed of Assignment were executed on November 7, 1983.

That arrangements were then completed with the ultimate purchaser of the C. D. and on the 18th of November he and Mr. Sim went to the Union Bank Suisse in Singapore to present the C. D. and related documents to the manager of the bank, to have the C. D. authenticated through the U. S. Embassy in Tokyo and the Japanese Government to the Mitsui Bank in Tokyo. But that the manager did not follow the instructions given him and as a result the Mitsui Bank denied the existence of the C. D. and said it must be a forgery; that as a result, the Singapore C.I.D. was called in and a complete investigation was done by the C.I.D. and the Japanese Embassy in Singapore.

That Mr. Siochi Iizuka (the holder of the C. D.) and his associates were arrested, together with himself, you (Mr. Horn) and others; that after a month of interrogation investigation and embarrassment, you, (Mr. Horn), he and others, except for the Japanese, were released; that it was recognized that those released were acting in good faith, based on the certification made by Ms. Lide of the U. S. Embassy in Japan.

That prior to leaving Singapore, you (Mr. Horn) and he met with Bill Moody, Consul at the U. S. Embassy in Singapore and requested Mr. Moody to assist you (yourself, Mr. Burns and your corporation) to recover the original Certificate of Cash Deposit and related documents from the Singapore Government for which documents Mr. Burns and you (Mr. Horn) held a receipt from Inspector Chai of the Singapore C.I.D.; and that Mr. Moody agreed to do this, putting the agreement in writing under the seal of the U. S. Embassy.

That in January, 1984, Mr. Sim requested that he return to Singapore saying that the Japanese were about to be released, and that the C. D. was going to be "cleared;" that he did return to Singapore and met with the parties involved, but the C. D. was not released; that throughout all this time, he and you (Mr. Horn) were placing your faith in the U. S. Embassy's certification, but the Embassy in Tokyo made the excuse that Ms. Lide was on leave and could not be reached to verify her signature.

That the Japanese, including Soichi Iizuka (the holder of the C. D.), were released; that Mr. Iizuka was no longer detained by the Tokyo authorities; and that to this date, no charges have been brought against Soichi Iizuka (the holder of the C. D.) or others, including the two bank officers who signed the certification.

That after the release of the Japanese, and at their request, he went to Tokyo and had numerous meetings with Mr. Iizuka and other party affiliates; that according to their statements, the C. D. is an authentic document and Mr. Iizuka was the rightful nominee of the Certificate; but in reality, the actual owner/owners is the Liberal Democratic Party of Japan; but that he was informed that the "powers that be," or, as the Japanese referred to as "the Boss," was not prepared to give the authority to the Mitsui Bank to "certify" the Certificate. Mr. Burns then continues in his affidavit, saying that he would testify to that account in his affidavit in a court of law.

The Evidence of Michael Sattelmaier. I have in my possession an Affidavit executed under oath by Michael Sattelmaier on October 27, 1986. Mr. Sattelmaier is president of Video Communications, Inc. Mr. Sattelmaier has contacts with a number of law enforcement officials, both foreign and domestic. You (Mr. Horn) and he are friends and have worked together on several matters. In his Affidavit, he states, among other things, in substance:

That on or about November 17, 1983 he received a telephone call from you (Mr. Horn) wherein you told him that the Certificate of Cash Deposit in the amount of $318 Billion Yen had been seized by the Singapore Police and that all parties involved had been placed under house arrest; that you (Mr. Horn) expressed your concern to him that the American Embassy in Tokyo would not confirm the certification of the documents and the endorsers thereof; that you (Mr. Horn) were very suspicious of the events taking place in Singapore and the actions of the American Embassy in Tokyo; and that you (Mr. Horn) requested him to attempt to determine the facts by contacting his (Mr. Sattelmaier's) associates in Tokyo and by talking to any federal officials who might shed light on the matter; and that he agreed to do so.

That he contacted a Mr. Tim Yamamoto, whom he knew well, in Tokyo and related that which had transpired and asked Mr. Yamamoto to examine into the matter, which he agreed to do; that later, after investigating rather deeply into the matter, Mr. Yamamoto told him that in his view the C. D. was authentic, and that the interviews Mr. Yamamoto had with Mr. Soichi Iizuka, (the owner of record of the C. D.) further confirmed Mr. Yamamoto's view of the authenticity of the C.D.; that apparently Mr. Iizuka told Mr. Yamamoto that when he was released by the Singapore authorities, he was treated as a dignitary by the Japanese ambassador in Singapore, and was escorted home in a grand fashion, (and was not charged with fraud or any criminal offense).

That Mr. Yamamoto arranged for him (Sattelmaier) to talk to Mr. Iizuka through an interpreter; that Mr. Iizuka stated in response to his question regarding its authenticity, that it was genuine and collectable by its legal owner; that the C. D. represented funds of the Liberal Democratic Party being held by the Mitsui Bank; that he (Mr. Iizuka) was the true owner of record of this C. D. and that he (Mr. Iizuka) had been instructed to fund this C. D. for the party purposes; that there had been some dispute internally between party factions, and now the leaders were attempting to nullify the transaction.

That Mr. Iizuka told him (Sattelmaier) that he had done nothing wrong in concluding the transaction (trying to dispose of it), and that if he had done anything wrong, he would surely have been arrested upon his return to Japan and prosecuted criminally; and that he had not been arrested or prosecuted. That he (Sattelmaier) asked Mr. Iizuka if he would be willing to testify in this country (the U.S.A.) regarding this matter, and he said he would.

At page 3 of this letter, I stated that the U. S. Mortgage and Trust Co., Inc. is undoubtedly the owner of the Certificate of Cash Deposit—but the question is whether or not this C. D. is a forgery, or is it valid? In my view, the evidence recounted hereinbefore demonstrates rather forcefully that the Certificate of Cash Deposit is valid and is not a forgery. It is only reasonable to conclude that Frances Lide, the Consul at the U. S. Embassy in Japan would not have taken lightly the responsibility of taking under oath the signatures of the bank officers and the attorney asserting:

"This is to confirm and certify that the above mentioned Cash Deposit Certificate is issued by the Mitsui Bank, Limited, Head Office, Japan," when that Cash Deposit Certificate amounted to the astronomical figure of 318 billion Japanese yen. She had the responsibility of assuring herself that these bank officers and the bank attorney were whom they purported to be, and undoubtedly, she did assure herself. Even a State Department official has stated (to John Binette) that Frances Lide was certifying that the bank officers and the attorney were precisely whom they purported to be. Ms. Lide's signature and the United States Seal rather strongly support the proposition that the Certificate of Cash Deposit is valid and is not a forgery.

Of great significance, in my view, is the evidence regarding the treatment accorded those Japanese individuals who are principals in the-matter of whether the Certificate of Cash Deposit was fraudulent (forged), or whether it was a valid instrument. The evidence is quite overwhelming, and could certainly be officially ascertained, that no charges, and no prosecution, have been made or brought against Soichi Iizuka, the depositor or holder of the Certificate. Likewise, no charges have been made and no prosecution brought against Eiji Usuyama and Akira Mishima, both shown on the certification by Frances Lide, as being Assistant Managers of the Mitsui Bank, Ltd., and similarly with respect to the attorney for the bank, Takashi Takahashi. It is inconceivable that, had these persons committed fraud that amounted to 318 Billion Japanese Yen, they would not have been prosecuted to the fullest extent.

Yet, the evidence is, and there seems to be no question of it, that no criminal action was brought against any of these individuals. Indeed, the evidence is that Soichi Iizuka was treated as a dignitary by the Japanese Ambassador in Singapore, and was escorted home to Japan in a grand fashion. Mr. Iizuka has indicated that he would be a willing witness to this whole matter. His most favorable testimony would be corroborated and supported by the fact that neither he nor any of the other three noted above were prosecuted. For had this been fraud, or had the Certificate of Cash Deposit not been valid, the fraud and forgery would have been of such magnitude that prosecution would surely have been mandatory. It must be remembered that the amount involved was 318 Billion Japanese Yen.

In addition to the evidence coming from Messrs. Burns and Sattelmaier concerning the fact of no prosecution having been brought, and to which Mr. Iizuka would also testify, these same persons' evidence provides the reason, very likely, why the Certificate of Cash Deposit is valid, and why no prosecution was brought. Mr. Iizuka and others told Mr. Burns and Mr. Sattelmaier <u>that the Certificate of Cash Deposit was valid; that he was the owner-nominee but that the funds represented those of the Liberal Democratic Party</u>. It is this reason, undoubtedly, that the present situation exists with the Certificate of Deposit— that the funds belong to the Liberal Democratic Party which it is apparently not willing to disclose at this time.

In view of that recounted herein, I iterate that it is my opinion that the U. S. Mortgage and Trust Co., Inc., now U. S. M. T., Inc., holds title to the Certificate of Cash Deposit and that the C. D. is a valid instrument, not a forged document.

Yours truly,

Willard C. McBride

The following résumé of Willard McBride shows his competency and background for evaluating the claims by Marion Horn and Five Star Trust:

RESUME
WILLARD C. MCBRIDE
4113 BLACKSNAKE DRIVE
HILLCREST HEIGHTS, MARYLAND 20748
450 - 5TH STREET, N.W., 9TH FLOOR WASHINGTON, D. C. 20001

1948 Accounting, taking daily trial balances.
Internal Revenue Service
Wilmington, Delaware

Revenue Agent 1949-1954. Made audits of taxpayers' income tax returns, both individual and corporation returns.

Tax Division, Department of Justice-1955-1983. Held the position of Trial attorney of Justice Attorney, then Reviewer, Washington, D.C. then Assistant Chief, Criminal Section, Tax Division, then Special Litigation Counsel in the Tax Division.

Prepared criminal income tax cases for trial, and then tried such cases, which trials were held in over 30 Judicial Districts in U. S. District Courts. Prosecuted about 100 and won convictions in all but about 10.

Reviewed and passed on (made decisions on) recommendations of case recommendations attorneys.

Conducted numerous Grand Jury investigations. Prepared material for criminal tax prosecution seminars, and lectured at such seminars in various cities over the United States. (Retired in July, 1983, and entered private law) practice in September, 1983).Private Law Practice

Defend persons charged with, under the name of or who may be charged with criminal tax violations; handle Attorney-at-Law civil tax matters; defend at: persons charged with whit 1815 H Street, N.W. collar crimes; bring suits Suite 1100 and defend in suits involving Washington, D. C. 20006 contracts, tort, divorce, etc. And Presently at 450 - 5th Street, 9th Floor Washington, D. C. 20001 Telephone: (202) 639-8929

Achievements and Outside Activities.

a. In 1950 I was selected to be one of 23 employees in the federal government to attend what was termed a "Second Career Development Program," covering a period of six months.

b. While at the Tax Division, Department of Justice, I received on three occasions the Sustained Superior Performance Award (monetary in nature, varying between $500.00 and $1,000.00); and received a special award which amounted to $5,000.00 on one occasion. Also, because of outstanding work in prosecuting cases most important to Internal Revenue Service, that Service gave me an award, even though I was at the Department of Justice, of $1,000.00.

In my church, The Church of Jesus Christ of Latter-day Saints (Mormon), have served in many positions, including eight years as a member of the Bishopric of Capitol Ward of that Church, and served five years on what is called the Stake High Council, as well as many other positions.

Investigative Report Requested by Five Star Trust

In 1987, J.R. Horn requested that an investigative trip be made to Japan regarding their willingness to admit the validity of a CD issued by the Mitsui Bank in Tokyo. Upon return, Alan Wolfley of New Canaan, Connecticut prepared a multi-page report stating the Japanese officials that he met knew about the Certificate of gold deposit and the cover-ups to deny their existence. The following is his report:

THIS REPORT WAS DONE BY ALAN WOLFLEY ON INVESTIGATIVE TRIP TO JAPAN FOR J R HORN

To: Memo for File
From: Alan Wolfley

During my 7 days in Tokyo from the morning of July 8, 1987 (Thursday) through noon on Wednesday July 15, 1987, I discussed the subject with more than 20 persons including the following:

Key (F) Friends
(A) Acquaintances
(C) Contacts (made for me by others)

Cabinet Offices

The Prime Minister - Yasuhiro Nakasone (A)
The PM's Secretariat Officer - (Councilor) Hideshi Honda (F)
Minister for Foreign Affairs - Kiichi Miyazawa (A)
Chief Cabinet Secretary - Masaharu Gotoda (F)
V-M of Finance for International Affairs - Togoo Gyoten (F)
Kozo Watanabe (F) Min, of Health and Welfare.

Former Cabinet Officers

Shintaro Abe - former Minister of Foreign Affairs; former head of MITI (A)
Takeo Fukuda - former Prime Minister (F) (An Abe backer)
Takeo Miki - former Prime Minister (A) (a member of the Komoto fraction)

Some of the others
Hideo Watanabe (from Niigata) - Parliamentary Vice Minister of MITI (home country of Tanaka) (C)
Shin Kanemaru (Tanaka) LDP Sec. General (Min. for Construction) (F)
Yukiyasu Matsuno (Tanaka) (Dir. Gr'l Nat'l Land) (C)
Takashi Hasegawa (Abe confidante) (LDP Min. for Transport) (F)
Masahura Gotoda - LDP Tanaka (C) (Director General - Nat'l Police Agency)
Mrs. Shintaro Fukushima (F) (widow of publisher of *Japan Times*).
Mr. "Ken" Iishi (F) House of Councilors.
Mr. Hisao Horinuchi (C) LDP - Chief of Audit Committee of House of Representative (DIET)

I did not meet:
Mr. Sasumu Nikaido - LDP Executive Council Chairman who is also running for PM;

Mr. Noboru Takeshita - LOP Secretary General also after PM post. 1987 is an important election year in Japan. Mr. Nakasone's term is coming to an end. Typical of Japanese politics is the ever present factions within the LDP (Liberal Democratic Party) that will determine who succeeds to the PM. In July 1987 these factions generally were:

(T) Stands for the Tanaka Faction (still strongest) gradually losing poser as the health and reputation of the old gentleman fades; but still powerful.

(M) For the Miyazawa Faction-

Kiichi Miyazawa - Recent Minister of Foreign Affairs and now Finance Minister.

Currently on top of the polls in the race for PM. The Miyazawa Faction is the second largest in LDP.

(N) For Nakasone Faction (3rd. largest) - considered, in the final analysis as a swing vote, most probably strongly behind Miyazawa.

(A) For Abe Faction. Shintaro Abe has been head of MITI (Minister of International Trade & Industry) ....otherwise known as "Japan, Inc." Also former Minister of Foreign Affairs.

(K) For Komoto Faction - relatively small but powerful beyond their numbers. Influential among those who have no factional affiliation.

Remember the election of a new Prime Minister will probably be held by the end of October 1987; if we intend to act we should do so soon.

My investigation reveals that only the Abe Faction was generally cognizant of the problem— and they did not appear to be sympathetic. They told me, "If you have a legitimate claim we encourage you to make it known publicly". My belief is that Mr. Abe, who by rights, talent and experience should be the next Prime Minister, will not be, knows it and is grasping at anything which will assist his possibilities even if it is to throw mud at everyone else in the race. We should be very careful with them.

The Tanaka group was very cagey. They know as for the rest: absolutely nothing.

The Miyazawa faction—where I probably know as many people as in the Tanaka group—were actually indignant that such a claim exists. They were vehement in their comments to me (Kowasaki, Ozawa, particularly - both LDP Diet members) "...It (The CD) must be fraudulent....circulating these rumors can be injurious to Japan and our Party ..."

The Abe faction's general hospitality and courtesy shown to me (and the CD) is suspect. We must be very careful. If you intend to take formal action of any kind one might consider sending copies to the ABE group. But be warned, fireworks would undoubtedly result.

Japan reveres and respects older people. Never more so than in the conduct of the affairs of the Diet, running the country.....it is the foundation block of the people and its national mores. "Older" or "Elderly" to the Japanese means "experienced, useful and wise". Anyone under 65 years of age is still considered, almost a youngster. If the CD were mine I would set out to employ, entice or otherwise engage respectful (USA) public servants who are now retired from service: Kissinger,

Gerald Ford, Robert Ingersoll (former US ambassador to Japan), William Simon (though "too young"), Griffin Bell, Robert Strauss, Stansfield Turner, etc.

If you can convince them that your CD is good you've won more than half the battle. But such a move costs money, requires a legal administrative search that will assist in convincing your consultant who or whomever they are that you've got something. That is your main problem: "credibility". The CD claim is so huge, the cast of characters heretofore generally so diverse and "curious" that taken together they raise a continual stream of question marks instead of taking the claim seriously. In my view some "labels" must be attached to what has gone on before—top flight and "name" legal assistance to research US and Japanese contract law and consultant advisors taken from list of people such as those set out above.

Lastly and alternately, it may well be that some significant payment against the CD will be made providing all negotiations are conducted on a covert basis. It seems to me that you cannot mix the two: covert and open or public negotiations. If the latter course is chosen, "labels" are essential. Obviously almost none are required if the other, more dangerous route is selected.

Alan Wolfley

Additional Information

Important points discussed in later conversations between A. Wolfley and J.R. Horn in July 1990, as stated in a report made by Mr. Horn, holder of the CD:

1. A. Wolfley informed J. R. Horn, prior to Donald Gregg appointment as ambassador to Korea that he had received a call from Mr. Gregg when it seemed Donald Gregg was not to receive the appointment, and he informed A. Wolfley to beware of Gen. Ferrera and his friends in higher places. This information was given to Gen. Ferrera, who then insisted that Gregg would get the appointment and he predicted the exact day and time Gregg would get the appointment. Which did happen as Ferrera predicted.

2. Recently as of July 1990, A. Wolfley received call from one of Shinatro Abe aids to inquire if Wolfley had been advised of conversations coming out of Kafiu, P.M. office. A. Wolfley said he had not been advised but stated to Shinatro Abe aide that we would like to resolve this situation and he, Abe aide said so would the people in Japan. End of conversation.

3. Mr. Wolfley is convinced that the CD is real and the events surrounding the certificate of deposit are 95% correct.

Another report of events was made by Marion Horn concerning the events surrounding CD number 4051100-92:

"Summary of events surrounding
Collection of CD # 4051100-92"

The following information surrounding the acquisition of CD #4051100-92 (ref. 118-65) by JR Horn, president of U.S. Mortgage and Trust Co., assigned to U.S. Mortgage and Trust (Bahamas) Ltd., (a Bahamian Co) in January 1987 and later assigned to Five Star Trust, an Isle of Man Trust, in December 1988.

The present trustees of Five Star Trust are J. R. Horn, executive trustee and main beneficiary to the trust, Alex Damelio, Jr. of Lexington, KY., and Ed Morrow of Middletown, Ohio. Mr. Lon Williamson, of Inez, KY. is a beneficiary to trust, and also holds directors' position and officers' positions in all the companies owned by Five Star Trust, which includes U.S.M.T., Inc., U.S. Mortgage and Trust Co. Ltd., International Financial Corporation, and U.S. Mortgage and Trust (Bahamas) Ltd.

Mr. Roberto L. Ferrera and William L. Clancy were trustees and officers of the above referenced companies until early part of 1990, when their positions were terminated for failure to comply with terms of the trust position. All corporate records are in hands of Ed Morrow, secretary of companies, and trustee of Five Star Trust. All of J. R. Horn and other pertinent documents were in William L. Clancy possession, but he has since notified Ed Morrow that someone broke into his office and stole only my files and the trust and related companies' records. So all records that were in Clancy's possession are now missing.

All corporate records were confiscated from offices in Lexington in 1986 by U.S. Dept. of Treasury and Customs, Cincinnati, Ohio, by Mr. Richard Waley, senior agent in charge. All records were lost or never returned. Mr. Waley was later reassigned and all agents involved to parts unknown. Several attempts were made by Willard C. Mcbride, attorney at law, Washington, D.C., who is retired prosecuting attorney for U.S. Dept of Justice, Tax Division, Washington, D.C. He now is semi-retired due to stroke and a heart attack occurring in 1989, but he is still available to advise in this matter. Mr. Mcbride did two title opinions on the CD #4051100-9; one in 1985 and in 1987, copies are attached hereto for reference.

The "specially treated" Japanese Yen certificate of deposit (c/d), number 4051100-92, ref. #118-65, face amount y318 billion Japanese yen, interest rate five percent (5%) payable semi-annually, issued by Mitzui Bank ltd., (Mitzui), head office, Tokyo, Japan, (copy of certificate of deposit attached hereto for reference)

No interest had been paid on the instrument since issued on Aug. 1, 1977, according to Iizuka. After purchasing the CD a letter was sent along with the deed of sale and bill of assignment to Mitzui Bank Ltd., head office, Tokyo, Japan for registering the CD as being transferred to U. S. Mortgage and trust Co., ownership, at head office of bank in Tokyo, Japan, sealed by said bank and the Japanese government, on Aug, 1, 1977, with Soichi Iizuka (Japan passport No. Mg 1333277) 2-26-12 Ohara, Setagaya-ku, Tokyo, Japan, as the owner of record but admittingly serving as a nominee for the liberal democratic party of Japan ("LDP").

Soichi Iizuka had served as district manager, Bunkyo Branch, Setagaya Ward, Welfare Corporation, Japan in 1977 and 1978 and a member of the Liberal Democratic Council and Liberal Democratic Party budget committee. Actually, Mr. Iizuka was appointed branch manager of the Bunkyo Branch on 1 March 1977 by Nanio Hiroyoshi, president of the National Social Welfare Council, Japan.

Soichi Iizuka, in his duties, was involved with, among others, the public service department of the Mitzui Bank Limited, and especially Mr. Itakuri Keiji, director, the Mitzui Bank Limited; Mr. Nanio Hiroyoshi, president of the National Social Welfare Council; Mr. Fukushi jigyodan, Bunkyo Branch, money payment guarantee documents; Mr. M. Ohira, Liberal Democratic Party president; Mr. Shigen Hori, speaker of House of Representatives; Mr. Yasui, speaker of House of Councilors; Mr. Kazu Kaneko, minister of finance; Mr. Tsutara Hashimoto, Minister of Health & Welfare; Mr. Hirazawa, Ministry of Finance, Financial Bureau chief; Mr. Seiji Tsutsumi, investor representative; Mr. Sato, investor representative; and I.R. Tanaka, Minister of Construction. Subsequently, Messrs. Sato and Tanaka served as Prime Ministers of Japan. Mr. Iizuka has affirmed over and over again that Mr. Tanaka was with him in the office of the president of the Mitzui Bank Limited at the time and witnessed the Y 318 billion CD being issued.

At one time, Mr. Iizuka, signing for the Liberal Democratic Party Council and Liberal Democratic Party Budget Committee, submitted a "loan consent and authorization" to the Mitzui Bank Limited for a 100,000,000 yen loan secured by a 318,000,000,000 yen face value fixed deposit. The conditions of the loan were to be for a period of five (5) years with interest about ten percent (10%) per year. Said loan consent and authorization contained what appears to be an expiry date of

18 March 1983, signed at Tokyo, Setagaya-ku, 11/1 Ohara 2-26-12.

Questions: could the above referenced 318 billion yen fixed deposit used to collateralize the 100 million yen loan have been C/D #4051100-92? Just how many 318 billion yen fixed deposit instruments did the Liberal Democratic Party have in its portfolio? None others known but they had several of varied amounts.

[U.S. Money into Japanese Political Party Slush Fund]

Well, among others, both Marion Horn, JR. and John Burns, were shown a "confidential registry," which listed some 137 or 139 such instruments. The funds for the deposits were alleged to have been paid to Japan as repatriation to Japan and Korea for housing from the U. S. Government and other countries. Instead of the money going into a "HUD" type program, the money went into a giant "slush fund" in the names of nominees for the Liberal Democratic Party in order to hide it. No wonder that party is so wealthy. It has been reported that the Japanese received some $23 to 25 billion reparation payments from the United States over a period of time. History shows that the Japanese are pretty sneaky. Remember Pearl Harbor????

Certificate of Deposit # 4051100-92 was acquired by U. S. Mortgage and Trust Company and/or assigns on November 7, 1983 through the execution of a "deed of assignment and bill of sale" with the owner of record, Mr. Soichi Iizuka and Mr. William Sim Meng Lyang (Singapore passport # 0000847/h) 30, Bendi Road, Jurong Town, Singapore 2262, trustee, and escrow agent for U. S. Mortgage and Trust Company and/or assigns.

Previous to executing the "deed of assignment and bill of sale", Mr. William Sim Meng Lyang had been appointed by Mr. Soichi Iizuka as his duly authorized attorney with powers of attorney to negotiate and make decisions regarding the purchase and sale of the c/d and subsequently was appointed trustee, and escrow agent for U. S. Mortgage and Trust Company and/or assigns to set up an escrow account in a prime bank in Singapore to handle the purchase and sale of the c/d.

On October 19, 1983, a sworn statement was subscribed to in writing in the form of "certificate (certification) of cash deposit" at the United States Embassy in Tokyo confirming and certifying that the c/d was issued by Mitzui and that it was a legitimate, genuine, legal, authentic and assignable document. The primary signatory to the "certification" was Mr. Soichi Iizuka, the owner of record. The attestors were two (2) bank officers of Mitzui in Japan, Mr. Eiji Usuyama, assistant manager (possibly manager) of the Ginza branch, 9-12, 1-chome, Ginzo chuo-ku, Tokyo, tel. Tokyo 561-5111, and Mr. Akira Mishima, assistant manager of the Jueon Branch, and Mr. Takashi Takahashi, an attorney who was reported to represent the Liberal Democratic) Party, with offices at Himawari General law Office, Ito building, 7f, 6-21, 3-chome kyobeshi chuo-ku, Tokyo, Japan 104, tel. Tokyo 567-4891. The signatory and attestors were identified by name, photograph and signature by Ms. Frances T. Lide, consul of the United States of America, who personally acknowledged and sealed the "certification" with ribbon.

On November 7, 1983, U. S. Mortgage and Trust Company and/or assigns issued a sight draft, No. 11783, payable to the order of Mr. William Sim Meng Lyang and/or assigns in the amount of $500 million for payment of the CD as provided in the "deed of assignment and bill of sale". Said sight draft was to be lodged with the Chase Manhattan Bank, Singapore, in escrow agent account #4051100-92.

William Sims had been appointed as escrow agent for U. S. Mortgage and Trust co. and a depository agreement was executed making him the escrow agent for company at Chase Manhattan Bank, Singapore. His personal account was used as the escrow account. USMT had made arrangements through Fajr Hamid Pacha, (Syria passport # sr/80 493-989), who had made arrangements for notification to Chase Manhattan Bank, Singapore, for approximately one billion USD to be available for covering the sight draft issued to William Sims, who also was acting as agent for Iizuka, by power of attorney, the sight draft was made payable upon validation and confirmation of CD by Mitzui Bank Ltd.

The commitment was sent to Chase Manhattan Bank Singapore from UBS Bank of Geneva, Switzerland, on behalf of Tamanco Saudi and Gulf Investment Group, who had agreed to purchase the CD for 80% of its value which included its back interest as well; this was to be adjusted after validation of CD was done.

The procedure for validation of CD was not followed by UBS Geneva, as directed by Iizuka; first through U. S. Embassy and then to proper parties in Mitzui Bank Ltd. Instead, UBS Geneva went direct to bank on bank to bank basis, and Mitzui denied ever issuing instrument.

This was a CD that was issued also by Japanese Government, countersigned and specifically used for a loan in 1979 by Iizuka for Liberal Democratic Party; an English translation is attached for reference. So, if the instrument was not real, how could they use it as collateral for a loan 4 years earlier? The CD also was registered in a special account according to Iizuka, backed up by gold certificates.

The commitment of funds to cover the sight draft was made to the escrow account of USMT at Chase Manhattan this irrevocable commitment was to remain in effect until 1100 hours, Singapore, Tuesday, 29th of Nov. 1983. The commitment was based upon validation of the CD by Mitzui Bank Ltd, to UBS Singapore by coded telex.

[Using FBI to Defraud Holders of CD's Arising from Japanese Plunder]

On Nov. 21, 1983, I, JR Horn, received a call from Mr. John Binette (former DIA agent) that we were going to be arrested for attempting to cash a fraudulent instrument, but not to worry, everything would work out ok. I told Mr. Burns and Mr. Sims and they felt that this was not true because Iizuka, Muto, and his niece were still at Hotel Paramount where we were all staying, and they assured us that the boss (Tanaka) would take care of the validation as agreed in our bill of sale.

On November 21, 1983, John Burns, who was Asst. Secretary of U.S. Mortgage and Trust Co., accompanied by Soichi Iizuka's nice, Kato, who was acting as interpreter, Mr. Motokichi, Muto (Japanese passport # mg 439860, issued 11.3.83) and Mr. Masharu Mizushina, 8-4-10 Seijo, Setagaya-ku, Tokyo-tu, Japan, tel. Tokyo 3-482-3822, along with William Sim Meng Lyang, went to the office of the Union Bank of Switzerland, ("UBS") in Singapore for the purpose of lodging the original CD and the validation of the CD by US Embassy, Tokyo, Japan.

It was at that time in the hands of attorney of Donaldson & Burkinshaw law firm in Singapore, who was acting as attorneys and custodians of the instruments, for lodging at UBS for validation at Mitzui Bank Ltd, Tokyo, Japan, so that the authentication could be verified. Whereupon, the assistant manager of UBS office contacted Mitzui Bank Ltd.

It is reported that he was advised by Mitzui that an instrument of that size must be a forgery. Further, the number given for that particular CD could not be found in their computer run. Remember, this was a specially treated instrument and co-signed by Gov. of Japan, and was pledge for a loan for Liberal Democratic Party 27th Dec. 1978. (A copy of literal translation of back-up documents is attached for reference. An original document in Japanese is in safekeeping)

If the CD was not issued, how could it be pledge for a loan prior to 1983 by Soichi Iizuka? Continuing, the Asst. Manager of UBS became suspicious that the CD might be a forgery. He called the Commercial Crime Division of CID after he was informed by Mitzui Bank Ltd, Tokyo, head office that the CD was not in their computer run.

The manager of the Singapore Branch UBS was the one who called in Singapore CID. Ironically, a circular had been issued shortly before by the Singapore Banking Commission alerting bank personnel to be aware of counterfeit foreign currencies, bank notes and the like.

And thus, the CID (Commercial Crime Division of Singapore police) placed Burns, Horn, who were at Paramount Hotel in Singapore, Iizuka, Mizushina, and William Sim Meng Lyang also under "house arrest" by picking up all their passports. Mr. Sim, a Singapore resident, was required to post a cash bond equivalent to $200,000 in U.S. currency. Mr. Muto, was a suspect of having official Japanese credentials, (he had shown official documents where he was on special leave from Minister of Finance Investigation Division, on special permission from emperor of Japan). Mr. Iizuka's niece was released immediately. Mr. Muto escaped to Malaysia with the confidential registry in his possession before returning to Japan.

The following documents were appropriated from Mr. John Burns after being returned by the attorney at bank of Singapore on 17th day of November, 1983 at the office of the UBS Bank in Singapore and a receipted to him for U. S. Mortgage and Trust Co., by inspector Chai Yong Seng, Commercial Crime Division, CID, and Singapore:

(a) Original Certificate of Time Deposit No. 4051100-92, ref. 118-65, issued by the Mitzui Bank Ltd., Japan.

(b) Original copy of the Certificate (certification) of Cash Deposit validated at the U. S. Embassy, Tokyo, Japan, dated 19th Oct. 1983, certifying that time deposit No. 4051100-192 is an original and authentic certificate; (Copy of validation attached for reference.)

(c) Original deed of assignment and bill of sale dated November 7, 1983 assigning and transferring ownership of the c/d to U. S. Mortgage and Trust Company and/or assigns from Soichi Iizuka;

(d) Original deed of assignment and bill of sale dated November 7, 1983 assigning and transferring ownership of the c/d to Fajr Hamid Pacha and/or assigns from U. S. Mortgage and Trust Company;

(e) Letter dated the 17th of November 1983 ref hmd/jh/u. 38959a from Donaldson & Burkinshaw (law firm in Singapore) to the president of U. S. Mortgage and Trust Company;

(f) Agreement of sale between William Sim Meng Lyang and J. R. Horn on the c/d signed by William Sim Meng Lyang:

(g) A copy of the letter of attorney from Soichi Iizuka to William Sim;

(h) A copy of the corporate resolution of U. S. Mortgage and Trust Company;

(i) A copy of the pay order for c/d #4051100-92 and the amendment thereto dated the 7th of November 1983.

[LDP Nominee Owner of CD]

On the other hand, the Japanese involved, who were heavily interrogated by the Singapore authorities, have contended and affirmed over and over again that they were released because the Singapore authorities learned that not only was the c/d a valid instrument but that Soichi Iizuka was the rightful holder of record even though, as he had acknowledged, he was a nominee for the Liberal Democratic Party of Japan and had only to return to the LDP the face amount of the c/d in

U.S. dollars believed to have been paid to the Japanese by the U.S. Treasury Department.

[Heavy Involvement of Japanese LDP Politicians]

A private investigator for U. S. Mortgage and Trust Company and/or assigns was told by a detective of the Commercial Crime Division, CID, Singapore, that he understood the attorney general of Singapore had closed and sealed the file. The actual status of the documents is uncertain. Real "foreign intrigue"! Logic says that the c/d was either real or a bogus. If real, Mitzui owes the USMT beneficiaries not only a bundle but possibly triple damages. If a bogus, then based on the affirmation of Soichi Iizuka and his friends in the Liberal Democratic Party, Mitzui perpetrated a fraud by deceit and misrepresentation on Soichi Iizuka and the Liberal Democratic Party of Japan. Further, the government of Japan is involved by complicity because their seal was on the c/d.

And get this; when a friend of Mr. Horn, who discussed the matter of the c/d with Mr. Shintaro Abe, presently the political head man of the Liberal Democratic Party of Japan, possibly the next prime minister, was asked, "What it would take to buy Mr. Horn," he was told "that he didn't know Mr. Horn could be bought," the subject was dropped. Further, Mr. Abe is Mr. Tanaka's boy!

The persons who were detained were held until December 23, 1983, when a release was issued and the cash bond posted by William Sim Meng Lyang was returned. A Japan government limousine picked up Soichi Iizuka and Masaharu Mizushina in Singapore and they were escorted to the airport as if they were dignitaries to return to Tokyo.

The address of the Singapore authority involved in the arrests, appropriation of documents and investigation is: Commercial Crime Division, Criminal Investigation Department, Robinson Road, Singapore 0106, Republic of Singapore. Possible case number is 468 CP103.

Reference to the investigation is Report No. A/32950/83. No charges were made against any of the persons detained. The chief investigation officer, Cheok Koon Seng, of the Commercial Crime Division, CID, Singapore, refused to reveal anything pertaining to the alleged investigation or even comment on the investigation to Messrs. Burns and Horn other than to say, when asked to return the documents, that had been appropriated, "They have been sent up to higher command".

At that time, the face value of the c/d in U.S. dollars was slightly in excess of \$1,200,000,000, excluding any accumulation of accrued interest. The face value of the c/d in U.S. dollars recently has been in excess of \$2,271,430,000 which, after payment of the \$500 million to Soichi Iizuka and/or assigns, would provide each of the above named beneficiaries, excluding any distribution of interest to them, an amount in excess of $590 million. Interestingly, if the $500 million plus all accrued interest were paid to Soichi Iizuka and/ or assigns, the transaction would not cost LDP one dollar.

The balance of the face value, $1,771,430,000, which would be payable to the U.S. Mortgage & Trust would come about because of the depreciation of the U.S. dollar and the increased value of the Japanese yen, now predicted by economists to be on its way to 100 yen to 1 dollar. If the exchange rate had been reversed during the interval between its issue and the present, there would be no issue to contend for.

As provided in instructions imprinted on the c/d, the officers of U. S. Mortgage and Trust Company sent a formal notification to Mitzui at the Ginza branch in Tokyo to the attention of Mr. Eiji Usoyama, manager, under date of November 19, 1983, of the change of ownership of said c/d and enclosed with said notice supporting evidence.

Under date of December 3, 1983, one Mr. Takashi Miyaji, deputy general manager, General Affairs Division, the Mitzui Bank Limited, head office, 1-2, Yurakucho 1-Chome, Chiyoda-ku, Tokyo 100, Japan, replied to the formal notification stating as follows:

Dear Sirs,

We have examined the enclosed photocopy of a Certificate of Deposit No. 4051100-92, dated August 1, 1977, and hereby confirm that we never issued the document and that the document is not genuine.

As for the certificate (certification) of cash deposit, a photocopy of which was also enclosed with your letter, we have no information concerning the origin of this document; but it appears to be a complete fabrication based on the forgery of the names "Eiji Usuyama" and "Akira Mishima".

As you did not inform us of the complete address for Singapore C.I.D. Inspector Chai Yong Seng, we authorize you to deliver a copy of this letter to the Singapore authorities if you so wish.

We hope this response is satisfactory.

Sincerely,

[Japanese Political Party's Improper Use of U.S. Repatriation Money]

Upon receipt of the above letter, the aforementioned beneficiaries set upon the Japanese who were involved in selling the c/d to provide further evidences of its authenticity. Mr. Soichi Iizuka and certain other members of the LDP, not only to prove their contentions about the c/d but "to save face", have provided certain evidence that the c/d is authentic and that Mitzui, the Liberal Democratic Party of Japan, the Singapore authorities, and possibly the United States Department of State are, and have been involved in a conspiracy to "cover up" and prevent revelation of the payments and illegal use of the repatriation money.

[Japanese Politician Using U.S. Repatriation Money to Buy Hawaiian hotel]

In one instance, it is alleged that a Mr. Osanu, who is known to be a close friend of Mr. Tanaka, formerly Minister of Construction and Prime Minister, used the C/D in question to collateralize a loan from a West German bank to purchase hotels in Hawaii. Secondly, it is almost unbelievable, if the C/D was not genuine and the signatures on the "certification" forgeries, that Soichi Iizuka was only called on the carpet by Mr. Tanaka to explain what he was going to do with the $500 million with Mr. Tanaka emphasizing to Mr. Iizuka how important it was that the entire matter be "quieted". Mr. Tanaka, in turn, advised Soichi Iizuka that he had to report his answer to the big boss, Mr. Kishi.

Interestingly, Messrs. Kishi, Sato, and Tanaka have served as prime ministers of Japan with Sato and Tanaka being charged with accepting "humongous" kick-backs. On 14 July 1983, Mr. Muto signed a distribution agreement with William Sim entitled "protocol of evidence" in respect of the sale of Certificate of Deposit No. 4051100-92 with face value of y 318,000,000,000 in which Mr. Muto agreed to pay 50% of his net intake of approximately US $400,000,000.

Further, there was discussion by the Japanese at one time that some seventy-two (72) prefectures (heads of prefects—similar to counties in the U.S.A.) in Japan were to receive payments from the residual value of the C/D when a major portion of the residual value was to have been paid to Soichi Iizuka and/or assigns. It was reported that such payments are a common practice in Japan.

Upon Messrs. Burns and Horn making an appeal to the United States Embassy in Singapore concerning their house arrest and the appropriation of the documents, their treatment can only be described as mystifying. Both were held on personal recognizance with $100 bond. Even more mystifying, they were hardly questioned about the C/D. In an attempt to prove to the Singapore authorities that the C/D had been validated by witnesses, Mr. Horn requested on November 18, 1983 that the U.S. Embassy in Singapore check with the U.S. Embassy in Tokyo concerning said validation.

On December 5, 1983, the following message was received at the U.S. Embassy in Singapore:

Embassy check consular receipts dated October 19, 1983 and found receipt #9247 made out to "Takahashi" for item 331 general notarial service. The account was transacted in Japanese yen with the total amount due yen 960, amount tendered yen 1,000 and change returned yen 40. Although the name corresponds with one of the persons listed reftel, we note that the surname Takahashi is probably one among the top ten most common Japanese names.

MANSFIELD

A memorandum by Marion Horn stated the following:

Other than to acknowledge that a notarial receipt had been issued on October 19, 1983, to a Mr. TAKAHASHI, the response said very little other than to raise a question if that receipt pertained to the alleged validation. Then, on December 15, 1983, the following message was received at the U.S. Embassy in Singapore from the U.S. Embassy in Tokyo:

Embassy has now received photocopies of documents pouched from Singapore November 23.

Mr. Yoshimura of the general affairs department of Mitzui Bank head office, 1-1 Yuraku-cho, Chiyoda ku, Tokyo 100 informed Embassy that he had earlier been in touch with the Interpol office in Tokyo and had been shown documents pertaining to this case. One of the documents was the certificate of cash deposit, a copy of which was forwarded under cover of Singapore's transmittal slip of November 23, 1983. He said that every document shown to him was forged. He said that the numbers appearing on the certificate were typed with a make of typewriter which is not used at the Mitzui bank. Furthermore, Mitzui bank does not have the type of account number shown on the certificate. He thought that a blank certificate had been photocopied and the particulars typed-on the certificate. Soichi Iizuka has no account with any Mitzui offices in Japan. The two bank officers, Messrs. Usuyama and Mishima, are assistant managers at the Ginza and Ueno branches but the signatures are not their signatures. Neither Mr. Yoshimura nor the embassy has been able to locate a lawyer called Takashi Takahashi.

3. Interpol has Mr. Yoshimura's statement which he believes has already been forwarded to Singapore by the national police Interpol office.

4. Consul Lide has now returned to Tokyo and has examined the photocopy of the affidavit. She has no recollection of performing this particular notarial act but believes that she did sign it. She is certain

that appropriate identification (normally either a Japanese driver's license which shows name and photograph or a passport) was presented for each person who signed. It is possible, however, that at least some of the signatures were added subsequent to October 19. It is also possible that the last paragraph was added subsequent to October 19.

5. Given that the basic document which the explanatory affidavit covers has proved to be fraudulent, the question of the genuiness of the consular notarial now appears to be immaterial.

Mansfield

We have no idea what documents were shown to Mr. Yoshimura in his claim "that every document shown to him was forged," but Mr. Iizuka has affirmed over and over again that he and Mr. Tanaka saw the president of Mitsui sign that C/D and that that C/D is authentic. If not, Mitsui issued to Mr. Iizuka a fraudulent document and that document, if fraudulent, was accepted by Mitsui and other alleged Lenders as collateral. Further, based on the testimony of persons who saw, held and felt the C/D, Horn, Burns, Binette, and Sims, it was no photocopy of a blank. It was observed to be an original print; the seals were real; and it showed evidence of having been in use or circulation—certainly not a new counterfeit.

Mr. Yoshimura grossly misrepresented the facts when he claimed that the person named on the C/D, Mr. Soichi Iizuka, had no account with Mitsui. He had several accounts, including credit cards. Mr. Yoshimura further claims that the signatures of the two bank officers of Mitsui on the "Certification" were not the signatures of Messrs. Usuyama and Mishima.

Question: How could Ms. Frances Lide have identified them by name, photograph and signature if they weren't who they represented themselves to be? It is really mystifying that neither Mr. Yoshimura nor the U.S. Embassy in Tokyo could locate Mr. Takashi Takahashi. He is a very prominent attorney in Tokyo.

It just so happens that John Burns still has the personal business card of Mr. Eiji Usuyama, Manager of the Ginza Branch of Mitsui, as well as the personal business card of Mr. Takashi Takahashi, who was identified as representing the Liberal Democratic Party of Japan at the time the Certification of the C/D was obtained at the U.S. Embassy in Tokyo.

Question: Can one imagine how a bright-minded, super selected person such as Ms. Frances T. Lide, Consul to the U.S. Embassy in Tokyo, could have such a short recall? In less than two months, this woman couldn't recall having notarized an instrument certifying to the validity of a bank obligation which had a face value in United States Currency in excess of One Billion Dollars. What a convenient loss of memory! She couldn't recall notarizing the "certification" but if she did, it's not only possible that some of the signatures were added subsequent to October 19. But it's also possible that the last paragraph was added subsequent to October 19. If those projected disclaimers aren't the product of warped brain waves, then one would wonder where they came from and for what reason.

Perhaps the shortcomings of Ms. Lide were recognized. Shortly thereafter, she was transferred from her post in Tokyo back to the States. In being traced, evidently her recall has improved because now she recalls enough that she doesn't want to talk about the "certification". Wonder why? (Ms. Lide was at US Embassy Canada 1989)

Ambassador Mansfield stated "that the basic document which the explanatory affidavit covers has proved to be fraudulent". The question is: Who proved it? What evidence was presented to the U.S. Embassy in Tokyo? What evidence was presented to the U.S. Embassy in Singapore? Why was no evidence presented to or shared with any of the USMT Beneficiaries?

Ambassador Mansfield stated "Interpol has Mr. Yoshimura's statement which he believes has already been forwarded to Singapore by the National Police Interpol Office".

Question: What was Mr. Yoshimura's statement? Why did Ambassador Mansfield accept his statement without benefit of documentation? In situations such as this it is often said that "something stinks in Denmark".

Well, in this instance, perhaps "something is rotten in Singapore and Tokyo". Mr. Yoshimura certainly misrepresented the facts relative to Soichi Iizuka having an account or doing business with Mitsui. The statement that "neither Mr. Yoshimura nor the Embassy has been able to locate a Lawyer called Takashi Takahashi" would appear true only if neither had attempted to locate him. Statements such as these indicate a complete "whitewash".

If the C/D is fraudulent or if the Embassy in Tokyo had received documented evidences which indicated its genuiness was subjected to question, why weren't such evidences revealed? Assuredly, if a fraud by deceit and misrepresentation were being perpetrated on a United States company and/or United States citizens involved in such company and the U.S. Embassy in Tokyo or Singapore were aware of it, one would think that fact would be communicated to the citizens from the Embassies, especially a fraud involving over One Billion Dollars.

Why was the matter "hushed up"? If, as alleged by Ambassador Mansfield, that the document was fraudulent, why were there no charges brought against any of the persons involved in attempting to authenticate it? Could it be that Mr. Yoshimura wasn't as informed about "special issue" time deposits as he should have been in representing Mitsui? And has the United States Department of State become involved by complicity in a "cover up" for the Liberal Democratic Party of Japan?

Mr. Soichi Iizuka was carrying on his person three (3) Japanese bonds at the time the group was picked up by the Singapore Authorities. These bonds were given to him by the Liberal Democratic Party for services to the Party, including serving as Nominee on the C/D. To this day, the Singapore Authorities have failed to return said Bonds to Mr. Iizuka. As a matter of fact, just recently, Mr. Iizuka implored John Burns to help him retrieve the bonds which are his personal property. Ah, yes, the beat of conspiracy and complicity goes on.

Question: Why would the Singapore Authorities hold Mr. Iizuka's bonds? Could it be they are evidence that the Liberal Democratic Party of Japan doesn't want revealed? No doubt, they have been declared fraudulent documents too. That might be a little difficult as they were once authenticated in the Philippines by the Mellon Bank. There is little doubt that "something" is mighty amiss. For good reasons.

Based on testimony of Mr. Iizuka, if the C/D was a forgery, then the Mitsui Bank Limited issued a fraudulent Certificate of Deposit in his name. Or, the C/D in question is "specially treated" with the regular bank officers of Mitsui being unaware of such "special" issues, which very likely aren't on "computer runs" as proclaimed by Mr. Iizuka. By no stretch of the imagination can one presume that if the C/D was a forgery that all persons would have been released by the Singapore Authorities.

Interestingly, when the group was picked up in Singapore, there were big headlines in the newspapers in Singapore and Tokyo about the arrests. However, upon release, the event wasn't covered in the news media. One would think that some reporter would have found the event newsworthy; or was the information on the releases intentionally withheld?

On August 2, 1985, U. S. Mortgage and Trust Company, through the law office of Willard C. McBride, filed a tort claim against the United States Department of State for negligent or wrongful action of the U.S. Embassy in Tokyo in reversing and setting aside its "validation" of a $1.2 Billion certificate of deposit on October 19, 1983. The claim was denied by administrative ruling of Mr. David P. Stewart, Assistant Legal Adviser, Office of International Claims and Investment Disputes, on March 21, 1986 "that in view of the invalidity of the document itself, the question of the genuineness of the consular notarial appeared to be immaterial".

Please Note: Mr. Stewart said "appeared" and that is only his opinion, not anyone else's. In summary, the Department of State contended that since the C/D itself had never been validated (by Mitsui we presume), there was nothing which could be reversed or set aside regardless of what Consul Lide did or did not do. Based solely on statements of Mr. Yasushi Yoshimura, presumably a Mitsui official with authority to address $1.2 billion controversies that the Certificate of Deposit was a forgery, and therefore, "there was no merit to the tort claim."

QUESTION: If we don't have the document, how can it be validated? How convenient for the U.S. Department of State to cope a plea that the genuiness of the consular notarial "appeared" to be immaterial in view of the invalidity of the document. Whose invalidity? There is no question that Ms. Lide notary didn't acknowledge-the-genuiness of the C/D. But she did acknowledge the identification and signatures of four (4) people who subscribed and swore that the C/D was a legitimate, genuine, legal, authentic and assignable document. Her acknowledgement is and should be testimony that those persons were who they represented themselves to be until otherwise proven.

If they weren't who they represented themselves to be, then the finger of blame is upon her. Certainly, the purchasers of the C/D relied upon the "certification" acknowledged by Ms. Lide. The Department of State would have to prove the invalidity of the document before Mr. Stewart's position can be considered as having any merit. The ready acceptance of the U.S. Embassy in Tokyo that (i) the C/D was a forgery and that (ii) the signatures of the two bank officers were not their signatures, as affirmed by Mr. Yoshimura's alleged statement to the National Police Interpol Office without that Embassy having received indisputable evidence to support said affirmation is baffling.

In fact, that Embassy unconditionally controverted a sworn statement of its own Consul, Ms. Frances T. Lide. Also, that Embassy with hardly a flicker of any eyelash controverted the sworn statements of four (4) other people. Was Mr. Yoshimura's statement sworn? Obviously, that Embassy really took to heart the affirmations made by Mr. YOSHIMURA whose position and rank of authority were never disclosed. He could be the guy from the General Affairs Department who changes the type in the typewriters used to type out 318 Billion Yen Certificates of Deposit for Mitsui as far as anyone knows because he most certainly isn't listed as an Officer of Mitsui in Polk's bank directory. Or perhaps he pushes a broom for Mr. Takashi Miyaji, Deputy General Manager, General Affairs Division, The Mitsui Bank Limited, to clean up the acts of senior officials who have been playing "footy footy" with senior officials of the Liberal Democratic Party of Japan. This much is certain.

The promises made to Messrs. Burns and Horn by Mr. William Moody of the U.S. Embassy in Singapore that he would retrieve all of the documents appropriated by the Singapore Authorities in order that they (Burns and Horn) could pursue proving the genuiness of the C/D never came about.

QUESTION: Just whose interests were the U.S. Embassies protecting? If the C/D was a forgery and Mr. Soichi Iizuka et al were attempting to perpetrate a fraud on the purchasers of the C/D, why weren't the evidences made available to Messrs. Burns, Horn, and William Sim Meng Lyang? Just what was discovered in the investigation instituted by the Singapore Authorities? Why won't they reveal what was uncovered. Why the cover up? The U.S. Embassies have a prime responsibility to represent the interests of U.S. Citizens. In this situation, it appears they have failed miserably.

All information from June 1987 is primarily through Fidesco De-Mexico, Col. Norman Grand, and Major Gen. Robert L. Ferrera. They have offices in Los Angeles, Ca. at 3250 Wilshire Blvd., Suite 900. Los Angeles, Ca. 90010, Phone: 213-382-0209, (Front Co. for CIA?)

Information contained up to this point was compiled in June 1987 by investigation of U.S. Mortgage and Trust Co., J. R. Horn, president. The information from this point of approximately June 1987 until June 1990 is by J. R. Horn:

In the fall of 1987, J. R. Horn received releases from John Burns, Williams Sims on all monies owed to them in their efforts to collect CD #4051100-92, with promises to reimburse each of them up to approximately $200,000 each upon collection of CD by USMT. Both signed releases to USMT/Horn and also, William Sims signed a release to USMT for all past monies due upon providing a standby L/C from Gulf Coast Casualty Ins. Co. which was done for $5 Million.

Copies of all these documents were forward to Col. Norman Grand, and Major Gen. Robert L. Ferrera, of Fidesco, for their files. All these files were supposedly stolen from Clancy office spring of 1990.

USMT opened an office in Dallas, TX to do individual Surety Bonding with Excel Surety Co, of Ft. Worth, TX., and Dominion Savings and Trust, acted as validation of the assets held by J R Horn, from U. S. Mortgage and Trust Co. Some individual bonding was done with Capital Exchange of Silver Springs, MD., Dr. Dean Manson, but all individual bonding stopped in Dec., 1987 and I, J. R. Horn, closed office in Dallas, Tx. and returned to Lexington, Ky.

In fall of 1989, sometime around September, a meeting was arranged through Norman Steining of Excel Surety Co., that a person from U. S. Dept. of Justice was in Dallas, TX and wanted to meet with me in regard to settling this CD. A meeting was set at Marriott Hotel, Downtown, Dallas, TX and at the meeting was Norman Steining, John Binette, myself, and the person (a black man) who stated he represented the Justices Dept., and on behalf of the CIA. He had been asked to meet with me to discuss this settlement. Mr. Norman Steining at 214-681-2424, has name of the individual. I had the meeting taped by Mr. John Binette, who still has the tapes.

I was told that after the election I would meet with Mr. Jim Baker and Controller of Currency and they would settle the transaction. I had previously been told by Col. Grand and Gen. Ferrera from Fidesco office in Tokyo that this was a rogue group of CIA who was trying to muscle in on the settlement and get credit through the parties in Defense Dept. who were making use of the funds. I never heard anymore from the party from Dept. of Justice after informing Gen. Ferrera of the proposal received in Dallas, Tx. (it was as if Ferrera waved the magic wand and he was gone.)

A Meeting was scheduled at Air Force Base near the LAX Airport in California at the Officers Club, with Major Gen. Robert L. Ferrera, Col. Norman N. Grand, John Binette and myself. This was first meeting with Grand and Ferrera, after conversing with them over six months. They would not meet anywhere at first except on a military base. The only people at the Officers Club were the four of us. Binette recorded the whole meeting secretly.

This was around early part of 1988. Ferrera and Grand assured us that the collection would have to be done covertly because U.S. Gov. and Japanese Gov. could not afford for this to be made public. This was first meeting with Ferrera and Grand. They set forth that they had spent large sums of money arranging for payment of the CD and we would have to cover expenses and monies from that point.

Col. Grand recommended that we form an offshore company somewhere like Bahamas and transfer title to the offshore company. This is when U. S. Mortgage and Trust (Bahamas) Ltd. came into existence. Five thousand dollars was paid to Julian Maynard, attorney at law, in Nassau, Bahamas for a charter like a bank and the name of U. S. Mortgage and Trust (Bahamas) Ltd. John Binette went to Nassau, Bahamas and completed the incorporation.

After the U. S. Mortgage and Trust (Bahamas) Ltd. Company was formed, all of its assets, which were those of U.S.M.T., Inc., which was the holding company for all assets of U. S. Mortgage and Trust co., were assigned to the Bahamas Company. The present officers and directors of U.S. Mortgage and Trust (Bahamas) Ltd., are the following: J R Horn, aka, Marion Horn Jr., Chairman of Board, President & CEO, Director, Mr. Ed Morrow, Secretary, Director, Mr. Lon E. Williamson, Executive V.P., & Director, Mr. Alex Damelio, Jr., Treasurer, & Director. Mr. Morrow and Mr. Damelio, are the active members of Five Star Trust, to whom all the assets and stock of U. S. Mortgage and Trust

Bahamas, Ltd. Ltd, was assigned in December 1988.

Mr. Ed Morrow has all the records the assignment of assets and stock to Five Star Trust (an Isle of Man trust), created in 1988, by Ed Morrow for heirs of John Booth, an ancestor of J R Horn, and Lon E. Williamson. Mr. J R Horn and his immediate family are direct beneficiaries of the Trust.

Mr. J R Horn holds the position of Executive Trustee, & Mr. Lon. Williamson, Asst. Trustee to Mr. Horn. Mr. Marion Horn, Jr., aka, J R Horn, owns no assets of any kind in his name; all interest he may have are the ownership of Five Star Trust. Elaine Horn, wife of J R Horn, holds assets in her own name and her assets and J R Horn, are individually owned. We have three children, Stuart Horn, Son, age 20, who has severe learning disability and epilepsy seizures, awaiting surgery and Sonya Horn, Daughter., age 17, awaiting to enter college at U of K, Lexington, Ky., she is working full time at Dawahares Dept., store, Lexington Mall, Lexington, Ky., and Starr D. Horn, Son, age 9. These people are beneficiaries of Five Star Trust.

Early part of 1988, a meeting was held at El Toro Marine Air Station, El Toro, CA in the Officers Living Quarters. Present at that meeting were J R Horn, John Binette, Bill Clancy, Col Norman Grand, Major Gen. Robert L. Ferrera. The purpose of this meeting was to give an up-to-date report on what was happening in Japan and D.C., and to deliver a letter from Mitsui Bank Ltd., to Shearson, Lehman, Bros in Beverly Hills, CA. confirming the validity of the Certificate of Deposit and signed by a bank officer of Mitsui. This signature was verified by Alan Wolfley, with Mitsui personnel to be a valid signature and there was a question whether or not he had the authority to confirm this much money.

[CIA Ferrera and DOD]

That letter is attached to this summary for reference. In January 30, 1989 a formal agreement was negotiated by Major Gen. Robert L. Ferrera with Dept. of Defense with Mitsui Bank Ltd., U. S. Government, Japanese Gov., and all other parties. It was agreed that Five Star Trust would be paid $320 Billion Japanese Yen and all back interest would go to International Freedom Foundation, (This was supposed to be a front company for CIA) at Credit Swiss Bank, Zurich, Switzerland.

The Original letter of agreement is in safekeeping. In July 1989, a letter was delivered to Mr. Horn confirming that over 400 Billion Japanese yen had been deposited to an account of Five Star Trust at the Bank of New Zealand, a copy is attached for reference. The original letter was in Bill Clancy hands and was stolen with our other records from his office, according to his statement to Ed Morrow.

In July 1989, Gen. Ferrera called at Bill Clancy's office and informed myself and Mr. Clancy that certain people wanted to use our account at the Bank of New Zealand to deposit funds into and out and they would pay to us one-third of the amount. I told Gen. Ferrera that I didn't want to be involved, but he insisted that this was for the benefit of our government and the development of third world countries, such as Mexico, Columbia, Argentina, Etc.

At this time I was asked if Alan Wolfley would like to be Ambassador to Japan. I contacted Mr. Wolfley and he agreed. I told Gen. Ferrera that we would agree to let them use our account if he felt it was in the best interest of our country, and Mr. Wolfley had agreed to accept the post in Japan. He had been offered the post during the Carter Administration but turned it down at that time due to business commitments he had in Japan.

I ask Mr. Wolfley to check with a friend of his, John P. Boegner, if he knew Baron Phillipe duDaphne, and he informed Mr. Wolfley that he did and had been in Jail with Baron during the Algerian War. In later part of July 1989 another letter addressed to U. S. Mortgage and Trust (Bahamas) Ltd. was issued by The Bank of New Zealand, referring to a deposit of over $12 Billion USD in AU that was on deposit in the Bahamas Co. This was supposedly the first payment of a larger one to be done which was delivered to Mr. Horn, later part of Feb. 1990 from General Ferrera at Cincinnati, Ohio airport, wherein three additional deposits were made to three different banks in the name of U. S. Mortgage and Trust (Bahamas) Ltd. Gen. Ferrera was the guardian of the funds for the Bahamas Company.

A copy of that letter is attached and additional letter authorizing J R Horn to withdraw funds from bank of New Zealand and the three other banks. A fax sheet is attached hereto also wherein an inquiry was made on the funds but as of this date June 21, 1990 no response.

Sometime in the summer of 1989 another letter was delivered to J R. Horn by General Ferrera that was addressed to Baron Phillipe du Daphne, from Admiral Gene R. La Rocque, attn: Gen. Robert L. Ferrera concerning the New Broom and Studebaker transaction, status report. This report specifically states the CD #4051100-92 is registered in World Bank, and that Admiral Gene R. LaRocque was the trustee of all records and documents regarding this situation.

I ask Gen. Ferrera why would he give me this document. He replied that "I have cancer and I don't know how long I will live and the more information you have, the more protection you will have if they (CIA) decide to double cross us. He further stated that Helms [CIA]was the one we had to watch, but that baron Guy Rothschild was a friend and would make the rest honor their word. Gen. Further informed me that Baron Guy Rothschild would deliver to me within a few weeks an insurance policy, which would serve to protect me if anyone decided to eliminate me.

I later received the documents in courier package from Ferrera; contained within was a confidential report from FBI addressed to Senator Ted Kennedy concerning this situation from beginning to end and a cover letter from Baron Guy Rothschild to myself giving the reason for sending me the report. A copy of that report is attached. The last page is missing from report that was signed, *Your Classmate*, to Kennedy.

[The Mexican Connection]

The Mexican connection began in 1989, with a trip to Mexico with Major Gen. Robert L. Ferrera, wherein Manolo Prieto, a friend of Gen. Ferrera lived and Luis Riverollo. Both had known Ferrera for over 20 years. The first meeting was with Mr. Bill Clancy, somewhere around spring of 1989 and we were on our way to New Zealand to finalize the collection of our funds. But we were to go by way of Mexico.

Ferrera wanted me to meet his two old friends and establish a working relationship at which time they proposed acquiring a city block in Mexico City and opening a gaming house with only the elite people of Mexico being members. It was later agreed that the Gov. of Mexico would give us a blanket permit for the whole country for a gambling book permit. I was not interested in getting involved in this gambling, but I later agreed with the understanding that all the income for myself and Five Star Trust would go toward a charitable foundation to be given to the poor in Mexico.

After a short time things began to drag on. I insisted that whoever Ferrera was talking to that we be paid at least the interest at Bank of New Zealand, which at that time was paying Five Star Trust 18% interest, and the only account receiving this amount of interest. While in Mexico on this trip he informed Mr. Sununu or whomever we wanted the interest and it was agreed that one month's interest would be paid, which came to around 70 million USD; this was 45 days, not one month. The monies were to be transferred to D.C. to be paid to Five Star Trust, but we never could get the funds confirmed or released.

Shortly thereafter came Greg Reynolds, of Reynolds, Beeby, & Magnuson, Attorneys at Law, Detroit, Michigan, who were interested in purchasing natural gas from Mexico. A meeting was set up in Las Vegas, Nevada to meet with Ferrera, Manolo Prieto, Reynolds, and another person from his law firm to discuss two items: the gaming permits in Mexico and the Natural Gas. Mr. Aggie Holm of Bechtel was present to discuss also the proposal of acquiring from Mexican Gov the right to build a land bridge cannel across the center of Mexico, wherein came the bank letter from ABN bank of Amsterdam, Netherlands, a copy of letter is attached for reference.

Out of this meeting came the initial creation of America Internationals Corporation, (a Mexican company), which I control or hold original stock of over 75%. Members of company are J R Horn, Robert L. Ferrera, and Raymond Lancaster, who assigned their stock to me. J R Horn, and Luis Riveroll, who also signed his stock to J R Horn. The only remaining stock holder outside is Manolo Prieto, who owns about 25%. This company has been issued a permit from Mexican Gov to build a 150 mile land bridge cannel across Mexico. I saw the permit but do not have a copy in English in my possession.

General Ferrera as recently as Monday, June 18, 1990 insisted that everything would be completed in satisfactory order as he predicted. He has been staying at a hotel in Mexico for over 6 months at 905-250-7700, room 3504.

The trustees of Five Star Trust have agreed to set up an office at 2220 Zandale Center, Suite 16, Lexington, Ky. 40503, Phone: 606-278-3339, for the Executive Trustee, J. R. Horn to operate from and try and bring this collection of CD to a conclusion.

Letters of inquiry have been sent to Office of President, Secretary Of State, Director of CIA, Secretary of Defense inquiring into the validity of the settlement letter given to J R Horn on Jan. 30, 1989, and no answers to these letters which were written in early spring 1990.

A separate certified letter was written to Chief of Staff, Mr. Sununu, and a response was sent back from aide Gary Radamaker, stating that Mr. Sununu had no knowledge of the attachments to the letters enclosed in our inquiry.

First of all, the letter received from Mr. Radamaker creates more suspicion because there was no phone number on the letter or reference letters and the answer did not deny anything, because the letters said Gov. Sununu did not know anything about the attachments; what attachments? There is clearly something wrong with the reply letter.

Letters were written to Senator Mitch McConnell for assistance, since he had agreed to assist several years ago; but no response to the letters sent to him as of this date and that was over two months ago, from June 21, 1990. Could it have to do with his campaign chairman Mr. Booth for Northern Ky., whose brother Bill Booth, a professor at Morehead State University, Dept. of Art, contacted Mr. Horn and stated that he had been asked by the highest level to look into this situation; referring to Mr. Sununu, the Oval Office.

Mr. Bill Booth and Larry Huffman (an attorney from Lexington, Ky., went to Tokyo, Japan, on my behalf, which was not authorized and they were informed as such). Terry Anderson, brother to Jerry Anderson (who acted as attorney to Trust for a short period of time until he was replaced due to inability to produce any concrete intelligent suggestions to the Trust).

This was quietly done because of Mr. Terry Anderson, attorney for State of KY for Workman Compensation, had taken data given to him by Jerry Anderson, who was acting as our counsel and advisor and gave it to Hiru Takeshita, nephew to former P.M. of Japan, who had offered Mr. Jerry Anderson anything he wanted in form of compensation as legal counsel for Japanese Companies to turn over our documents to them.

This is main reason he was terminated. Jerry Anderson, through his brother Terry Anderson, gave to Japanese all copies of documentation that belong to Five Star Trust and J R Horn, without first getting permission from the Trust. The Trust wanted to file a formal complaint against Jerry Anderson and Terry Anderson with State Bar Association but this has been delayed to find out exactly they were trying to accomplish.

Mr. Ed Morrow is convinced that Jerry Anderson has not acted in manner that an attorney should and we should report him to State Bar Association. This we have not done and will not do until we are sure his motives were not honorable.

Mr. Raymond Lancaster, who acted as assistant to Mr. J. R. Horn for over a year beginning late in 1988 and going into early 1990, when he got married and left for Houston, Texas with his new bride. He introduced Mr. Horn to Mr. Anderson to act as temporary counsel and that he wanted to arrange a meeting with the Japanese party of Hiru Takeshita, who wanted to get hold of confidential tapes that were in hands of an associate, Mike Sattelmair, of Richmond, Va.. The tapes involves high ranking Japanese confirming that Congressman Carroll Hubbard has made several inquiries to Dept. of Defense and Mr. Sununu, and no definite answers as of yet. But they say that Mr. John MacElroy is not in Dept of Defense but they didn't say he did not work for Government, and they recommended that we report this to Dept. of Justice.

I wrote Carroll Hubbard and asked him to forward materials I had given him on to the Justice Dept. and see what they would do and find out about this situation. This was done first of June 1990.

I went to Washington, D. C. to meet Mr. Bill Jennings, former FBI Agent retired, who was doing contract work for Dept. of Defense, CID, and gave him a complete file to look into. I was accompanied to the first meeting by Stuart Sigmon from Princeton, W. Va, who was a roommate in college.

Mr. Jennings agreed to look into the situation. Second meeting was a month later, and Keith Jones of Lexington, Ky. accompanied me to Leesburg, Va., where we met Mr. Jennings at Ramada Inn, Manassas,

Va. A full and complete package was given him surrounding this situation. Last information received from Bill Jennings as of June 21, 1990, is that Ferrera has cancer and has very little time left. He stated that the Japanese and other parties would continue to deny any knowledge of the Certificate of Deposit #4051100-92.

As of this date, June 22, 1990, I have been contacted by Gen. Ferrera, who wants to meet with me in Cincinnati., Ohio, June 30 & 31, 1990, to discuss the collecting of the funds owed to Five Star Trust, and its subsidiary companies.

I am attaching hereto a list of letters and documents which we have received over the past seven years regarding CD #4051100-92. Please note that the documents herein displayed have been placed into the hands of U.S. Congressman Carroll Hubbard of Kentucky and certain documents into U.S. Attorney General's hands for investigation. Certain of the documents have been referred to herein have been placed in hands of special prosecutor office Washington, D. C. also for investigation.

General Ferrera's whereabouts as of August 6, 1990 is with John Binette of Biddeford, Maine, who is in process of acquiring a offshore bank. General Ferrera has communicated with the office of Five Star Trust twice within last three months and last communication was the last of July 1990, wherein he stated he was still working to resolve the payment of the Certificate of Deposit and related deposits owned by Five Star Trust and or its subsidiary companies.

This is English translation of Japanese records where CD # 4051100-92 was pledged for a loan. The originals are in safekeeping.

Source Document Page TITLE/TRANSLATIONS

1 Refers to Money Payment Guarantee Document - Top Secret

2 Money Payment Guarantee Documents - 27 December 1978 Fukushi Jigyodan, Bunkyo Branch, Setagaya Ward Welfare Corporation

District Manager Iizuka

As a result of an investigations concerning restitution of money repayment for Bunkyo Branch in the Finance Council in the reporting to the Budget Committee of the House of Councillor; and House of Representatives which accepted the petition and report on 22 December 1978.

3 Finance Council:

Liberal Democratic Party President Ohira M,

Speaker of' House of Representatives Hori, Shigen
Speaker of House of Councillors Yasui
Minister of Finance Kaneko, Kazu
Minister of Health & Welfare Hashimoto, Tauter
Ministry of Finance, Financial Bureau Chief Hirazawa
Investor Representative Sutsumi, Seiji
Investor Representative Sato

4. Official Notarial verification of the inscribed seal (signatt of the Liberal Democratic Party President – Ohira

5 Official Notarial verification of the inscribed seal (signatt of the Investor Representative (SATO)

6 Official Notarial verification of the inscribed seal (signatt of the Minister of Health 6 Welfare (Hashimoto).

Official Notarial verification of the inscribed seal (signatu of the Investor Representative (Tsutsumi).

8. 00658 Payment to the representatives by each district of the Bunkyo Branch was decided as stated below, and the guarantee of restitution money payment was granted.

Record

1. Interest Bearing Government Bonds - 5,600,000,000 Yen
1. Restitution Money - 5,600,000,000 Yen
1. Discount Industrial Bank (Debentures) New bonds) 5,600,000,000 Yen
1. Payment Commencement Date - 16 January, 1974

In order to clearly define the decision recorded above, the government and the Finance Council Committee put their inscribed seal on the guarantee.

9 Emergency Circular

In the Fiscal Year 1977, Budget Committee, as a result of the reinvestigation by said Council Committee due to the consecutive occurrences of incidents to concerned persons concerned with the Bunkyo Branch, the need to prevent such incidents was strongly felt and the decision was adopted with the complete agreement of the full committee that individual grants pertaining to the purpose for which the previously decided Social Welfare Project investments are spent will be handled by the Public Service Department.

Within the Diet, there has been news of problems with abuse of the name of the National Social Welfare Council, and since there has been opposition from various quarters because of those incidents, handling by the below recorded public services is authorized strictly within the objectives of the council.

Managing Orgunizatiun - Mitzui Bank Public Service Department

TO : National Social Welfare Council

FROM : Liberal Democratic Party Council Liberal Democratic Party Budget Committee

Loan Consent and Authorization

At this time, I delegate all authority to the Mitsui Bank to loan 100,000,000 yen secured by 318,000,000,000 Yen issued as fixed deposit face value.

Conditions

1. Period - over five (5) years.
1. Interest – about ten (10%) per year.

18 March, 1983

Tokyo, Satuguya-Ku, Ohura 2-26-12

Signed - Iizuka Shuicue

10 To: Liberal Democratic Party Budget Committee

National Social Welfare Council

24 November 1977

With the coldness of autumn, we hope you will be in ever more continued health in your diligent government service.

We would like to thank you very much in designating our bank au the bunk handling social welfare project investments for the National Social Welfare Council.

Today, we have received from the Ministry of Finance the designated grant of ten (10%) of the total amount for ordinary savings by individual under the management of the local department chief, National Social Welfare Council. This was transmitted to the local representatives at our brunch office on 28 November, 1977.

Signed - Mitsui Bank

Itakura Keiji, Director

Transaction at U.S. Military Base

The following is reference to financial transactions occurring on July 19, 1988 at the Officer Club, Marine Air Station, El Toro, California. At this meeting, a check on the Mexican bank Fidesco was given to Col. Norman Grand by J. R. Horn for expenses incurred with CD #4051100-92.

National Association Notice to Customers:

P.O BOX 1290
Fort Worth. Texas 78101-1290

Fort Worth, Texas
J.R. Horn, Purchaser

Fidesco De Mexico/Col. Norman Grand $17,100,00

Official Check:
Expenses estimated paid to Fidesco, Col. Grand, Mgen. Robert l. Ferrera from 1988 up to Present June 1990

From J.R. Horn:	52,300.00
Phone Charges:	13,300.00 (This also includes half R. Lancaster)
Charges Cards;	25,000.00
Pocket Cash;	3,500.00

From: Alex Damelio, Jr.

5,000.00 estimated from credit receipts

From: Ione Williamson

10,000.00 estimated from credit card receipts and Western Union Transfers.

William L. Clancy, CPA, estimated he wired close to $125,000.00 to Gen. Robert L. Ferrera from monies received from bonding contracts. $125,000.00.

Since none of records are available, there is no way to verify this amount.

Mr. Ed Morrow: 15,000.00, Amount to Fidesco, Col. Grand.

Estimated Amount: $249,100.00 sent or given to Fidesco, Col Grand and Megan.

Robert L. Ferrera.

A fax from Marion Horn refers to the transfer of funds from one of his accounts to General Ferrera, a CIA asset.

U. S. MORTGAGE & TRUST (BAHAMAS) LTD.

SUBSIDIARY COMPANY OF FIVE STAR TRUST

FIVE STAR TRUST

FAX COVER SHEET

J R Horn-President

Date: June 18, 1990

Fax number: 65-225-6880

To: NMB Bank (Singapore) Ltd.

Att: Wong Chin Au, Director: Phone: 65-2204644
Battery Road 30-02 No of Pages: 3.
Standard Chartered Bank Bldg.
Singapore 0104

From: Mr. J. R. Horn, Executive Trustee of Five Star Trust, and President and CEO of U.S. Mortgage and Trust (Bahamas) Ltd.

USA Address is 2220 Nicholasville Road, Suite 16, Lexington, Ky. 4050. Phone: 606-278-3339 FAX: 606-278-2684

Comments:

Dear Mr. Wong Chin Aun:

I am attaching to this fax cover sheet a letter from General Roberto L. Ferrera, who as a Trustee of Five Star Trust and as Executive Vice President of U. S. Mortgage and trust. (Bahamas) Ltd. has informed me that these funds were transmitted to an account at Credit Suisse Bank Zurich, Switzerland, Banque de Paris et des pays bas, Paris, France and Lloyds Bank Plc., London, England.

The amount of the funds were to be deposited to an account under General Ferrera name on behalf of Marion Horn, Jr. (U.S. mortgage and trust (Bahamas) Ltd. at the bank where they are now on deposit.

Since these funds are the property of U.S. Mortgage and trust (Bahamas) Ltd. and/or JR Horn, we do hereby request that the funds hereinabove transmitted to the banks indicated be notified that U.S. Mortgage and Trust (Bahamas) ltd. Has requested that arrangements be made to redeposit the funds into a special account for U. S. Mortgage and Trust (Bahamas) Ltd./JR horn, president at the banks where the funds are now on deposit. We would like for you to handle this on our behalf. Also, to furnish us with all information necessary to complete this transfer.

SIGNED: Marion Horn, aka, JR Horn
President & CEO of USMT Bahamas

Executive Offices:
J. R. Horn, Executive Trustee Landale Office Center
2220 Nicholasville Road Lexington, KY 40503

Administrative Offices:
Edwin P. Morrow, Trustee
Financial Planning Building 2507 North Verity Parkway
Middletown, OH 45042-0430
(513) 424-1656 FAX: 5752

The following affidavit related to a meeting between escrow officer and Marion Horn relating to the transfer of funds:

STATE OF FLORIDA
COUNTY OF BROWARD

Richard H. Sowden, Sr. Executive Escrow Officer of Private Escrow & Transfer Company, Ltd., who after first being duly sworn by me states that the legal U.S. mailing address of the company is C/O. U.S. Administration, One Hundred Five Northeast First Court, Dania Beach, Florida. 33OO4-2816.

Further depose and says the following is true and accurate to the best of his knowledge, and under the penalty of perjury:

On the 27th day of August, 1999 I had a meeting with Mr. Marion JR Horn representing Five Star Trust, in room 1423 of the Double Tree Guest Suites on East Sunrise Boulevard, Ft. Lauderdale, Florida. At that Lime I was given and asked to take possession and escrow an original document wet-stamped Original and Confidential from Golden Eagle Holdings, Ltd. to a large multinational corporate group dated 28th of July 1999.

This document was an authorization to make deposits into a numbered Bahamian bank account in the name of Golden Eagle Holdings, Ltd. These deposits are to be in the form of an advance loan in the amount of Ten Million U.S. Dollars and paid from existing assets of Five Star Trust. This authorization is executed by Marion Horn. Jr. and wet stamp with the corporate seal of Golden Eagle Holdings, Ltd., and accepted on 30-7-99 by a director of the International Corporate Group.

Positive due diligence statements between the two parties, to myself, or in my presence, has confirmed sufficient assets and capability to warrant and complete such a sizable advance. It is further my understanding a review is being conducted by a big five accounting firm, and that some of these advance fund were to be used to help offset some of the expense for the completion of such a continued review.

I am actively participating in the preparations for the transfer of funds to Five Star Trust, and attest such transfers are due to be scheduled imminently.

I have been asked to confirm both the document content and the ongoing activity subsequent to its execution. Further, be advised this original document, or facsimile copy are not in my immediate possession or control, as per escrow agreement, instructions and client confidentially warrant.

Further Affiant Sayeth Naught

Richard H. Sowden, as Senior Executive Escrow Officer for Private Escrow & Transfer Company, Ltd.

Endless Connections with Government Personnel

A confidential letter from the office of the U.S. Secretary of Defense to General Robert Ferrera relating to the culpable position that the government of Singapore had been put in as a result of seizing a certificate of gold deposit issued by the Mitsui Bank of Japan and turning it over to Japanese officials:

OFFICE OF THE ASSISTANT SECRETARY OF DEFENSE
WASHINGTON, D. C. 20301-2400

January 15, 1988

CONFIDENTIAL

International
Security Affairs

General Robert L. Ferrera
Far East Command
7-23-17 Roppongi, Minato-Ku, Tokyo, Japan

Re: Certificate of cash deposit # 4051100-92
Issued by Mitsui bank, ltd., Japan
Principal: U.S.M.T., Inc.

Dear General Ferrera:

This office has just completed the second stage of the investigation you last assigned and the following is an up-dated evaluation of the present status. As you have requested and as the restrictions of this office requires, this is an unofficial report and anything beyond an "off-the-record" application would be considered a breach of security. With this unnecessary word of caution (which I trust you will understand and forgive) I hereby state that:

1) The government of Singapore has fully, yet privately, acknowledged that they are in a culpable position. By the fact of admitting the confiscation of the above referenced CD and turning that property over to particular officials of the government of Japan and not to the representative of U.S.M.T, from whose possession it was taken.

2) Said government of Singapore wishes this matter settled, quietly and without any national loss of prestige.

3) Due to your direct intervention, it has been recently decided by the authorities of the government of Japan, to seek a resolution of this matter and negotiate for the payment of everything appropriately due on said CD.

4) Both governments have agreed that for political expediency, negotiations and final, settlements should be turned over to the private sector and avoid any risk of governmental exposure.

5) They have, therefore, accepted your well-planned proposal and request that one of the corporations, which act under your dire control, be exclusively and independently responsible for the settlement of the matter.

6) The several government leaders involved in reaching this decision includes [redacted] and from Japan.

7) As your proposal indicated, your privately held corporate entity will proceed to engage the services of an international law firm, after your submission of a list of such firms, for approval by the combined government authorities. That said firm will follow the precise procedures for negotiations and settlement as will be prepared by said, combined governmental authorities.

Finally, General, I must advise you because of our longstanding friendship, to be very, very careful. As you are so well known by your reputation for caution and foresight, you are the one man I would rely upon for meeting and beating the opposition to the successful conclusion of this ratter. The opposition that you are so much more familiar with than I.

Please do not hesitate to call upon me at any time. Incidentally, I wish to take this opportunity to thank you for the splendid present you sent for Helen's birthday. She will treasure it always. It truly exemplifies your eye for beauty and your friendship for us. Thanks again.

One last word, general, about the matter at hand. Some of the most respected experts in this sort of exercise have suggested that the surest route to failure, particularly when two Asian governments are so deeply involved, is to attempt to hurry the matter along. Any hint of impatience, they claim, could be disastrous.

With all of my sincere best wishes and hopes of seeing you soon,

With the deepest respect,
Cordially yours,

[redacted]
Rear admiral, U.S.N.

Another letter from the Assistant Secretary of Defense John J. Mac Elroy in the office of the Assistant Secretary of Defense to Major General Robert Ferrera addressed and the involvement of multiple U.S. departments and the president of the United States—who at that time was President George H.W. Bush. [That fits in with Bush's covert activities that I write about in another book, *Defrauding America*.]

The letter recognized Horn's ownership of the CD issued by Japan's Mitsui Bank. A good question is why would the U.S. Defense Department would be involved with a private financial arrangement between a Japanese Bank and a U.S. citizen unless that certificate of gold deposit had a relationship to the gold plundered by the Japanese Army during World War II.

OFFICE OF THE ASSISTANT SECRETARY OF DEFENSE
WASHINGTON. D. C. 20301-2400
30 JANUARY, 1989

RE: STUDEBAKER

CONFIDENTIAL

To : Major General Robert L. Ferrera
c/o : Central Intelligence Agency Office
Federal Building
Westwood, California

VIA: Hand-Deliver in Top Secret Pouch

FROM : John J. Mac Elroy
Assistant Secretary of Defense
International Security Affairs

Dear Sir:

I have been assigned the official task of being the direct contact with you regarding the Studebaker matter. In this regard, I shall, when so ordered, be speaking for the combined offices of the Secretaries of State and Defense, the director of the Central Intelligence Agency and the White House.

I have been instructed by Secretary of State Baker to inform you that it is the unanimous decision of the above named offices and that of the chief of staff, Mr. Sununu, for the Oval Office, that the matter of concern to all, Studebaker be finalized immediately upon the conclusion of the impending official visit of president Bush to Japan and to other Far East locations scheduled as of now for the latter part of the week of 20 February, 1989. This is so being handled in this manner to allow those persons concerned in this affair with Mr. Marion horn, a.k.a. "J. R. Horn," to thus secure their position with regards to their individual participatory status, as is outlined in the following paragraphs.

This office, in full representation of the Oval Office, has been in direct communication with Lord Sir Walter duke, the director general of the bank of New Zealand, at their home office located in Wellington, and have notified him that any and all funds regarding the Studebaker Project be released to yourself and to Mr. Horn upon clearance from the government of Japan, which will be given upon the termination of the visit of President. Bush to that area. All parties concerned, in all, three nations involved are in accord that this is the best schedule for the handling of Studebaker, for the sake of international security and for the utmost secrecy and full protection of all involved. As well as the protection of the entities of all.

All are in full agreement to accept your proposal for the disbursement of funds to Mr. Horn, as well as the forfeiture of any rights of Mr. Horn of any legal action against any of the individuals or countries involved in this affair at any time in the future. In exchange for this forfeiture of rights by Mr. Horn, he is to receive the sum of three hundred billion Japanese Yen (300,000.000.000 JY) as his full and total share of the proceeds from what would have been the purchase of the time deposit No. 4051100-92, issued in error by the Mitzui bank Ltd, Japan. It is fully understood by you, General, in representation of Mr. Horn, there no longer exists any such time deposit. Nor any certificate of cash deposit associated with same.

All documentation concerning the whole of this affair has been destroyed. Again for the protection of all concerned, we further wish to inform you, General, that all concerned are fully aware of the lack of validity and substance to the monetary papers and procedures taken by Mr. Horn to attempt the purchase of the tine deposit No. 4051100-92, but we understand and accept the fact that he also was duped while acting in total good faith. It is further accepted that Mr. Horn is to receive the additional sum of twenty billion Japanese Yen (20,000,000,000 JY) as punitive compensation and any expenditures incurred in the finalization of this affair.

The Bank of New Zealand is under implicit instructions to deliver those funds to Mr. Horn in whatever world currency is so designated by you at the time of collection.

It is further understood, and accepted by all concerned, that any and all interest earned by the time deposit No. 4051100-92, had that time deposit not been issued in error by the Mitzui bank Ltd, Japan, will be paid by the Mitzui Bank Ltd, Japan, for one of their clients as if the document in question had been legally issued. This interest shall be paid at the rate of five percent p.a. (5%) from 1 august, 1977, until 19 January, 1989, inclusive, and the interest shall be compounded. The sum of interest due shall be paid into the account of the international freedom fund, at the main office of Credit Suisse in Zurich. Switzerland.

The bank of New Zealand, as of this date, is in full possession of all the monetary documentation concerned to finalize this transaction when the clearance is so given by the government of Japan.

If there are any questions concerning this communication, please contact this office, in person, within the immediate next forty eight (48) hours using the security codes assigned to you.

Because of the highly sensitive nature of this matter, general, it must be insisted that you continue to be the only representative for Mr. Horn, his company, his interests, and his front trust. Until such time as you sign over all rights of the funds to him before the proper authorities in New Zealand.

In closing, general, I have been further ordered by the Oval Office to remind you that there has been a substantial amount of security lapses from persons associated with Mr. Horn. You have stated, and we accept, that all such inquiries have been done without the knowledge or permission of Mr. Horn, and we have up to now accordingly so ignored them. However, general, if these "lapses" do not stop fully and immediately, we feel that the danger of a leak on this most delicate matter is potentially immense, and in such case. The oval office would disassociate itself and disavow any knowledge of the Studebaker Affair, as would all cabinet members and nations concerned.

I have been asked by Secretary of State Baker to request that you be kind enough to inform Mr. Horn that the appointment of mutual interest has been fully approved, and will be submitted to congress at the appropriate time.

Thank you and Mr. Horn for your understanding/ and we are all looking forward to entertaining both of you at the white house/ when this is concluded.

Sincerly,

John J. MacElroy, (Detached Service)
Assistant Secretary of Defense
International Security Affairs
(On assignment)

Accepted:

Robert L. Ferrera
For/ J.R. Horn, et. Al.
(Verb. App. by all conc.)

TOP SECRET & HIGH PRIORITY TOP SECRET

The following letter was sent by Mitsui Bank, Ltd, Main Office, Tokyo, Japan, at the request of Fidesco, Tokyo, for U.S. Mortgage and Trust (Bahamas) Ltd, Five Star Trust, by Major Gen. R.L. Ferrera and Norman Grand (Phone 213-382-0209). President of Fidesco was Mr. Wantabe, and referred to Cash Deposit Certificate number 40500-92. It included reference to Mitsui Bank Certificate of Deposit No. 4051100-92.

Date: February 28, 1988.

Toshino Kasumoto
% Shearson Lehman Brothers, Inc.
166 North Canon Drive
Beverly Hills, California 90210

Mr. Kasumoto: CONFIDENTIAL

In reply to your most recent inquiring the status of the above quoted certificate of deposit, please accept the following:

This certificate of Deposit, number 4051100-92, was issued by the Mitsui Bank Limited, at our head office here in Nihon, as ordered by the Government of Nihon, and treated with the most delicate of matters.

On instructions of Government, this bank issued the Cash Deposit Certificate in question for the amount of Y 318,000,000,000.00 (Three Hundred & Eighteen Billion Yen), bearing an annual simple interest rate of 5% (Five Percent) per annum. The date of this issuance was the 1st of August, 1978.

There has been much investigation of this matter, and as per instructions of the Government, and the General, you must understand our reluctance to much discussion in this matter, and to the official reply to your request. Upon our having cleared your request with the General, we are permitted to inform you of the status, as of this writing.

The government of Nihon, as well as the Government of Singapore have arrived at the mutual decision that this matter must be concluded with the most rapid haste, and they have further agreed with the General that a totally uninterested third party be the link between both governments. This to allow for the honorable actions of both governments, as well as keeping the General in the background, and protecting the present recognized owner of the Cash Certificate of Deposit legal owner of this Certificate of Deposit, Number 4051100-92 Mr. Marion Horn, Jr., a citizen and present resident of the United States of America, thru the U.S. Mortgage and Trust (Bahamas) Ltd., formally U.S. M.T. Inc./U.S. Mortgage and Trust Corporation, and therefore, this institution does confirm the above unconditionally.

P.S. Omoi tatta ga Kichinichi

The following letter from a member of the Rothschild banking dynasty to U.S. General Robert Ferrera made reference to the unusual secret discussions between Baron Philipe du Daphne,[91] and U.S. General (and CIA asset) Robert Ferrera, calling for confidentiality and making reference to former CIA Director George H.W. Bush. Examine the significance of that banking connection between a major European bank and a member of the U.S. military and CIA as it relates to huge quantities of gold deposits in banks.

Organisation for Economic Cooperation and Development

Telephone : 524 82.00
Telegrammes: Descentre
Teles : 62 140 Ocoe Paris

---

[91] Baron Phillipe du Daphne, April 13, 1903 to January 20, 1988.

Reference: MTD/UN3998

Centre De Developpement
Development Centre

4 November, 1988

Le President, Baron Phillipe du Daphne.

CONFIDENTIAL

To: General Robert L. Ferrera
Hand Deliver

Via: Consul General, San Francisco, California, U.S.A.

Bon Ami, Robaire:

In response to your telephonic request of this immediate past 2 November present, I am most honoured to report to you the following—which we both understand is a most delicate matter which must continue in our confidence.

I have contacted the president of Mitzui Bank Ltd., as well as the chairman of said board of directors, and after much dialogue, they finally agreed to inform me that the certificate issued by their bank on August 1, 1977, with Identification Number 405100-92, for the benefit of Soichi Iizuka, Reference # 118-65, for the amount of y 318,000,000,000.00 (three hundred & eighteen billion Japanese yen) is non-existent, having been destroyed on the strict orders of the former prime minister of Japan. This was done, so I have been informed, under strong agreement betwixt the governments of Japan and the United States. All other papers pertaining to this transaction have also been destroyed. This, I must say, is most irregular, and not really in keeping with banking procedures.

I then proceeded to call my friend____, the United States Secretary of State, and under the utmost of caution, he gave to me the information that the possible next president of the United States Mr. George Bush was the individual that could most acquaint me with the agreement made by both nations. The secretary further cautioned me to be most careful, for many persons had perished who were associated with this matter. The secretary called Mr. Bush, and I have been informed by him that upon his taking the oath of office (not "if"), he will personally meet with you and give "carte blanche" to you concluding this matter—

but not before. Please call me, my dear *bon ami.*

The following was a message from U.S. Navy Admiral Gene R. LaRocque[92] to U.S. Major General Robert L. Ferrera, relating to New Broom and Studebaker operations, calling for utmost secrecy:

A Personal Message from Admiral Gene R. La Rocque
TOP SECRET TOP SECRET

Baron Phillipe du Daphne, President,
Organisation For Economic Cooperation & Development
Paris, France

Subject: "New-broom" & "Studebaker"

Re: Status Report

Attention: MGen. Robert L. Ferrera,

-----HAND DELIVER----

My Very Valued Friend:

It is rather odd for me to start a report, to you, with the invocation of the National Security Act, with which both of us are most acquainted. Never-the-less, I must invoke the NSA to you, and place this memorandum in a "top secret" category. This is done to conform with the direct orders of the Baron du Daphne, who is to receive this original, and of Mister Helms, who will receive first copy.

As the trustee of all of the records and documents on the "New Broom" and "Studebaker" projects, it is felt by them that I am the one to give you an "over-view" of the total subject operations. I must again caution you, General, that in this instance there must not be any security lapses on your part. You will read this report and destroy it immediately. If any part, or all of this report, ever comes to the fore, we will disavow any knowledge of it and put forth the same effort that we instituted with the Iran/Contra North affair. I might add that despite our

---

[92] U.S. Navy Rear Admiral Gene R. La Rocque joined the U.S. Navy in 1940 (the same year that I joined the Navy) and served on the U.S.S. Macdonough when the Japanese attacked Pearl Harbor on December 7, 1941. He founded the Center for Defense Information. He was disillusioned with the U.S. invasion of Vietnam and retired in 1972. La Rocque and his colleagues testified several times before Congress and he was in frequent touch with national and international political leaders.

very close and valued friendship, General, the results would be the same, if there is a security leak. I have been given instructions that you can relay, in private, to Mr. Marion horn (a.k.a. J.R. Horn) whatever you deem is necessary, but only in a verbal form, for security reasons, with your full responsibility.

There is no need to go over again that with which all concerned are aware of, i.e. that. Certificate of Cash Deposit #114051100-92, purported to have been issued by the Mitzui Bank Ltd, for the amount of 318,000,000,000.00 (three hundred and eighteen. Billion Japanese yen), does not exist. There is documentation on file with the Mitzui bank Lts., the files of both governments—Japan and Singapore—the proper police agencies of both, and the world banking community, as well as the World Bank archives, to substantiate the official stance of all concerned that the CD was a stolen instrument, and that a fraud of international ramifications was being attempted by those involved.

This documentation is fully endorsed by the legally binding notarized statements given to the Japanese government by those who helped perpetrate this deed. It is most fortunate that those statements were given, for since this affair was attempted, all, save one, have taken their lives, in one form or another, in keeping with the Japanese tradition of "dishonor". I might add a personal note here, that Mr. Horn, in view of the Japan authorities, was an unsuspecting foreign businessman who was used by the perpetrators, and he was, and is, in no manner involved with any illegal act in this matter.

When Mr. Horn, thru various and sundry means, attempted to collect on this fraudulent instrument, which he felt that he was to purchase, all documentation in his possession was taken as evidence. That documentation was destroyed in a subsequent fire at CID headquarters in Singapore. This was a most fortunate happenstance, for thus Mr. Horn can never be accused by anyone of being a co-conspirator in this fraud.

During the immediate past few years, Mr. Horn, thru his representatives, attempted again to collect on this fraudulent Mitzui Bank Ltd. CD, feeling that he was in some manner the victim of the bank and the Japanese government. As you are well aware of, my friend, Mr. Horn met with a wall, as did all of his "representatives." I will not report to you how you became involved, General, but when you did, it gave to Mr. Horn the only opportunity that he could ever have for the collection of anything on the "Studebaker" matter.

It had become a very sensitive affair, because the criminals had the foresight to register the stolen CD with the World Bank, and thus with all documentation being unavailable due to fires, acts of god, misplacing, lost, etc., the records of the World Bank still show such a document, but without any documentary evidence to substantiate any claim.

When you persisted in following this up, and met with the persons concerned in many countries, it was finally agreed by all, that indeed, your plan for the peaceful solution to this affair had merit. By your plan all governments and all individuals could save "face" and Mr. Horn could in some manner be compensated financially for his time and money well spent on this, as well as any inconvenience he may have endured.

I wish to say at this time, general, that those funds that you have arranged for his trust to receive are simply given for the sake of international harmony, for any "noise" made on this would only serve to embarrass many innocent people and friendly governments, before the courts would rule that it indeed was a fraud, as all of the documentation that still exists would show.

My orders are to state in this report that the telephonic surveillance on all concerned in this matter shows that you, General, have at all times relayed to Mr. Horn only that which you have been told, even during those moments when you have informed those involved that you did not accept that which you were being told. By my being ordered to insert this paragraph, I am given to understand that perhaps your word is being questioned by some, and if that is the situation, I am personally surprised that you have just not "walked away" from "Studebaker", for if there is one American whose word-is accepted world-wide, it is you.

I remember, during Vietnam, when you used the alias of "Colonel David Hackworth", how your true self came across—no punches pulled, only the bottom line. I personally pray that I am in error in this judgment that you are being questioned, for you do not deserve it under any circumstances.

"Studebaker" was an entity unto itself, brought about by your suggestions for the "saving-face" solution. "Operation New-Broom" had been in the fire for some time prior to your involvement, and was a totally different entity. However, the last piece of the puzzle for the perfect termination of "New-Broom" was still missing until Mr. Helms and Baron du Daphne both agreed that the route that you had arranged for the funds going to Mr. Horn and/or his trust, was an ideal vehicle to use for the termination of "New-Broom", for any future questions that might come about would be answered by the agreement that you signed with the government representatives of Singapore, regarding the payment of damages to Mr. Horn. Your insistence that minimum payment amount be inserted, but a maxim be left out, gave the perfect opportunity for those funds from "New-Broom" to be disbursed as need be.

We, in our business, General, pride ourselves in saying that fate plays a hand in our success or failure, but that we have the ability to "help" direct the fates. In this instance, fate stepped in with the acquaintance relationship between Mr. Horn and Dr. C. K. Lee. We wish to be emphatic in our statement that Dr. Lee and Mr. Horn are both fully innocent of any wrong-doing in the affair now called "New-Broom". Fate saw to it that Dr. Lee would be used to try and legalize certain funds thru Japanese Certificates of Deposit. The proper authorities had to step in and make it impossible for Dr. Lee to continue in his misguided efforts. However, it was felt that having obtained the documentation from Dr. Lee, we could let him again venture into the banking circles to see if he would lead us to anyone who might be attempting to "step-in," General, we helped "fate" and you, Mr. Horn, and Dr. Lee met.

You, General, were approached with the suggestion that we be allowed to use the same route that you used for "Studebaker", and the records show that you agreed, on the condition that a minimum of 25% of the total amount of monies legalized be paid to a Bahamian corporation, controlled by Mr. Horn. It was understood that the broom would sweep clean in five total attempts, due to the vast amount of dirt to be swept. The first was concluded and that portion belonging to Mr. Horns' company was deposited for safekeeping with his "Studebaker" funds, but in this instance, in the form of AU rather than yen. It was further agreed that the person in command of "New-Broom" final phases would be Mr. Sununu, for he is nearest, at this time, to the President, and he was handling, to a great degree, the final "okay" on the "Studebaker" matter.

This office, as well as Mr. Helms and the Baron du Daphne were of the opinion that phase two of the five, had been fully completed in the manner that you set up, and that the 25% due to Mr. Horns' company had again been paid in the previous form: AU in New Zealand. Thus, my friend, we were all rather perplexed when you called in a most angry fashion, almost as bad as in your Mexico City call, and informed Mr. Sununu that you had had enough and all had to be completed immediately. We could not understand why you would press for completion of "Studebaker" when you had been informed that "Studebaker" would not be terminated and collected until the conclusion of "New-Broom". We are now well aware that you accepted the deadline of the 19th of June. However, given the circumstances now in vogue, when the 18th would arrive, you would be called by Mr. Sununu and informed that due to "international affairs" there would be a further delay of ten to fifteen days.

This I can fully guarantee to you, general, for I, above everyone concerned, know how long it will take to conclude "New-Broom" with full security to all, and it will not he finished by the 19th of June. With the fortunes of "fate", you called upon your long friendship with the Baron and asked for his help, and thus we found that we were getting two totally different versions of phase two of "New-Broom"... Mr. Sununu was informing us that all was as originally planned and that you were fully aware of the second deposit of AU. As a matter of information for you, General, the AU did go through the New Zealand bank.

I personally inquired thru code of the amount of AU in the New Zealand account of the Horn company and found that there had not been any amount added to it since phase one. I have concluded a complete and most covert investigation of this and have found that Mr. Sununu has at all times fully intended to divert your 25% for his personal use, and has not been totally honest with us, nor with you for that matter. It is the final decision of Mr. Helms, Baron du Daphne, the Japanese P.M. and the former head of our CIA that the best manner to handle this is to play along with Mr. Sununu and those that are allied with him. We will let him finish operation "New-Broom" totally, and at that time, we will transfer ownership in his AU account to whatever account Mr. Horn so indicates. When all is concluded, Mr. Horn will have quadrupled his "Studebaker" funds. At this time, I cannot give you a date for the conclusion, and thus, your collection of "Studebaker" funds, but it will not he before ten banking days, nor will it be longer than thirty banking days. That is the word of Mr. Horns' new partners, the Baron and Mr. Helms.

We have agreed to that which I have stated, and it will be up to your ability to keep Mr. Horn calm and not allow him to start causing any ripples in the ocean. It is true that if he did, it would be cause of great embarrassment to many very important world leaders, past and present, but in the end, the only one that would have to fall would be you, General. That was fully brought out to you at the start, and you fully went along with it, as I would have had I been in your stead. We have no doubts, that when you verbally explain to Mr. Horn that which I am sending here-in to you, he will continue to fully cooperate with us as he has in past. However, General, you must be sure that those around him who would like to be little napoleons of power and wealth refrain from trying to force Mr. Horn in taking steps that would try and force policy on us.

Any more of that type of pressure will be reason to think about taking steps to alleviate the pressure origins. The Baron does not need the worry, Mr. Helms will not accept the worry, and you and Mr. Horn do not deserve the worry; so please excerpt a stronger effort to keep the fringe element on the fringe. We fully exclude Mr. William Clancy from this, for we accept him as n spokesperson with you, General, and with Mr. Horn. We accept Mr. Williamson and Damelio, Jr. As very close allies of Mr. Horn, but not as the inner circle with you and Clancy. We place Mr. Alan Wolfley in a category of "senior advisor", but in view of that which is to be for Mr. Wolfley, we strongly recommend that he be kept as just that—a friendly advisor. Please be aware that in the future every single enemy, plus those that will be and are, envious of Mr. Wolfing will investigate all that they can to discredit him, and putting him with "New-Broom" or "Studebaker" might open up Pandora's box. We recognize no others as being involved.

Now a rather touchy situation has arisen. I refer to the suspected "contract" on Mr. Wolfley. I will have explained to you all there is to know on that matter, on the phone, and for the time-being, suffice to say that the person responsible, Mr. Sununu, and others, will be given their due niche in the passing of time. For now, we must all just accept and go along, for as the government is concerned, the original plans for Mr. Wolfley will be carried out to the fullest.

In closing remember how these funds came about, thus the need for the utmost secrecy, and also remember that no one individual is above the welfare of the nation. I will expect your call within 48 hours for I know that you will be conferring with Mr. Horn. Further, it has just come to my attention from the telephone surveillance that Mr. Slater received a call on your proposed journey to D.C. call Mr. Sununu and inform his office of this, and you will be informed of the delay. Play along with them, and cancel your trip. His health will give out soon. I will further say that my sending this by personal messenger, with a copy to you, will facilitate security, and thus easier to deny if anything does go wrong, which we do not anticipate.

In closing, I am instructed to inform you that Mr. Helms and the Baron du Daphne have both stated that now it is a "trio in bed together", with the addition of Mr. Horn. When this is all concluded, they intend to meet with Mr. Horn, and have him take charge of the funding of needy governments. Regards and a fond embrace from your friend, and please forgive the errors, for I am not a typist, and I was ordered to do this personally.

Gene La Ra Rocque

TOP SECRET READ AND DESTROY

An April 24, 1989, letter from Richard Armitage[93] to Major General Robert Ferrera from the Office of the Assistant Secretary of Defense referred to Triangle and Studebaker, showing that Ferrera was representing Five Star Trust, and showing the involvement of the CIA, the State Department, and Japanese politicians.

OFFICE OF THE ASSISTANT SECRETARY OF DEFENSE
WASHINGTON, D. C.
20301-2400
24 April, 1989

T 0 P S E C R E T — DEFENSE DEPT. POUCH

Robert L. Ferrera (For your eyes only)
Mgen. Office of Special Services
c/o 3250 Wilshire Blvd., Suits # 900
Los Angeles, California, 90010

Re: Understanding of Agreement on Triangle/Studebaker

Dear Sir:

This is a confirmation on the verbal agreement reached this past Week-end, April 22nd & 23rd, inclusive, at the conference held at Valdez, Alaska. If there are any are differences with your understanding, please inform the undersigned vie the code arranged.

It is the understanding of the undersigned that you represent Five Star Trust, as confirmed by J.A.B. III, and in that capacity you have concluded a contract for the joint Japanese-Singapore venture to build for them a chain of luxury hotels under the name of "Studebaker", for which Five Star Trust is to be paid the sum of money as agreed in the Certificate of Cash Deposit issued by the Mitsui Bank, Lmt., reference No. 4051100-92, to one Suichi Iizuka, a Japanese National, for assignment to a Mr., Marion Horn, a.k.a. J. R. Horn, of Lexington, Kentucky.

The undersigned has confirmed with Mr. Horn that Five Star Trust, thru your involvement, has caused the full payment of the above mentioned certificate be made via a bank in New Zealand, and that said funds are awaiting the release code from the Japanese P.M. and from the Oval office, It has further been confirmed that interest for the first

[93] Richard Armitage was a CIA agent in Vietnam and later with the State Department. Some of my sources that worked near him described his role in drug smuggling and other CIA activities. I describe some of his activities in *Defrauding America* and *Drugging America*.

quarter of this year, earned by those funds, has now been forwarded to Washington, D.C. for final disbursement to you, for Five Star Trust.

It is the further understanding of the undersigned, that you—General, are fully empowered to speak for the Five Star Trust, and in that capacity, you have been made aware that the "Golden Triangle" Construction Co. Lmt., represented by General Khun Sa, of Burma, has also done some work for various Far East nations, using the same materials and the same suppliers as Five Star Trust. The Director of the Managing Company in Va., for your materials, Mr. H, and the present Director, have both been informed by the majority stockholder of the Va. Company, Mr. H that the disbursement of the Five Star Trust funds be held back until Gen. Khun Sa can close the "Golden Triangle" operations totally, in the Far East, and they are both in complete accord with this decision, for they also feel that this is the best manner to handle this most delicate operation due to the possible international ramifications that could ensue if any of this were to become public knowledge at this most critical and delicate time.

The undersigned is fully aware that you, General, have been placed in a rather delicate position, for in effect, you have had to agree to the delay. I think you put it rather well at the meeting when you stated that the Company was putting you and Five Star Trust in a position similar to the old army: "I went a volunteer-you just volunteered" situation. Please believe me General, there is no other way in which this can be done and still have a total security blanket over both projects, which at a security expert, you must agree, is our primary concern.

I wish to further state that having read the dossier of Mr. Marion Horn, I feel that he also is a true patriot and will sacrifice within reason for his country, and this delay is within reason. This is our moment of truth. If we continue to cooperate, as Five Star Trust has done in the past, General Khun Sa[94] and his associates will be fully closed down by the time period of 1 May and 14 May inclusive, with a target of 1 May, 1989. At that time we will implement Phase Two of our agreement, the immediate release of all of the funds now in New Zealand and in Washington D.C. that are being held for Five Star Trust.

As this is being written, General, word has reached us thru official channels that Prime Minister Noboru Takeshita has fully accepted our suggestion that he resign his office. We, at this time, have no knowledge of the person that will replace him, but we feel that a strong possibility is that Masayoshi Ito will be named. You, however, informed us in Valdez that you felt that the replacement, if any, would be

[94] Gen. Khun Sa was a major drug trafficker and named in many books on thee subject.

Maseharu Gotoda. We have, at the present, no idea as to whom will cause the release of the funds. I strongly suggest that you arrange an immediate trip to Tokyo and have the Prime Minister delay his resignation until after Five Star has received the release of the funds.

In closing General, I feel that I can be fully candid in what I write, for I know that the contents of this letter will never be released, and in that spirit I wish to state that is has been a total honor for me to finally meet the "elusive and mysterious" General, code name "Eagle." I can inform you that even as this is being sent, there are many in Washington trying to identify the "General". I have met you, and I still do not know who you are. On the other side of the coin, Sir; I cannot understand how you, in your position, could take leave of your duties to devote yourself to the business of a private citizen.

We know that you are not being paid, and yet your loyalties appear to be primarily with Five Star Trust and Mr. Horn. Perhaps one day we can discuss this, if both of us survive. We are on opposite sides of the coin, General, but I respect you and I pray the feeling is returned. Your word is acceptable to all, as I hope mine is to you, and in that spirit. I wish to warn you that there are certain elements that feel you have stepped or their toes, as well as those that do not want to see Mr. Horn or Five Star collect their funds, and thus claim them for their own use. These elements have offered a great deal of money for you, General, for without you, they feel they can win. Beware of the "friends" of your Mr. Horn who are no longer within his inner circle, and beware of those in the Bureau that feel you have "embarrassed" the service. I, for my part, must help to keep you safe, for without you, Mr. S., Mr. H., and myself are left in limbo. Finally, steps have been taken to wipe out any reference to Mr. Horn from any international publications as well as any complaints, etc., with any government agency.

Richard Armitage

Copy: Mr. B., H., S. & Gen. Sa

Because of his State Department position, the abbreviations used for receiving copies can be assumed to be (a) George H.W. Bush; (b) General John Singlaub, and (c) Khun Sa, a major drug smuggler from the days of the Vietnam War, as described in numerous books on the subject).

A July 4, 1989, letter to Major General Ferrera from Bank of New Zealand referred to Five Star Trust and the involvement of the United States, Japan, and New Zealand, in those funds, and including the names of Rothschild banker Baron du Daphne, confirming the existence of the Five Star Trust, Marion Horn's ownership, and Mitsui Bank in Tokyo.

Bank of New Zealand
International Banking Division

BANK OF NEW ZEALAND
P.O. Box 2392
Wellington, New Zealand

July 4, 1989

Major General R. L. Ferrera
c/o 3399 Tates Creek Road, Suite 105
Lexington, Kentucky 40502
United States of America

RE: 5 Star Trust Account

Personal Delivery
Honourable General:

On the most explicit instructions from Baron du Daphne, Commander R. Croix de Guerre, and per your personal request, I personally make available to you the information that follows, with the full understanding that the data contained herein is for the information of Mr. Marion Horn, Jr., a resident of the State of Kentucky and an associate of Baron du Daphne. This data will not be confirmed without the prior authorization of Baron du Daphne.

This will confirm to you, General, that our bank is the Trust Holder of an account for the "Five Star Trust," of whom you are a trustee. As such, we hold a deposit in our bank, to the favour of Five Star Trust, a Top Secret Number account, in an amount that exceeds 400,000,000,000 J/Y (Four Hundred Billion J/Y Japanese Yen).

This account is the sole and exclusive property of Five Star Trust, free of any encumbrance, and is to be released to your signature, in the presence of Mr. Marion Horn, Jr. at such time as we received the coded clearance for said release from the representatives of the Governments of Japan, Singapore, and the United States of America, as well as yours.

The said representatives are the Prime Minister of Japan, as of July

1, 1989, the Baron du Daphne replaces Mr. Sununu for the United States. We further state that any and all interest earned by this deposit is to be paid to Five Star Trust, less the sum sent to America previously, for future payment, to Five Star Trust.

It is our further understanding that the aforementioned release is scheduled to take effect on or about the first day of August 1989.

We pray we have been, in some small manner, of service to you, General, and we look forward to again meeting with you on Tuesday, 11 July, 1989, and also with Mr. Horn at the future time of the release of the funds.

Your obedient servant,

Lindsey Pyne
Chief Executive Officer
Bank of New Zealand

cc: Baron du Daphne
Edward Ong
P.M. Office, Japan

The following letter from ABN Bank in The Netherlands to Mexican president C. Salinas, with a copy to the U.S. Embassy, referred to an agreement between major bankers and the involvement of Marion Horn:

ABN Bank

32, Vijzelstraat
P.O. Box 669
1000 EG Amsterdam
The Netherlands
2 September, 1989
Special re-type 2

C. Salinas-G. President,
Estados Unidos Mexicanos,
Palacio National,
Mexico, D.F., Mexico

HAND DELIVER

CC: Embassy of the United States of America
Mexico City, Mexico.

Dear Mr. President Salinas:

As per our agreement with General Roberto Ferrera, and at the personal request of Baron Guy Rothschild, we take this opportunity to confirm to Your Excellency that on Friday last, 1 September, 1989, an international consortium of banks agreed to enter into a joint funding venture, with the sole purpose of making available investment and construction capital to the International Investment and Bank Group, Limited, Zurich, Baron Guy Rothschild and Marion Horn Esq., co-chairmen of the Board of Directors.

Our bank, the Algemene Bank Netherland N.V., has joined with the Credit Suisse, CitiCorp/City Bank, Development Bank of Singapore, Netherland Bank, N.V., Bank of New Zealand, Banque Nationale de Paris, Chase Bank International, Deutsche Bank, National Westminster Bank, Royal Bank of Scotland, and the Word Bank in this joint-venture, and we have been further honoured by being chosen to act in the role of "Flagship Bank:"

It was further decided at the meeting of 1, September, to make available the sum of $750,000,000,000.00 Dlrs., U.S. of 3 (Three) years, to international Investment & Bank Group, Lmt. These funds are to carry a flat interest of 2.75% per annum, for a 30 (Thirty) year period, with interest only paid yearly, in arrears, with the principle due and payable at the termination of the 30 year loan period.

Baron Rothschild has requested that the funds be deposited in the Rothschild/Horn bank, the Eurc-Latin American Bank Limited, Gillet House, 55, Basinghall Street, London, EC2V5EN, for further transfer of same to the credit of U.S. Mortgage and Trust (Bahamas) Ltd., Mr. J.R. Horn (a.k.a. Marion Horn) sole Signator.

We are making all this information available to your Excellency because it is the firm intention of Mr. Horn to use the majority of these funds to help the Third-world nations, with Mexico as his first priority. With Horns' plans in mind, we feel that we must take these steps to inform you that this is a firm bank commitment to Mr. Horn, et. al., so that Your Excellency will feel secure in not accepting the proposal for funds that are to be made to your office by the Prime Minister of Japan on the Monday hence. We are aware that the Prime Minister is to present to you a proposal for the building and financing of a "land-bridge" across the Isthmus of Tehuantepec, and other proposals, but Mr. President, please consider this letter prior to any decision.

Most Sincerely

D. De Bruyne

Chairman

The following message from Baron Phillipe duDaphne to General R. Ferrera refers to the highly secret matter "Studebaker" matter:

Tokyo 23437
Via: Sealed Envelope, Hand-delivered by Major General

R. Ferrera

Dear Sir:

Please forgive my audacity, and perhaps my strong desire for total security in this matter, but Le Baron is convinced that you strongly share my sentiments. I do not, under any circumstances what-so-ever wish to give the impression that I do not trust General Ferrera by my sending these documents under the security of the seal. On the contrary, I trust the General with my life, and his honour and his word have always been accepted. I say this to erase any doubts that might appear as to my very strong positive feelings toward the General. As you read that which Richard and I have enclosed, you will understand the reasons for security.

Bon Ami "J.R.", both Mister Helms and I are of the opinion that the documentation enclosed should be shared with you, so we have taken the liberty to send to you the copies you now possess. The original is in our Paris vault, one copy in my personal bank vault, and one copy is held by Richard. There are no other copies, and we strongly insist that there not be any more made. You do understand, Bon Ami.

Richard and I have known for a long time now that certain elements have desired to bring us down, and we have had a rather definitive idea as to the identities of those persona, but even with all that, we were both astounded when we learned that Senator E. Kennedy had requested a TOP SECRET report on our project. We were further shocked when we saw also a complete dossier (well, almost complete) on General Ferrera.

We have come by these documents by having one of our covert agents "liberate" the documentation from the vault in the home of Senator Kennedy, and we have also had all tapes and copies at the Federal Bureau of Investigation destroyed. The Senator cannot report the "borrowing" because he would then have to divulge his own covert operations against President Bush.

No, Bon Ami. This is one of those operations when all must remain silent. We cannot, and will not, help the General in his financial problems, for to do so would endanger "Studebaker", and that we shall never do, for those funds and the others in AU will help save this earth. We are trying to meet our stated deadline for clearing of the 24/25 July. But if we cannot, we do not want you to worry bon-ami, for the delay will only be short, if any.

We shall all meet most shortly—Richard, you, and your friend.

Baron Phillipe duDaphne

The following writing was from Baron Phillipe du Daphne to Marion Horn and Ferrera, making reference to CIA and State Department Richard Armitage, John H. Sununu,[95] the Prime Minister of Nipon:

CENTRE DE DEVELOPPEMENT
DEVELOPMENT CENTRE
28 July, 1989

94, rue Chardon Lagache
75016 PARIS

Le President, Baron Phillipe du Daphne.

CONFIDENTIAL
Diplomatic Pouch

To: Marion Horn, Jr., (J.R. Horn)
Lexington, Kentucky,
United States of America

Via: World Court of Justice, United Nations
To Consul General, Republic of France, San Francisco, CA.
USA
Hand-deliver to addressee by Maj Gen. R.L. Ferrera ONLY

Bon Ami, Marion:

Please forgive this most unorthodox method of having this delivered to you, but Richard and I, with Guy in concurrence, feel that the

---

[95] John H. Sununu was the White House chief of staff for President George H.W. Bush.

urgency of this message, and the expediency that must be used, constitutes a sufficient reason to this approach. As you know, Bon Ami, under all other circumstances we would not let anything of this importance, and confidentiality, be delivered from us to you by any other than General Ferrera, with direct delivery from us to you.

As I explained to you in my last brief communication, we have set up collection schedules prior to this latest one, and we have changed them, mostly at the very last minute, because everything was not perfectly balanced. I did inform you, J.R., that all was in readiness, but that you should be prepared for the eventuality of a necessary delay. Well, Bon Ami, all three of your associates in this matter (Richard, Guy, and I) are in complete agreement that we cannot move with your release until the final bridge is burned behind us, and that fire has now been set and the bridge is burning.

We did hear as the question was put to Mr. Alan Wolfley,[96] his feelings regarding his best possible person to assume the post of Prime Minister of Nippon. Under normal circumstance, we would not hesitate to so recommend him to the Liberal Democratic Party, but we must be most careful, because Mr. Wolfley's choice does not want to discuss the C.D. matter at all.

In view of this lack of cooperation, we have relegated him to second choice, as of this writing. Our top recommendation must now be Ryutaro Hashimoto, the Secretary General of the L.D.P. At our urging, a caucus of the party lawmakers is to be held on August 8, and at that time, Hashimoto will be picked as a replacement for Prime Minister Sosuke Uno.

We will continue to excerpt pressure behind the bamboo doors on Mr. Wolfley's choice, but we must act on the assumption that there will be no change in his position. Soon after the August 8th caucus, there will be called a special session of Parliament and Hashimoto will win routine approval. We have seen to that.

We must, therefore, put off your collection date in Washington, D.C. until after the August 8 date. We cannot at this time, Bon Ami, give you the exact day and time for your collection, but we can say that it will be the very day following the naming by Parliament of our man. This must be so if we are to have full control in the future. We might break the news to you that you are going to collect all at one time. That is, D.C., N.Z., and Singapore (AU).

At this time, we have also decided to inform you of the steps that will be taken by all of us from this moment on. We are now all together

---

[96] Alan Wolfley is a major contributor for the Republic party and a fund raiser.

in the proverbial life-boat, all safe, and we must not capsize it, or we will drown. I, for one detest swimming, so I must insist on the safety of the boat. You, J.R., will serve as the wealthy investor, industrialist, etc. etc., and world bon vivant, with as much of a mysterious cover as we can establish for you. This will entail your accepting the plaudits of the public and press for your many projects that will help humanity and the free world.

In plain French, Bon Ami, you will be the "face" of our little group with the world. (I deplore the description by General Ferrera of the "front-man". You are not to be a "front man", but rather, as our full partner, you shall be our spokesperson and our image unto the public). This will commence with the land bridge in Mexico, and many other projects that will suddenly be presented to you.

The choice of projects shall be in your hands, except on those occasions when we need to accept or reject a project. Those instances will be at a minimum. Baron Guy will "smooth" out any problems in your obtaining "project loans" from the top financial institutions in the world. The "loans" will be those AU funds that we have "liberated" from Sununu and Armitage. You are never to use one single centime of your personal funds—C.D. or otherwise for any project after you collect.

My trusted friend, Richard, will do all of the planning and the arranging with the governments involved, making sure that all the paper work and permits that you may require are in order. I will use the Centre De Development for the International negotiations. In the very near future, Bon Ami, you will form with our help and funds, the "International Bankers Trust, Lmt.", which will be the roof over various banks that we are in the process of obtaining for U.S. Mortgage and Trust, Lmt., Bahamas. Amongst them, we have reserved for you, 35% of the stock in the NZ bank that at the present has your C.D. funds in trust for you. You will also "buy" at least 33% of any bank controlled by us as well as the Rothschilds, plus various banks that we intend to control by August 8th.

In Mexico, we have arranged for the government to approve the sports book wagering along the border to-the United States. We had this granted to Jorge Hank Rhon, the owner of the racing emporium in Tia Juana Mexico. This permit is issued with 11 branches along the border, and thus takes the pressure off of your book permit that now awaits you in Mexico City. We own Jorge Hanks and his permit and he has pre-transferred ownership to your Mexican S.A., to be used after you get the betting book in Mexico City. This announcement should be released very soon.

I want you to send General Ferrera to Singapore, where he must take personal count of the AU bricks that have been added to your holdings since he was last there. There is being held for you AU in the amount of 75 BILLION dollars in AU as of yesterday's second London close. This is the one-third asked for by the General from the total "liberated".

This amount may increase as we find other bank accounts. When the General does this, you must then have him here in Paris, or in London, on August 7, for your final instructions on collection. We do wish that we could somehow alleviate the financial problems you are facing, but we must insist that you continue to arrange for capital in the same manner that you have in the past, for by so doing, nobody will ask any questions. Further, we want to inform you that some of those to be associated with you will be from the U.S. branch of La Cosa Nostra. Have no fear for we are aware of it and in control.

Merci, Bon Ami,

Baron Phillipe duDaphne

The following letter from the assessor confirms the existence of the account and funds in it.

27th of May, 1997

Mr Alvaro Chavez
Assessor
Grupo San Jose S.A.

Personal delivery

Dear Mr. Chavez,

In response to your request, the Central Bunk of Costa Rica has informed us that the account number 4051100-92 ref 118-65 maintains funds in dollars superior to 9 digits.

Said account that is with credit Suisse, at the Zurich Branch, can only guarantee the blocking of funds when the respective banking codes are used.

Sincerely,

Mr. Zaida Chavarria C.
Manager of International Department

Certification

This is to certify that the attached translation is, to the best of my knowledge and belief, a true and accurate rendition into English of the original document written in Spanish.

Sergio Sanabria,
California, this 27 day of May, 1997.
Sworn to and subscribed before me on this 27th day of May, 1997.
Notary by Dale C. Leake

The following letter from Denver attorney Warren Goss to Marion Horn relates to a planned meeting and completion of a financial transaction, with a copy to Jim Georges.

E. Warren Goss, III
Attorney At Law
5375 Western Avenue
Boulder, CO 80301

Licensed in Colorado — Telephone (303)444-0460
And Texas — Fax (303) 444-0675

August 15, 1997

J.R. Horn
Via fax at 606/269-3078 or 606/352-2647

Gentleman:

Please be advised that I will meet you in Atlanta Tuesday morning the 19th of August. I will be arriving Atlanta at 7:18 a.m. on flight 551 on Delta Airlines and will be prepared to move forward and I will have with me two other individuals with authority to bind this transaction and to implement immediately. I will plan on meeting you all at your convenience in Atlanta and I would think that we need to meet either at the Airport or at some location closely adjacent thereto. I have a flight out at 9:40 p.m. and I would hope that we'll be able to take care of all business during the day. I look forward to meeting with you.

Sincerely,

Warren Goss
EWG\ksb

cc: Jim Georges

[Handwritten note on copy: 11/8/99 (year?). Initial letter setting up meeting in Atlanta, GA at Sheraton Hotel at Airport, with Jr Horn, Terry Black, Clarence Kingry, Warren Goss, James Georges and Mr. Kain, Friend Warren Goss.]

In a January 19, 19909, letter, General Ferrera and Fidesco informed Multiple Southwest Investment Corporation that he was the guardian holder on funds in the Bank of New Zealand Bank in Wellington, New Zealand, and that there the funds are in excess of two trillion dollars.

FIDESCO
(Mexico), S.A.

Fomento
Industrial
Eoonomico y
Coordinados

January 19, 1990

U.S. Mailing Address
3250 Wilshire Blvd.
Suite 900
Los Angeles, CA 90010
Phone: 213 382-0209
FAX 213 487-2411

Multiple Southwest Investment Corp.
Dr. Dean Manson & Norman Staining
12830 Hillcrest Road #11
Dallas, Texas, 74230

Re: U.S. Mortgage & Trust (Bahamas) Ltd., and Five Star Trust (Isle of Man) balance sheet of Jan, 9, 1990

Dear Dr. Manson & Mr. Staining,

As per my telephone conversation this day with Mr. Staining and Mr. J. R. Horn, aka (Marion Horn Jr.), I hereby make available to you, Dr. Manson and Mr. Staining, that I Major General Robert Ferrara, Executive V. President and Director of U.S. Mortgage and Trust (Bahamas) Ltd, and Trustee of Five Star Trust, for whom I am the Guardian

Holder at the Bank of New Zealand, Wellington, New Zealand. Wherein there is on deposit in excess of two billion U. S. Dollars ($2,000,000,000.) on deposit.

I hope this letter of verification as to the liquid assets of U. S. Mortgage & Trust (Bahamas) Ltd., and Five Star Trust satisfy your requirements of validation of Balance Sheet of U.S. Mortgage and Trust (Bahamas) Ltd. /Five Star Trust, dated January 9, 1990.

I look forward to meeting both of you face to face this Sunday, January 21, 1990 at the Delta Crown Room at the Dallas International Airport.

Respectfully,

Fidesco (Mexico) S.A.

Major General Robert L. Ferrera
President and Director

RLF/mj

A February 27, 1990 fax from NMB Bank to General Ferrera of U.S. Mortgage and Trust (Bahamas) relates to the transfer of one billion dollars in gold bullion involving "former" CIA asset Gen. Roberto Ferrera and Baron Guy Rothschild.

NMB BANK

Fax Transmission

TO:	U.S. Mortgage and Trust (Bahamas) Ltd.
	General Roberto Ferrera
ATTN:	General Roberto L. Ferrera Suite 3726
Fax No.	(621) 22452
Date:	27 FEB 1990

No of pages: 2

Sirs:

We respectfully confirm to you that the transfer of the following has been completed as indicated:

ACCT # 036/90/YB/GR transmitted to main office Credit Suisse Bank Zurich, USD $ 1,000,000,000 (one billion. dollars US); your new account coded to you prior.

ACCT. II 036/90/YB/GR transmitted to main office Banque De

Paris Et Des Pays Bas, Paris, France USD $ 1,250,000,000 (one billion two hundred fifty million dollars US); Your new account coded to you prior.

ACCT. # 37/90/YB/GR/AU transmitted to main office, Lloyds Bank PLC, London England, 725,342 AU bars of 12.5 K weight, 999.5, Rothschild Hallmark; Your new account coded to you prior.
Best Regards,

WONG CHIN AUN
Director

c.c. Baron Guy Rothschild, Personal
Rothschild Banque, Paris France

A To-Whom-It-May-Concern writing by Fidesco, Mexico and Major General Robert L. Ferrera confirmed the existence of funds in the Bank of New Zealand for Five Star Trust:

FIDESCO
(Mexico), S.A.
Fomento
Industrial
Eoonomico y
Coordinados

CONFIDENTIAL
March 2, 1990

TO WHOM IT MAY CONCERN:

I, Mgen Robert L. Ferrera, do hereby confirm unconditional and irrevocable, that the monies on deposit at the bank of New Zealand, Wellington, New Zealand are the deposits of Five Star Trust and U.S. Mortgage and Trust (Bahamas) Ltd./Marion Horn, Jr., aka, J.R. Horn, of Lexington, Kentucky, USA.

I, Mgen. Robert L. Ferrera, further state and confirm that the monies on deposit at Credit Suisse Bank, Zurich, Switzerland, in the amount of $1,000,000,000 (one billion U.S. dollars), acct. #036/90/YB/GR, are the funds of JR Horn, U.S. Mortgage and Trust (Bahamas) Ltd. and he has complete authority to do whatever he wishes with these funds.

ACCT. # 036/90/YB/GR, main office Banque de Paris et des pays bas, Paris, France, on deposit in USD, $1,250,000,000 (one billion two hundred and fifty billion U.S. dollars) for and on behalf of Marion Horn, Jr., aka JR Horn, u. s. mortgage and trust (Bahamas) ltd.

Acct. #37/90/YB/GR/AU, main office, Lloyds Bank Plc, London-England 725342, au bars of 12.5 k weight, 999.5, Rothschild Hallmark, for deposit for U. S. Mortgage and Trust (Bahamas) Ltd./Marion Horn, Jr., Aka, JR Horn, President & CEO.

Let this letter serve as your complete authority to withdraw or transfer the monies or deposits to any bank you so desire.

Sincerely,

Director, Fidesco
And Trustee of Five Star Trust, Executive Vice President of U.S. Mortgage and Trust (Bahamas) Ltd.

A proposed settlement from Jim Georges to Five Star Trust with copy to attorney Terrell Black, August 29, 1997:

TRANS TECH
TRANS/TECH HOLDINGS COMPANY. LTD. INC.

August 29, 1997

"Five Star Trust, Ltd."
C/o Five Star Investments, Ltd.
(A Five Star Trust Company)
2230 Idle Hour Center, Suite #201
Lexington, Kentucky 40504

Attn: Mr. Marion Horn, Jr.
President & CEO
(Executive trustee of Five Star Trust)

C/o and sent to;
Mr. Terrell L. Black, Esq.
Tilford, Dobbins, Alexander, Buckaway & Black Attorney's at Law
1400 One Riverfront Plaza sent via fax & fedex #4386375302
Louisville, Kentucky 40202

Revised structure of transaction for 5-Star Trust

Dear Mr. Black:

Pursuant to our recent conversation of today and some of the issues you have raised requesting some additional consideration on several items, such as Escrow, Deposit of Funds in U.S. Bank, etc., which I will address in the following text. These issues were relayed to me by Mr. Warren Goss, from discussion you have had with him over the past couple of days.

Please understand, as I stated to you today and to Warren in prior discussion, this is not a negotiation as in a Union Contract, it is a very delicate issue and a tremendously large matter and it must be kept strictly confidential from all positions and sides and be handled in a very well executed series of documents.

The additional area of concern as we discussed and I raised the issue with Warren after our meeting in Atlanta, the escrow agent. My suggestions for this is to utilize a Bank for the Custodial Trust of the Sealed Documents, the contents only being known to the 4 parties and not even to the Escrow Agent. If we choose an Escrow Agent, it should be a person or attorney, that you as Representative of the Trust, Warren and I are totally comfortable with and is very Trustworthy.

There are many issues to still discuss, such as the manner of purchase of the trust or the insertion of new trustees, which I will advise you of my position after I have reviewed the trust agreement.

My main concern is that we reach an understanding of the basic terms of the transaction, and that this letter of understanding is executed by all parties and that I have a copy in my possession by close of business, September 2, 1997. This will allow me to advise the proper Government Authorities and Officials, that we have reached an accord and binding contracts.

The basic terms of the transaction are as follows;

Trans/Tech Holdings Company, Ltd., inc. will purchase Five Star Trust for $3.5 Billion United States Dollars. The alternative is to purchase the rights to Five Star Trust and insert a new Executive Trustee and Board of Trustee's. This method will be defined after Trans/Tech Holdings Company, Ltd., Inc. and its Officers have reviewed the Trustee Agreement. The Purchase Price will be paid out over 35 years at an investment rate of $100 Million per year.

The investment of $100 Million per year will return 280% per year paid in equal amount twice a month over 12 months.

The Beneficiaries of Five Star Trust will have to re-invest 55% of the initial payout back into the investment program and they will receive 280% on that amount, this creates a compound effect and will continue for the first five years of the term of the contract payout.

During this period of payout, 35 years, the entire sum of $3.5 Billion will be blocked in a secure account, in the control of First International Private Bank, within its corresponding bank, Citibank, New York City, New York. This block fund will be established within 30 to 45 days after full execution of the contract, and exchange of escrow funds for documents.

If any default occurs on the part of TTHC, the blocked funds will be released to the beneficiaries of the purchase and sale contract for Five Star Trust. This will be covered under a separate default agreement and made an exhibit to the overall purchase and sale agreement or the agreement to insert new trustee's and board members.

If all the conditions of the contract are met without any default on the part of the Beneficiaries for Five Star Trust, the block funds amount of $3.5 billion United States Dollars will be release to the beneficiaries at the end of the term of the contract of 35 years, as a good faith bonus.

If all of the conditions of the contracts are met without any default on the part of the Beneficiaries for Five Star Trust, especially the breach of confidentiality, then Trans/tech Holdings Company, Ltd., Inc., through its subsidiary, First International Private Bank, will Grant permission for the bank to remit the principal amount of investment of $100 million for every year and the end of each 5 year period. This condition will remain in effect for the first 25 years of the contract. The effect is an additional income to the beneficiaries of $2.5 billion.

I cannot guarantee the amount of money, until I have reviewed all of the documents involved and have had several additional meetings with government officials but I would agree to place a sum of money in escrow with the bank of our choice. The sum of money will be placed in escrow within approximately 4 weeks after the contracts have been executed. The funds will be release within 2 weeks after the documents have been turned over to Trans/Tech Holdings Company, Ltd., Inc., this will be approximately 30 days before the start of the initial transaction funding.

I cannot guarantee a full tax exemption and I will not even try to discuss it with the IRS, but I can probably arrange a similar situation, (no guarantee) that I already have and that is a small percentage of the gross paid on all funds coming into the U.S., before receiving any money.

Please review this structure and if you have any questions please advise, prior to discussing with you client. I would like to have a verbal acceptance, a signed acceptance sent via Fax with seals affixed and the two of the originals returned via FEDEX.

The entire package is worth between $19 and $23 Billion Dollars over the term of the contract, without consideration for the amount of assets that will be created for the Beneficiaries of the Trust.

Thank you for your continued cooperation and I await your reply.

Sincerely yours,

R. Georges, Jr. President

CC: Warren Goss, Esq.

The following is a notarized statement by Clarence Kingery and Marion Horn relating to Five Star Trust relating to Blackeagle:

CONFIDENTIAL INFORMATION
This Update on Blackeagle Story

Date: 22nd day of March 2006 and notarized by Grover N. Jones. Those four pages are attached hereto updates the meeting in Florida with Maurice Moore and Associates:

Clarence Theodore Kingery, Jr.,
8608 Sturbidge Drive
Cincinnati, Ohio 45236
Phase: (513) 791-7077

I, the Undersigned, Clarence Theodore Kingery, Jr., and Marion Horn, Jr., severalty and jointly do hereby swears to the statement declared herein, being of sound mind, do make this format declaration and affidavit of my own free will and accord this 23rd day March 2006. I further do swear to the statement herein given ís true and correct to the best of my knowledge and recollections.

On, the 26 of February 2006, I, Clarence Theodore Kingery, Jr., and Mr. Marion Horn, Jr. Ex. Trustee of Five Star Trust, with address at 3620 Park Point Dr., Lexington, KY 40509, were jointly present and attending meeting at the Vacation Village Resort, Weston, Florida, wherein we met with Mr. Maurice Moore, former ambassador to the United Nations from Commonwealth of Bahamas; also present was Mr. H. Moore the brother of Maurice Moore, who stated he was an employee for the US District Attorney office of Miami, Florida.

Mr. Maurice Moore was there to confer with Mr. Marion Horn, Jr., and myself, regarding the collection and release of cash or gold assets in the name of Five Star Trust (An Isle of Man Trust), which Mr. Marion Horn Jr., was the Executive Trustee and sole signature to all the foreign US dollar accounts of Five Star Trust identified possibly by account number 405110092 (Ref. 1.1145).

Ambassador Maurice Moore, and associate Burton Miller, who also was present, had been given an agreement by Mr. Marion Horn, Jr., to pay to Mr. Maurice Moore and his associates 33 1/3% of any and all monies recovered by their efforts for Five Star Trust. This was not an exclusive agreement, since a previous non-exclusive agreement existed between Five Star Trust/Marion Horn, Jr. and Walter Moore, of Freeport, Bahamas, a brother to Ambassador Maurice Monte, wherein that agreement had been signed by Mr. Marion Horn. Jr., and co-signed and approved by Banister Kevin M. Russell, Attorney for Marion Horn, Jr. /Elaine B. Horn, the heirs of Five Star Trust and the trust itself. Mr. Walter Moore claimed to have formal connections to agencies of US government, via the US dept. of Justices, and had been meeting with representatives of the US Government, according to Mr. Marion Horn, Jr., and Mr. Kevin M. Russell, legal counsel.

The agreement with Mr. Walter Moore called for Mr. Walter Moore to collect some $31 Million USD that was owed to Five Star investments Ltd., a subsidiary of Five Star Trust, of which I am secretary and treasury of Five Star Investments Ltd. Also, Walter Moore of Freeport, Bahamas (Phone: 305-503-5933), was authorized to collect and move up to Five Billion USD ($5,000,000,000.00) to an account of Kevin M. Russell, and Co. at First Caribbean International Bank, Bay St., Nassau, Bahamas.

Mr. Walter Moore had confirmed to Mr. Horn and Kevin M. Russell, as well as to Maurice Moore and Burton Miller that Walter Moore had personally checked the money in the system owed to Five Star Investments Ltd. from Nigerian government, and had made trips to Cuba to meet with the Ambassador of Nigeria to clear up the release of these funds to Mr. Kevin M. Russell account.

For this, Mr. Moore and associates would receive twenty (20%) per cent of the gross amount recovered. For moving and collecting the money from Barclays Bank PLC, Isle of Man, which Walter Moore had selected since he had previously someway confirmed that Five Star Trust/Marion Horn Jr. had deposits in excess of this amount on deposit.

Mr. Walter Moore confirmed that he has formal permission from the US Government Treasury to move up to Two Billion USD on his sole signature. For this movement Mr. Moore and his partners would receive a fee of not less than Two Billion USD, and that amount to be finally approved and determined by the officials of the US Government permitting fees and brokerage fees such as these.

[84 Worldwide Bank Accounts for Five Star Trust]

During our meetings with Ambassador Maurice Moore, his brother, who works for the US district attorney of Miami, Florida, it was determined that through their Ambassador Moore, his brother, and their high sources, that Five Star Trust has in excess of 84 worldwide bank accounts. The amount in these accounts was not disclosed, but it was disclosed that in the account at Barclays Bank PLC, Isle of Man, that there were one hundred and thirty-five billion USD ($135,000,000.00) on deposits. Further it was stated by Ambassador Moore that the banker at Barclays Bank PLC had been dipping into this account on his own and that he would be agreeable to move up to one billion US to any account we, Five Star Trust, selected.

This information was relayed to individuals in Europe who indicated that they would be glad to accept this amount for and on deposit for Five Star Trust and open an account on our behalf, subject to the final transfer of these funds, which would be declared clean, clear funds of non-criminal origin.

This was tabled until after the weekend of 27 of February 2006 wherein I and Mr. Horn returned back to our homes in Kentucky and Ohio.

Also, while at the meeting in Florida with Ambassador Maurice Moore, his brother and Burton Miller (who was former Mayor of Freeport, Grand Bahamas, Bahamas. until recently), Mr. Moore, the Ambassador Brother and the Ambassador Moore confronted Mr. Horn, that he was taking funds out of one of the accounts in Germany at the tune of $150.000.00 per day and had been for some years.

Mr. Horn said, "Are you referring to the account of FST at Deutsche Bank?"

"No," replied Ambassador Moore, "the account at Dresdner Bank, Ag., Frankfort, Germany."

Prior to our departure, Ambassador Maurice Moore and Burton Miller requested that Mr. Marion Horn, Jr., Ex. Trustee of Five Star Trust, voided the pending agreement between Five Star Trust/Marion Horn, Jr. and his brother Walter Moore, on the statement that his brother Walter Moore had informed him and Burton Miller, that he, Walter Moore and other high officials of US government, were going to take control of all these accounts without my knowledge and approval, and that Five Star Trust would receive nothing.

At that time, Mr. Marion Horn stated that he had given to Mr. Wailer Moore, an advance of Five Thousand Dollars ($5,000.00) to pay him to cover his expenses in his travel to obtain the release of Five Star Investments Ltd., and Five Star Trust assets.

Mr. Burton Miller of Freeport, Mr. Maurice Moore of Freeport, Bahamas, and Maurice's brother, Moore, who worked for the US district attorney office in Miami, FL., told Mr. Horn that he should do this immediately.

Mr. Horn attempted to contact Walter Moore at his address and via his legal counsel, but no response. Therefore, a notice was given to Walter Moore and Maurice Moore as well, that as of 10th of March 2006, all agreements with both of them would be null and void and no longer in effect

This notice was done by US registered mail to their official address or their legal counsel's official address. It is hereby noted as of this date 22nd day of March 2006, NO binding agreement exist formally with either Maurice Moore and/or his brother Walter Moore, both of Freeport, Bahamas.

Affiant Sayeth noth:

Signed this 22nd day of March 2006.

By, Clarence T. Kingery, Jr. and Marion Horn, Jr., jointly and severally on behalf of themselves and Five Star Trust (An Isle of Man Trust).

/s/ Clarence Theodore Kingery, Jr., Individually

/s/ Mr. Marion Horn, Jr., Individually & Ex. Trustee of Five Star Trust

State of Kentucky
Country of Fayette
City of Lexington

On this 22nd day of March 2006, appeared before me, Clarence Theodore Kingery, Jr., and Marion Horn, Jr., both are personally known to me to be the person or persons whose name is subscribed to the within instruments, and acknowledged to me that Clarence Kingery, Jr. and Marion Horn, Jr. executed the same in his authorized capacity and that by their signature on the instrument, the person, or the entity upon behalf of which the person acted, executed the instrument.

My commission expires: 4th of October 2007.

/s/ Mr. Grover N. Jones
Notary Public at Large
State of Kentucky
United States of America
Notary Seal
End of Affidavit

Horn Hiring Former Federal Official

In 2006, Marion Horn hired Texas attorney Mark C. Conrad to represent him in obtaining access to Five Star Trust Accounts. (I had known Conrad for many years and found him knowledgeable about intrigue and misconduct in government.) The following is a copy of a letter sent by Conrad to former President H.W. Bush. The reason for addressing Bush was that prior information showed that he was involved in the covert activities hiding gold retrieved by the OSS/CIA in the Philippines.

Unknown to Conrad, I had become a confidante to the titular head of a secret CIA proprietary based in Honolulu and had learned that the CIA had secret bank accounts for people such as Vice President George H.W. Bush and Richard Armitage. This information is in my book, *Explosive Secrets of Covert CIA Companies.* Conrad's letter follows:

Mark C. Conrad
Assistant Professor Criminal Justice

Troy University-Dothan Campus
P.O. Box 8684
Dothan, AL 36304

April 29, 2006

President George H.W. Bush
10000 Memorial Drive Suite 900
Houston, Texas 77024

In re: Marion "Jr." Horn, Five Star Trust (Isle of Man)

Dear Mr. President:

I have been retained by Mr. Marion Horn, Jr., of Lexington, Kentucky, who is the Executive Trustee of Five Star Trust (An Isle of Man Trust), to resolve a number of still existing disputed matters between Mr. Horn/Five Star Trust, and various domestic and foreign entities. According to Mr. Horn, in the past, intermediaries or brokers represented to Horn their past and current affiliation/association with you and various U.S. Government agencies. These individuals represented their ability to resolve these outstanding Matters.

These parties negotiated and entered into signed notarized agreements with Mr. Horn, but for some reason or other they were unable to finalize or complete their agreements. Mr. Horn is now of the opinion, after our long discussion that it would be best to resolve this matter without any court actions that would give the impression that we are ready to declare war to resolve this matter. That is not his intention. He only wants to resolve this matter, as it pertains to him, quietly once and for all. Mr. Horn accepted my idea that first approach you to request your assistance in resolving this nester quietly and confidentially, before having to seek remedies in various courts. Mr. Horn and I feel that any publicity will be harmful to a number of individuals and probably cause this matter to never be completely settled. Mr. Horn and I both, feel you are the one person who would know how to resolve this matter for the best of all concerned.

So that you know who I am, I would like to reintroduce myself to you. Betty and "Corky" Green are personal friends of my wife and me and attended my retirement dinner in 1998. I am the (now retired) Supervisory Special Agent that made arrangements for Betty and your good friend, the late Jack Steele to fly tally on the U.S. Customs Blackhawk helicopter while you were vice President. Jack and Betty invited my wife and me to the luncheon at your church when you officially released your autobiography *Looking Forward*. If necessary, Betty can provide additional information to you as to the assistance I unofficially provided to your office on a couple of occasions in the past.

Mr. Horn is desirous of resolving all matters that involve him (and FST) and while I have been intentionally circumspect, I am authorized to engage in discussions to resolve all matters involving Mr. Horn quietly.

Thanking you in advance for your time and consideration, I am,

Sincerely,

Mark C. Conrad

cc: Marion "JR" Horn

The letter by Conrad to former President George H.W. Bush referred to circumspect, meaning matters that the public should not know about. In response to that letter, Bush denied—naturally—any knowledge of the "circumspect" matters and if he did, he did not wish to be involved directly or in the matter. The subject was too serious for Bush to have said anything that even remotely referred to what had been the world's greatest financial fraud that now involved multiple countries and dozens of worldwide banks. The reply follows:

Office of George Bush

June 21, 2006

Dear Mr. Conrad:

On behalf of President Bush., thank you for your letter of April 29.

I apologize for the delay in responding.

Unfortunately, sir, President Bush is not able to be of assistance to you and your client, Mr. Horn. Although we have no idea what the "existing disputed matters" to which you refer might be, I can tell you that it would not be appropriate for Mr. Bush to be involved in any way, directly or indirectly. He wishes you and your client well and thanks you for writing.

Sincerely,
Linda Casey Poepsel
Assistant to President Bush

Mr. Mark Conrad
Assistant Professor of Criminal Justice
Troy University-Dothan Campus
Post Office Box 8684
Dothan, AL 36304

10000 Memorial Drive, Suite 900, Houston, Texas 77024
Phone (713) 686-1188 • Fax (713) 683-0801

The following letter from Washington, D.C. lawyer Scott Hodges relates to Marion Horn, seeking information:

Scott A. Hodes, Attorney At Law
Post Office Box 42002
Washington DC 20015
www.infoprivacylaw.com

Member DC and MD Bars INFOPRIVACYLAWS@YAHOO.COM

June 27, 2006

Kathy J. Lyerly
Special Agent in Charge
Freedom of Information & Privacy Acts Branch
United States Secret Service
246 Murray Drive, Building 410
Washington, D.C. 20223

Re: Freedom of Information/Privacy Acts Requests—2004015

Dear Ms. Lyerly:

By letter dated March 17, 2006, notified you that I now represent Marion Horn Jr. on his FOIA/PA request to your office. I attached to my March 11, 2006 letter a copy of Mr. Horn's authorization allowing you to discuss this request with me.

On two previous occasions I spoke with someone in your office concerning the status of the request. On June 23, 2008, an individual who claimed to be a supervisor in your office claimed there was no record of my letter or Mr. Home authorization and as such no one could provide me with an update to the status of Mr. Horn's request. I left a message for you to contact me to discuss this, but I have not heard from you as of this date.

As you know, Mr. Horn sent his request to your office on April 20, 2004. Your office has assigned this request file numb 20040215. Over two years has passed since the request was submitted and Mr. Horn has still not received the requested material. I believe Mr. Horn has waited much longer than is reasonable for these records.

I am enclosing the original of Mr. Horn's authorization allowing me to represent him on this matter. Please contact me to let me know you have received It and also to let me know the status of his request.

Additionally, I ask that you release the records to me so that I can review them before passing them on to my client.

I look forward to speaking to you concerning this request. If you have any questions concerning this matter, feel free to contact me at your convenience.

Sincerely,

Scott A. Hodes
cc; Marion Horne, Jr.

enclosure

[Mr. Horn's hand written comments on this page: Ken, these files, if I can obtain their release, will show FST accounts. I feel SS is withholding these files from release due to information contained in them. Plus the obstruction of justice for withholding critical evidence. JR.
PS: These files were scheduled for release last week but did not happen.]

The following affidavit was made by William Stanley relating to "Stonewood Trust for which Marion Horn was signatory, requesting a status report on the account:

STONEWOOD TRUST

Est. 1947

29676 Avante
Laguna Niguel, CA 92677
Phone: 949-363-1464
Fax: 949-363-7434

Copies of this Letter shall be Accepted as Original
Until the Original is Delivered or Required to be Delivered

LETTER OF ACKNOWLEDGEMENT

TO WHOM IT MAY CONCERN:

Or this 13th day of September 2007, I, William G Stanley, USA Passport 221877608, with official address at 29676 Avante, Laguna Niguel, California 92677, and the Authorized signature of Stonewood Trust, a private trust, do hereby make the following affidavit of my own free will and accord.

I do solemnly swear that after conferring with my bankers and traders who have conferred with their contacts inside the three subject banks namely: Bank of Scotland, Edinburgh, Credit Suisse Bank, Main Branch, Zurich, Switzerland, and Deutsche Bank AG, Headquarters Office, Frankfurt, Germany, they have recommended the following:

Mr. Stanley should request to have Mr. Horn, the sole signatory for these accounts of the Five Star Trust in those subject banks, to instruct the banks to add the name William G. Stanley holding USA passport# 221877608 as a signatory to these accounts.

They further stated that Mr. Horn should request the banks to send the signature cards to their branch banks or corresponding banks in Southern California where Mr. Stanley should be invited in to affix his signature on the signature cards in their presence and have those branches return the executed signature cards by inter-branch courier to their headquarters in Europe.

Further, they recommended Mr. Horn request when the account signature process has been recorded, that the bank send an acknowledgment latter so stating to Mr. Horn along with a new print screen showing the current status of the account and signatures thereto. I have requested and accepted the attached bank letters referred to as Exhibits—A, B and C, hereto regarding the three banks.

I further state that I have requested from Mr. Marion Horn, Jr. and Five Star Trust the approval and official authorization to add my signature, William G. Stanley to the account at .... Horn, Jr.

Also, I agree to perform any and all legal acts, as agreed by both parties, that Mr. Marion Horn, Jr. may instruct and approve in regard to any of these banks and accounts.

I, William G. Stanley, personally and on behalf of Stonewood Trust, do hereby sign this letter of acknowledgement and agreement this s 13th day of September 2007 of my own freewill and accord.

/s/ William G. Stanley, Director of Stonewood Trust
Passport Number: USA # 221877608

Attached Exhibits
A, B and C bank letters hereto are made part of this acknowledgment.

Acceptance of the above acknowledgement

Date: accepted this 14th day of September 2007, by Marion Horn, Jr. executive trustee of Five Star Trust and agreed that copies of this acknowledgement above and the attached bank letter exhibits, A, B, & C, shall be accepted under the same terms and conditions.

/s/ Marion Horn, Jr. Executive Trustee

<u>Notary Acknowledgement</u>

On this 14th day of September 2007, before me, Grover N. Jones, Notary Public at large, State of Kentucky, USA, appeared Marion Horn, Jr. Executive Trustee of Five Star Trust, who is personally known to me and did sign the above acceptance.

My commission expires: 8th October 2008.
/s/Mr. Grover N. Jones
Notary Public at Large, KY

The following resolution by the trustees of Five Star Trust related to the approval of a note:

<u>FIVE STAR TRUST</u>

Isle of Man Trust (Domiciled Underneath Despen Trust Ltd.)
(Reg. # 287/99 Nevis, W.I.)
Attn: Marion Horn, Jr. Executive Trustee
Official Address: C/O: Despen Trust Ltd.
Attn: Dexter Bowrin, Managing Director-Despen Trust Ltd.

P.O. Box 625 Charleston, West Indies
Phone: 869-469-1016, Fax: 869-469-0826
Email: despen@caribsur.com

TRUST RESOLUTION

EXHIBIT —A (Attached to Promissory Note #23057)

On this 16th day February 2008, a special meeting of the Board of Trustees of Five Star Trust (Nevis, W.I.), was called to order by Marion Horn, Jr. Executive Trustee and Clarence T. Kingery, Jr., individual trustee and secretary of trustees kept the minutes of the meeting.

All the voting trustees were in attendance, in person or by telephone conference or other communications.

A general discussion was held and a motion made and duly seconded approving the approval of issuance of a International Promissory Note Number: 23057, to be effective and valid upon receipt of $13,000,000.00 (Thirteen Million USD) as a loan to Trust for one hundred and twenty (120) days, to pay for legal expenses to recover assets of Five Star Trust worldwide.

The note is for a payment of $52 Million USD, or a 4X1, return if paid within ninety days, and if extended beyond this time period a maximum of one billion USD ($1,000,000.000, 00), as additional compensation to be paid as and when assets of Five Star Trust are recovered by legal counsels headed by Mr. Mark Conrad, Attorney at Law, Springs, TX. USA. It was further approved that Mr. Marion Horn, Jr. Executive Trustee of Five Star Trust be authorized to sign the promissory note #23057 and any other documentation to receive this loan.

As additional collateral, Five Star Trust will issue to lender a formal authorization to withdraw the payment of this note 23057 by lender if for any reason Five Star Trust is unable to make the payment of the note herein issued. The lender will be able to select the bank of its choice and confirm that the funds are available to pay the note at that bank, and that Mr. Marion Horn, Jr. is the signature on that account, as Aegis Capital Corporation has already done herein and made part of this loan repayment. (Attached Updated Promissory note #23057 dated 16th February 2008; and made part of this Resolution)

A vote was taken, passing a requisite majority of this board.

Emails and/or facsimile copies shall in each and every situation be considered as originals and shall be legal and binding document until replaced with the original, if necessary and/or required.

With no other business to come before the trust the meeting was adjourned. Signed:

Signed: Clarence T. Kingery, Jr., Individual Trustee and Secretary of

Trust

Signed: Marion Horn, Jr. Executive Trustee, USA Passport # 4038857898

SAMPLE—INTERNATIONAL PROMISSORY NOTE

Note Number 23057

Date: February 16th, 2008

Pay to the Order of Lender-Payable to Bearer $52,000,000.00

FIVE STAR TRUST

Five Star Trust will issue as collateral to lender a banking authorization to lender to electronically draw down from a bank of lenders choice from the list of banks previously validated and confirmed existence of sufficient capital to pay this note. This authorization to electronically draw down the payment to cover promissory note no. 23057. If for any reason Five Star Trust is unable to pay its obligations of the promissory note #23057, lender if he so chooses will be given ample time to confirm for his own satisfaction the existence of Five Star Trust bank account and availability of funds at bank he wishes to draw down the repayment of this note

Date: 16th February 2008

To: lenders bank and banking coordinates wiring instructions

Instructions: please draw down via electronic transfer from account of Five Star Trust/Marion Horn, Jr. Executive trustee, and signature to the account at bank of your choice from the list previously given you. Example, Deutsche Bank AG, Frankfurt, Germany, Account number: 4051100-92, pin number: 8942, amount: $42,000,000.00 (forty-two million U.S. dollars)

To be withdrawn and transferred into lenders account at lenders bank, location of lenders bank and account: bank info to be inserted

Account number: Account # to be inserted
Account Name: Account Name to be inserted
Authorized and Approved by Marion Horn, Jr.

Marion Horn, Jr. Executive Trustee, Five Star Trust
USA Address: 3620 Park rote Drive Lexington, KY 40509, USA,
Phone: 859-266-0730, Fax: 859-422-5023, cell: 859-229-7199,
Email: fivestartrust@gmail.com

The following is a letter Marion Horn wrote to a friend:

MARION HORN JR
3620 Park Pointe Drive
Lexington, Kentucky 40509, USA
Tel. (59) 266-0730, Cell: (859) 948-7642, Fax: (859) 422-5023
Email address: jrhom8942@hotrnail.com

Monday, 20th August 2007

Ref: Authorization and Limited Power of Attorney (A One Eyed Man in the Land of the Blind can be King)

Dear Ken:

I got your letter today with your formal request for authorization to act on behalf of myself and Five Star Trust. I had already sent you a couple of LPOA, but not sure that they were exactly what you needed, so I have gotten he Notary to come today and notarize signatures to a Service Agreement between FST/myself and you, regarding the accessing and recovery of assets of FST.

Also, I enclosed a separate agreement with LPOA wherein you were authorized to probe, scan, printout and move funds of FST in accounts worldwide. As you know the partial list of accounts is small compared to the accounts worldwide.

The last estimate was there was something like 300 or more. I am not sure how many there actually are but I am sure the T boys and Agency know. I don't know how long they can do what they are doing and get by with it but I assume that as long as they have no conscious of what is right or wrong, they will continue to do it as long as they wish.

I believe that someday we all must acknowledge what we do. The accounts of FST are worldwide and the man who had done the last scan and had them compiled was Mr. Bill Siwy, a friend of Alice Rivlin, former Vice Chairman of Federal Reserve and friend of my former attorney Lew Rivlin, Alice's former husband. Bill has or had the printouts but I was informed that he was told to disappear and he did but I believe he is still alive as is Gen. Robert L Ferrera as well.

I do herby authorize you to act in any way that is in the best interest of myself and our Trust and company, Five Star Investments La, you have the account of Five Star Investments Ltd. at bank of America, and you can wire whatever amount you wish to this account. Also another account will come to you as stated before with the reference validation of the code I spoke to you about to acknowledge it came from me.

I hope this is what you require and you are able to use it to the benefit of myself, yourself and our family and Trustees.

Regards,

M Horn, Jr.
Executive Trustee
Five Star Trust (Isle of Man Trust)
Enclosed: Two original agreements and Two LPOA attached thereto.

FIVE STAR TRUST (Isle of Man Trust)-
US Tax Id #61-6234232
CIO: Kevin M. Russell & Co., Attorneys and Counselors at Law
#15 Lillian Court, (Off Royal Palm Way), Lucaya Beach, P.O. Box F42021
Freeport, Grand Bahamas, Bahamas

Tel.: (242) 373-9740/41, Fax: (242) 373-1429, email: info@russlawbahamas.com

The Director,
IMF Office, Washington, D.C. USA
Five Star Trust
Mark Conrad, Attorney At Law, Dothan, AL
USA Address: P.O. Box 22711
Marion Horn, Jr., Ex. Trustee-Five Star Trust
Lexington, KY 40522

January 19, 2007
Number of pages: Three (3)
Office: 859-266-0730-Cell /859-948-7642
Fax: (859) 422-4903

Request Assistance in Obtaining Release Of
Funds and Assets Worldwide Banks
jrhorn8942@hotmail.com

Dear Sir:

I, Marion Horn, Jr., Executive Trustee of Five Star Trust (An Isle of Man Trust) US Tax ID No. 61-6234232, write in regard to requesting your assistances in obtaining the release of our assets worldwide, in many major worldwide banks, which includes, bank accounts at UBS, Geneva, Switzerland, Credit Suisse, Zurich, Switzerland, AU the major German Banks, all the major French banks, ABN Ambro Bank, Netherlands, and Ing Bank, and most all the major English banks, including Barclays Bank, Isle of Man, HSBC Bank, Jersey, Channel Isles, UK. There are many more banks that have our accounts, which total as many as eighty-four, according to our intelligences and reports.

These worldwide accounts are all US Dollar accounts, except for the precious metals that are on deposit in many areas of the world, including Switzerland, Singapore, and England. The accounts are all the same account number which is 4051100-92 (Ref. 11865), under the name of Five Star Trust/Marion Horn, Jr., Executive Trustee and sole signature.

We have secured the service of an attorney Mr. Mark Conrad, who is a former Homeland Security agent (retired) of 27 years who is presently assisting our trust. We would like you to contact us and or Mr. Conrad, whose Limited power of attorney is attached hereto for your references; and if you require further information please contact me immediately.

We hereby seek the appropriate intervention of the IMF via their auditors assigned to UK, Germany, France and Netherlands, to help us in our location and release of our assets worldwide, and especially the US Banks, Citibank, Chase and Bank America.

Thank you very much for your kind attention to this matter and your anticipated urgent cooperation.

Regards,
Five Star Trust

Horn, Jr., Executive Trustee

NOTICE: Attached hereto: Passport & KY Drivers license of Marion Horn, Jr., 3620 Park Pointe Dr., Lexington, KY 40509, USA, Phone: (859) 266-0730, Cell: (859) 948-7642, Fax: (859) 422-5023, Email: jrborn8942@hotmail.com. Attached hereto also is the power of attorney issued to Attorney Mark Conrad by Marion Horn Jr, Ex. Trustee of Five Star Trust.

Marion Horn giving Attorney Mark Conrad a limited power of attorney to act on Horn's behalf and that of Five Star Trust:

LIMITED POWER OF ATTORNEY
For Attorney at Law David Mark Conrad on
Behalf of Marion Horn, Jr.

I, Marion Horn. Jr. hereby authorize David Mark Conrad and attorney at law, licensed to practice law in the State of Texas, United States of America, a limited power of attorney and authorize him to:

Make any inquiries and obtain information on behalf for or any of my businesses listed below with any government Agency including but not limited to that of the United Sates, the European Union and its member states, New Zealand, or Mexico.

Make any inquiries under the United States Freedom of Information Act or Privacy Act, and take any action, worldwide, including any legal action necessary to identify, secure and protect funds or otherwise identified assets, in any of my personal or business accounts or where I am shown as a signatory to the accounts, in any banking or financial institutions, wherever located.

My identifiers are as follows:

Name: Marion Horn
DOB: [redacted]
SSN: [redacted]
Driver's license: [redacted]

My related businesses are:

Five Star Trust (Isle of Man)
Five Star Investment, Ltd (Belize, Central America) & Commonwealth of Bahamas

If there are any questions, Mr. Conrad's contact points are:

Mark Conrad BS MS JD
Attorney at Law (Texas)
Assistant Professor of Criminal Justice
P.O. Box 8684
Dothan, AL 36301
Fax: 3334-671-8532 Cel: 832-326-7086
Email address: markconrad_law@hotmail.com

Texas Bar Number: 24014497

This authorization is valid until December 31, 2007, unless revoked by me earlier.

/s/ Mr. Marion Horn, Jr., aka J.R. Horn. Date: 15th April 2006.

Sworn to and subscribed to before me this the 15th day of April 2006, by Marion Horn, Jr., who is personally known to me.

/s/ Grover N. Jones

County of Fayette, State of Kentucky

United States of America My commission expires on 4th October 2007

In an e-mail message to this writer, Marion Horn stated:

General Robert L. Ferrera, who is legally dead in USA, but still much alive under another name and now living in Oslo, Norway, or possible New Zealand. His new name is Lauren W. Rosier, Special Advisor to G8. He controls the accounts of FST worldwide which are around 825 more or less, even though he is not legally authorized to do so. It is done through subordinates etc.

A Caveat About Marion Horn

The documents shown in this chapter were provided to me by various sources and reveal important information on various matters relating to the topic of this book. However, Marion Horn had repeatedly refused to answer important questions and refused to provide any meaningful documentation. Among the questions presented to Horn, that he refused to answer, were the following:

- Details about his financial background that could have put him in position to purchase a CD issued by the Mitsui Bank in Tokyo.
- Request for documentation related to the purchase of the CD.
- The approximate price paid for the CD that would provide some information about the enormous financial wealth required of the person or group making the purchase.
- How the CD from the Mitsui Bank in Tokyo become the source of many bank accounts?

Horn was cooperative *until* he was asked these specific questions and request for documentation. His refusal to response to simple but important matters raises a question about his role in these matters. But the documentation reveals important information about the key issues.

CHAPTER TEN

Effects of Covert Schemes on United States

What is stated in this book about the culture of people in control of key segments of the U.S. government is serious. For most people, it may be difficult to connect this culture with what exists today in the United States. In most of my other books, the relationship between the endemic corruption and endemic cover-ups is easier to visualize.

These pages provide only a small fraction of the available documents and writings revealing such matters as:

- Horrific brutality of the Japanese that has been kept from the American public, due to the need to cover up for covert and corrupt actions by people in various overt and covert U.S. government entities.
- U.S. politicians and U.S. media have instead limited their attention to wartime atrocities upon the Nazi treatment of the Jews in Europe.
- War plunder that had been seized by the invading Japanese from a dozen countries, from 1937 to 1945, and hidden in Japan and the Philippines, have been covered up by U.S. personnel.
- Japanese war criminals responsible for horrific crimes against U.S. prisoners of war were corruptly shown as innocent, and even rewarded, making a mockery of the suffering of their victims.
- War plunder that should have been returned to the rightful owners were confiscated by U.S. personnel and that hidden in Japan was protected by the same scheme concocted by the same personnel.
- Banks throughout the world became a knowing party in the conspiracy and fraud, and protected by U.S. politicians and Department of Justice employees.
- People who tried to expose the corruption came under brutal attack by Department of Justice personnel—a common occurrence.
- The consequences of this culture, shown in this book, had many other and far worse consequences for the United States and its peo-

ple. Some of these consequences are detailed and documented in my other books.

What You Can Do

The first step is to show a serious interest in these matters and become informed. And with the vast cover-ups, disinformation, and blatant lying by U.S. politicians, media personnel, and political pundits, this requires a little effort. In searching for information, don't be misled by wild conspiracy theories and go where facts can be found, including courageous insiders who speak out in defense of the country.

Sadly, fewer people read such books (preferring trivia reading), rarely read newspapers (which is one small step to becoming informed). Therefore, the future is bleak, made possible by the corruption detailed here and in the books, the cover-ups, and the public's indifference to their responsibilities.

The corruption has by now progressed to such an extent, and the public's obsession with trivia and the general decline in morals, makes it highly unlikely that conditions do reverse instead of steadily increasing. For the American public, they need only look for one of those at fault by looking in the mirror.

Comparison Between the German Public Under Adolf Hitler and the American Public Under Their Corrupt Leaders

A poem written by Martin Niemoller, relating to how Germans tolerate Adolf Hitler is especially suitable to most Americans today:

First they came for the Jews, and I did not speak out, because I was not a Jew. Then they came for the Communists, and I did not speak out, because I was not a Communist.

Then they came for the trade unionists, and I did not speak out, because I was not a trade unionist. Then they came for me, and there was no one left to speak out for me.

Pastor Martin Niemöller

Pastor Martin Niemöller (1892–1984) first supported the rise of Adolf Hitler, and then upon learning the truth, and objecting, he was imprisoned. He wrote a poem about the state of denial of Germans about what Hitler was doing. Probably no better example could be shown than what has been done to the American people, in their name, while they ignored the outrages.

CHAPTER ELEVEN

Sampling of Documents

Because copies of documents are often hard to read, I have taken the contents from the documents and formatted them for easier reading. This section contains copies of some of the documents for the readers' viewing. The documents listed here are only a sampling of what I have and what are available in various places.

CROWN COMMODITY HOLDING
INTERNATIONAL
151 SAN JOSE, CALAMBA, LAGUNA

19 JULY 1995

HON. CHAIRMAN/PRESIDENT
C/O DRESNER BANK
SINGAPORE

AUTHORITY TO VERIFY

GENTLEMEN:

THIS AUTHORIZES ______________ ______________ TO CONDUCT A "SOFT PROBE" OF THE ACCOUNTS LISTED HEREUNDER TO WIT

NAME OF BANK	:	DRESNER BANK, SINGAPORE
PRIVATE CODE NO.	:	A112934
METAL ACCOUNT NO.	:	10-583127-333
ACCOUNT NAME	:	RAMON POIRROTTE/ALFREDO R. DE RAMOS
CLIENT CODE	:	UEB INDUSTRIES MEX
SECURITY CODE	:	36-90 UEB INDUSTRIES PT. LTD
FAX NO.	:	65-222-9593

SUCH VERIFICATION/CONFIRMATION/PROBE WILL BE PERFORMED BY ______________ ANY BULLION OFFICER OF ______________

DESIGNATED BANK

YOUR UTMOST COOPERATION IN THIS REGARD IS HIGHLY APPRECIATED. WE ARE

VERY RESPECTFULLY YOURS,

ALFREDO DE RAMOS
PASSPORT NO. L380283
OWNER'S SIGNATORY

REPUBLIC OF THE PHILIPPINES
QUEZON CITY

SUBSCRIBED AND SWORN TO BEFORE ME THIS 13TH DAY OF JULY 1995 IN THE CITY OF QUEZON CITY, PHILIPPINES, AFFIANT EXHIBITING TO ME HIS PASSPORT NO. L380283 ISSUED AT MANILA ON OCTOBER 15, 1992 AND VALID UNTIL 1997

MA. ELENA R. CASTILLO
NOTARY PUBLIC
PTR NO. 2314542/1.09.95
QUEZON CITY
UNTIL DECEMBER 31, 1996

DOC. NO. 55
PAGE NO. 12
BOOK NO. 1
SERIES OF 1995

P.1/1

(15)

JAN.18 '89 15:15 UBS ZURICH

FAX IN

Union Bank of Switzerland

Schweizerische Bankgesellschaft
Union de Banques Suisses
Unione di Banche Svizzere

8021 Zurich
45 Bahnhofstrasse
P.O. Box
Telephone 01 234 11 11
Cable address: Bankunion
Telex 813 811/822 802

Direct dialing 01 234 28 48

Our ref.	Your letter of	Your ref.	Date
Special Trust Counseling SVZE-VAR/AMS			January 18, 1989

Dear Sir,

Estate of the late Mr. Severino G. Sta. Romana and aliases

We acknowledge receipt of your telefax of January 17, 1989 with enclosures in the above-mentioned matter.

Under the banking secrecy law in our country we are not authorized to furnish any information unless complete documents proving the legitimacy of such a request are presented to us. Kindly submit to us certified and sealed copy of the Letters of Administration issued by the Court of First Instance of the City of Manila which in our opinion is the only competent authority for the case in question appointing Miss Flordeliza T. Sta. Romana as the Administratrix of the above estate.

However, we like to point out that this statement is a general one which is made without checking whether the above-mentioned deceased held accounts with us or not.

Yours faithfully,

Union Bank of Switzerland

W. Haas
First Vice President

Dr. E. Varkonyi
Assistant Vice President

Letter by UBS Bank, dated January 18, 1989, referring to estate of Severino G. Sta. Romana and aliases.

THIS CHECK WAS HAND DELIVERED TO **COL. NORMAN** GRAND P- 114
AT THE MARINE AIR STATION, OFFICEKS CLUB. EL TOKO. CA.. JULY 19, 1988
BY J. R. HOKN FOR EXPENSES TO COLLECT CD 154051100-92

Nnational Association Notice to Customers:
P.O BOX 1290
Fort Worth, Texas 78101-1290
P.0 BOX 1390
Fort Worth July 15. 1988

Fort Worth. Texas
J R HORN
PURCHASER

FIDESC0 DE MEXICO/ COL. NORMAN GRAND $17.100.00*

OFFICIAL CHECK

EXPENSES ESTIMATED PAID TO FIDESCO, COL. GRAND & MGEN. ROBERT L. FERKERA
FROM 1988 up to Present June 1990

FROM J. R. HORN:	52,300.00
Phone Charges :	13,300.00 (This also includes half R. Lancaster)
Charges Cards:	25,000.00
Pocket Cash:	3,500.00

FROM: ALEX DAMELIO, JR.
5.000.00 estimated from Credit Receipts

FROM: LON E. WILLIAMSON
10.000.00 estimated from credit card receipts and Western Union Transfers.

WILLIAM L. CLANCY, CPA, ESTIMATED HE WIRED CLOSE TO $125,000.00 to
Gen. Robert L. Ferrera from monies received from Bonding Contracts. $125.000.00
SINCE NONE OF RECORDS ARE AVAILABLE THEIR IS NO WAY TO VERIFY THIS AMOUNT
MR. ED MORROW: 15.000.00. Amount to Fidesco. Col. Grand.
ESTIMATED AMOUNT: $249.100.00 SENT OR GIVEN TO FIDESCO, C'OL GRAND
AND MGEN. ROBERT L. FERRERA.

CREDIT SUISSE MAIN BRANCH. Zurich. Switzerland
Amount deposited to FIVE STAR TRUST ACCOUNT is in excess of 1.6 Trillion USD
in July 1996 verbal information given by Manfredo Manesseti of Italy-Vatican Bank,
Representative, via R. Breedlove of Orem. Utah-Ref. Dimitri Leone, of Italy.

REGISTER No. 80

MARRIAGE CONTRACT

Municipality of Pateros .... Province of Rizal

	Husband	Wife
Full name of contracting parties	SEVERINO G. STA. ROMANA	LUZ C. RAMBANO
Age	36 yrs. 8 mos.	36 yrs. 6 mos.
Nationality	Filipino	Filipina
Residence	T. Sulit, Pateros, Rizal	T. Sulit, Pateros, Rizal
Single or divorced	Widower	Single
Name of father	Marcelo Sta. Romana	Hilario Rambano
Nationality	Filipino (dec.)	Filipino
Name of mother	Valeria Garcia	Obigaria Casido
Nationality	Filipina (dec.)	Filipina
	Rogelio Guzman	Jose Velasquez
Residence	Sta. Ana, Manila	Cubao, Quezon City
	n/a	n/a
	n/a	n/a
	n/a	n/a

Marriage: Municipal Mayor

Date of marriage: February 15, 1974

Marriage solemnized by: Hon. Nestor V. Ponce

Mayor .... (b) .... Pateros, Rizal

WE HEREBY CERTIFY: That I, Severino G. Sta. Romana and Luz C. Rambano on the date and at the place above given, of our own free will and in the presence of the person solemnizing this marriage and of the two witnesses named of age, take each other as husband and wife.

I, Nestor V. Ponce, Mayor, certify: That on the date and at the place above written the aforesaid Severino G. Sta. Romana and Luz C. Rambano were with their mutual consent lawfully joined together in matrimony by me in the presence of said witnesses, both of age; and I further certify that marriage License No. ...., issued at .... on ...., 19.... of said parties, was exhibited to me or no marriage license was exhibited to me, this marriage of an exceptional character performed under Art. 76 of Rep. Act 386; and that consent to such marriage was duly given, as required by law, by the person or persons above mentioned.

IN WITNESS WHEREOF, we signed, (or marked with our fingerprint) this certificate ... day of February 1974.

(Contracting Party) (Contracting Party)

HON. NESTOR V. PONCE
(Judge, Justice of the Peace, Mayor, Priest, Minister, etc.)

WITNESSES

APR 11 1988
CERTIFIED TRUE COPY
MANILA, PHILIPPINES

verified by Juan

Marriage license between Luz C. Rambano and Severino G. Sta. Romana Page 474

OFFICE OF THE ASSISTANT SECRETARY OF DEFENSE

WASHINGTON, D.C. 20301-2400

24 April, 1989

T O P S E C R E T -- D E F E N S E D E P T. P O U C H

Robert L. Ferrere (For your eyes only)
MGen. Office of Special Services
c/o 3250 Wilshire Blvd., Suite #900
Los Angeles, California, 90010

Re: Understanding of Agreement on Triangle/Studebaker

Dear Sir:

This is a confirmation on the verbal agreement reached this past week-end, April 22d & 23rd, inclusive, at the conference held at Valdez, Alaska. If there are any differences with your understanding, please inform the undersigned via the code arranged.

It is the understanding of the undersigned that you represent FIVE STAR TRUST, as confirmed by J.A.B. III, and in that capacity you have concluded a contract for the joint Japanese-Singapore venture to build for them a chain of luxury hotels under the name of "Studebaker", for which FIVE STAR TRUST is to be paid the sum of money as agreed in the Certificate of Cash Deposit issued by the Mitsui Bank, Lmt., reference No. 4051100-92, to one SUICHI IIZUKA, a Japanese National, for assignment to a Mr. Marion Horn, a.k.a. J. R. Horn, of Lexington, Kentucky.

The undersigned has confirmed with Mr. S. that FIVE STAR TRUST, thru your involvement, has caused the full payment of the above mentioned certificate be made via a bank in New Zealand, and that said funds are awaiting the release code from the Japanese P.M. and from the Oval office. It has further been confirmed that interest for the first quarter of this year, earned by those funds, has now been forwarded to Washington, D.C. for final disbursement to you, for FIVE STAR.

It is the further understanding of the undersigned that you, General, are fully empowered to speak for the FIVE STAR TRUST, and in that capacity, you have been made aware that the "Golden Triangle" Construction Co., Lmt., represented by General Khun Sa, of Burma, has also done some work for various Far East nations, using the same materials and the same suppliers as FIVE STAR TRUST. The Director of the Managing Company in Va., for your materials, Mr. B., and the present Director, have both been informed by the majority stockholder of the Va. company, Mr. H. that the disbursement of the FIVE STAR funds be held back until Gen. Khun Sa can close the "Golden Triangle" operations totally, in the far-east, and they are both in complete accord with this decision, for they also feel that this is the best manner to handle this most delicate operation due to the possible international ramifications that could ensue if any of this were to become public knowledge at this most critical and delicate time.

The undersigned is fully aware that you, General, have been placed in a rather delicate position, for in effect, you have had to agree to the delay. I think you put it rather well at the meeting when you stated that the Company was putting you and FIVE STAR in a position similar to the old army "I want a volunteer-you just volunteered" situation. Please believe me General, there is no other way in which this can be done and still have a total security blanket over both

OFFICE OF THE ASSISTANT SECRETARY OF DEFENSE

WASHINGTON, D. C. 20301-2400

T O P S E C R E T -- T O P S E C R E T

Page 2 of 2 ------Triangle/Studebaker (4/24/89)

---

projects, which as a security expert, you must agree, is our primary concern.

I wish to further state that having read the dossier of Mr. Marion Horn, I find that he also is a true patriot and will sacrifice within reason for his country, and this delay is within reason. This is our moment of truth. If we continue to cooperate, as FIVE STAR has done in the past, General Khun Sa and his associates will be fully closed down by the time period of 1 May and 14 May, inclusive, with a target of 1 May, 1989. At that time we will implement phase two of our agreement, the immediate release of all of the funds now in New Zealand and in Washington D.C. that are being held for FIVE STAR TRUST.

As this is being written, General, word has reached us thru official channels that Prime Minister Noboru Takeshita has fully accepted our suggestion that he resign his office. We, at this time, have no knowledge of the person that will replace him, but we feel that a strong possibility is that Masayoshi Ito will be named. You, however, informed us in Valdez that you felt that the replacement, if any, would be Masaharu Gotoda. We have, at the present, no idea as to whom will cause the release of the funds. I strongly suggest that you arrange an immediate trip to Tokyo and have the Prime Minister delay his resignation until after FIVE STAR has receved the release of the funds.

In closing General, I feel that I can be fully candid in what I write, for I know that the contents of this letter will never be released, and in that spirit I wish to state that is has been a total honor for me to finally meet the "elusive and mysterious" General, code name "Eagle". I can inform you that even as this is being sent, there are many in Washington trying to identify the "General". I have met you, and I still do not know who you are. On the other side of the coin, Sir, I cannot understand how you, in your position, could take leave of your duties to devote yourself to the business of a private citizen. We know that you are not being paid, and yet your loyalties appear to be primarily with FIVE STAR and Mr. Horn. Perhaps once day we can discuss this, if both of us survive. We are on opposite sides of the coin, General, but I respect you, and I pray the feeling is returned. Your word is acceptable to all, as I hope mine is to you, and in that spirit I wish to warn you that there are certain elements that feel you have stepped on their toes, as well as those that do not want to see Mr. Horn or FIVE STAR collect their funds, and thus claim them for their own use. These elements have offered a great deal of money for you, General, for without you, they feel they can win. Beware of the "friends" of your Mr. Horn who are no longer within his inner circle, and beware of those in the Bureau that feel you have "embarrased" the service. I, for my part, must help to keep you safe, for without you, Mr. B., Mr. H., and myself are left in limbo. Finally, steps have been taken to wipe out any reference to Mr. Horn from any international publications as well as any complaints, etc., with any goverment agency.

RICHARD ARMITAGE
U.S. Asst. Sec. of Defense

copy: Mr. B., H., S. & Gen. Sa

IRREVOCABLE SPECIAL POWER OF ATTORNEY
ANNEX "B"

ONE THOUSAND TWO **HUNDRED (1,200)**, IN TRANCHES ON ONE HUNDRED (100) METRIC TONS OR MORE

A.	DEPOSITORY BANK:		Societe De Banque Suisse Swiss Bank Corporation Paradelplatz 6, Zurich Switzerland
B.	PRIVATE NUMBER CODE:		A - 112934
C.	CODE NUMBER:		429 - 3284 - 5
	1. S.D.C. CODE NAME		SEEFLED
	S.B.C. CODE NO.		15 - 2504111
	S.B.C. NAME		SEEFLEDSTRASSE
	2. S.B.C. CODE NAME		SCHWANMENDICEN
	S.B.C. CODE NO.		524 - 402244
	S.B.C. NAME		WINTERTHURERSTRAYSE
	3. S.B.C. CODE NAME		DELIKON
	S.B.C. CODE NO.		399 - 3124521
	S.B.C. NAME		SCHAFFHAUSERSTRASSE
D.	BANK OFFICER		
	Title		President
E.	TELEPHONE NO.		2251111
F.	DEPOSITORY CODE NO.		A - 112934

UBS ACCOUNT	AMOUNT	CODE NOS.	TROY OUNCE
1. OERLIKON	$ 339M	01-312-4521	(1,695,000,000)
2. SCHWAMENDIN	524M	GEN-01402-244	(2,620,000,000)
3. WITIKON	185M	01-534-800	(2,425,000,000)
4. ALTSTETTEN	682M	01-621-020	(3,410,000,000)
5. HONGG	160M	01-564-435	(8,000,000)

REFERENCE: GOLD VOLUME CERTIFICATE - U.B.S. (38 CERTIFICATES)
ACCOUNT: OOLD DEPOSIT (10,000 MT)
GOLD BARS DEPOSITED AT KLOTEN BULLION VAULT
UNION BANK OF SWITZERLAND, BAHNHOFSTRASSE 45 ZURICH

- VAULT NO. 88 RW RP
- ABA ACCOUNT NOL G725-70367-D U.B.S.
- PRIVATE CODE NO. A112934
- CODE NO. 429-3284-5
- MASTER ACCOUNT NO. 7257
- IN 200 CRATES ON PALLET NOS. 1392 THRU 1397, LOT NOS. 72413 THRUS 72422, MARKED TO CONTAIN AU PRECIOUS METAL WITH J & M HALLMARK STAMP.

MAR-30-93 FRI 11:51 FAX NO. 8174440384 P.03

CANDELARIA V. SANTIAGO
P.O. BOX 1439
AZLE, TX. 76098

Telephone (817) 444-2400 FAX: (817) 444-0384

Reference: CODE SCORPIO-83-JP-114-ocd-cvs

I, Candelaria V. Santiago, Philippine Passport No. L 164476, seller of record, under penalty of perjury, with full responsibility, offer the following AU metal for sale exclusively to: FAISAL HOLDING LTD.

Commodity:	AU Metal (Gold)
Quantity:	16,000 metric tonne (approx)
Discount:	6%
Purity:	99.95%
Specifications:	12.5 kg bars
Procedures:	Swiss Procedures

BANKING INFORMATION:
Union Bank of Switzerland
Bahnhofstrasse 45
CH-8021 Zurich

LOCATION OF ALL DOCUMENTS: All located within Union Bank of Switzerland

BANK OFFICER:	Assigned by Faisal Holding Ltd.
VAULT:	ZUR-Main-NS-pmgr
METAL ACCOUNT:	RC:KLGZ-5-21392-1
CERTIFICATE ACCOUNT:	Subsidiary Accounts Attached to Referenced Metal Account, Union Bank Switzerland, Bahnhofstrasse 45. CH-8021 Zurich
PIN CODE:	BC: C-476539

I, Candelaria V. Santiago, do hereby authorize a duly appointed representative, or bank officer, of Faisal Holding Ltd. to access all accounts/documentation pertaining to this transaction in order to verify metal, documentation and title.

I Candelaria V. Santiago, do hereby authorize Faisal Holding Ltd. to appoint a Bullion Officer at Union Bank of Switzerland, Bahnhofstrasse 45, CH-8021 Zurich, to oversee this transaction.

In witness whereof I have hereunto set my hand, this 26th day of April 1993.

Candelaria V. Santiago
Philippine Passport No. L 164476

Annex 'A' Page 2

DRESDNER BANK, Franfurt, Germany
B.C. 050-005
Dated: 06-141981
ACCT. A.I.U. 8256
Book 140-04715

CODE NAME: "DERYKON"
Bank Officer: Chairman of the Board
Acct. No. : 01-484-321
Reference Code Name: "SCHEFAAUSERTRASSES"
COMPANY : DIAZ AND POERROTTE ENTERPRISES OR
NANNETTE COOLY ENTERPRISES
OWNER : DON JOSE ANTONIO DIAZ
BANK ADDRESS: BAHNHOFSTRASSE
45, 8001 Zurich, Switzerland

CODE NAME: "SQUUVANEDIENEN"
Reference Code Name: "WINTERTHORNESTRASSE"
Bank Officer : Chairman of the Board
ACCOUNT NO. : 01-402-244
OWNER : DON ANTONIO DIAZ
COMPANY : DIAZ AND POERROTTE ENTERPRISES
or NANNETTE COOLY ENTERPRISES
BANK ADDRESS : BAHNHOFSTRASSE
45, 8001 Zurich, Switzerland

UBS ACCOUNT	AMOUNT	CODE NOS.
1. H O I D	$ 1M	AMMARTPLATZ
2. R O M E R H O P	1M	01-252-4634
3. S E E F E L D	15M	01-250-4111
4. W E R D G U T	79M	01-242-7573
5. W I E D I K O N	155M	01-737-0131
6. A L B I S R E I D E N	8M	-
7. B A N H O F P A S S A G E	7M	01-271-331
8. B E L L E V U E	1M	-
9. B L E I C H E R W E G	30M	01-208-5111
10. F L U N T E R N	80M	01-475-747
11. F R E I L A G E R	39M	-

UBS
Bank Account No. 15-25040111-75267-C10
Reference Code: SEEFELDS/SEEFELDS/FRASSE
DEPOSITORY NO. A-112834562-A-7

SANWA BANK CENTRAL DISTRICT
Hongkong
Account No. 916-002358-4

PO SANG BANK, Central District
Hongkong
Account No. 681-112785

Office of the President
of the Philippines
Malacañang

HIGHLY CONFIDENTIAL:

MAY 3, 1983

THE FOREIGN BUYERS/FIDUCIARY BANKS=

KIND ATTENTION: MR. DANIEL W. SWIHART
BUYERS' ATTORNEY-IN-FACT
ENGINEERING CONSTRUCTION CO. LTD.

SUBJECT : SCHEDULED PRESENTATION OF BNK DRAFTS AND OTHER BANKS INSTRUMENTS, ETC.

Gentlemen:

Below are very, very and strictly classified and confidential and in the name of "CODE ONE" of the Fourth Republic of the Philippines thru his most trusted women in the sales of these Hottest commodity by the name of Konsehala Candelaria V. Santiago, we wish to inform you of the followi...

1. That either May 11 or 12, 1983 you and your buyers' banks officials may present personally to the prime local servicing bank designated by "CBRP" thru "CODE ONE", the banks drafts original copies or unconditional/irrevocable hard several copies of banks guarantees with "verifiable signatures" of said prime banks for the buyers, for the total sums as payments for the 716,045 pieces of 12.5 kilos each bar, 4x4x16, 24 carat, fineness 999.9% with complete export documents and clearances and with specifications of good london delivery;

2. That price as approved by "PN-1518254" will be US$442.OO per troy ounce conditioned that US$400.00 net for "CBRP"/KONSEHALA C.V.SANTIAGO/ASSIGNEE", AND US$30.OO per troy ounce for "R.B. MARASIGAN/R.B. MARALIT/ASSIGNEE" (OR US$22.OO per troy ounce VIPS'; US$6.5O securities/with prime banks guarantees/tax free thru PN-1518254 name; US$1.50 per troy ounce for "RAMON B. MARASIGAN/RB MARALIT/P.A. PASCUAL/PN-1518254 ...

3. That upon presentation of banks drafts, etc. cited in No. 1 to personally ... PN-1518254, Secret-seller's primelocal servicing bank will confirm au... and all about everything to your buyers' banks abroad.

Any secret documents you'll receive from us, don't xerox it or show it to any ... except your concerned buyers/banks, or else we'll cancel the sales of 716,... pieces with you -- without notice.

BY THE AUTHORITY OF "CODE ONE/K-CVS"

Authorized signature

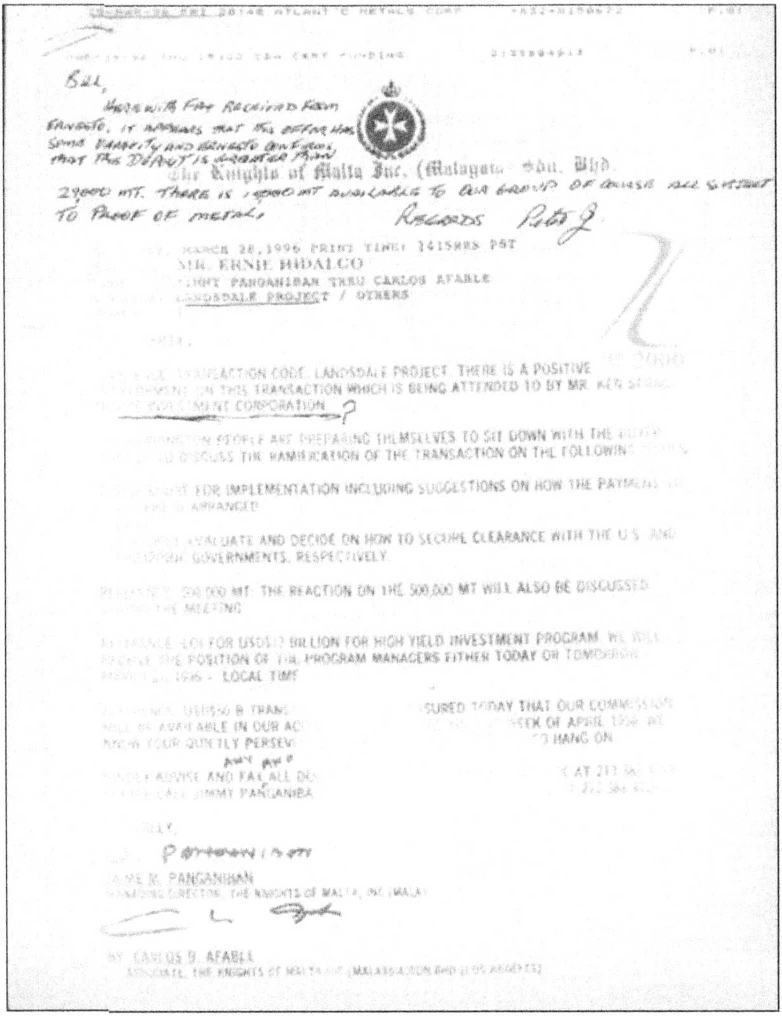

Bill,

Herewith fax received from Ernesto, it appears that the offer has some validity and Ernesto confirms that the deposit is greater than 29000 MT. There is 10000 MT available to our group of course all subject to proof of metal.

Regards Peter J.

The Knights of Malta Inc. (Malaysia) Sdn. Bhd.

MARCH 28, 1996 PRINT TIME: 1415HRS PST

MR. ERNIE HIDALGO

JIMMY PANGANIBAN THRU CARLOS AFABLE

LANDSDALE PROJECT / OTHERS

TRANSACTION CODE: LANDSDALE PROJECT. THERE IS A POSITIVE DEVELOPMENT ON THIS TRANSACTION WHICH IS BEING ATTENDED TO BY MR. KEN ... INVESTMENT CORPORATION. ?

... PEOPLE ARE PREPARING THEMSELVES TO SIT DOWN WITH THE BUYER ... TO DISCUSS THE RAMIFICATION OF THE TRANSACTION ON THE FOLLOWING ...

... FOR IMPLEMENTATION INCLUDING SUGGESTIONS ON HOW THE PAYMENT ... IS ARRANGED.

... EVALUATE AND DECIDE ON HOW TO SECURE CLEARANCE WITH THE U.S. AND ... GOVERNMENTS, RESPECTIVELY.

... 500,000 MT: THE REACTION ON THE 500,000 MT WILL ALSO BE DISCUSSED ... THE MEETING.

... LOI FOR USD$1? BILLION FOR HIGH YIELD INVESTMENT PROGRAM. WE WILL RECEIVE THE POSITION OF THE PROGRAM MANAGERS EITHER TODAY OR TOMORROW ... LOCAL TIME.

... USD$50 B TRANS... ...SURED TODAY THAT OUR COMMISSION WILL BE AVAILABLE IN OUR AC... ...WEEK OF APRIL 1996. WE KNOW YOUR QUIETLY PERSEV... ...TO HANG ON.

... ADVISE AND FAX ALL DO... ...AT 213 ... CALL JIMMY PANGANIBA... ...213 ...

...LY,

JAIME M. PANGANIBAN

MANAGING DIRECTOR, THE KNIGHTS OF MALTA, INC (MALAY...)

BY: CARLOS B. AFABLE

ASSOCIATE, THE KNIGHTS OF MALTA INC (MALAYSIA ... AND LOS ANGELES)

G-1

MATEO

INVESTMENT LIMITED

(OFFSHORE CORPORATION)

~~58 LEEDS STREET~~
~~GULLIVER~~
~~TOWNSVILLE, AUSTRALIA, Q4812~~
~~PHONE (077) 751796~~

80 Broad Street
Monrovia, Liberia

February 26, 1985

IRREVOCABLE LETTER OF UNDERTAKING

To the Beneficiary

Mr.
A/C No. FASDUN/425, PRUDENTIAL BANK, UN AVENUE
MANILA, PHILIPPINES.

In reference of the loan against collateral under Transaction Code 213-LUMA-30K/P-239428 ISS 23101978 with the sale and exchange of Volume of USDLRS THREE HUNDRED BILLION (US$300-B), we irrevocably and unconditionally accept with full responsibility on closing of the above-mentioned transaction without protest on notification and promise to commit and agree to pay against this original letter of undertaking as fee in sum of USDLRS ONE HUNDRED EIGHTY SEVEN MILLION FIVE HUNDRED THOUSAND (US$187,500,000.00).

This Irrevocable Letter of Undertaking will be exchanged by cash money after the finalization of the transaction between the Borrower and Lender, and/or the funds have been received by Clearing House Account.

This Irrevocable Letter of Undertaking shall be automatically unvalid and void if the transaction is not materialized, without any recourse, unless the transaction goes through.

Sincerely yours,

KEE WING LUN
Passport No. R 100669
Issued on Nov. 8, 1983
Issued at Brisbane, Australia
Authorized Signature for
Clearing House under A/C
[illegible]
No. Z-88306 GUANGZHOU
AMERICAN EXPRESS BANK.

G.I.

Office of the President
of the Philippines
Malacañang

HIGHLY CONFIDENTIAL;

MAY 3, 1983

THE FOREIGN BUYERS/FIDUCIARY BANKS=

KIND ATTENTION: MR. DANIEL W. SWIHART
BUYERS' ATTORNEY-IN-FACT
ENGINEERING CONSTRUCTION CO. LTD.

SUBJECT : SCHEDULED PRESENTATION OF BNK DRAFTS AND OTHER BANKS INSTRUMENTS, ETC.

Gentlemen:

Below are very, very and strictly classified and confidential and in the name of "CODE ONE" of the Fourth Republic of the Philippines thru his most trusted woman in the sales of these Hottest commodity by the name of Konsehala Candelaria V. Santiago, we wish to inform you of the following:

1. That either May 11 or 12, 1983 you and your buyers' banks officials may present personally to the prime local servicing bank designated by "CBRP" thru "CODE ONE", the banks drafts original copies or unconditional/ irrevocable hard several copies of banks guarantees with "verifiable signatures" of said prime banks for the buyers, for the total sums as payments for the 716,045 pieces of 12.5 kilos each bar, 4x4x16, 24 carat, fineness 999.9% with complete export documents and clearances and with specifications of good london delivery;

2. That price as approved by "PN-1518254" will be US$442.OO per troy ounce conditioned that US$400.00 net for "CBRP"/KONSEHALA C.V. SANTIAGO/ ASSIGNEE", AND US$30.OO per troy ounce for "R.B. MARASIGAN/R.B. MARALIT/ASSIGNEE" (OR US$22.OO per troy ounce VIPS';US$6.50 securities/ with prime banks guarantees/tax free thru PN-1518254 name;US$1.50 per troy ounce for "RAMON B. MARASIGAN/RBMARALIT/P.A. PASCUAL/PN-1518254"

3. That upon presentation of banks drafts, etc. cited in No.1 to personally to PN-1518254, Secret-seller's primelocal servicing bank will confirm au-stock and all about everything to your buyers' banks abroad;

Any secret documents you'll receive from us, don't xerox it or show it to any one except your concerned buyers/banks, or else we'll cancel the sales of 716,045 pieces with you -- without notice.

BY THE AUTHORITY OF "CODE ONE/K-CVS"

Authorized signature

nicholaus senn
c. wilhelm christians
carl hermann letemeyer
International Lawyers – Consultants ZURICH SW

03 · 10 · 89 L–18H

Clem F. Santiago +

BANK	ACC. NO.	AMOUNT
STANDARD CHARTERED INT'L TRUSTEE LIMITED LONDON	4 77 22 P	$ 47 BILLION
BANK OF CHINA HK	5555 20 1HE	$ 12 BILLION ✓
CITICORP NY	LVI 820975 TI	$ 9 BILLION
BANK OF EAST ASIA HK	78 9520 · 37 · 0	$ 3 BILLION

CERTIFIED CORRECT:

CARL HERMANN LETEMEYER

Received Originals – 11.21.90

21 nov 90
Copy from Original

AUTHENTICATION
CERTIFIED AS XEROX COPY
OF THE ORIGINAL AS PRESENTED
ON NOVEMBER 21, 1990

RICARDO L. BUHN

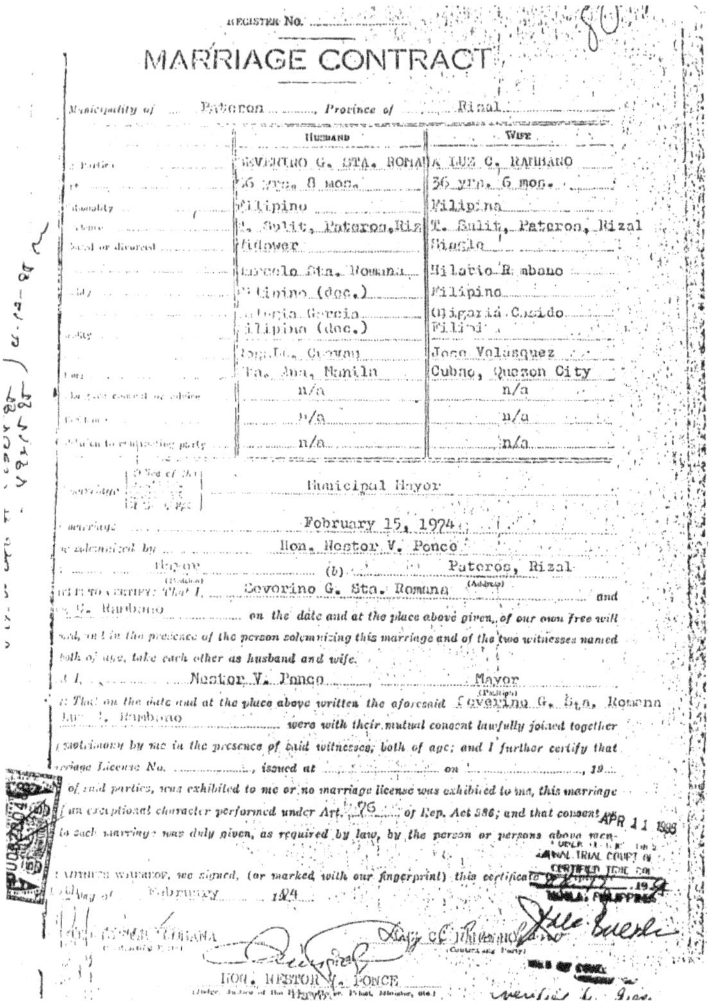

REGISTER No.

MARRIAGE CONTRACT

Municipality of Pateros, Province of Rizal

	HUSBAND	WIFE
Parties	SEVERINO G. STA. ROMANA	LUZ C. RAMBANO
	36 yrs. 8 mos.	36 yrs. 6 mos.
Nationality	Filipino	Filipina
Residence	T. Sulit, Pateros, Riz	T. Sulit, Pateros, Rizal
Single or divorced	Widower	Single
	Marcelo Sta. Romana	Hilario Rambano
	Filipino (dec.)	Filipino
	Valeria Garcia	Gigaria Casido
	Filipina (dec.)	Filipina
	Leonardo Guzman	Jose Velasquez
	Sta. Ana, Manila	Cubao, Quezon City
	n/a	n/a
	n/a	n/a
Relation to contracting party	n/a	n/a

Municipal Mayor

February 15, 1974

Solemnized by Hon. Nestor V. Ponce

Mayor (b) Pateros, Rizal

WE HEREBY CERTIFY: That I, Severino G. Sta. Romana and Luz C. Rambano on the date and at the place above given, of our own free will and in the presence of the person solemnizing this marriage and of the two witnesses named both of age, take each other as husband and wife.

And I, Nestor V. Ponce, Mayor

That on the date and at the place above written the aforesaid Severino G. Sta. Romana and Luz C. Rambano were with their mutual consent lawfully joined together in matrimony by me in the presence of said witnesses, both of age; and I further certify that Marriage License No. ...., issued at .... on ...., 19..., of said parties, was exhibited to me or no marriage license was exhibited to me, this marriage of an exceptional character performed under Art. 76 of Rep. Act 386; and that consent to such marriage was duly given, as required by law, by the person or persons above mentioned.

IN WITNESS WHEREOF, we signed, (or marked with our fingerprint) this certificate .... day of February 1974.

SEVERINO STA. ROMANA (Contracting Party)

LUZ C. RAMBANO (Contracting Party)

HON. NESTOR V. PONCE

APR 11 1986

CERTIFIED TRUE COPY

MANILA, PHILIPPINES

HIGGS & JOHNSON
COUNSEL & ATTORNEYS-AT-LAW

Sandringham House
P.O. Box N-[illegible]
Nassau, Bahamas

Tel: (809) [illegible]
Fax: (809) [illegible]
Cables: Lex, Nassau
Telex: 20150 Lex

Partners: Philip C. Dunkley; [illegible]

Associates: [illegible]

Our Ref: PCD/jek 10/143 Your Ref:

VIA TELEFAX 1-212-575-0799 ORIGINAL BY POST

1st July, 1992

Ms. Eleanor Jackson Piel,
36 W-st Forty-fourth Street,
New ork, N.Y.
[illegible] U.S.A.

Dr : Ms. Piel,

Re: Estate of Severino Sta. Romana

I refer to your letter dated 29th June, 1992 the contents of which we note.

As you are aware, Sir Leonard Knowles has obtained a grant of the Estate in The Bahamas and under authority of that grant is bringing action against Citibank and Cititrust in The Bahamas to recover assets of the Estate here. Our instructions are that there are no assets in The Bahamas.

In any event, so long as the grant in favour of Sir Leonard Knowles stands, we must recongise his (and only his) authority to represent the Estate in The Bahamas. It has occurred to us that Mrs. Romana may have some right to challenge the Bahamian grant, although she may be reluctant to do so since there are no assets in The Bahamas.

Assuming that our instructions are correct that there are no assets in The Bahamas, then it must follow that the action brought by Sir Leonard Knowles, as administrator of the Estate against Citibank and Cititrust, must fail. It is likely that the Bahamian Court will order the Estate (or Sir Leonard Knowles) to pay the reasonable legal fees and expenses of Citibank an Cititrust. Accordingly, there is a possible liability against the Estate which may be of interest to your client to protect against.

We look forward to your reply.

Yours faithfully,
HIGGS & JOHNSON
Philip C. Dunkley

A

B

Z

Made in United States
North Haven, CT
12 September 2025

72812729R00232